Why Do You Need This New Edition?

If you're wondering why you should buy this edition of *The Skilled Reader*, here are 6 good reasons!

① Review each chapter on-the-go with our new *Chapter Review Cards.* Easy to tear out and take with you wherever you need to study—on the bus, at your job, in the library—*Chapter Review Cards* boil each chapter down to the fundamentals, making them the perfect tool to check your comprehension or prepare for an exam.

② Understand what you need to learn with *Learning Outcomes* at the beginning of each chapter. New Learning Outcomes begin each chapter to help you focus on the key skills you need to learn to understand and apply to become a skilled reader.

③ Write about what you read with new *What Do You Think?* writing prompts. Do you think cell phones should be allowed in the classroom? How do you think the biotech industry will change society? In short, what do *you* think about today's issues?

Throughout the book, new *What Do You Think?* questions challenge you to respond to today's issues as explored in our longer reading selections at the end of each chapter and in Part Two: Additional Readings.

④ Explore new topics in our many new readings. New topics include building good communication skills, developing good study skills, participating in your community, managing your finances, and many more! With over 25 percent of the readings and accompanying activities new to the edition, you will find topics that help you build new skills to master not only reading, but your life.

⑤ Master finding the main idea and its supporting details. The table of contents has been rearranged to teach these related topics in order—making it easier for you to learn these fundamental skills.

⑥ Take your reading online with our new *Connect to MyReadingLab* features. New *Connect to MyReadingLab* sections provide directions for accessing activities for additional practice on Pearson's MyReadingLab program.

PEARSON
Longman

Third Edition

The Skilled Reader

D. J. Henry
Daytona State College

Longman

Boston   Columbus   Indianapolis   New York   San Francisco   Upper Saddle River
Amsterdam   Cape Town   Dubai   London   Madrid   Milan   Munich   Paris   Montreal   Toronto
Delhi   Mexico City   Sao Paulo   Sydney   Hong Kong   Seoul   Singapore   Taipei   Tokyo

Editor in Chief: Eric Stano
Senior Acquisitions Editor: Kate Edwards
Editorial Assistant: Lindsey Allen
Associate Development Editor: Erin Reilly
Senior Supplements Editor: Donna Campion
Marketing Manager: Tom DeMarco
Production Manager: Ellen MacElree
Project Coordination, Text Design, and Electronic Page Makeup: Nesbitt Graphics, Inc.
Cover Designer/Manager: Wendy Ann Fredericks
Cover Photo: © Masterfile Corporation. All rights reserved.
Photo Researcher: Rona Tuccillo
Senior Manufacturing Buyer: Dennis J. Para
Printer and Binder: Quad/Graphics-Taunton
Cover Printer: Lehigh-Phoenix Color/Hagerstown

For permission to use copyrighted material, grateful acknowledgment is made to the copyright holders on pp. 561–562, which are hereby made part of this copyright page.

Library of Congress Cataloging-in-Publication Data

Henry, D. J. (Dorothy Jean)
  The skilled reader / D.J. Henry. -- 3rd ed.
      p. cm.
  Includes index.
  ISBN 978-0-205-78087-7
  1. Reading. 2. Critical thinking. I. Title.
  LB1050.H433 2011
  428.4'0711--dc22

                          2010038327

ISBN-10: 0-205-78087-3   (student ed.)

ISBN-13: 978-0-205-78087-7   (student ed.)

ISBN-10: 0-205-81934-6 (instructor's ed.)

ISBN-13: 978-0-205-81934-8 (instructor's ed.)

2 3 4 5 6 7 8 9 10—QGT—14 13 12 11

Longman
is an imprint of

www.pearsonhighered.com

Brief Contents

v

Detailed Contents

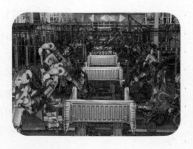

PART TWO

Additional Readings   427

Preface

Dear Colleagues:

In our college's library hangs a poster that bears the face of Fredrick Douglass and the following words: "Once you learn to read, you will be forever free." The poster serves as a daily reminder of two ideals: Reading empowers an individual's life, and our work as reading instructors is of great and urgent importance. Many of our students come to us lacking the basic skills that make skilled reading and clear thinking possible. Too often their struggles have left them unable to find much joy or success in working with the printed word. For them, text is a barrier. *The Skilled Reader,* Third Edition, has been designed to address these challenges.

New to This Edition

The following changes have been made to *The Skilled Reader*, Third Edition, to help students become skilled readers and critical thinkers.

- **New order for the Main Ideas and Supporting Details Coverage.** Based on extensive feedback from instructors across the country, the order of presentation has been rearranged to bring the main ideas and supporting details coverage together, closer to the beginning of the book. The table of contents now progresses from Topics to Stated Main Ideas, to Implied Main Ideas, to Supporting Details—more in line with the way instructors nationwide present these topics. Of course, each chapter is still self-contained, allowing instructors to easily teach these important topics in any order they choose.

- **New chapter review cards.** New chapter review cards will make studying more accessible and efficient by distilling chapter content down to the fundamentals, helping students to quickly master the basics, to review their understanding on the go, or to prepare for upcoming exams. Because they're made of durable cardstock, students can keep these Review Cards for years to come and pull them out whenever they need a quick review.

- **New Learning Outcomes.** Each chapter now opens with learning outcomes keyed to Bloom's taxonomy. Learning outcomes help students to understand why they are learning the material and help them to set goals for their learning.

- **New "Connect to MyReadingLab" features.** New *Connect to MyReadingLab* sections offer specific activities tied to chapter content for use as lab activities or additional outside-of-class practice. Never search for an appropriate online activity again: *Connect to MyReadingLab* provides easy-to-follow click paths and descriptions of specific MyReadingLab activities and how they fit with chapter content.

- **More attention to the connection between reading and writing.** Part Two now opens with a 6-Step Reading/Writing Action Plan that encourages students to see reading as a chance to enter a conversation with the writer and helps students to see how the reading process and the writing process work together to help them participate in this conversation.

- **New "What Do You Think" writing prompts.** Found at the end of longer reading selections throughout the book, our new "What Do You Think?" writing prompts challenge students to respond to the issues explored.

- **New Reading Level Indications in the Annotated Instructor's Edition.** The reading level of all selections within our Review and Mastery Tests, Additional Readings, and Combined Skills Tests are now indicated in the Annotated Instructor's Edition (levels are not indicated in the student edition).

- **New Longer Reading Selections.** In addition to four new longer readings in Part Two, over 25 percent of the reading selections and accompanying pedagogy throughout the text have been revised, giving students new reading material that is lively, up to date, and thought-provoking.

- **New Design.** In addition to appearing more modern and mature, the new design visually clarifies the text's different features to help students navigate and find the content they are looking for with greater ease.

- **Reorganized Appendix C: Word Parts.** A new approach to Appendix C: *Word Parts* taps into and expands upon students' prior knowledge by offering 114 of the most frequently used word parts. This new approach lays the foundation for meaningful and manageable instruction within the limited time of any given semester. Mastering this list will give students command of thousands of words.

Guiding Principles

The Skilled Reader, Third Edition, was written to develop in students the essential abilities that will enable them to become skilled readers and critical thinkers.

Practice and Feedback

An old Chinese proverb says, "I hear and I forget. I see and I remember. I do and I understand." We all know that the best way *to learn* is *to do.* Thus, one of the primary aims of this text is to give students plentiful opportunities to practice, practice, practice!

For every concept introduced in the book, there is an **explanation** of the concept; an **example** with an explanation of the example; and a **practice or sets of practices**. Each chapter also has **brief skill applications**, **four review tests**, and **four mastery tests**.

High-Interest Reading Selections

For many, enthusiasm for reading is stimulated by reading material that offers high-interest topics written in a direct, energetic style. Every effort has been made to create reading passages in examples, exercises, reviews, and tests that students will find lively and engaging. Topics are taken from popular culture and textbooks; some examples are music, sports figures, interpersonal relationships, gangs, movies, weight loss, drug use, nutrition, inspiration and success stories, role models, stress management, football, and aerobics.

Integration of the Reading Process and Reading Skills

Skilled readers blend individual reading skills into a reading process such as SQ3R. Before reading, skilled readers skim for new or key vocabulary or main ideas. They create study questions and make connections to their prior knowledge. During reading, skilled readers check their comprehension. For example, they annotate the text. They notice thought patterns and the relationship between ideas. They read for the answers to the questions they created before reading. After reading, skilled readers use outlines, concept maps, and summaries to review what they have read and deepen their understanding. Students are taught to integrate each skill into a reading process in Part One.

In Chapter 1, "A Reading System for Skilled Readers," students are introduced to SQ3R. In every other Part One chapter, students actively apply SQ3R strategies in "Before Reading" and "After Reading" activities. "Before Reading" activities are pre-reading exercises that appear at the beginning of each chapter. These activities guide the student to review important concepts studied in earlier chapters, build on prior knowledge, and preview upcoming material. "After Reading" activities are review activities that appear after the review tests in each chapter. These activities guide students to reflect upon their achievements and assume responsibility for learning.

Comprehensive Approach

The Skilled Reader, Third Edition, offers several levels of learning. First, students are given an abundance of practice. Students are able to focus on individual reading skills through a chapter-by-chapter workbook approach. In each of the skills chapters of Part One, Review Test 4 offers a multiparagraph passage with items on all the skills taught up to that point. In addition, Chapter 1 ("A Reading System for Skilled Readers") teaches students how to apply their reading skills to the reading process before, during, and after reading by using SQ3R. Students also learn to apply all the skills in combination in Part Two, "Additional Readings," and Part Three, "Combined-Skills Tests." The aim is to provide our students with varied and rich opportunities to learn and practice reading skills and to apply reading processes.

Textbook Structure

To help students become skilled readers and critical thinkers, *The Skilled Reader,* Third Edition, introduces the most important basic reading skills in Part One and then provides sections of additional readings (in Part Two), combined-skills tests (in Part Three), and reading enrichment (in Part Four).

Part One, Becoming a Skilled Reader

Essential reading skills are introduced individually in Part One to help students become skilled readers.

- Chapter 1, "A Reading System for Skilled Readers," guides students through the stages of the SQ3R reading process. Each step of this process is explained thoroughly with ample opportunities for practice and mastery. The aim is to show students how to apply the skills they acquire in each of the skills chapters before, during, and after reading.

- Chapter 2, "Vocabulary in Context," fosters vocabulary acquisition during reading by using a mnemonic technique: SAGE stands for **S**ynonyms, **A**ntonyms, **G**eneral context, and **E**xamples.

- Chapter 3, "Vocabulary-Building Skills," develops language skills by demonstrating how to determine word meanings from prefixes, roots, and suffixes. The chapter also provides extensive instruction in dictionary skills.

- Chapter 4, "Topics and Main Ideas," offers both verbal and visual strategies to help students see the building-block relationship between topics and main ideas.

- Chapter 5, "Locating Stated Main Ideas," builds on the foundation laid in the previous chapter by explaining strategies to locate main ideas along with extensive practice in doing so.

- Chapter 6, "Implied Main Ideas," furthers students' understanding of the main idea by explaining the unstated main idea and offering extensive practice in identifying implied main ideas.

- Chapter 7, "Supporting Details," identifies the differences between major and minor details. This chapter uses a visual method to demonstrate the increasing level of specificity in a paragraph from topic sentence to major details to minor details.

- Chapter 8, "Outlines and Concept Maps," reinforces the skills of locating main ideas and identifying major and minor supporting details. This chapter teaches the students the structure of a text by offering instruction and practice with outlines and concept maps.

- Chapter 9, "Transitions and Thought Patterns," introduces the fundamental thought patterns and the words that signal those patterns. Students are given numerous opportunities to practice identifying the signal words and their relationship to the thought patterns they establish. The chapter includes the time order, space order, listing, and classification patterns.

- Chapter 10, "More Thought Patterns," introduces the more complex thought patterns and the words that signal those patterns. Just as in Chapter 9, students are given extensive practice opportunities. Chapter 10 introduces the comparison-and-contrast pattern, the cause-and-effect pattern, the generalization-and-example pattern, and the definition pattern.

- Chapter 11, "Inferences," addresses this advanced skill carefully by dividing the necessary mental processes into understandable units of activity. Students are taught the basic skills necessary to evaluate an author's purpose and choice of words.

Part Two, Additional Readings

Part Two is a collection of ten reading selections followed by skills questions designed to give students real reading opportunities and the opportunity to gauge their growth as readers. This section begins with a key discussion about the relationship between reading and writing and offers a few pointers on basic writing skills. The readings, which include magazine articles and textbook excerpts, were chosen to engage, encourage, and motivate the reader. Each selection is followed by skills questions so that students can practice all the skills taught in Part One. The skills questions are followed by "What Do You Think?" writers' prompts so that students can practice critical thinking by reacting and responding to the issues explored in the readings.

Part Three, Combined-Skills Tests

Part Three is a set of ten reading passages and combined-skills tests. This section offers students ample opportunity to apply reading skills and strategies and to become more familiar with a standardized testing format to help prepare them for exit exams, standardized reading tests, and future content course quizzes, tests, and exams.

Part Four, Reading Enrichment

Supplementary material is provided here for three important skills.

- Appendix A, "ESL Reading Tips," addresses some of the particular challenges of students who are learning English as an additional language. Students first learn about the difference between literal and figurative language. They then learn how to understand idioms, similes, and metaphors to become skilled readers. Since every chapter of *The Skilled Reader,* Third Edition, teaches specific skills and strategies that are helpful to students learning to read English, students are first guided through a survey of the entire textbook.

- Appendix B, "Reading Graphics," offers basic guidelines for reading and analyzing graphics, followed by specific examples and explanations of tables, line graphs, bar graphs, pie charts, diagrams, and pictograms.

- Appendix C, "Word Parts," is an in-depth list of prefixes, roots, suffixes, their meanings, and sample words. This section supplements Chapter 3, "Vocabulary-Building Skills."

Chapter Features

Each chapter in Part One features elements that work together to help students become skilled readers.

Learning outcomes: New to this edition, each chapter opens with learning outcomes to help students preview and assess their progress as they master chapter content.

Before Reading About . . . : "Before Reading About . . ." activities appear at the beginning of Chapters 2–11 in Part One. These activities are pre-reading exercises based on SQ3R: they review important concepts studied in earlier chapters, build on prior knowledge, and preview the chapter. The purpose of "Before Reading About . . ." is to actively teach students to develop a reading process that applies individual reading skills as they study.

After Reading About . . . : "After Reading About . . ." activities appear after Review Test 4 in Chapters 2–11 of Part One. Based on SQ3R, "After Reading About . . ." activities teach students to reflect on their achievements and assume responsibility for their own learning. These activities check their comprehension of the skill taught in the chapter. Students learn to integrate individual reading skills into a reading process; they learn the value of reviewing material; and finally, students create a learning journal that enables them to see patterns in their behaviors and record their growth as readers.

Instruction, example, explanation, and practice: The chapter skill is broken down into components, and each component is introduced and explained. Instruction is followed by an example, an explanation of the example, and a practice. Each of these components has its own instruction, example and explanation, and practice exercises.

Textbook
Skills

Textbook Skills: As the last section of each chapter's instruction, students are shown the ways in which the skills they are learning apply to reading college textbooks. These activities, signaled by the icon to the left, present material from a college textbook and direct the student to apply the chapter's skill to the reading passage or visual. In a concerted effort to prepare students to be skilled readers in their content courses, activities that foster college textbook skills across the curriculum are also carefully woven throughout *The Skilled Reader,* Third Edition. The Textbook Skills icon signals these activities.

Visual Vocabulary: The influence of technology and media on reading is evident in the widespread use of graphics in newspapers, magazines, and college textbooks. Throughout *The Skilled Reader,* Third Edition, visual vocabulary is presented as part of the reading process, and students interact with these visuals by completing captions or answering skill-based questions. The aim is to teach students to value photos, graphs, illustrations, and maps as important sources of information.

Applications: Brief application exercises give students the opportunity to apply each component of the reading skill they've just acquired.

Review Tests: Each chapter has a total of four review tests. Review Tests 1 through 3 are designed to give opportunity for practice on the specific skill taught in the chapter; Review Test 4 offers a multiparagraph passage with questions based on all the skills taught up to and including that particular chapter. Review Tests 3 and 4 also give "What Do You Think?" writing prompts so that teachers have the opportunity to guide students as they develop critical thinking skills.

Mastery Tests: Each chapter also includes four Mastery Tests. Most of the Mastery Tests are based on excerpts from science, history, psychology, social science, and literature textbooks.

Chapter Review Cards: New to this edition, a chapter review card is included for each chapter. The chapter review serves as a comprehension check for the reading concepts being taught.

The Longman Teaching and Learning Package

The Skilled Reader, Third Edition, is supported by a series of innovative teaching and learning supplements. Ask your Pearson sales representative for a copy, or download the content at **www.pearsonhighered.com/irc.** Your sales representative will provide you with the username and password to access these materials.

The **Annotated Instructor's Edition (AIE)** is a replica of the student text, with all answers included. 0-205-81934-6.

The **Instructor's Manual,** prepared by Mary Dubbé of Thomas Nelson Community College, features teaching strategies for each textbook chapter, plus additional readings that engage students with a variety of learning styles and encourage active learning through class, group, and independent practices. Each chapter includes an introduction designed to hook the students, reproducible handouts, and study-strategy cards. Also included is a ten-item quiz for each chapter. A supplemental section provides a sample syllabus, readability calculations for each reading in *The Skilled Reader,* Third Edition, five book quizzes to encourage independent reading and the creation of book groups, sample THEA and Florida State Exit Exams, and a scaffolded book review form. ISBN 0-205-82472-2.

The **Lab Manual,** prepared by Mary Dubbé of Thomas Nelson Community College, is designed as a student workbook and provides a collection of 65 activities that provide additional practice, enrichment, and assessment for the skills presented in *The Skilled Reader*, Third Edition. The activities for each chapter include practice exercises, one review test, and two mastery tests that mirror the design of *The Skilled Reader*, Third Edition, and emphasize the reading skills and applications students need in order to succeed in college. The lab activities give students realistic practice, encourage them to use the strategies they have learned, and offer an opportunity for students to continue to build a base of general, background knowledge. This lab manual can be used to strengthen students' reading skills, to allow them to assess their own progress, and to measure their success and readiness for college level reading. The lab manual is available packaged with *The Skilled Reader*, Third Edition, for an additional cost. ISBN 0-205-82473-0.

MyReadingLab (www.myreadinglab.com) MyReadingLab is the first and only online learning system to diagnose both students' reading skills and reading levels. This remarkable program utilizes diagnostic testing, personalized practice, and gradebook reports to allow instructors to measure student performance and help students gain control over their reading. Specifically created for developmental students, MyReadingLab is a website that provides diagnostics, practice, tests, and reporting on student reading skills and student reading levels. Student reading skills are improved through a mastery-based format of exercises and tests. Exercises include objective-based questions, open-ended questions, short answer questions, combined skills exercises and more. Student reading level is assessed through a Lexile framework (developed by Metametrics™, an educational measurement expert). Once diagnosed, students are assigned a Lexile number, which indicates their reading comprehension skills, and throughout the program, the Lexile number rises as the students' reading level improves. The result of this skills and level combination is a personalized student study plan to address individual needs and quantifiable data that measures individual student reading level advancement.

Acknowledgments

As I worked on the third edition of this reading series, I felt an overwhelming sense of gratitude and humility for the opportunity to serve the learning community as a textbook author. I would like to thank the entire Longman team for their dedication to providing the best possible materials to foster literacy. To every person, from the editorial team to the representatives in the field, all demonstrate a passion for students, teachers, and learning. It is a joy to be part of such a team. Special thanks are due to the following: Kate Edwards, Acquisitions Editor, and Erin Reilly, Developmental Editor, for their guidance and support; Kathy Smith with Nesbitt Graphics, Inc. for her tireless devotion to excellence; Ellen MacElree and the entire production team for their work ethic and gracious attitudes, including Genevieve Coyne. I would also like to thank Mary Dubbé for authoring the Lab Manual and the Instructor's Manual that supplement this reading series.

For nearly twenty-five years, I worked with the most amazing group of faculty from across the State of Florida as an item-writer, reviewer, or scorer of state-wide assessment exams for student learning and professional certification. The work that we accomplished together continues to inform me as a teacher, writer, and consultant. I owe a debt of gratitude to this group who sacrificed much for the good of our students.

I would also like to acknowledge two of my colleagues at Daytona State College: Dustin Weeks, Librarian, and Sandra Offiah-Hawkins, reading professor. As Tennyson extols in "Ulysses," these are the "souls that have toiled, and wrought, and thought with me."

Finally, I would like to gratefully recognize the invaluable insights provided by the following colleagues and reviewers. I deeply appreciate their investment of time and energy: Tina Ballard, Elgin Community College; Janet Brotherton, Cedar College of the Dallas County Community College; Debbie Felton, Cleveland State Community College; Danette Foster, Central Carolina Community College; Vicci Fox, Pima Community College; Doug Holland, Pima Community College; Linda Mininger, Harrisburg Area Community College; Robbi Muckenfuss, Durham Technical Community College; and Betty Payne, Montgomery College.

D. J. Henry
Datytona Beach, FL

Becoming a Skilled Reader

A Reading System for Skilled Readers

1

LEARNING OUTCOMES

After studying this chapter you should be able to do the following:

1. Define prior knowledge.
2. Describe and illustrate SQ3R.
3. Discuss your reading process.
4. Assess your comprehension of the key reading concepts described in the chapter.
5. Evaluate and explain the importance of what you have learned.
6. Apply what you have learned to your reading process.

Many people think that reading involves simply passing our eyes over words in the order that they appear on the page. But reading is much more than that. Once we understand the **reading process**, we can follow specific steps and apply strategies that will make us skilled readers.

Reading is an active process during which you draw information from the text to create meaning. When you understand what you've read, you've achieved **comprehension** of the material.

> **Comprehension** is an understanding of information.

Before we examine the reading process in detail, it is important to talk about the role of prior knowledge.

Prior Knowledge

We all have learned a large body of information throughout a lifetime of experience. This body of information is called **prior knowledge**.

Knowledge is gained from experience and stored in memory. Everyday, prior knowledge is expanded by what is experienced. For example, a small child hears the word *hot* as her father blows on a spoonful of steaming soup. The

3

hungry child grabs for the bowl and cries as some of the hot liquid spills on her hand. The child has learned and will remember the meaning of *hot*.

> **Prior knowledge** is the large body of information that is learned throughout a lifetime of experience.

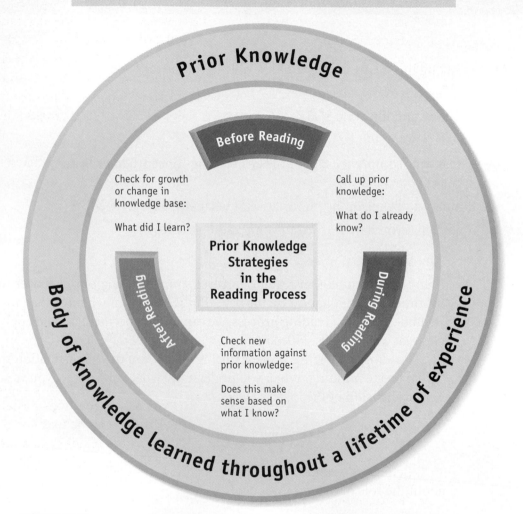

Prior Knowledge

Before Reading

Check for growth or change in knowledge base:

What did I learn?

Call up prior knowledge:

What do I already know?

After Reading

During Reading

Prior Knowledge Strategies in the Reading Process

Check new information against prior knowledge:

Does this make sense based on what I know?

Body of knowledge learned throughout a lifetime of experience

EXAMPLE Read the following paragraph. In the space provided, list any topics from the paragraph about which you already have prior knowledge.

A computer virus is programmed to raid and attack existing computer programs. The virus is sent by an e-mail or activated through a download. The virus program then infects the whole computer system. The virus attaches itself to other programs in the computer and copies itself. Some computer viruses are terrible; they erase files or lock up systems. Viruses must not go untreated.

_____

_____

_____

EXPLANATION If you know about computer programs, this passage makes more sense to you than it does to someone who does not understand how computer programs work. However, even if you do not know much about computers, you may have helpful prior knowledge about some of the ideas in the passage. For example, most of us have been sick with a virus. We understand that a virus can affect our entire body, and we recognize the need for treatment to help the body repair itself. Our prior knowledge about human viruses helps us understand how serious a computer virus can be.

The more prior knowledge we have about a topic, the more likely we are to understand that topic. The more you know, the easier it is to learn. This is why skilled readers build their knowledge base by reading often!

PRACTICE 1

Read the passage, and answer the questions that follow it.

The Micro and Macro Views of the World

[1]Just as doctors specialize in different branches of medicine, so economists specialize in different branches of economics. [2]This field of study is divided into two parts. [3]**Microeconomics** (micro) is the study of the choices that individuals and businesses make. [4]Micro also studies how these choices work together. [5]In addition, the micro view focuses on how governments influence these choices. [6]The following questions reveal a few examples of micro issues. [7]Will you buy a flat screen or traditional television? [8]Will Sony sell more PlayStations if it cuts the price? [9]Will a cut in the income tax rate encourage people to work longer hours? [10]Will a hike in the gas tax lead to smaller automobiles? [11]Are MP3 downloads killing CDs? [12]**Macroeconomics** (macro) is also the study of choices made by individuals, businesses, and governments. [13]However, macro focuses on the total effects of these choices. [14]This branch of study looks at the national economy and the worldwide economy. [15]The following questions reveal a few examples of macro issues. [16]Why did production and jobs expand so slowly in the United States in the early 2000s? [17]Why are incomes growing much faster in China and India than in the United States? [18]Why are Americans borrowing more than $2 billion a day from the rest of the world?

—Adapted from Bade & Parkin, *Foundations of Economics*, 3rd ed., p. 14.

1. What did you already know about economics? That is, what was your prior knowledge about economics? _____

2. Was this an easy passage to understand? How does your prior knowledge about economics affect your understanding of this passage?

   _____

3. List the statements in the passage that you had no prior knowledge about.

   _____

VISUAL VOCABULARY

The difference between micro-economics and macroeconomics is similar to the difference between two views of a display of drummers in a sports stadium. Which photograph stands for the micro view? Which one represents the macro view? Use "micro view" or "macro view" to label each photograph.

Photo 1: A single participant

_____

Photo 2: The patterns formed by the joint actions

_____

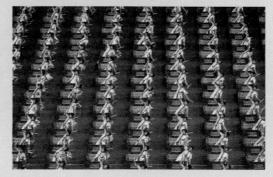

The Reading Process

Prior knowledge helps the skilled reader get a head start on the reading process. Skilled readers break reading into a three-step process. Each step uses its own thinking activities.

1. Before reading, look over or preview the material. (Previewing brings up prior knowledge.) Ask questions about the material you are about to read.

2. During reading, test your understanding of the material.

3. After reading, review and react to what you have learned.

One well-known way to apply this reading process is called **SQ3R.**

SQ3R stands for
Survey
Question
Read
Recite
Review

SQ3R activates prior knowledge and offers strategies for each phase of the reading process. The following graphic illustrates the phases of the reading process through SQ3R. Skilled readers repeat or move among phases as needed to repair comprehension.

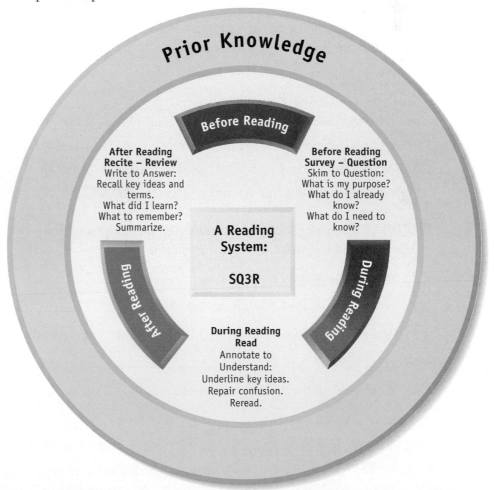

Before Reading: Survey and Question

Survey

Quickly look over, or **skim**, the reading passage for clues about how it is organized and what it means.

To skim effectively, look at *italic* and **boldface** type and take note of titles, introductions, and headings. Also look at pictures and graphs. Finally, read the first paragraph, summaries, and questions. Each of these clues provides important information.

> **Glossary**
>
> **skim** read quickly

Question

To aid in comprehension, ask questions before you read. The following list of prereading questions can be used in most reading situations:

- What is the passage about?
- How is the material organized?
- What do I already know about this idea? (What is my prior knowledge?)
- What is my purpose for reading?
- What is my reading plan? Do I need to read everything?
- What are the most important parts to remember?

EXAMPLE   Before you read the following passage word for word, skim the passage and fill in the following information.

1. What is the passage about? _____

2. What do I already know about this topic? _____

3. What is my purpose for reading? What do I need to remember? _____

   _____

4. What ideas in the passage are in **bold** type? _____, _____,

   _____, and _____

5. After reading the passage, study the picture, and complete the caption by filling in the blank.

Racing for Safety

The challenge for each Indianapolis 500 car team is the same every year. Designers need to develop a race car that is safe, durable, and competitive in different racing conditions. Durability is required to complete the 16-race schedule. In addition, cars must meet the demands of four different types of racing circuits, with each course requiring a different aerodynamic and mechanical setup.

Street: A narrow, temporary course ranging from 1.6 to 2.1 miles in length, with tight turns and a long straightaway. The Long Beach circuit (lap record, 108 mph) tests the durability of the gearbox, braking system, and low-speed acceleration.

Road: Laguna Seca Raceway (lap record, 112 mph) is an example of a road course with hills. A road course is a wide-open track that ranges in length from 1.9 to 4 miles. It has both slow and high-speed corners and is wide enough for passing. The suspension system, downhill braking, and power are stressed on this type of course.

Short Oval: Phoenix International Raceway (lap record, 172 mph) is a 1-mile-long oval track. Short straightaways and banked turns are typical of this type of track. The short oval tests the suspension and aerodynamic setup of the car.

Speedway: The speedway is an oval track with banked turns and long straightaways. The one-lap record at the Michigan International Speedway (2-mile oval) is 234 mph. At Indianapolis (2.5-mile oval), the record is 232 mph. High sustained speed requires aerodynamic efficiency.

VISUAL VOCABULARY

The Mazda Nagare concept car is both beautiful and aerodynamic.

The best synonym for

aerodynamic is _____.

   a. powerful.
   b. sleek.
   c. durable.

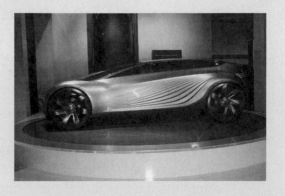

The job of the team engineer is to prepare a competitive, safe car that can be adjusted quickly. Currently, the Indy cars are considered the safest race cars in the world.

—Adapted from "Car Development," *NAS Systems Development at NASA Ames Research Center,* 27 Aug. 2001. 24 Aug. 2009. http://www.nas.nasa .gov/About/Education/Racecar/development.html

EXPLANATION

1. *What is the passage about?* The title of the passage gives us a clue: "Racing for Safety." So does the first paragraph. This passage is about the need to make race cars safe for four different types of tracks.

2. *What do I already know about this idea?* This answer will vary for each reader. Racing fans already know a great deal that will help them understand the details in this passage. Others may not follow the sport. Yet most of you probably drive or ride in cars and can relate to the need for safety on different types of roads, so you can connect your driving experience to the information in the passage.

3. *What is my purpose for reading?* You read to learn new information. *What do I need to remember?* You might need to remember the four types of racetracks.

4. *What ideas in the passage are in **bold** type?* The four types of racetracks are in bold: street, road, short oval, and speedway.

Applying the Before Reading Step: "Before Reading" Activities

The "Before Reading" activities in this book will help you turn reading skills into reading strategies. The rest of the chapters in Part One start with a "Before Reading" activity. These activities use SQ3R strategies. Sometimes, the activity directs you to review skills taught in earlier chapters. At other times, you are asked to skim the chapter and create study questions. Then you answer these questions as you read about the skill. For example, in Chapter 4's **Before Reading About Topics and Main Ideas,** you will create several questions based on the learning outcomes. Notice that every chapter has a set of learning outcomes listed under the chapter's title.

During Reading: Read and Annotate

After you have surveyed and asked questions about the text, it's time to read the entire passage.

Read

As you read, think about the importance of the information by continuing to ask questions:

- Does this new information agree with what I already knew?
- Do I need to change my mind about what I thought I knew?
- What is the significance of this information? Do I need to remember this?

In addition to asking questions while you read, acknowledge and resolve any confusion as it occurs.

- Create questions based on the headings, subheadings, and words in **bold** print and *italics*.
- Reread the parts you don't understand.
- Reread when your mind drifts during reading.
- Read ahead to see if the idea becomes clearer.
- Determine the meanings of words from the context.
- Look up new or difficult words.
- Think about ideas even when they differ from your own.

Annotate

Make the material your own. Make sure you understand it by repeating the information.

- Create a picture in your mind or on paper.
- Restate the ideas in your own words.
- Mark your text by underlining, circling, or highlighting topics, key terms, and main ideas. (See pages 428–429 for more information about how to annotate.)
- Write out answers to the questions you created based on the headings and subheadings.
- Write a summary of the passage or section.

EXAMPLE   Before you read the following passage, take the time to use your surveying skills by answering the following questions.

1. What is the passage about? _____

2. What do I already know about this topic? What is my prior knowledge?

_____

_____

_____

3. What is important about this passage? What do I need to remember?

_____

_____

_____

4. What are the words in **bold** type? _____, _____,

and _____

As you read, monitor your understanding or comprehension. Highlight key words and ideas. Once you have surveyed the information, read the passage. Record the answers to the questions based on the ideas in **bold** print.

Drug Abuse: *A, B, C*

5. What new or difficult words do I need to look up?

_____

_____

6. How does alcohol act as a depressant?

_____

_____

Drug abuse is a serious problem in modern society. Drugs are available at school, on the street, and even in our homes. Depression, stress, and peer pressure can make the use of drugs as an escape very appealing. Three drugs in particular—alcohol, barbiturates, and cocaine—cause millions of people great loss of income, health, and peace of mind. One way to combat drug abuse is to learn some facts about these drugs.

Alcohol is a depressant that affects the central nervous system. It slows the action of nerve cells called *neurons*. Alcohol numbs the part of the brain that controls behavior. It makes the user feel happy and relaxed. However, as little as $1\frac{1}{2}$ ounces of alcohol affect the body and judgment. Muscle control is lost, and speech becomes slurred. Some people become loud and violent; others insist on driving. Too much alcohol taken in during a short period of time can cause breathing to

7. How do barbiturates act as a depressant?

_____

_____

8. How does cocaine act as a stimulant?

_____

_____

stop, which can lead to coma or even death. Alcohol is the oldest and most commonly used social drug.

Barbiturates are also depressants that affect the central nervous system. In small doses, they relieve tension. In large doses, they cause a deep sleep. A large dose that does not result in sleep causes a feeling of being high. This feeling is similar to the effect of alcohol. Barbiturates can be grouped by how long their effect lasts. The longest-lasting barbiturates stay in the body for 6 to 24 hours. The short-term barbiturates last 3 to 6 hours and are the most widely used. These are the ones doctors give to people who complain about sleep problems. Barbiturates are often used in suicide attempts.

Cocaine is a stimulant that causes short, intense bursts of energy. When cocaine is taken into the body by chewing coca leaves, stomach acids reduce the effect. However, when the drug is sniffed through the nose or injected directly into a vein, the drug becomes more dangerous. Mild use causes confusion and anxiety. A large dose leads to dizziness, tremors, and convulsions. Overdoses cause the heart to stop and breathing to cease.

EXPLANATION Compare your answers to the ones given here. Your wording and examples may be different.

Before Reading: Survey and Question

1. The passage is about drug abuse.

2. Details of your prior knowledge will vary.

3. What is important to remember are the characteristics of the three types of drugs and the dangers of each drug.

4. The words in **bold** type are *alcohol*, *barbiturates*, and *cocaine*.

During Reading: Read and Annotate

5. Words you need to look up may include *depressant*, *neurons*, *stimulant*, and *convulsions*.

6. Alcohol slows down the brain and causes loss of muscle control. Loss of muscle control causes unclear speech and poor driving. Alcohol can cause a person to become violent or to make poor decisions and can lead to a coma or death.

7. Depending on the dose and type, barbiturates can help a person relax, cause a deep sleep, or lead to coma or death.

8. Cocaine causes confusion, anxiety, dizziness, tremors, and convulsions. Cocaine in large doses brings the heart and lungs to a stop.

9. Identify here any ideas you needed to reread to understand the passage.

_____

 ## After Reading: Recite and Review

Once you have read the entire selection, go back over the material to review it.

Recite

As part of your review, take time to think and write about what you have read.

- Connect new information to your prior knowledge about the topic.
- Form opinions about the material and the author.
- Record changes in your opinions based on the new information.
- Write about what you have read.

Review

- Summarize the most important parts.
- Revisit and answer the questions raised by headings and subheadings.
- Review new words and their meanings based on the way they were used in the passage.

PRACTICE 2

Now that you have learned about each of the three phases of the reading process, practice putting all three together. Think before, during, and after reading. Apply SQ3R to the following passage. Remember the steps:

- **Survey:** Look over the whole passage.
- **Question:** Ask questions about the content. Predict how the new information fits in with what you already know about the topic.
- **Read:** Continue to question, look up new words, reread, and create pictures in your mind.

■ **Recite:** Restate the ideas in your own words. Write out questions and answers, definitions of words, and new information.

■ **Review:** Think about what you have read and written. Use writing to capture your opinions and feelings about what you have read.

Before Reading: Survey and Question

The following passage is adapted from a Report by the Centers for Disease Control (CDC). Skim the passage and answer the following questions.

1. What is this passage about? _____

2. What do I already know about this topic? _____

3. What do I need to remember? _____

_____

4. What ideas are in *italic* print? _____,

_____, _____

During Reading: Read and Annotate

As you read this report from the CDC, answer the questions in the margin.

5. What are some examples of *new technology?*

_____

_____

_____

6. What is *technology lingo?*

_____

_____

_____

_____

_____

Electronic Aggression: Problem and Solution

Technology and youth seem meant for each other. Both are young, fast paced, and ever changing. In the past, teens readily accepted technology, such as record players, TVs, cassette players, computers, and VCRs. However, in the last two decades, there has been an explosion in *new technology*. Cell phones, iPods, MP-3s, DVDs, and PDAs (personal digital assistants) are now a part of everyday life. And young people are eagerly using these new tools. This new technology has also added new words to our vocabulary. For example, *technology lingo* such as instant messaging ("IMing"), blogging, and text messaging are now familiar terms. Despite the clear benefits of new technology, many are concerned about the dangers it poses for young people.

One such danger is *electronic aggression.* Electronic aggression is similar to bullying. It is a personal attack. But this attack is carried out through technology. Examples are teasing, telling lies, making fun of someone, making rude or mean

7. What are some examples of technology lingo?

_____

_____

_____

_____

8. What is *electronic aggression*?

_____

_____

_____

_____

_____

comments, spreading rumors, or making threats. This aggression takes place through email, a chat room, instant messaging, a website, blogs, or text messaging. Electronic aggression is a form of violence committed with the use of electronic devices. Youth must be protected against it.

To respond to this concern, some states and school districts have established policies about the use of cell phones on school grounds. And they have created policies to block access to certain websites on school computers. Many teachers have taken action individually. They spot-check the websites accessed by their students.

Caregivers can also make a difference. Young people spend a good part of their day in school, but the most influential people in their lives are their caregivers. Peers are a very close second, but caregivers are still first. However, adults and youth have different views about technology. For example, adults see the Internet as a tool to find information. In contrast, young people see the Internet as a place to visit. To bridge this gap, caregivers must talk with their children. Concerned caregivers ask their children where they are going and who they are going with whenever they leave the house. They should take the same approach when their child goes on the Internet. Parents should check to see which sites their children visit and to whom their children are talking while on the Internet. Young people are sometimes reluctant to disclose victimization. They fear their use of the Internet and cellular phone will be limited. Caregivers should talk with their teens to come up with a fair solution to prevent or deal with the victimization. The teen should not be punished for his or her victimization.

—Adapted from U. S. Department of Health and Human Services. *Electronic Media and Youth Violence: A CDC Issue Brief for Educators and Caregivers.* Centers for Disease Control and Prevention. 2008 24 Aug. 2009 http://www.cdc.gov/ncipc/dvp/YVP/electronic_agression_brief_for_parents.pdf.

After Reading: Recite and Review

9. What actions have school districts taken to protect youth from electronic aggression? _____

_____

_____

10. What actions should caregivers take to protect their children from electronic aggression? _____

_____

_____

_____

Applying the After Reading Step: "After Reading" Activities

"After Reading" activities will help you turn reading skills into reading strategies. "After Reading" activities appear in Chapters 2–11 as a final review and comprehension check before the mastery tests. After you have completed the review tests, you will be asked questions that focus on your studies. These questions ask you to reflect on what you have learned about the skill taught in the chapter. As you write your answers, you are creating a learning log or journal that tracks your growth as a reader.

Textbook Skills

Before, During, and After Reading—Asking Questions and Recording Answers

A vast number of textbooks use titles, headings, **bold** print, and *italics* to organize ideas. A skilled reader applies the questioning and annotating steps to these pieces of information. For example, before reading, turn titles and headings into questions. Write these questions out. During or after reading, write out the answers to these questions.

EXAMPLE   Before you read the following passage from a health textbook, skim the information and write out four questions based on the title and the words in **bold** print. After you read, answer the questions you have created.

Three Types of Eating Disorders

Throughout our lives, most of us wage a running battle with food. We eat too much, we gain weight, and a few days go by when we are not concerned about what we are putting into our mouths and what all that food is doing to our hips, our buttocks, or other body parts. On occasion, over one-third of all Americans are obese and obsessed with diet.

For a growing number of people, chiefly young women, this obsessive bond with food develops into a persistent, chronic eating disorder known as **anorexia nervosa**. Anorexia is a condition marked by deliberate food restriction and severe, life-threatening weight loss. **Bulimia nervosa** is an eating disorder marked by binge eating, which is followed by improper steps to avoid weight gain. These steps include purging (self-induced vomiting), laxative abuse, or excessive exercise. **Binge eating disorder** (BED) is an eating disorder of regular binge eating, without steps to avoid weight gain. Binge eaters are clinically obese.

—Donatelle, *Access to Health*, 7th ed., p. 280.

1. _____

_____

2. _____

_____

3. _____

_____

4. _____

_____

EXPLANATION   Compare your questions and answers to the ones given here.

1. *What are the three types of eating disorders?*

   The three types of eating disorders are anorexia nervosa, bulimia nervosa, and binge eating disorder (BED).

2. *What is anorexia nervosa, and what is it marked by?*

   Anorexia nervosa is the severe restriction of food intake, marked by an avoidance of food and dangerous weight loss.

3. *What is bulimia nervosa, and what is it marked by?*

   Bulimia is binge eating and then taking drastic steps to avoid gaining weight.

4. *What is binge eating disorder, and what is it marked by?*

   Binge eating disorder is binge eating without any steps to avoid weight gain, resulting in obesity.

PRACTICE 3

Textbook Skills

Before you read the following passage from an interpersonal communication textbook, skim the information and write out *five* questions based on the title and the words in **bold** print. After you read, answer the questions you have created.

Self-Awareness and the Four Selves

Since you control your thoughts and behaviors to the level that you understand who you are, it's crucial to develop a high sense of self-awareness. We can begin this discussion by looking at the four selves.

Your Open Self. Your **open self** represents all the information, behaviors, attitudes, feelings, desires, motives, and ideas that are you. The type of information might vary from your name and sex to your age, religion, and batting average. The size of your open self changes based on the situation you are in and the people you are with. Some people may make you feel comfortable. To them, you would open yourself wide. To others, you might want to leave most of yourself closed and unknown.

Your Blind Self. Your **blind self** represents all the things about yourself that others know but of which you are not aware. These may include your habit of rubbing your nose when you get angry, your defense mechanisms, and your repressed experiences. You can shrink your blind area, but you can never totally get rid of it.

Your Hidden Self. Your **hidden self** contains all that you know of yourself but that you keep to yourself. This area includes all your secrets. This includes everything you have not revealed and seek actively to hide.

Your Unknown Self. Your **unknown self** represents truths that exist but that neither you nor others know. We infer this unknown self from dreams, psychological tests, or therapy. For example, through therapy you might become aware of your need for acceptance.

—DeVito, *Messages: Building Interpersonal Communication Skills*, pp. 42-43
© 1999. Reproduced by permission of Pearson Education, Inc.

1. _____

_____

_____

_____

_____

2. _____

_____

_____

3. _____

_____

_____

4. _____

_____

_____

5. _____

_____

_____

_____

APPLICATIONS

Application 1: Prior Knowledge

Read the paragraph, and answer the questions that follow it.

Cellular Phones

For most people, cell phones are a welcome addition to a busy, on-the-go lifestyle. Cell phones offer many benefits. Because of wireless phones, parents are more likely to keep up with their teenage children. Drivers faced with roadside emergencies can reach help. Some cell phones even allow access to e-mail and the Internet. This access helps workers stay in touch with their offices. However, cell phones also present some real problems. Dialing while driving takes attention from the road, and in an instant, a car can drift off the road or into oncoming traffic. Talking while driving presents the same risk. Surprising or bad news can cause the driver to think about the conversation instead of the traffic. In addition, a new study reveals that driving while texting on a cell phone or smartphone is very dangerous. In fact, a person who is texting is 23 times more likely to be involved in a crash than drivers who are not texting. Finally, some experts fear cell phones because cell phones use radio frequency waves. These experts question the safety of constantly putting radio frequency waves close to the head. Overall, cell phones do offer many benefits, but they may also present some risks.

1. What is your prior knowledge about the benefits of cell phones? _____

_____

_____

_____

2. What is your prior knowledge about the dangers of cell phones? _____

_____

_____

_____

3. What is your reaction to the information about the safety of using cell

phones? _____

_____

_____

Application 2: Before Reading

Survey the passage by answering the following questions.

1. What is the passage about? _____

_____

2. What do I already know about these ideas? _____

_____

3. What do I need to remember? What is my purpose for reading? _____

_____

_____

4. What words are in **bold** type? _____, _____, and

_____

Three Steps to Success

Successful people tend to follow three steps to achieve their goals.

Setting goals is the first step. Success comes from a clear goal, and a clear goal comes from a strong desire. For example, to successfully lose 10 pounds and keep those pounds off, a person must first want to do so. This goal is based on the strong desire to look and feel better.

Staying focused is the second step. For example, a student sets a clear goal to earn a high grade in a class, understanding that the grade represents a level of knowledge. Cheating on a test or assignment for a higher grade would distract from the goal of becoming educated. Staying focused leads to hard work and follow-through.

Solving problems is the final step to success. The path to every goal has a set of barriers or problems that need to be overcome. Sometimes the barrier is a lack of a skill. At other times, the problem may be an attitude or habit that needs to be changed. Often unplanned events must be dealt with. No matter what the barrier, successful people find ways to solve the problem and reach the goal. Successful people set goals, stay focused, and solve problems.

Application 3: During Reading

As you read the following passage, record your answers to the following questions.

1. What new words do I need to look up? _____

   _____

2. What are the three types of cloning? _____

   _____

3. What is another name for therapeutic cloning ? _____

   _____

4. What ability do stem cells have? _____

   _____

5. Why are doctors and scientists excited about stem cells? _____

   _____

   _____

Three Types of Cloning and Stem Cells

Cloning describes the processes used to create an exact genetic replica of another cell, tissue, or organism. The copied material has the same genetic makeup as the original. The copied material is referred to as a clone. The most famous clone was a Scottish sheep named Dolly.

There are three different types of cloning. First, gene cloning creates copies of genes or segments of DNA. Second, reproductive cloning creates copies of whole animals. Third, therapeutic cloning creates embryonic stem cells. Therapeutic cloning is also called "embryo cloning." The goal of this process is not to clone human beings. Instead the goal is to harvest stem cells from the cloned embryo.

Stem cells are cells with the ability to develop into many different types of cells in the body. They serve as a repair system for the body. There are two main types of stem cells: One type is the embryonic stem cell. And the other type is the adult stem cell.

Doctors and scientists are excited about stem cells. Studying stem cells may help explain the causes of serious conditions such as birth defects and cancer. Stem cells may one day be used to make cells and tissues for therapy of many diseases. Stem cells may help cure Parkinson's disease, Alzheimer's disease, spinal cord injury, heart disease, diabetes and arthritis. Researchers hope to use these cells to grow healthy tissue. The new tissue will replace injured or diseased tissues in the human body.

—Adapted from "Cloning." MedlinePlus. 13 July 2009.
http://www.nlm.nih.gov/medlineplus/cloning.html.

VISUAL VOCABULARY

Based on the information in the passage, Dolly the sheep is an example of

_____ cloning.

a. gene
b. reproductive
c. therapeutic

Application 4: After Reading

Read the passage, practicing your before reading and during reading skills. Once you have finished reading the selection, answer the questions that follow it.

Gangs

Although gangs can be found anywhere these days, two of the best known are the Crips and the Bloods from California. To cope with the problems gangs bring to a community, it is important to understand what a gang is and why people join gangs.

Why join a gang? There are at least five reasons that gangs are attractive to young people. First, some young men thrill at the idea of parties, girls, and drugs, which they assume gang membership will provide. Second, gangs often satisfy the desire to escape poverty by providing money for food and clothes through drug dealing and theft. Third, some young people crave power and respect and see gang membership as a way to gain both. Fourth, some feel the need to belong to and be accepted by a peer group or regard the gang as the family they never had. Fifth, some people join gangs for protection against the violence in their neighborhood.

What is a gang? Most gangs share at least five traits. First, like the Crips and the Bloods, gangs have names. Even large gangs like these two have smaller groups with local names. Second, most gangs mark out a territory with graffiti. The graffiti are a way of warning enemies or advertising a drug sale. Third, gangs are known for their violence. Often the violence starts over a trivial issue like an insult. Violence can also be a part of initiation into the gang, or it can occur as the gang commits another crime such as robbery. Fourth, the bond between members is deep. Gang members become almost inseparable. The strength of the gang comes from the amount of time the members spend together. Finally, gangs usually wear clothing, tatoos, or other items to identify their gang affiliation.

1. What five things make gangs attractive?

   a. _____

   b. _____

   c. _____

   d. _____

   e. _____

2. What five traits do most gangs share?

a. _____

b. _____

c. _____

d. _____

e. _____

VISUAL VOCABULARY

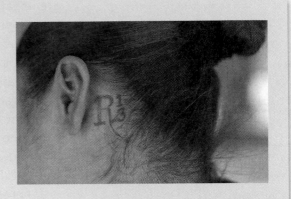

Gang members often use tattoos to show their gang *affiliation*.

The best synonym for

affiliation is _____.

  a. individuality.
  b. membership.
  c. affection.

REVIEW TEST 1

Score (number correct) _____ × 10 = _____ %

Before and During Reading

A. Before you read, survey the passage by skimming for the following information.

1. What is the passage about? _____

2. What are the ideas in *italics*? _____, _____,

_____, and _____

3. What do I already know about this topic? _____

_____

4. What do I need to remember? _____

_____

B. Read the passage. As you read, answer the accompanying questions.

Tropical Rain Forests

5. How much of the earth's surface do tropical rain forests cover?

_____

6. What percentage of the earth's species live in tropical rain forests?

_____

7. What is the effect of rich soil and a hot, wet climate?

_____

_____

8. What are hot spots?

_____

_____

9. What is destroying tropical rain forests?

_____

_____

10. How many species become extinct each year?

_____

The _beauty and value_ of tropical rain forests are their great diversity of life. Tropical rain forests cover about 6 percent of the earth's surface and are home to half of the world's species.

Of all the known insects in the world, 80 percent are found in tropical forests. Several factors explain why so many different types of life thrive in tropical forests. _Rich soil_ and a _hot, wet climate_ create ideal growing conditions. Heavy rainfall and abundant energy from the sun produce dense plant growth. Some tropical rain forests have more variety of life than others. Forests that have a great variety of life are known as _hot spots_. Hot spots contain more than one-fourth of all forest plant species. The different species that live in a tropical rain forest need one another to survive. Insects and birds pollinate flowers, allowing fruit to develop. And the fruits of the forest feed the animals and people who live there.

Sadly, human action is rapidly destroying these havens of life. For example, over the past decade, worldwide tropical rain forests have shrunk by about 23,000 square miles each year. Most of the loss has been due to logging or to clearing land for farming. The rapid destruction of these forests is causing many species to go extinct, as their homes disappear. Experts believe that as many as 25,000 species become extinct each year. Most of them are disappearing before they are even discovered and named. If this is true, organisms are becoming extinct at an alarming rate. And in the future, the Earth will have far fewer species than are currently present.

A tropical rain forest is a *haven* of life.

The best synonym for *haven* is

_____.

   a. port.
   b. refuge.
   c. wilderness.

REVIEW TEST 2

Score (number correct) _____ × 20 = _____ %

Before and During Reading

A. Before reading, survey the following excerpt from the website, and answer these questions.

   1. What is my purpose for reading? _____

_____

   2. What kinds of information should I be looking for to understand and remember? _____

_____

_____

B. Read the information. As you read, answer the following questions.

   3. What is the main ingredient in this dish? _____

   4. How does Calorie-Count rate this dish? _____

_____

   5. Which of the following words best describes the ratings for the levels of cholesterol and sodium? _____ healthful _____ unhealthful

calorie-count
from About.com Health

Calories in SOUTH BEACH DIET FROZEN ENTREES ENTREE- CAPRESE STYLE CHICKEN WITH BROCCOLI & CAULIFLOWER
Frozen Entrees

Manufactured by South Beach Diet

Add item to food log
Create a free account

Nutrition Facts
Serving Size 1 serving (297.0 g)

Amount Per Serving	
Calories 250	Calories from Fat 72
	% Daily Value*
Total Fat 8.0g	**12%**
Saturated Fat 2.0g	**10%**
Cholesterol 95mg	**32%**
Sodium 1350mg	**56%**
Total Carbohydrates 12.0g	**4%**
Dietary Fiber 3.0g	**12%**
Sugars 6.0g	
Protein 35.0g	
Vitamin A 15% •	Vitamin C 25%
Calcium 20% •	Iron 10%

* Based on a 2000 calorie diet

Tags - south beach, lunch, dinner

Nutritional Analysis

Nutrition Grade

42%
confidence

B-

Bad Grade?

Bad points
High in cholesterol
Very high in sodium

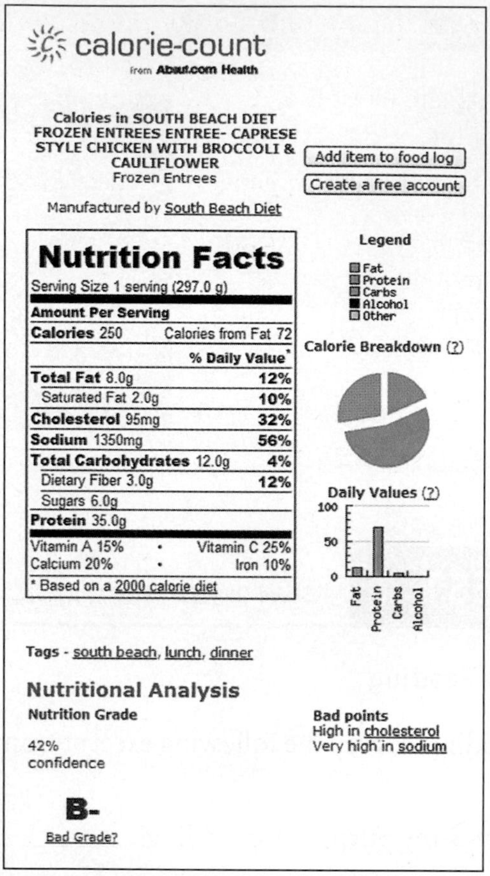

Source: © 2010 About.com (http://caloriecount.about.com) All rights reserved.

REVIEW TEST 3

Score (number correct) _____ × 20 = _____%

Before, During, and After Reading

A. Before reading, survey the poem, and answer the following questions.

1. What is this poem about? ____________________

____

____

2. What do I already know about this topic? ____________________

____

____

B. Read the poem. As you read, answer the accompanying questions.

3. How many people are identified as "Nobody"?

_____

4. How is a "Somebody" described?

_____

I'm Nobody! Who are you?
Are you—Nobody—too?
Then there's a pair of us!
Don't tell! They'd banish us—you know!

How dreary—to be—Somebody!
How public—like a Frog—
To tell your name—the livelong June—
To an admiring Bog!

—Emily Dickinson, 1861. Reprinted by permission of the publishers and the Trustees of Amherst College from *The Poems of Emily Dickinson,* Thomas H. Johnson, ed., Cambridge, Mass.: The Belknap Press of Press of Harvard University Press, Copyright © 1951, 1955, 1979, 1983 by the President and Fellows of Harvard College.

C. After you have read it, put the poem into your own words. Use two or three sentences.

5. _____

_____

REVIEW TEST 4   Score (number correct) _____ × 10 = _____%

Before, During, and After Reading

A. Before reading the passage, survey the information. Answer the following questions.

Textbook Skills

    1. What is this passage about? _____

B. Now read the passage. As you read, answer the accompanying questions.

_____

2. What can you do to make conflict more productive?

_____

_____

Before and After a Conflict

Make conflict with your partner truly useful. Use these ideas both for preparing for the conflict ahead of time and for using the conflict as a method of growth after the conflict.

3. Why should you fight in private?

_____

_____

_____

_____

_____

4. Why should you only fight about problems that can be solved?

_____

_____

_____

_____

5. What can you learn from the conflict?

_____

_____

_____

_____

_____

6. What does it mean to keep the conflict in perspective?

_____

_____

_____

7. Why reward each other?

_____

_____

Before the Conflict

Fight in private. When you air your conflicts in front of others, you create a wide variety of other problems. You might not be willing to be totally honest when others are present. You may feel you have to save face and win at all costs. This might lead you to use strategies to win the argument rather than to solve the problem. Also, you run the risk of embarrassing your partner in front of others. Embarrassment may lead to bitterness and anger.

Focus on the problem. Make sure you are both free of other problems and ready to deal with the conflict at hand. Confronting your partner when she or he comes home after a hard day of work may not be the right time for resolving a conflict. Choose a good time to deal with your conflict.

Know what you are fighting about. Sometimes people become so hurt and angry that they lash out just to vent their frustration. The problem at the center of the conflict is merely an excuse to express anger. For example, getting upset over the uncapped toothpaste tube is not the real problem. The underlying problem may be a need to feel respected.

Fight about problems that can be solved. Fighting about past behaviors or about family members over which you have no control doesn't help. Instead, it creates additional problems. Any attempt at resolution is doomed since the problems can't be solved.

After the Conflict

Learn from the conflict. Think about the process you went through in trying to resolve the problem. For example, can you identify the fight strategies that aggravated the situation?

Keep conflict in perspective. Be careful not to blow it out of proportion. In most relationships, conflicts actually occupy a very small part of the couple's time, and yet in their recollection, they often loom extremely large. Don't view yourself, your partner, or your relationship as a failure just because conflicts sometimes arise.

Attack your negative feelings. Often such feelings arise because unfair fight strategies were used to challenge the other person—for example, blame or verbal attacks. Resolve to avoid such unfair tactics in the future, but at the same time, let go of guilt or blame for yourself or your partner.

Reward each other. Increase the exchange of rewards and cherishing behaviors. These will show your positive feelings and that you're over the conflict and want the relationship to survive.

—DeVito, *Messages: Building Interpersonal Communication Skills*, pp. 297–298
© 1999. Reproduced by permission of Pearson Education, Inc.

C. Now that you have read the passage, answer the following question by filling in the blanks.

What are the steps to making conflict useful?

Before the conflict:

8. _____
Focus on the problem.
Know what you are fighting about.
Fight about problems that can be solved.

After the conflict:

9. _____
Keep conflict in perspective.
Attack your negative feelings.

10. _____

After Reading About a Reading System for Skilled Readers

Now that you have read and studied A Reading System for Skilled Readers, take time to reflect on what you have learned before you begin the Mastery Tests. Think about your learning and performance by answering the following questions. Write your answers in your notebook.

- How has my knowledge base or prior knowledge about the reading process changed?

- Based on my studies, how do I think I will perform on the Mastery Test(s)? Why do I think my scores will be above average, average, or below average?

■ Would I recommend this chapter to other students who want to learn more about the reading process? Why or why not?

Test your understanding of what you have learned about the reading process by completing the Chapter 1 Review Card in the insert near the end of your text.

CONNECT TO PEARSON **myreadinglab**

To check your progress in meeting Chapter 1's learning outcomes, log in to **www.myreadinglab.com** and try the following activities.

■ The "Memorization and Concentration" section of MyReadingLab ties the use of prior knowledge to your ability to focus on and remember what you have read. To access this resource, click on the "Study Plan" tab. Then click on "Memorization and Concentration." Under the heading "Review Materials," choose option #3 "Model: Concentration and Memorization."

■ The "Active Reading Strategies" section of MyReadingLab offers an overview, model, slide show, practices, and tests about the reading process. To access this resource, go to MyReadingLab.com. Click on the "Study Plan" tab. Then choose "Active Reading Strategies" from the menu.

■ The "Reading Textbooks" section of MyReadingLab offers an overview, model, slide show, practices, and tests about the reading process and text-books. For example, to learn about how to survey a textbook, click on "Reading Textbooks." Then, under the heading "Review Materials," choose option #2 "Model: Reading Textbooks." To learn more about applying SQ3R to textbook reading, choose option #3 "Model: SQ3R."

To measure your mastery of the content of this chapter, complete the test in the "Active Reading Strategies" section and click on Gradebook to find your results.

Before you read the following passage from a textbook on physical fitness, skim the information and write out *five* questions based on the words in **bold** print. Then read the passage and answer the questions you have created.

Textbook
Skills

Weight Training

Weight training is an excellent way to control weight, tone muscles, and build bones. However, many people begin lifting weights with very little understanding about the proper way to get the most out of a workout. Understanding a few workout terms will help you execute your workout routine.

Repetitions or reps. Repetitions are the number of times that you perform an exercise. For example, one rep for a bench press occurs when you pick up the bar, lower it, pause, and lift it up. If you perform that same movement a second time, you have completed a second repetition.

Sets. A set is a series of repetitions that ends when the muscle reaches muscular failure. Muscular failure occurs when the buildup of lactic acid in the muscle makes it impossible to complete another rep with proper form.

Rest interval. A rest interval is the amount of time you rest between sets. For example, a rest interval of 60 seconds means you sit inactive for 60 seconds before beginning another set.

Modified compound supersets. A modified compound superset occurs when you pair exercises, usually for opposing muscle movements or opposing muscle groups (such as push and pull). First, you perform one exercise, rest, and then perform the second exercise. For example, first you do the biceps, then do the triceps. Then you rest and return to the first exercise.

Supersets. A superset is a combination of exercises performed right after each other with no rest in between. There are two ways to do this. The first way is to do two exercises for the same muscle group at once. The second and best way to superset is by pairing exercises of opposing muscle groups.

—Adapted from Villepigue & Rivera, *The Body Sculpting Bible for Women: The Way to Physical Perfection*, p. 46.

1. _____

_____

_____

2. _____

_____

_____

3. _____

_____

_____

4. _____

_____

_____

_____

5. _____

_____

_____

A. Survey the passage below before reading it, and answer the following questions.

1. Who is this passage about? _____

2. What are the nine ideas in **bold** print and *italics*?

_____

_____

_____

_____

_____

_____

_____

_____

_____

B. Now read the passage. As you read, answer the accompanying questions.

3. How did Banneker show his love of learning?

_____

_____

_____

4. How did Banneker show his love of work?

_____

_____

_____

Benjamin Banneker: A True Genius

Benjamin Banneker, born a free black man, lived in Elliot Mills, Maryland, from 1731 until 1806. His life was marked by a love of learning, a love of work, and a love of justice.

A love of learning. Banneker had to teach himself. Throughout his childhood, he spent most of his days working beside his mother and father in their tobacco fields. His farm duties meant that he could attend school only during the winter months. Banneker's love of learning was evident even in his early years. In a one-room school, he learned reading, writing, and mathematics. He excelled in *mathematics*. He was curious about everything, and he spent much of his time observing the sky, earth, clouds, rain, and seasons. He read as much and as often as

5. What is an almanac?

_____

_____

_____

_____

_____

6. How many years did Banneker write and publish his almanac?

_____

_____

7. What did President Washington appoint Banneker to?

_____

_____

_____

_____

8. How did Banneker show his love of justice?

_____

_____

_____

9. What was the attitude of slave owners?

_____

_____

10. What about Banneker impressed Thomas Jefferson?

_____

_____

he could. However, books were scarce. So most of what he learned, he had to learn firsthand.

A love of work. As much as Banneker loved to learn, he also loved to use his knowledge. He became a hardworking and successful _farmer_. He was also an inventor, writer, and publisher. For example, by the time he was 22, he had built a handmade clock. This clock was probably the _first clock made on American soil_. He shaped the clock and each gear out of hardwood with a knife, and the clock kept time for more than 20 years.

From 1792 until 1802, Banneker _wrote and published his own almanac_. An almanac is a book that shows the times the sun sets and rises, phases of the moon, and times of high and low tides. Farmers used almanacs to help them in many ways. For example, a farmer could reset a stopped clock or plan the best time to plant a crop.

Banneker's success brought him to the attention of the president, George Washington. The United States was about to build the nation's capital. _President Washington appointed Banneker_ to the team of civil engineers and surveyors who would _plan the nation's capital_. Banneker helped select the sites for the U.S. Capitol building, the U.S. Treasury, and the White House. At one point in the process, the plans for the capital disappeared. President Washington feared the work would not be finished. However, Banneker had memorized the plans, and the work continued.

A love of justice. Although Benjamin Banneker was a free black man, racial limits were placed on free blacks as well as slaves. Slave owners tried to convince the nation that blacks were not as smart or hardworking as whites. Many whites began to fear well-educated free blacks. Banneker was the _first black person to take a stand against the unfair treatment of blacks_. In fact, he wrote a letter to Thomas Jefferson. Jefferson, the author of the Declaration of Independence, owned slaves. In his letter, Banneker talked about Jefferson's owning slaves. Along with the letter, Banneker sent a copy of his almanac. Banneker's education and success impressed Jefferson.

A. Survey the following passage before reading it. Answer these questions.

Textbook
Skills

1. What is this passage about? _____

2. What are the ideas in **bold** print? _____, _____,

_____, _____, _____, and _____

3. What do I need to remember about this passage? _____

_____

B. Now read the passage. As you read, answer the accompanying questions.

4. What was the New Deal?

_____

_____

_____

_____

_____

5. For what reforms does Eleanor Roosevelt deserve credit?

_____

_____

_____

6. In what roles did women predominate prior to the Great Depression?

_____

_____

_____

The New Deal, Women, and Minority Groups

The New Deal: The term *New Deal* refers to the programs President Franklin D. Roosevelt created to deal with the problems of the Great Depression of the 1930s. These programs were designed to provide relief, recovery, and reform.

The First Lady: Eleanor Roosevelt deserves much of the credit for the reforms aimed at helping minorities. Mrs. Roosevelt was the first president's wife to take a strong public stand on these issues. She supplied moral strength to the New Deal. The First Lady worked hard to convince her husband and the government to hire skilled women and African Americans. In 1933 alone, she traveled 40,000 miles. She visited families and checked on welfare programs. Some thought she was more courageous than her husband. She did not hesitate to take a public stand on civil rights. For example, the Daughters of the American Revolution refused in 1939 to allow the black contralto Marian Anderson to sing in Washington's Constitution Hall. As a result Mrs. Roosevelt arranged for her to perform a concert on the steps of the Lincoln Memorial on Easter Sunday.

Women: Women made some progress under the New Deal. Prior to the Depression, women had dominated both social work and voluntary associations.

7. How did Harold Ickes support civil rights?

_____

_____

_____

_____

8. How did the Farm Security Administration try to help Mexican Americans?

_____

_____

_____

9. How did federal grant money help Native Americans?

_____

_____

_____

_____

Women worked hard to provided charity for the poor and unemployed. The same skills were needed to combat the Depression. Thus, women joined the throngs of professionals who rushed to Washington to work in New Deal programs.

African Americans: Roosevelt named Mary McLeod Bethune, an African American educator, to the advisory committee of the National Youth Administration (NYA). Thanks to her efforts, African Americans received a fair share of NYA money. The Works Progress Administration (WPA) was colorblind. The WPA was a federal program. The WPA put millions of jobless people to work. These workers built or repaired bridges, highways, and parks. Blacks in northern cities benefited from its work relief programs. Harold Ickes, a member of Roosevelt's cabinet, was a strong supporter of civil rights. He placed several African Americans on his staff. He also poured federal funds into black schools and hospitals in the South.

Mexican Americans: The New Deal offered Mexican Americans some help. The Farm Security Administration created camps for migrant farm workers in California. The WPA hired jobless Mexican Americans on relief jobs. Many, however, did not qualify for relief because they had no home address. Additionally, migrant farm workers were not able to collect benefits under workers' compensation or Social Security.

Native Americans: The Indian New Deal was the only bright spot in President Roosevelt's treatment of minorities. President Roosevelt created the Indian Emergency Conservation Program (IECP). This program hired more than 85,000 Native Americans. In 1934, Congress passed laws to help Native Americans. They were allowed to buy new land. They were allowed to have their own government. They were able to follow their customs. And they were allowed to speak their own language. That same year, federal grants gave money to schools, hospitals, and social services to help Native Americans.

—Adapted from Martin et al., _America and Its Peoples: A Mosaic in the Making_, 3rd ed., pp. 848–849.

C. Now that you have read the passage, answer the following question.

    10. What were the three purposes of the New Deal? _____,

                _____, and _____

A. Survey the following passage. Answer the following questions.

1. What is the passage about? _____

2. What is the purpose for reading this passage? _____
_____

B. Now read the passage. After you read, answer the following questions.

3. What are the two types of reality shows discussed in the passage?
_____
_____

4. According to researchers what is the number one reason viewers watch reality shows? _____

5. What are three of the social values held by viewers of reality shows?
_____

Reality Television

Reality television has come into its own. On any given evening, millions of viewers tune in to some type of reality show. *Dancing with the Stars, Survivor, The Bachelor, What Not to Wear, Extreme Makeover: Home Edition* are just a few examples. Why are reality shows so popular?

Some researchers suggest that the number one reason viewers tune in is to relieve stress. Viewers just want to relax and escape from everyday worries. In addition, fans seem to enjoy talking about a shared television event with others. Call it the water-cooler effect. Other researchers point to the audience voting system as a strong draw. Fans want to play a part and affect the outcome of the show. In all, researchers agree that reality television fans tune in to shows that reflect their own social values, such as suspense, personal identity, or romance. A brief look at just two types of reality programs reveals these values.

Elimination and Game Shows

Elimination and game shows include dating-based competitions, top skill and job searches, and sports. Examples range from *The Bachelor*,

America's Next Top Model, Celebrity Apprentice, American Idol, Project Runway, to *Survivor.* These reality shows often cast somewhat diverse groups. The purpose is to see whether conflict or harmony will result. Contestants often win by developing alliances and strategic relationships. And watching the deals and game-play unfold can be great fun.

Renovation, Self-Improvement, and Makeover Shows

The renovation show makes over part or all of a person's living space. For example, each week, *Extreme Makeover: Home Edition* makes over the home of a family in difficulty for reasons beyond their control, such as a natural disaster or a family member with a serious illness. The viewers meet the family, hear the heart-wrenching story, and watch the builders make the family's dream come true. Finally, the viewers watch as the family discovers each new living space. Likewise, the self-improvement show focuses on people who want to improve some part of their lives. Examples include *What Not to Wear, Celebrity Fit Club,* and *Supernanny.* In this type of show, the viewers meet the subjects in their current state of being. Then experts meet with, advise, train, and encourage the subjects to improve. Finally, after training, the subjects meet with their family, friends, and the experts. Together, they review the changes made in the lives of the subjects.

VISUAL VOCABULARY

─────────── Which type of reality show is *The Biggest Loser?*

   a. renovation
   b. self-improvement

Vocabulary in Context

LEARNING OUTCOMES

After studying this chapter you should be able to do the following:

1. Define vocabulary.
2. Classify context clues.
3. Describe how you have always handled new words as you read.
4. Assess your comprehension of context clues.
5. Evaluate and explain the importance of what you have learned.
6. Apply what you have learned about context clues to your reading process.

Before Reading About Vocabulary in Context

Chapter 1 taught you the importance of surveying material before you begin reading by skimming the information for **bold** or *italic* type and noting graphs, charts, and boxes. Throughout this textbook, key ideas are emphasized in bold or italic print where they appear in the passage. Often they are also set apart visually in a box that gives the definition or examples of the term. Skim this chapter for key ideas in bold or italic print and ideas highlighted in boxes. Refer to these key ideas and create at least six questions that you can answer as you read the chapter. Write your questions in the following spaces (record the page number for the key term in each question):

_____? (page _____)

_____? (page _____)

_____? (page _____)

_____? (page _____)

_____? (page _____)

_____? (page _____)

Compare the questions you created with the following questions. Then write the ones that seem most helpful in your notebook, leaving enough space between each question to record the answers as you read and study the chapter.

What is vocabulary (page 42)? What is a context clue (page 43)? What is a SAGE approach (page 43)? What are synonyms (page 43)? What are the signal words for synonyms (page 43)? What are antonyms (page 46)? What are the signal words for antonyms (page 46)? What does the term *general context* mean (page 49)? What are the signal words for examples (page 51)? What is visual vocabulary (page 53)?

The Importance of Words

Words are the building blocks of meaning. Have you ever watched a child with a set of building blocks, such as Legos? Hundreds of separate pieces can be joined together to create buildings, planes, cars, or even spaceships. Words are like that, too. Individual words have meaning. Words properly joined create greater meaning. A large set of building blocks increases the size and number of items a child can build. Likewise, a large set of words expands your ability to create meaning.

> **Vocabulary** is all the words used in a language as a whole.

How many words do you have in your **vocabulary**? By the age of 18, most people know about 60,000 words. During your college studies, you will most likely learn an additional 20,000 words. Each subject you study will have its own set of words.

Learning so many new words may seem overwhelming. However, as you add words to your vocabulary, you increase your skill and pleasure in reading. You first learned words by interacting and practicing. You heard the word; you connected the word to its meaning; you heard the word again and again; you used the word. A skilled reader follows that same pattern.

Context Clues: A SAGE Approach

Skilled readers learn new words in a number of ways. One way is to use **context clues**. The meaning of a word is influenced by the words surrounding it—by its context. Skilled readers use context clues to learn new words.

A **context clue** is the information that surrounds a new word, and is used to understand its meaning.

Four most common types of context clues are:

- Synonyms
- Antonyms
- General context
- Examples

Notice that the first letter of each type of context clue, reading down, spells the word *SAGE*. *Sage* means "wise." Using context clues is a wise—a SAGE—reading strategy.

Synonyms

A **synonym** is a word that has the same or nearly the same meaning as another word. For example, the words *funny* and *humorous* are synonyms. Many times, an author will place a synonym near a new or difficult word as a context clue to the word's meaning. Often the words *or* and *that is* introduce the synonym. Sometimes a synonym is used later in the sentence. A synonym may also be set off with a pair of dashes, a pair of parentheses, or a pair of commas before and after it.

Synonym Signal Words	
or	that is

EXAMPLES Each of the following sentences has a key word in **bold** type. In each sentence, circle the synonym for the word in **bold**.

1. Thousands of years ago, our ancestors lived as **nomadic,** or roaming, tribes.

2. These **primitive**—uncivilized—people used magic to survive. For example, they used magic to find food, to stay healthy, to understand nature, and to please their gods.

3. Slowly, people settled down and formed **urban** (city) cultures, such as Egypt, Greece, and Rome.

4. In urban areas, making magic became a **specialized,** or skilled, line of work.

VISUAL VOCABULARY

Graffiti is a common sight in many _____ areas.

a. primitive
b. urban
c. specialized

EXPLANATIONS

1. The synonym for **nomadic** is *roaming*. Notice that the synonym *roaming* immediately follows the word *nomadic* and has the word *or* before it. The phrase *or roaming* is set off with a pair of commas.

2. The synonym for the word **primitive** is *uncivilized*. The synonym *uncivilized* immediately follows the word *primitive*. It is set off with a pair of dashes.

3. The synonym for the word **urban** is *city*. The synonym *city* immediately follows the word *urban* and is enclosed in parentheses.

4. The synonym for **specialized** is *skilled*. Notice that the synonym *skilled* immediately follows the word *specialized* and has the word *or* before it. The phrase *or skilled* is set off with a pair of commas.

PRACTICE 1

Each of the following sentences contains a word that is a synonym for the word in **bold**. Circle the synonym in each sentence.

1. The ankh was a magical **icon** or symbol to the ancient Egyptians. It stood for both physical life and the afterlife.

2. Ancient Egyptians were concerned about life after death. They developed ways of **mummifying** (preserving) bodies. This custom mixed physical and magical steps.

3. In ancient Egypt, Taweret was the goddess of childbirth. She kept mothers safe from physical harm and evil **sorcery**—witchcraft.

4. Around 500 B.C.E., the Persians worshipped fire. Often priest-magicians used a bundle of special twigs known as the barsom. They used the barsom to keep **ceremonial** or official flames burning.

5. Hecate was the ancient Greek goddess of the underworld. The **patron**, or supporter , of witchcraft and magic, she tormented humans as she roamed the earth at night with a pack of red-eyed hell hounds.

6. In ancient Greece, people visited a sacred grove at Delphi. A priestess would give magical answers to their questions or predict their future. This priestess became known as the Delphic **Oracle** (prophet).

7. Ancient Romans used **talismans**—charms—to ward off evil.

8. One Roman talisman was the cockatrice. The cockatrice was a **mythological**, or make-believe, serpent; it was supposed to be able to kill with its stare.

9. Another talisman was the pinecone. The pinecone was a symbol of the god Dionysus. He was often linked to the wild **rituals** or practices of witches.

10. Sometimes, Romans decorated bronze nails with magic symbols. These nails may have been used in spells. Most likely, an **incantation** (chant or prayer) was spoken as the nail was slowly hammered into a wooden surface.

VISUAL VOCABULARY

In today's society, many people use a rabbit's foot as ——————.

   a. an icon.
   b. a ritual.
   c. a talisman.

Antonyms

An **antonym** is a word that has the opposite meaning of another word. For example, *heavy* and *light* are antonyms. So are *early* and *late*. Antonyms help you determine a word's meaning by showing you what the word does *not* mean. Antonyms are usually introduced with words and phrases of contrast or difference. Contrast words such as *not* or *unlike* often act as signals that an antonym is being used. These signal words alert you to expect a change.

Antonym Signal Words				
as opposed to	however	not	rather than	yet
but	in contrast	on the other hand	unlike	

Sometimes antonyms can be found next to the new word. In those cases, commas, dashes, or parentheses may set them off from the new word. At other times, antonyms are placed in other parts of the sentence to emphasize the contrast between the ideas.

EXAMPLES In each sentence, circle the antonym for the word in **bold**. In the blank, write the letter of the word that best defines the word in **bold**.

_____ **1.** Trying to save money by putting off going to the doctor may have a **detrimental**, not helpful, result.
   a. useful   c. positive
   b. harmful   d. pleasant

_____ **2.** A person possessed of **fortitude** rather than indecision has great purpose and strength.
   a. kindness   c. success
   b. determination   d. honor

_____ **3.** Sandra was a **sociable** child; in contrast, her sister was very shy.
   a. annoying   c. loving
   b. cute   d. outgoing

_____ **4.** One physical sign of starvation is a **distended**, not flat, stomach.
   a. swollen   c. hard
   b. shrunken   d. soft

EXPLANATIONS

1. The antonym for **detrimental** is *helpful. Detrimental* means (b) "harmful." Notice the signal word *not* and the pair of commas before and after the antonym phrase.

2. The antonym for **fortitude** is *indecision. Fortitude* means (b) "determination." Notice the signal words *rather than.*

3. The antonym for **sociable** is *shy. Sociable* means (d) "outgoing." Notice the signal words *in contrast.* Also note that the antonym *shy* appears at the end of the sentence.

4. The antonym for **distended** is *flat. Distended* means (a) "swollen." Notice the signal word *not* and the set of commas that signal the antonym *flat.*

PRACTICE 2

In each sentence, circle the antonym for the word in **bold**. In the blank, write the letter of the word that best defines the word or phrase in **bold**.

_____ 1. Instead of being so **severe** in your attitude, please try to be more open-minded.
   a. rigid   c. gentle
   b. unhappy   d. depressed

_____ 2. In short stories, some characters remain **static** (not dynamic) in their beliefs and actions.
   a. shocking   c. fixed
   b. changing   d. confused

_____ 3. Mothers Against Drunk Driving urges young people to **abstain from**—rather than indulge in the use of drugs and alcohol.
   a. enjoy   c. apply
   b. avoid   d. learn

_____ 4. Beyond rational thought, a person suffering from anorexia nervosa has a **fixation** with being thin.
   a. interest   c. obsession
   b. diet   d. failure

_____ 5. In contrast to the leanness of anorexia, obesity is marked by **adiposity.**
   a. fattiness   c. thinness
   b. size   d. weight

_____ **6.** Julie Ann refused to remain **illiterate**; instead she worked to become well educated.
- a. poor
- b. uneducated
- c. helpless
- d. depressed

_____ **7.** Paul's reactions to problems seem to be expressed by a **dearth**, not an excess, of emotions.
- a. lack
- b. surplus
- c. dread
- d. acceptance

_____ **8.** The **obscurity** of Professor Bailey's lecture was in direct contrast to the clarity of Professor Brown's presentation.
- a. certainty
- b. success
- c. vagueness
- d. stupidity

_____ **9.** The employee received not a **commendation** but a rebuke for working overtime.
- a. punishment
- b. warning
- c. reward
- d. demand

_____ **10.** The identical twins Roger and Ted have very different attitudes; Roger remains **complaisant**, unlike Ted, who is often disobedient.
- a. unruly
- b. wild
- c. obedient
- d. weak

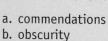

VISUAL VOCABULARY

Members of the 1st Battalion, 227th Aviation Regiment of the U.S. Army, including former prisoners of war CW2 David Williams and CW2 Ronald Young (L), earned _____ for their service in Operation Iraqi Freedom. Medals shown are (L to R): Bronze Star; Air Medal with Valor: Purple Heart and the Prisoner of War Medal.

- a. commendations
- b. obscurity
- c. rebukes

General Context

Often you will find that the author has not provided a synonym clue or an antonym clue. In that case, you will have to rely on the **general context** to figure out the meaning of the unfamiliar word. This requires that you read the entire sentence, or read ahead for a few sentences, for information that will help you understand the new word.

Information about the word can be included in the passage in several ways. Sometimes a definition of the word may be provided. Often vivid word pictures or descriptions of a situation can give a sense of the word's meaning. At times, you may need to figure out the meaning of an unknown word by using prior knowledge, logic, and reasoning skills.

EXAMPLES In the blank, write the letter of the word that best defines the word in **bold**.

_____ **1.** The children lived in **squalor**: soiled and stained clothes covered every piece of furniture, dirty dishes filled the sink and cluttered the stove and counters, the floor was sticky with food, and the house smelled of rotted food, sweat, and urine.
   a. confusion   c. freedom
   b. filth   d. hope

_____ **2.** Kashada decorated her room with a **hodgepodge** of posters of everything from country music stars to hard rock groups.
   a. unity   c. mixture
   b. theme   d. group

_____ **3.** A climber must think about the harmful impact high mountain **elevations** can have on her body.
   a. heights   c. widths
   b. depths   d. scenes

EXPLANATIONS

1. **Squalor** means (b) *filth*. The details of this passage vividly describe a very dirty place: *soiled, stained, dirty, cluttered, sticky, smelled,* and *rotted*.

2. **Hodgepodge** means (c) *mixture*. Kashada doesn't seem to have a favorite kind of group or music. Instead she seems to collect posters based on a wide range of taste.

3. **Elevations** means (a) *heights*. The words *climber, high,* and *mountain* all suggest height.

Each of the following sentences has a word in **bold** type. In the blank, write the letter of the word that best defines the word in **bold**.

_____ **1.** Too often, the **indigenous** people of the rain forests are considered backward; however, they have lived successfully in their homelands for thousands of years.
a. native
b. poor
c. uneducated
d. displaced

_____ **2.** California power companies had **blackouts** because there was not enough energy to supply the residents' electrical needs.
a. fainting spells
b. power failures
c. rate hikes
d. lower prices

_____ **3.** Rebecca was accused of **slander** when she spread lies about Ross after they broke up.
a. stalking
b. damage to a person's reputation
c. burglary
d. hatefulness

_____ **4.** Jordan demonstrated his **agility** when he caught the football, turned in midair, outran the defense, and scored a touchdown.
a. clumsiness and fear
b. determination
c. quickness and grace
d. courage

_____ **5.** The **perimeter** of a figure is the total distance around the edge of the figure.
a. border
b. inside
c. center
d. value

_____ **6.** Marie smiled and whistled as she **obligingly** helped her father wash the car.
a. resentfully
b. agreeably
c. reluctantly
d. skillfully

_____ **7.** Mark and Sandi made no advance plans for their trip; they simply **meandered** across the country for two weeks.
a. ran
b. drifted
c. rushed
d. drove

_____ **8.** The **emergence** of the butterfly from its cocoon surprised and delighted the young child.
a. beauty
b. appearance
c. change
d. shape

_____ **9.** Kaye **coerces** the other children to give their allowance to her by threatening to beat them up.
  a. forces   c. helps
  b. limits   d. discourages

_____ **10.** The Lincoln Memorial in Washington, D.C., is an **enduring** reminder of the strength, wisdom, and sacrifice of Abraham Lincoln.
  a. temporary   c. humble
  b. lasting   d. final

Examples

Many times, an author will show the meaning of a new or difficult word with an example. Often the signal words *such as, including,* or *consisting of* introduce the example as a context clue. Colons and dashes can also indicate examples. Sometimes the example is incorporated into the sense of the sentence.

Example Signal Words		
consisting of	for instance	like
for example	including	such as

EXAMPLES Using example clues, choose the correct meaning of the word in **bold**.

_____ **1.** Many wealthy people take up **altruistic** causes; for instance, film star Angelina Jolie volunteers as a spokesperson with the United Nations on the behalf of refugees.
  a. unselfish   c. political
  b. horrible   d. harmful

_____ **2.** Sports figures, including Le Bron James, Jimmie Johnson, and Maria Sharapova, become **paragons** of excellence in our society.
  a. people   c. heroes
  b. role models   d. rulers

_____ **3.** The player seemed **suspended** in midair as she jumped as high as the basket to score the winning point in the game.
  a. pushed   c. slapped
  b. shocked   d. hanging

EXPLANATIONS

1. **Altruistic** means (a) *unselfish*. The phrase "for instance" signals that Angelina Jolie is an example.

2. **Paragons** are (b) *role models*. The word "including" signals a list of examples of sports figures who are role models or paragons.

3. **Suspended** means (d) *hanging*. "Jumped as high as the basket" shows that the player's feet were off the ground.

PRACTICE 4

Using example clues, choose the correct meaning of the word in **bold**.

_____ 1. Many television ads use **fallacious** thinking—such as half-truths and exaggerations—to sell products.
   a. factual
   b. deceitful
   c. honest
   d. creative

_____ 2. People from different parts of the United States speak using different **dialects**, including the fast, clipped northern accent and the slow southern drawl.
   a. language patterns
   b. value systems
   c. interests
   d. jobs

_____ 3. **Illicit** drugs, like marijuana, cocaine, and heroin, bring great wealth to those who buy and sell them in large amounts for a living.
   a. dangerous
   b. legal
   c. illegal
   d. expensive

_____ 4. **Lagomorphs** (which include rabbits and hares) used to be thought of as rats.
   a. animals with scales
   b. animals with wings
   c. animals with large front teeth
   d. animals without fur

_____ 5. Mrs. Powell served a plate of tasty **hors d'oeuvres** that included cheese, crackers, and bite-size meatballs before dinner.
   a. main courses
   b. appetizers
   c. desserts
   d. drinks

_____ 6. **Salutations**, such as "Hello," "How do you do?," and "How are you?," are common courtesies.
   a. insults
   b. snubs
   c. greetings
   d. questions

_____ **7.** Carbon monoxide, chlorine vapor, and ammonia are **noxious** chemicals that can cause severe health problems or lead to death if not handled properly.
a. harmless
c. natural
b. expensive
d. poisonous

_____ **8.** Some authors use **pseudonyms**; for example, American author Mark Twain's real name was Samuel L. Clemens.
a. disguises
c. false names
b. body guards
d. autographs

_____ **9.** A **chronic** illness, such as asthma or arthritis, usually gets increasingly worse.
a. short-term
c. painful
b. long-term
d. curable

_____ **10.** **Predators**, such as owls, catch and eat other animals.
a. birds
c. hunters
b. animals
d. victims

Textbook Skills

Visual Vocabulary

Textbooks often make information clearer by providing a visual image such as a graph, chart, or photograph. Take time to study these visual images and their captions to figure out how each one ties in to the information.

EXAMPLE Read the following passage and study the graphic from a college biology textbook. Use context clues to answer the questions that follow.

Rain Shadows

Mountains change rainfall patterns. When water-laden air is forced to rise as it meets a mountain, it cools. Cooling reduces the air's ability to retain water. And the water is released as rain or snow on the windward (near) side of the mountain. The cool, dry air is warmed again as it travels down the far side of the mountain. The warmed air absorbs water from the land and creates a local dry area called a rain shadow.

—Adapted from Audesirk, Audesirk, & Byers, *Biology: Life on Earth*, 8th ed., p. 585.

▲ Mountains modify rainfall patterns and create rain shadows.

Source: Figure 29–5 Mountains Create Rain Shadows from Audesirk, Audesirk, & Byers, *Biology: Life on Earth*, 8th ed., page 585.

1. The best meaning of the word *modify* (in the caption for the graphic) is
_____.

     a. change.   b. create.   c. halt.

2. The synonym for *windward* (in the paragraph) is _____.

3. The best synonym for the word *prevailing* (in the graphic) is _____.
     a. changing.   b. weakening.   c. controlling.

EXPLANATIONS

1. The best meaning of the word *modify* is (a) *change.*

2. The synonym for *windward* is *near.* Notice this synonym is set off in parentheses.

3. The best synonym for the word *prevailing* is (c) *controlling.*

PRACTICE 5

Read the following passage from a college biology textbook. After you have read the paragraph, answer the questions and complete the caption for the photograph.

Types of Clouds

Clouds are classified based on their form and height. Three basic forms are recognized: cirrus, cumulus, and stratus. **Cirrus** clouds are high, white, and thin. They can occur as patches composed of small cells or as delicate veil-like sheets or extended wispy fibers that often have a feathery appearance. **Cumulus** clouds consist of globular individual cloud masses. They normally have a flat base and rising domes or towers. Such clouds are frequently described as having a cauliflower structure. **Stratus** clouds are best described as sheets or layers that cover much or all of the sky. While there may be minor breaks, there are no distinct individual cloud units.

—Adapted from Lutgens and Tarbuck, *Foundations of Earth Science*, 5th ed., p. 585.

_____ **1.** What is the best meaning *globular*?
   a. flat   b. round   c. wispy

2. What context clue(s) did you use to determine the meaning of *globular?* _____

_____

The cloud depicted in the photograph is a _____ cloud.
   a. cirrus   b. cumulus   c. stratus

APPLICATIONS

Application 1: Synonyms as Context Clues

Read the following information taken from a college introduction to algebra text-book. To test your comprehension of key terms, complete the activities that follow.

Textbook Skills

- In geometry we study sets of points. A geometric figure is simply a set of points.

- A **segment** is a geometric figure consisting of two points, called end-points, and all points between them. The segment whose endpoints are A and B is shown here. It can be named $\overline{AB}$ or $\overline{BA}$.

A   B

■ We get an idea of a geometric figure called a ray by thinking of a ray of light. A ray consists of a segment, say $\overline{AB}$, and all points X such that B is between A and X, that is, $\overline{AB}$ and all points "beyond" B. A ray is usually drawn as shown below. It has just one endpoint. The arrow indicates that it extends forever in one direction.

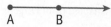

A B

■ Two rays such as $\overset{\leftrightarrow}{PQ}$ and $\overset{\leftrightarrow}{QP}$ make up a line. The line named PQ is shown here.

P Q

■ Lines in the same plane are called coplanar. **Coplanar** lines that run alongside each other and do not intersect are called **parallel**.

■ Lines that cross are called **intersecting** lines.

■ An angle is a set of points consisting of two **rays**, or half-lines, with a **common endpoint** or vertex.

—Adapted from Bittinger & Beecher, *Developmental Mathematics: College Mathematics and Introductory, Algebra,* 7th ed., pp. 384–385.

Match the term to its synonym. Some synonyms will not be used.

_____ **1.** ray   a. segment   e. coplaner

_____ **2.** common endpoint   b. alongside   f. half-line

_____ **3.** parallel   c. crossing

_____ **4.** intersecting   d. vertex

VISUAL VOCABULARY

This field of tulips is laid out in

_____.

a. parallel lines.
b. intersecting lines.
c. angles.

Application 2: Antonyms as Context Clues

In each sentence, circle the antonym for the word in **bold**. In the blank, write the letter of the word that best defines the word in **bold**.

_____ 1. **Comprehension**, unlike confusion, results in knowledge.
    a. understanding   c. studying
    b. ignorance   d. work

_____ 2. If a part of a chromosome is lost, the remaining chromosome has a **deletion**, not an addition.
    a. added part   c. finished part
    b. missing part   d. important part

_____ 3. Charlie Anne has a **phobia** for dogs, yet she tries to act as if she has some liking for them.
    a. courage   c. fear
    b. concern   d. joy

_____ 4. **Obese** people (unlike thin people) may suffer social problems because of their weight.
    a. tall   c. skinny
    b. overweight   d. rejected

_____ 5. **Geriatric** citizens are concerned about the cost of health care; in contrast, youthful citizens are concerned about finding a job.
    a. elderly   c. helpless
    b. young   d. independent

Application 3: General Context as a Clue

Write the letter of the word that best defines the word in **bold**.

_____ 1. Suddenly, there was a **lull** in the hard-driving rain and wind; after hours of hearing the howling wind, the silence was strange.
    a. increase   c. pause
    b. outbreak   d. strength

_____ 2. Katie's **belligerence** surprised everyone. She threw her book across the room, glared at Chris, and then pushed him to the floor.
    a. carefulness   c. courage
    b. hostility   d. honesty

_____ 3. The pupil of the eye **dilates** to adjust to darkness, sometimes becoming as large as the eye's iris.
    a. closes   c. agrees
    b. opens   d. contracts

_____ **4.** John's **sentimental** card expressed his deep and undying love for Amy.
   a. cheap
   b. unemotional
   c. emotional
   d. expensive

_____ **5.** After eating three helpings of turkey and dressing, four helpings of sweet potatoes, and three pieces of pumpkin pie, Andy's hunger was **satiated**.
   a. increased
   b. permanent
   c. satisfied
   d. worsened

Application 4: Examples as Context Clues

Write the letter of the word that best defines the word in **bold**.

_____ **1.** The use of **mnemonics** is a good way to remember something by putting a name on it; for example, SAGE stands for _synonyms, antonyms, general context_, and _examples_.
   a. memory tools
   b. note-taking tools
   c. discussion tools
   d. reviewing tools

_____ **2.** The **axial** skeleton of a human being includes the bones of the trunk, head, and neck.
   a. bottom
   b. inner
   c. central
   d. limb

_____ **3.** A **spherical** object is a solid object on which all points on its surface are the same distance from the center of the figure; for example, the sun and the earth are spherical objects.
   a. large
   b. heavy
   c. round
   d. oval

_____ **4.** The **characteristics** of cocaine withdrawal include depression, irritability, and strong cravings.
   a. denials
   b. symptoms
   c. barriers
   d. goals

_____ **5.** Many types of **reflexes** are present at birth, including the moro or startle reflex, walking or stepping reflex, and the grasping reflex.
   a. automatic responses
   b. thoughtful responses
   c. planned responses
   d. unhappy responses

REVIEW TEST 1   Score (number correct) _____ × 10 = _____%

Using Context Clues

A. Read the sentences, and answer the questions that follow them.

Putting your work off until the last minute will have **adverse**—negative—effects on your learning.

 1. What does **adverse** mean?
- a. helpful
- b. harmful
- c. long-term
- d. short-term

 2. Identify the context clue you used.
- a. synonym
- b. antonym
- c. general context
- d. example

John took a **menial** job in the company, hoping to train and work his way into a more skilled and higher-paying position.

 3. What does **menial** mean?
- a. important
- b. better
- c. unskilled
- d. high-paying

 4. Identify the context clue you used.
- a. synonym
- b. antonym
- c. general context
- d. example

Inebriated from the effects of drinking too many beers, Marsha staggered through the house, unable to find any of the light switches or walk in a straight line.

 5. What does **inebriated** mean?
- a. sober
- b. drunk
- c. happy
- d. confused

 6. Identify the context clue you used.
- a. synonym
- b. antonym
- c. general context
- d. example

B. Using context clues, write the definition for each word in **bold**. Choose definitions from the box. Use each definition only once.

concluded	ground-breaking	mutual	worry

7. In a healthy marriage, giving should be **reciprocal**, not one-sided.

Definition of **reciprocal**: _mutual_

8. The **angst**, or anxiety, of giving her speech weighed heavily on LaToya.

Definition of **angst**: _worry_

9. Although Justin and Robert were best friends, Justin refused to speak with or even look at Robert. After a few days of being ignored or treated rudely by Justin, Robert finally **inferred** that he had somehow angered his friend.

Definition of **inferred**: _Concluded_

10. At a time when men were the ones to hold most of the high-powered jobs, a few women enjoyed **innovative** careers; for example, Ruth Handler created the Barbie doll, and Margaret Knight invented a machine that made the first flat-bottomed paper bag.

Definition of **innovative**: _ground breaking_

REVIEW TEST 2

Score (number correct) _____ × 5 = _____%

Using Context Clues

Choose the best definition for each word in **bold**. Then identify the context clue used in each passage. A clue may be used more than once.

Context Clues

> **S**ynonym
> **A**ntonym
> **G**eneral context
> **E**xample

The **folly** of youth stands in stark contrast to the wisdom of age.

_____ **1.** The word **folly** means
a. strength.   c. foolishness.
b. happiness.   d. decisions.

2. Context clue: _____

Some recovering alcoholics still think they can control their habit. They believe they can start and stop drinking at any time. But after they have stopped, taking even one drink is a **perilous** decision.

_____ **3.** The word **perilous** means
a. dangerous.   c. good.
b. hopeful.   d. funny.

4. Context clue: _____

A fat, orange moon hung low against a velvet black sky. A mist of fog swirled around the lamppost, and a black cat ran across the street. A werewolf howled. The **eerie** scene made me walk a little faster.

_____ **5.** The word **eerie** means
a. beautiful.   c. relaxing.
b. spooky.   d. inspiring.

6. Context clue: _____

Some old **superstitions** are told in childhood sayings, for example, "Step on a crack, break your mother's back"; "Break a mirror, have seven years of bad luck"; and "If your nose itches, you're going to have company soon."

_____ **7.** The word **superstitions** means
a. facts.   c. false ideas.
b. details.   d. wise sayings.

8. Context clue: _____

Simone carefully dressed for the prom; she **donned** her best shoes, a new gown, and her mother's pearls.

_____ **9.** The word **donned** means
a. borrowed.   c. put on.
b. bought.   d. laid out.

10. Context clue: _____

Jeremy Bletz wandered in the desert for three weeks. **Dehydrated**, he looked for water by cutting open a cactus.

_____ **11.** The word **dehydrated** means
     a. thirsty.   c. hungry.
     b. tired.   d. lost.

12. Context clue: _____

The drug addict who does not seek help may **regress** into more serious drug use; however, recovery is possible with counseling, hard work, and support from loved ones.

_____ **13.** The word **regress** means
     a. succeed.   c. depress.
     b. turn back.   d. overcome.

14. Context clue: _____

Jane's fingerprints at the scene **refuted**, not proved, her innocence.

_____ **15.** The word **refuted** means
     a. confused.   c. denied.
     b. doubted.   d. approved.

16. Context clue: _____

Some creatures can **regenerate** parts of themselves, such as a starfish growing a new arm or a lizard growing a new tail.

_____ **17.** The word **regenerate** means
     a. break off.   c. grow back.
     b. reattach.   d. relax.

18. Context clue: _____

A short temper, constant fatigue, and a sense of hopelessness may be **symptomatic** of depression.

_____ **19.** The word **symptomatic** means
     a. characteristic.   c. hurtful.
     b. supportive.   d. stylish.

20. Context clue: _____

REVIEW TEST 3   Score (number correct) _____ × 10 = _____%

Using Context Clues

A. Using context clues, write the definition for each word in **bold**. Choose definitions from the box. Use each definition only once.

corruption ✓	refused	view
match ✓	use of words that imitate sounds	worth imitating

1. The professional dancers on *Dancing with the Stars* **synchronize** their movements so that they seem to move as one person.

   Definition of **synchronize**: _match_

2. The **vice**, or evil, of violence threatens our schools across the nation.

   Definition of **vice**: _corruption_

3. Dr. Martin Luther King Jr. was an **exemplary** human being; he was a man of strength, wisdom, and compassion.

   Definition of **exemplary**: _worth imitating_

4. The **vista** from Diamond Head in Honolulu, Hawaii, is a breathtaking sight as the sun rises.

   Definition of **vista**: _view_

5. Sybil **rebuffed** her brother's offer to lend her money with a brusque "no thanks."

   Definition of **rebuffed**: _refused_

6. **Onomatopoeia**, evident in words such as *sizzle*, *crackle*, *buzz*, and *whirr*, helps a reader's mind hear an idea while a text is being read.

   Definition of **onomatopoeia**: _____

B. Read the following passage from a college psychology textbook. Answer the questions that follow.

Textbook
Skills

¹Declarative memory is a type of long-term memory. ²Declarative memory stores facts, information, and personal life events. ³This information can be brought to mind with words or in the form of images. ⁴Then the information is declared or stated. ⁵There are two types of declarative memory. ⁶On the one hand, **episodic** memory records events as they have been experienced. ⁷It is somewhat like a mental diary, a record of the events in your life. ⁸Using episodic memory, a person might say, "I remember being in Florida on my vacation last spring, lying on the sand. ⁹I soaked up some rays and listened to the sound of the waves rushing to shore." ¹⁰On the other hand, **semantic** memory stores general knowledge or objective facts and information. ¹¹Semantic memory is involved when a person recalls that Florida is bounded by the Atlantic Ocean on the east and the Gulf of Mexico on the west. ¹²It is not necessary to have ever visited Florida to know these facts. ¹³Semantic memory is more like an encyclopedia or dictionary than a personal diary.

—Adapted from Wood, Wood, & Boyd, *Mastering the World of Psychology*, 3rd ed., p. 182.

_____ **7.** What does **episodic** mean?
  a. constant   c. temporary
  b. spoken   d. experienced

_____ **8.** Identify the context clue you used.
  a. synonym   c. general context
  b. antonym   d. example

_____ **9.** The word **semantic** refers to
  a. the meaning of words.   c. the comparison of ideas.
  b. experienced events.   d. imagined details.

_____ **10.** Identify the context clue you used.
  a. synonym   c. general context
  b. antonym   d. example

WHAT DO YOU THINK?

Which type of long-term memory do you rely upon most often: episodic or semantic memory? Do you think most people rely on one type of long-term memory more than the other? What situations or types of information would best be stored by episodic memory or semantic memory? Assume you have an elderly relative or friend who is suffering with memory issues, and you want to increase the quality of his or her life through stimulating contact. Write a letter to this person about a recent event of importance. Use both episodic and semantic memories to discuss the importance of the event.

REVIEW TEST 4

Score (number correct) _____ × 20 = _____%

Using Context Clues

Textbook
Skills

Read the following passage adapted from a college sociology textbook. Apply context clues to each of the words in **bold** print, and answer the questions that follow the passage.

"So, You Want to Be Yourself?" Cloning in the Coming Biotech Society

¹No type of society ends abruptly. ²The edges are fuzzy, and one overlaps the other. ³As the information society matures, it looks as though it is being overtaken by a biotech society. ⁴Let's try to peer over the edge of our current society to catch a glimpse of the one that may be coming. ⁵What will life be like? ⁶We could examine many issues, but since space is limited, let's consider just one: cloning.
⁷Consider this **scenario**:

⁸Your four-year-old daughter has drowned, and you can't get over your sorrow. ⁹You go to the regional cloning clinic, where you have stored DNA from all members of your family. ¹⁰You pay the standard fee, and the director hires a **surrogate** mother to bring your daughter back as a newborn.

¹¹Will cloning humans become a reality? ¹²Since human embryos have already been cloned, it seems inevitable that some group somewhere will complete the process. ¹³If cloning humans becomes routine—well, consider these scenarios:

- ¹⁴Suppose that a couple can't have children. ¹⁵Testing shows that the husband is **sterile**. ¹⁶The couple talk about their dilemma, and the wife agrees to have her husband's genetic material implanted into one of her eggs. ¹⁷Would this woman, in effect, be rearing her husband as a little boy?

- [18]Or suppose that you love your mother dearly, and she is dying. [19]With her permission, you decide to clone her. [20]Who is the clone? [21]Would you be rearing your own mother?
- [22]What if a woman gave birth to her own clone? [23]Would the clone be her daughter or her sister?

[24]When genetic duplicates appear, the questions of what humans are, what their relationship is to their "parents," and indeed what "parents" and "children" are, will be brought up at every kitchen table.

Source: Based on Kaebnick 2000; McGee 2000; Bjerklie et al. 2001; Davis 2001; Weiss 2004; Regalado 2005.

For Your Consideration

[25]As these scenarios show, the issue of cloning brings up **profound** questions. [26]Perhaps the most weighty concerns the future of society. [27]Let's suppose that mass cloning becomes possible.

[28]Many people object that cloning is immoral, but some will argue the opposite. [29]They will ask why we should leave human reproduction to people who have inferior traits—genetic diseases, low IQs, perhaps even the **propensity** for crime and violence. [30]They will suggest that we select people with the finer characteristics—high creative ability, high intelligence, compassion, and a propensity for peace.

[31]Let's assume that scientists have traced these characteristics—as well as the ability and appreciation for poetry, music, mathematics, architecture, and love—to genetics. [32]Do you think that it should be our moral obligation to populate society with people like this? [33]To try to build a society that is better for all—one without terrorism, war, violence, and greed? [34]Could this perhaps even be our evolutionary destiny?

—Adapted from Henslin, *Essentials of Sociology: A Down to Earth Approach*, p. 95 © 2007 Pearson Education, Inc. Reproduced by permission of Pearson Education, Inc.

_____ **1.** What does **scenario** mean in sentence 7?
  a. scheme
  b. outline
  c. situation
  d. idea

_____ **2.** What does **surrogate** mean in sentence 10?
  a. original
  b. substitute
  c. model
  d. donor

_____ **3.** What does **sterile** mean in sentence 15?
  a. clean
  b. sick
  c. productive
  d. infertile

_____ **4.** What does **profound** mean in sentence 25?
   a. important   c. common
   b. shallow   d. negative

_____ **5.** What does **propensity** mean in sentence 29?
   a. love   c. tendency
   b. skill   d. dislike

WHAT DO YOU THINK?

What do you think of when you read the term *biotech*? How would you explain the relationship between an information society and a biotech society? Do you think a biotech society will be much different from our current society? How could cloning change society as we know it today? How could cloning affect our everyday lives? Assume you are applying for an academic scholarship to pay for your tuition and books. To compete for the scholarship you must write an essay that explains the impact of technology on society. Write an essay that predicts what our future society might be like and how it might differ from current society.

After Reading About Vocabulary in Context

The reading system you learned in Chapter 1 will help you comprehend and retain large sections of information, such as this textbook chapter about vocabulary skills. Now that you have read and studied the chapter, take time to reflect on what you have learned before you begin the Mastery Tests. Check your comprehension of what you have studied. Answer the following questions. Write your answers in your notebook.

   What did I learn about vocabulary in context?

   What do I need to remember about vocabulary in context?

   How has my knowledge base or prior knowledge about vocabulary in context changed?

Test your understanding of what you have learned about Vocabulary in Context by completing the Chapter 2 Review Card on the insert near the end of your text.

CONNECT TO myreadinglab

To check your progress in meeting Chapter 2's learning outcomes, log in to **www.myreadinglab.com**, and try the following activities.

- The "Other Resources" section of MyReadingLab offers an overview of each of the topics below, an audio dictionary, activities, exercises and quizzes, spelling activities, and flashcards.

- To access this resource, go to the "Other Resources" on the Home page of MyReadingLab. Click on the link labeled "Vocabulary Website." Under "select your level," choose the link labeled "Beginner." Click on "Context Clues."

- To access this resource, go to the "Other Resources" on the Home page of MyReadingLab. Click on the link labeled "Vocabulary Website." Under "select your level," choose the link labeled "Beginner." Click on "Synonyms."

- To access this resource, go to the "Other Resources" on the Home page of MyReadingLab. Click on the link labeled "Vocabulary Website." Under "select your level," choose the link labeled "Beginner." Click on "Antonyms."

- To access this resource, go to the "Other Resources" on the Home page of MyReadingLab. Click on the link labeled "Vocabulary Website." Under "select your level," choose the link labeled "Beginner." Click on "Context Clues."

- To access this resource, go to the "Other Resources" on the Home page of MyReadingLab. Click on the link labeled "Vocabulary Website." Under "select your level," choose the link labeled "Beginner." Click on "Context Clues."

To measure your mastery of the content in this chapter, complete the test in the "Vocabulary" section and click on Gradebook to find your results. To access this resource, click on the "Study Plan" tab, then choose Vocabulary from the menu.

A. The following passages are from a chapter in the textbook *Communication @ Work*. Read each passage, and answer the questions that follow.

Textbook
Skills

When working, how late is "late" for a meeting? How early is "early" for dinner? North Americans become **intolerant** after waiting for about ten minutes. But in some South American countries it is excusable if you show up four hours late.

_____ **1.** What does **intolerant** mean?
    a. unforgiving   c. angry
    b. patient   d. curious

_____ **2.** Identify the context clue you used.
    a. synonym   c. general context
    b. antonym   d. example

Kinesics reflects the values of a culture. For example, in a Japanese company, if a person sits quietly, others assume that the person is thinking and will not interrupt. If the person stands and moves about, others will interact more freely.

_____ **3.** What does **kinesics** mean?
    a. attitude   c. body movement
    b. conversation   d. thoughts

_____ **4.** Identify the context clue you used.
    a. synonym   c. general context
    b. antonym   d. example

"Cultural **chauvinism**" is the belief that one's culture is the only way to live. Cultural chauvinism is an intolerance of values, customs, and traditions different from one's own.

_____ **5.** What does the word **chauvinism** mean?
    a. value   c. prejudice
    b. indifference   d. tolerance

_____ **6.** Identify the context clue you used.
    a. synonym   c. general context
    b. antonym   d. example

B. Using context clues, write the definition for each word in **bold**. Choose definitions from the box. Use each definition only once.

fail	manners	space	timeliness

7. When working in another country, visitors risk making a negative impression unless they adapt their use of **spatial** distances. In one program, some Englishmen were trained to stand closer to Arabs, make more eye contact, touch more, and smile more.

Definition of **spatial**: _____

8. Numerous websites and travel guides discuss customs and communication. These guidelines help prepare people to follow business **etiquette** across cultures.

Definition of **etiquette**: _____

9. **Err** on the side of being too formal, rather than too informal. Develop relationships slowly.

Definition of **err**: _____

10. Learn the culture's use of time and the practice of **punctuality**. Northern Europeans, Americans, and Japanese are the most punctual. In contrast, southern Europeans, Hispanics, Middle Easterners, and Filipinos are more relaxed about time.

Definition of **punctuality**: _____

—Adapted from Kelly, *Communication
@ Work*, pp. 128–129.

Name _____ Section _____

Date _____ **Score** (number correct) _____ × 10 = _____%

Read the following passage adapted from the college sociology textbook *Women, Men, and Society*. Then answer the questions that follow it.

Textbook
Skills

Gender and Housework: Who Does What?

[1]When it comes to housework, research consistently shows that wives spend more time on these chores than husbands do—as much as five times more hours per week, in fact. [2]Of course, this may not seem unfair if spouses are exchanging services according to the traditional marriage contract: She does the housework and he works in the paid labor force for their financial support. [3]However, this arrangement applies to only a small percentage of couples today.

[4]Most married women, like their husbands, are **employed** outside the home. [5]Although husbands in two-earner families spend more time on housework than men who are the only breadwinners, they still do less than their wives. [6]Husbands typically express a willingness to "help" their wives with the housework, but even among two-earner couples, the commonly held belief of both men and women is that housework is "women's work." [7]This is true no matter what other demands wives have on their time.

[8]Interestingly, men are less tolerant of gender **inequality** in the workplace than in their own homes. [9]Consequently, employed wives end up working what is called the "second shift." [10]They are wage earners for part of the day and then come home to still more, **albeit** unpaid, work.

[11]In fact, if you ask full-time homemakers what kind of work they do, they usually reply, "I don't work; I'm a housewife." [12]This is a **striking** answer, for housework, which is important and necessary work, is not considered real work. [13]Even the woman who is doing housework doesn't think of it as real work. [14]One reason housework is not considered real work is that it is **unspecialized**, covering by some guesses more than eighty different tasks. [15]It is also never ending; in a sense, it is never fully finished. [16]No sooner is a chore completed than it must be done again. [17]This is because housework produces items and services for immediate **consumption**.

[18]Another reason housework is not thought of as "real" work is that unlike work in the paid labor force, there is no fixed work schedule for housework. [19]Homemakers rarely get time off, not even holidays—who, for instance, cooks those large holiday meals? [20]Housework also differs from what we usually think of as real work in that it is **intertwined** with love and feelings of care. [21]It is also **privatized**. [22]We see people leaving their houses to go to work; we see them in public on the job. [23]But housework is done **in isolation** in the home, and much of it is done when other family members are elsewhere.

[24]And of course, one of the main reasons housework is not considered real work is that it is unpaid. [25]In a society such as ours, individuals' **status**—how much people are

valued by others as well as by themselves—often is measured by how much money they make.

—Renzetti/Curran, *Women, Men, and Society,* pp. 164–165 © 1999 Pearson Education, Inc. Reproduced by permission of Pearson Education, Inc.

_____ **1.** What does **employed** mean in sentence 4?
    a. working   c. roaming
    b. staying   d. looking

_____ **2.** What does **inequality** mean in sentence 8?
    a. fairness   c. strength
    b. unfairness   d. weakness

_____ **3.** What does **albeit** mean in sentence 10?
    a. although   c. so
    b. and   d. for example

_____ **4.** What does **striking** mean in sentence 12?
    a. hitting   c. weak
    b. powerful   d. sick

_____ **5.** What does **unspecialized** mean in sentence 14?
    a. special   c. broad, general
    b. hard   d. focused

_____ **6.** What does **consumption** mean in sentence 17?
    a. waste   c. work
    b. use   d. play

_____ **7.** What does **intertwined** mean in sentence 20?
    a. broken apart   c. woven in
    b. free   d. replaced

_____ **8.** What does **privatized** mean in sentence 21?
    a. made public
    b. controlled by a person or private group
    c. controlled by the government
    d. made secret

_____ **9.** What does **in isolation** mean in sentence 23?
    a. alone   c. in large groups
    b. in small groups   d. out of fear

_____ **10.** What does **status** mean in sentence 25?
    a. worth   c. work
    b. height   d. friends

Read the following passage adapted from the college communications textbook *Listening: Attitudes, Principles, and Skills.* Then answer the questions that follow it.

Concept Versus Fact Method of Listening

[1]This method of listening focuses your attention on the main points of the message. [2]To use the **concept** versus fact technique, draw a vertical line down the center of your paper. [3]On the left side, jot down the speaker's main points as they occur. [4]In the right column, indicate any supporting evidence, examples, and other information used to **clarify** those concepts. [5]If the rate of presentation becomes too fast to get everything recorded, you will be able to make informed decisions about what information to include in your notes.

[6]Not only is the concept versus fact method easy to use, it also provides a quick **reference** when you need to recall information later on. [7]Study the example below. [8]This chart was created by listening to a speech about the effects of the sun.

Effects of Sun

Concept	Fact
[9]The sun is harmful (main **topic**)	
[10]Greeks' view of sun exposure—recognized only the benefits	Hippocrates—sun for health Herodotus—necessary for recovery
[11]Today's scientific facts are different—sun viewed as harmful	Tan is response to solar damage Sun has a negative **cumulative**—not single—effect
[12]Sun has many harmful effects	Heat stress—cramps, dizziness Heat exhaustion—nausea, faintness Heatstroke is life-threatening Skin and hair damage Stay away 10 A.M.–3 P.M. Sun is stronger at high altitudes
[13]Damage can be prevented	Tan slowly Wear a sunscreen

—Brownell, *Listening*, pp. 123–124 © 2002 by Pearson Education, Inc.
Reproduced by permission of Pearson Education, Inc.

_____ **1.** What does **concept** mean in sentence 2?
   a. idea   c. fact
   b. dream   d. myth

_____ **2.** What does **clarify** mean in sentence 4?
   a. argue   c. explain
   b. deny   d. create

_____ **3.** What does **reference** mean in sentence 6?
   a. source   c. opinion
   b. recommendation   d. memory

_____ **4.** What does **topic** mean in sentence 9?
   a. subject   c. fact
   b. support   d. paper

_____ **5.** What does **cumulative** mean in sentence 11?
   a. small   c. dangerous
   b. total   d. healthy

Read the following passage adapted from a library book about the life of the prophet Mohammad. Then answer the questions that follow it.

The Founder of Islam

1   The prophet Muhammad ibn Abd Allah lived more than fourteen hundred years ago. His life affected world history. And he still inspires people living in every corner of the world. He is the founder of Islam. The followers of Islam, Muslims, honor him as the person through whom Allah (the Arabic word for God) spoke to humankind. Muhammad preached that there was only one God. Muhammad also led believers to do good deeds, as taught in their holy book, the Koran. Muslims also **revere** him because of his extraordinary life.

2   Today, Islam has more than a billion followers across the world. It is the second largest religion in the world—after Christianity. It is also the fastest growing religion in the world. Many people link Islam with Arabs. Yet, the three countries with the most Muslims are Indonesia, Pakistan, and Bangladesh. Since the 1950s, large numbers of Muslims have also **emigrated** to Europe and America. In Europe and North America, they have become a vital and rapidly growing minority.

3   Five times a day believers face Mecca, the holy city of their religion, and pray, "La ilaha illa Allah . . . Muhammad rasul Allah." "There is no god but Allah. Muhammad is the messenger of Allah."

4   Who was this man? And why has his life affected so many people for so long? Not only a wise spiritual leader, Muhammad was also a good businessman, a loving husband and father, a skilled military **strategist**, and a smart politician. He was very involved in the world in which he lived.

5   Despite his fame, very few facts are known about the years of Muhammad's life before he began to receive spiritual **revelations** at the age of forty. No known written accounts exist from that time. There is also very **sparse** information about the first years when he began to win converts in Mecca.

6   Much of what we know about Muhammad comes from the Koran, the holy book of Islam. The Koran is made up of verses revealed to him during his lifetime. The Koran gives rules for daily living. It acts as a guide

for spiritual practices. And it offers hints about Muhammad's life. As Muhammad received the revelations, he told them to his followers.

—Adapted from Tower-Oliver, Marilyn, *The Importance of Series–Muhammad*, pp. 10–13 © 2003 Gale, a part of Cengage Learning, Inc. Reproduced by permission www.cengage.com/permissions.

_____ **1.** What does **revere** mean in paragraph 1?
    a. obey   c. adore
    b. follow   d. scorn

_____ **2.** What does **emigrated** mean in paragraph 2?
    a. started   c. turned
    b. returned   d. moved

_____ **3.** What does **strategist** mean in paragraph 4?
    a. observer   c. traitor
    b. planner   d. soldier

_____ **4.** What does **revelations** mean in paragraph 5?
    a. disclosures   c. mysteries
    b. secrets   d. rules

_____ **5.** What does **sparse** mean in paragraph 5?
    a. dense   c. very little
    b. fragile   d. abundant

Vocabulary-Building Skills

3

After studying this chapter you should be able to do the following:

1. Define word parts.
2. Illustrate vocabulary-building skills.
3. Analyze and define words.
4. Assess your comprehension of vocabulary-building skills.
5. Evaluate the importance of what you have learned.
6. Apply vocabulary-building skills to expand vocabulary.

 Before Reading About Vocabulary-Building Skills

Two kinds of vocabulary-building skills are learning about word parts and using the dictionary and other similar resources. To aid your study, set up a note-taking system like the one that follows. Refer to the learning outcomes and headings throughout the chapter, and create headings such as the following on notebook paper:

Key Term	Definition (or type of information)	Example
Word parts	Definition	Example
Roots (page 78)		
Prefixes (page 78)		
Suffixes (page 78)		

Dictionary	Type of Information	Example
Guide Words (page 87)		
Spelling (page 89)		
Syllabication (page 89)		

Leave enough space between each key term to record the definition and example as you read the chapter. Skim the chapter and record the page number where each key term is defined. Be sure to use all the key terms to complete your note-taking system.

Word Parts

Just as ideas are made up of words, words are also made up of smaller parts. Learning about *word parts* can help you learn vocabulary more easily and quickly. Furthermore, knowing the meaning of the parts of words helps you understand a new word when you see it in context. In fact, word parts can help you unlock the meaning of thousands of words. A single word part may appear in hundreds or even thousands of different words. If you know the meanings of several parts of a word, you can often figure out the meaning of the word as a whole.

Root	The basic or main part of a word. Prefixes and suffixes are added to roots to make a new word. Example: *spect* means "look"
Prefix	A group of letters with a specific meaning added to the beginning of a word or root to make a new word. Example: *in-* means "into," so 　　　　*inspect* means "look into"
Suffix	A group of letters with a specific meaning added to the end of a word or root to make a new word. Example: *-ator* means "one who," so 　　　　*spectator* means "one who looks"

For example, the word *restatement* has three parts, and each part has its own meaning. The first part, the prefix *re-*, means "again"; the second part, the root *state*, means "say"; and the third part, the suffix *-ment*, means a condition of being. Thus a *restatement* is "something that is said again."

The overall meaning of the word changes if one part of the word changes. For example, in the word *overstatement*, the prefix is now *over-*. The prefix *over-* means "excessive" or "exaggerated." The new word means "something that is said in an exaggerated way."

A word can have two or more parts. For example, *prehistoric* has three parts. The first part of *prehistoric*, the prefix *pre-*, means "before"; the second part, the root *historia*, means "inquiry, learned"; the third part, the suffix, *-ic*, means "related to." *Prehistoric* means being related to times before formal learning was recorded or written.

This chapter defines and explains each of the three word parts in depth and offers you ample opportunity to practice combining word parts to explore meanings. Furthermore, Appendix C in the back of this book provides an additional list of word parts and their meanings for further study.

Many of the words in the English language are based on two other languages: Greek and Latin. Greek and Latin divided words into the following three parts: **roots**, **prefixes**, and **suffixes**. Skilled readers understand how the three word parts join together to make additional words.

EXAMPLES The following group of word parts contains a root, a prefix, and a suffix. Make two new words by combining the word parts. The meaning of each part is in parentheses. *You don't have to use all the parts to make a word.*

Prefix: *im-*   (in)
Root: *port*   (carry)
Suffix: *-ation*   (action)

1. _____

2. _____

EXPLANATIONS

1. **Import**: The root *port* ("carry") joins with the prefix *im-* ("in"). The new word means "carry in."

   Companies in the United States now **import** many of their supplies from other countries.

2. **Importation**: The prefix *im-* ("in"), the root *port* ("carry"), and the suffix *-ation* ("action") join to form a word meaning "the action of carrying in."

   Another kind of **importation** results when people move here and bring their own customs with them.

PRACTICE 1

Study the word parts. Using the meanings of the prefixes, the root, the suffixes, and context clues, put each word into the sentence that best fits its meaning. Use each word once.

Prefix	Meaning	Root	Meaning	Suffix	Meaning
in-	in, into	*spect*	look	*-acle*	quality
retro-	backward			*-ive*	of, like, related to
				-tion	state of being

spect = "look"

inspect	inspection	retrospective	spectacle

1. To sell copies, some magazines turn the private life of a famous person into a public _____.

2. Many famous people complain about this public _____ of their lives.

3. Why is the public so eager to _____ the private lives of famous people?

VISUAL VOCABULARY

Fans offered a _____ of Michael Jackson's career as they gathered to mourn his death.

  a. inspection
  b. retrospective
  c. spectacle

Roots

The **root** is the basic or main part of a word. Many times a root combined with other word parts will create a whole family of closely related words. Even when the root is joined with other word parts to form new words, the meaning of the root does not change. Learning frequently used roots will help you develop a strategy for decoding the meaning of many new words. A list of common roots starts on page 557.

EXAMPLES The root *tract* means "drag" or "pull." Study the following words. Using the meaning of the root *tract* and the context of each sentence, put each word into the sentence that best fits its meaning. Use each word once.

tract = "drag, pull"

contract	extracted	traction	tractor

1. The _____ pulled the oak tree, roots and all, out of the ground.

2. The shoe factory and its workers agreed on a _____.

3. Cocaine is a drug _____ from the coca plant.

4. After he injured his back, Alex was placed in _____.

EXPLANATIONS Each word contains the root *tract* ("drag" or "pull"), and each word uses the meaning of "drag" or "pull" differently. The additional word parts—prefixes and suffixes—create the different meanings. However, the meaning of the root word and the context of the sentence should have helped you choose the correct word for each sentence.

1. **Tractor:** A tractor is a machine that pulls or drags objects.

2. **Contract:** A contract is a legal record that pulls people together into agreement.

3. **Extracted:** Extracted means "pulled out."

4. **Traction:** Traction pulls broken bones together by means of a special device.

PRACTICE 2

Study the following words. The root *socius* means "companion, ally, associate," as in **society**. Using the meaning of the root socious and context clues, put each word into the sentence that best fits its meaning. Use each word once.

antisocial	socialism	socialite	sociologist	unsocial

1. Kaleem wants to be a _____; he enjoys studying about groups of people and how they live.

2. Duncan never played with other children or went to school, so he remains _____ and enjoys being alone.

3. Many think that the government-run Medicare program is a form of _____.

4. Chris Brown said he was ashamed of his _____ behavior toward Rihanna. He regrets hitting her.

Kim Kardashian is a popular

_____ who enjoys being in the spotlight.

   a. socialite
   b. sociologist
   c. unsocial

Prefixes

A **prefix** is a group of letters with a specific meaning added to the beginning of a word or root to make a new word. Although the basic meaning of a root does not change, a prefix changes the meaning of the word as a whole. A list of common prefixes starts on page 558.

   For example, the prefix *ex-* means "out" or "from." When placed in front of the root *tract* (which means "pull" or "drag"), the word *extract* is formed. *Extract* means "pull or drag out." The same root *tract* joined with the prefix *con-* (which means "with" or "together") creates the word *contract*. A *contract* is a legal way to pull people together.

   The importance of prefixes can be seen in the family of words that comes from the root *port,* which means "carry." Look over each of the following prefixes and their meanings. Then, in the examples given, note the change in the meaning of the whole word.

Prefix	Meaning	Root	Meaning	Example
ex-	out, from	*port*	(carry)	Oil is one **export** from the Middle East.
im-	in, into			Many countries **import** French wines.
re-	back, again			Bill's credit **report** was good.

EXAMPLES Using the meanings of the prefixes, root, and context clues, put each word into the sentence that best fits its meaning. Use each word once.

Prefix	Meaning	Root	Meaning
e-	out, from	mit	send, let go
per-	through		
sub-	under, from below		

mit = "send, let go"

emit	permit	submitted

1. Jane _____ her request for a vacation to her boss.

2. Malcolm hoped his father would _____ him to use the car Saturday night.

3. Some factories _____ dangerous fumes.

EXPLANATIONS

1. **Submitted**: The prefix *sub-* means "under" or "from below." The root *mit* means "send." Jane is recognizing the authority of her boss by asking for the vacation time, so her request was "sent from below."

2. **Permit**: The prefix *per-* means "through." The root *mit* means "let go." Therefore, *permit* means "let go through." Malcolm hoped that his father would let his request for the car go through.

3. **Emit**: The prefix *e-* means "out of" or "from." The root *mit* means "send." Therefore, *emit* means "send out": Some factories send out fumes into the air.

PRACTICE 3

Study the meaning of each of the following prefixes and roots.

Prefix	Meaning	Root	Meaning
de-	down, away, reversal	press	put, arrange
ex-	out, from	tort	twist
re-	again		

Create four words by joining these prefixes and roots.

1. _____

2. _____

3. _____

4. _____

False views and expectations can

_____ a person's ability

to achieve.

   a. express
   b. depress
   c. repress

Suffixes

A **suffix** is a group of letters with a specific meaning added to the end of a word or root to make a new word. Although the basic meaning of the root does not change, a suffix can change the type of word and the way a word is used. (A list of common suffixes starts on page 559.) A word may contain more than one suffix. Look at the following examples.

Root	Meaning	Suffix	Meaning	Word	Meaning
bio	life	*-logy*	study of	*biology*	study of life
		-ist	person	*biologist*	person who studies life
		-ical	related to	*biological*	related to biology

EXAMPLES Using the meanings of the root, suffixes, and context clues, put each of the words in the box into the sentence that best fits its meaning. Use each word once.

Root	Meaning	Suffix	Meaning
pos	to place, put	*-ible*	capable of
		-ive	of, like, related to, being
		-tion	action, state
		-ture	quality, state

pos = **to place, put**

position	positive	possible	posture

1. Miguel applied for a sales _____ with a real estate office.

2. He made a _____ impression during his interview.

3. His _____ was confident and professional.

4. The future he hopes for seems _____.

EXPLANATION

1. The answer is *position*. Miguel is looking for a place to work.

2. The answer is *positive*. His skills and attitude related well to the job.

3. The answer is *posture*. The way he stood and sat made him seem confident and professional.

4. The answer is *possible*. Miguel is capable of making his hopes come true.

PRACTICE 4

Using the meanings of the roots, suffixes, and context clues, put each word in the box into the sentence that best fits its meaning. Use each word once.

Root	Meaning	Suffix	Meaning
col, com, con	with, together	*-ate*	action
		-ive	of, like, related to, being
		-or	doer
		-tion	state, action

collate	collection	collective	combination	connection

1. Daniela stayed late in the office to _____ the report for a meeting the next day.

2. The report offers a large _____ of customer surveys.

3. The final report gives a _____ view of the surveys.

4. The company wants a better _____ with its customers.

5. Daniela plans to talk about a _____ of problems and solutions based on the report.

VISUAL VOCABULARY

A copy machine can _____ documents.

a. collector
b. collate
c. collection

Additional Word Parts

A skilled reader wisely invests time and effort in studying word parts and their meanings. Appendix C in the back of this book provides an additional list of word parts and their meanings for further study.

The Dictionary

Remember, some experts believe that most people by age 18 know around 60,000 words. Experts also believe that most adults actually use between 25,000 and 50,000 words. That seems like a large number, yet the English language has over one million words. Skilled readers use a dictionary to understand new or difficult words.

> **Most dictionaries provide the following information:**
>
> - Guide words (the words at the top of each page)
> - Spelling (how the word and its different forms are spelled)
> - Syllabication (the word divided into syllables)
> - Pronunciation (how to say the word)
> - Part of speech (the type of word)
> - Definition (the meaning of the word, with the most common meaning listed first)
> - Synonyms (words that have similar meanings)
> - Etymology (the history of the word)

All dictionaries have guide words at the top of each page. However, dictionaries differ in the way they give other information about words. Some dictionaries give more information about the origin of the word; other dictionaries give long lists of synonyms. In addition to print dictionaries, computer technology has caused the development of electronic dictionaries. Dictionaries now come on CD-ROMs and as Web-based formats that are available through the Internet. Each dictionary will explain how to use its resources in the first few pages or in an introduction.

How to Find Words in the Dictionary

Guide words help you find a given word. **Guide words** are a pair of words printed in bold at the top of every page of a dictionary. Guide words show the first and last word printed on that page. Below is a copy of the top of a page from *Merriam-Webster's Collegiate Dictionary, Eleventh Edition.*

> **24 aged • aggressive**
>
> **aged** \'ā-jəd, 'ājd; 'ājd *for 1b**adj* (15c) **1** : grown old: as **a** : of an advanced age <an ~ man> **b**: having attained a specified age <a man ~ 40 years> **2** : typical of old age — **ag·ed·ness**\'ā-jəd-nəs\ *n*
> **age–group** \'ā-j-ˌgrüp\ *n* (1904) : a segment of a population that is of approximately the same age or is within a specified range of ages
> **age·ism** *also* **age·ism** \'ā-(ˌ)jiəzm\ *n* (1969) : prejudice or discrimination against a particular age-group and esp. the elderly — **age·ist** *also* **age·ist** \-jist\ *adj*
> **age·less** \'āj-ləs\ *adj* (1651) **1** : not growing old or showing the effects of age **2** : TIMELESS, ETERNAL <~ truths> — **age·less·ly** *adv* — **age·less·ness** *n*

Source: By permission. From *Merriam-Webster's Collegiate® Dictionary,* 11th Edition © 2010 by Merriam-Webster, Incorporated (www.Merriam-Webster.com).

The guide words are *aged* and *aggressive*. These guide words tell you that the words on this page fall alphabetically between them. When you are looking up a word, use the guide words to determine if the word you need is located on that page.

EXAMPLE Place a check beside the three words that would appear on the page with the guide words **aged • aggressive.**

___affirm   ___agency   ___aggravate   ___age-old   ___airplane

EXPLANATION The guide words **aged • aggressive** tell you that all the words on this page will begin with the letters *ag*. Thus *affirm* and *airplane* will not be found on this page of the dictionary.

PRACTICE 5

In each of the following items, a pair of guide words is followed by five other words. Place a check next to the three words in each set that would be found on the page with the guide words that are given.

1. chairman • champ

___cesspit   ___chamber   ___challenge   ___chalet   ___cicada

2. pant • paper money

___papaw   ___pupil   ___pantry   ___popular   ___pantsuit

3. gender • genet

___gene   ___genesis   ___gladly   ___general   ___gimmick

How to Read a Dictionary Entry

The following entry from *Merriam-Webster's Collegiate Dictionary, Eleventh Edition,* will be used as an example for the discussions about the kinds of information a dictionary provides.

> **stol·id** \\'stä-ləd\ *adj* [L *stolidus* dull, stupid] (ca. 1600) **:** having or expressing little or no sensibility **:** UNEMOTIONAL   **syn** see IMPASSIVE —
> **sto·lid·i·ty** \\stä-'li-də-tē, stə-\ *n* — **stol·id·ly** \\'stä-ləd-lē\ *adv*

Source: By permission. From *Merriam-Webster's Collegiate® Dictionary,* 11th Edition © 2010 by Merriam-Webster, Incorporated (www.Merriam-Webster.com).

Spelling and Syllables

The spelling of the word is given first in bold type. The word is also divided into syllables. A **syllable** is a unit of sound that includes a vowel. In our sample entry, *stolid* is divided into two syllables: *stol-id*.

Variants are given at the end of the entry. These are very helpful when letters are dropped from or added to the entry word to create another word. Variants of the word *stolid* are *stolidity,* which has four syllables (*sto-lid-i-ty*), and *stolidly,* which has three syllables (*stol-id-ly*).

EXAMPLES Use a dictionary to break the following words into syllables. In the space provided, rewrite each word, using a dot (•) to separate the syllables.

1. mural _____

2. extradite _____

3. immediately _____

EXPLANATIONS

1. Mural has two syllables: *mu · ral.*

2. Extradite has three syllables: *ex · tra · dite.*

3. Immediately has five syllables: *im · me · di · ate · ly.*

PRACTICE 6

Use a dictionary to break the following words into syllables. In the space provided, rewrite each word, using a dot (•) to separate the syllables.

1. inset _____

2. mutable _____

3. myology _____

4. psychoneurosis _____

Pronunciation Symbols and Accent Marks

Right after the word itself, the word's pronunciation is given in parentheses. The entry for *stolid* shows this information: **'stä · ləd**\\. Notice that accent marks and pronunciation symbols are used.

An **accent mark** is a dark mark above a word that looks like a slanted apostrophe or a tiny vertical bar ('). The accent mark indicates the syllable that gets the most emphasis when the word is spoken. For the word *stolid*, the dictionary places the accent mark before the first syllable, which means that the first syllable gets the emphasis. Often an additional stress mark, positioned below the syllable rather than above it, will indicate that a word has a lighter stress placed on that syllable.

EXAMPLES Study these words, and answer the questions that follow them.

1. **tri · bal** \'trī-bəl\

   a. How many syllables are in *tribal*? _____

   b. Which syllable is stressed? _____

2. **mo · men · tous** \mō-'men-təs\

   a. How many syllables are in *momentous*? _____

   b. Which syllable is most strongly stressed? _____

3. **man · do · lin** \ˌman-də-'lin\

   a. How many syllables are in *mandolin*? _____

   b. Which syllable is most strongly stressed? _____

EXPLANATIONS

1. **Tribal** has two syllables, and the first syllable is stressed.

2. **Momentous** has three syllables, and the second syllable is most strongly stressed.

3. **Mandolin** has three syllables, and the third syllable is most strongly stressed.

Note: Dictionaries vary in their use of accent marks; some dictionaries use bold and regular type to show the difference between the stressed syllables. Some dictionaries place the accent mark before the stressed syllable, and others place it after the syllable. Be sure to get to know your dictionary's approach.

Pronunciation symbols indicate the sounds of consonants and vowels. Dictionaries provide a pronunciation key so that you will understand the symbols used. Following is a sample pronunciation key:

> **Pronunciation Key**
>
> \ə\ **abut** \ᵊ\ **kitten**, **F** table \ər\ **further** \a\ **ash** \ā\ **ace** \ä\ **mop, mar**
> \au̇\ **out** \ch\ **chin** \e\ **bet** \ē\ **easy** \g\ **go** \i\ **hit** \ī\ **ice** \j\ **job**
> \ŋ\ **sing** \ō\ **go** \ȯ\ **law** \ȯi\ **boy** \th\ **thin** \t̲h̲\ **the** \ü\ **loot** \u̇\ **foot**
> \y\ **yet** \zh\ **vision beige** \k̲, ⁿ, œ, ᵫ, ʸ\ *see* Guide to Pronunciation

Source: By permission. From *Merriam-Webster's Collegiate® Dictionary,* 11th Edition © 2010 by Merriam-Webster, Incorporated (www.Merriam-Webster.com).

Note that each letter and symbol is followed by a sample word. The sample word tells you how the letter represented by that symbol sounds. For example, \ā\ (long *a*) sounds like *a* in *ace.* And \ĭ\ (short *i*) has the sound of the *i* in *hit.* The symbol that looks like an upside-down *e* (ə) is called a *schwa.* The schwa has a sound like *a* and *u* in **ab**u**t.**

Different dictionaries use different symbols in their pronunciation keys, so be sure to check the key of the dictionary you are using.

EXAMPLES Using our sample pronunciation key, answer questions about the following words. Write the letters of your answers in the given spaces.

_____ **1. pit · fall** \'pĭt-ˌfôl\
The *i* in *pitfall* sounds like the *i* in

   a. *hit.*　　　　　　　b. *ice.*

_____ **2. ra · di · um** \'rā-dē-əm\
The *a* in *radium* sounds like the *a* in

   a. *ash.*　　　　　　　b. *ace.*

_____ **3. in · sole** \'ĭn-ˌsōl\
The *o* in *insole* sounds like the *o* in

   a. *boy.*　　　　　　　b. *go.*

EXPLANATIONS

1. The *i* in *pitfall* is a short *i* sound as in (a) *hit.*

2. The *a* in *radium* is a long *a* sound as in (b) *ace.*

3. The *o* in *insole* is a long *o* sound as in (b) *go.*

PRACTICE 7

Using your dictionary, find and write in the pronunciation symbols and accent marks for each of the following words.

1. acrobat _____

2. constrain _____

3. migrate _____

4. presume _____

5. vary _____

Parts of Speech

Dictionary entries tell you what part of speech a word is—noun, verb, adjective, and so on. The part of speech is abbreviated and printed in italics. Your dictionary provides a full list of abbreviations. The following box lists the most common abbreviations for the parts of speech:

Common Abbreviations for the Parts of Speech			
adj	adjective	*prep*	preposition
adv	adverb	*pron*	pronoun
art	article	*vi, vt*	verb (intransitive,
conj	conjunction		transitive)
interj	interjection	*v aux*	verbal auxiliary
n	noun		

Review the dictionary entry for *stolid*.

stol·id \'stä-lied\ *adj* [L *stolidus* dull, stupid] (ca. 1600) **:** having or expressing little or no sensibility **:** UNEMOTIONAL **syn** see IMPASSIVE — **sto·lid·i·ty** \stä-'li-də-tē, stə-\ *n* — **stol·id·ly** \'stä-ləd-lē\ *adv*

Source: By permission. From *Merriam-Webster's Collegiate® Dictionary,* 11th Edition © 2010 by Merriam-Webster, Incorporated (www.Merriam-Webster.com).

As the entry indicates, the word *stolid* is an adjective. The two variants of the word are identified as a noun (*stolidity*) and an adverb (*stolidly*).

EXAMPLES   Use your dictionary to identify the parts of speech for each of the following words. A word may be used as more than one part of speech.

1. pardon _____

2. without _____

3. rust _____

EXPLANATIONS

1. Pardon can be used as a noun or as a transitive verb.

2. Without can be used as a preposition, an adverb, a conjunction, or a noun.

3. Rust can be used as a noun, an intransitive verb, or a transitive verb.

PRACTICE 8

Use your dictionary to identify the parts of speech for each of the following words. A word may be used as more than one part of speech.

1. benefit _____

2. set _____

3. well _____

Definitions

Most words have more than one meaning. When more than one definition is given in the dictionary, each meaning is numbered. The most common meaning is listed first. The dictionary may also provide examples of sentences in which the word is used.

EXAMPLES   Three definitions are given for the verb form of the word *stand*. In the space provided, write the letter of the definition that best fits the meaning of the sentence.

    a. a large seating area for spectators in a sports stadium

    b. be in a particular place

    c. attitude or opinion

_____ **1.** Some fans will stand in line for hours to see their favorite performer.

_____ **2.** Paula took a stand against ticket scalping.

_____ **3.** The stand collapsed under the weight of the fans.

EXPLANATIONS

1. The correct answer is (b) "be in a particular place."

2. The correct answer is (c) " attitude or opinion."

3. The correct answer is (a) "a large seating area for spectators in a sports stadium."

PRACTICE 9

Examine the following words, their definitions, and a sentence using each word. In the space provided, write the number of the meaning that best fits each sentence.

cross   **1.** pass from one side to the other   **2.** make or put a line across **3.** combine the qualities of two things

_____ **1.** Jane is going to **cross** the river on her homemade raft.

sage   **1.** a person known for being wise   **2.** an herb in the mint family used in flavoring foods

_____ **2.** Rubbing a turkey with **sage** before cooking adds a savory flavor.

Synonyms

Often at the end of an entry, synonyms are given. A **synonym** is a word whose meaning is similar to that of another word. For example, a synonym for *angry* is *irate*. The abbreviation for *synonym* is *syn*. You may find it helpful to look up the synonym, too.

The entry for *stolid* includes this note: "**syn** see IMPASSIVE." If you look up *impassive*, you will find a list of synonyms for the words *impassive* and *stolid*.

Etymology

Etymology is the study of a word's history. This information follows the part of speech and is found in brackets. In the entry for *stolid*, some facts about the word's history are given. Inside the brackets is the following information: "L *stolidus* dull, stupid." The letter *L* stands for *Latin*. The word *stolidus* is the Latin word from which the word *stolid* came; in Latin, its meaning was "dull" or "stupid." The entry also gives the date when a word was first recorded in a dictionary: "(ca. 1600)." The abbreviation *ca.* means "approximately," so the word *stolid* was first recorded in English around the year 1600. If even an approximate date cannot be given, the dictionary may indicate the century instead of the year, using the abbreviation *c*: thus "(16c)" would indicate that the word entered the English language in the 16th century.

Textbook Skills

Textbook Aids for Learning Content Words

Content Words

Many students think they should be able to pick up a textbook and simply read it. However, a textbook is written for a content or subject area, such as math, history, or English. Each content area has its own vocabulary. For example, a history textbook takes a different approach than a literature textbook. Different courses may use the same words, but the words often take on new or different meanings in the context of the content area.

EXAMPLES The following sentences all use the word *portfolio*. For each sentence, write the letter of the course that would use the word in its context.

_____ 1. The **portfolio** included works of oils, watercolors, and chalk and line drawings.
　　　　　　a. introduction to art
　　　　　　b. business
　　　　　　c. English

_____ 2. A wise investor creates a **portfolio** of a wide range of investment stocks and bonds.
　　　　　　a. introduction to art
　　　　　　b. business
　　　　　　c. English

_____ 3. You will be required to turn in a **portfolio** that includes prewrites, drafts, and final copies of all your essays.
　　　　　　a. introduction to art
　　　　　　b. business
　　　　　　c. English

EXPLANATIONS Use context clues to determine your answers.

1. The word *portfolio* in this sentence is used in the area of art. So this term could be used in an introduction to art course (a).

2. The word *portfolio* in this sentence is used in the area of business or economics (b).

3. The word *portfolio* in this sentence is used in a writing class (c).

Glossaries

Each subject or content area, such as science, mathematics, or English, has its own specialized vocabulary. Therefore, many textbooks provide an extra section in the back of the book called a *glossary*. A **glossary** is a list of selected language used in a specific area of study. Like a dictionary, a glossary is an alphabetized list of words, their spellings, and their meanings. However, unlike a dictionary entry, a glossary does not give parts of speech, word origins, or different forms or definitions of the word. In fact, the meanings given in a glossary are limited to the way in which the word or term is used in that content area.

EXAMPLE   Read the following two word lists. Identify each one as follows:
      G = Glossary entry   D = Dictionary entry

_____ List 1:

Balanced budget A budget in which the legislature balances expenditures with expected revenues, with no deficit.

Barbary Wars Conflicts the United States fought in the early eighteenth century with North African states against their piracy.

Bicameral legislature A legislature divided into two houses: the U.S. Congress and the state legislatures are bicameral except Nebraska, which is unicameral.

—O'Connor et al., *American Government: Continuity and Change*, 2004 Texas Ed., p. 1050.

_____ List 2:

¹as·ter·oid \\'as-tə-,ròid\ *n* [Gk *asteroeidēs* starlike, fr. *aster-*, *astēr*] (1802) **1 :** any of the small rocky celestial bodies found esp. between the orbits of Mars and Jupiter **2 :** STARFISH
— **as·ter·oi·dal** \\,as-tə-'ròi-dəl\ *adj*
²asteroid *adj* (1854) **1 :** resembling a star <~bodies in sporotrichosis> **2 :** of or resembling a starfish
asteroid belt *n* (1952) **:** the region of interplanetary space between the orbits of Mars and Jupiter in which most asteroids are found

Source: By permission. From *Merriam-Webster's Collegiate® Dictionary*, 11th Edition © 2010 by Merriam-Webster, Incorporated (www.Merriam-Webster.com).

EXPLANATION   The first list is a glossary from a history textbook. The terms and meanings are specifically related to U.S. history. The second list is from *Merriam-Webster's Collegiate Dictionary, Eleventh Edition*. The second list includes much more information about the words, such as the pronunciation marks and several definitions of each term.

PRACTICE 11

Read the following sample from a glossary. In the spaces provided, write **T** if the statement is true and **F** if the statement is false.

Glossary

Absorption: Occurs when a drug reaches the bloodstream from surrounding tissue or organs
Abuse potential: Ability of a drug to give pleasure or pain; this ability increases the likelihood that the user will continue to use the drug and become dependent
Addictive personality: Character traits that may put an individual at risk for addictive behaviors, such as drug addiction, eating disorders, compulsive gambling, or other compulsive behaviors
Bazuko: Cocaine paste that is mixed with tobacco and smoked
Cold turkey: Abrupt withdrawal from an addictive drug without the help of other drugs to lessen withdrawal symptoms; most commonly linked with heroin withdrawal

—Adapted from Fishbein/Pease, *The Dynamics of Drug Abuse,* pp. 395-397 © 1996
Allyn and Bacon. Reproduced by permission of Pearson Education, Inc.

_____   **1.** Surrounding tissues and organs do not absorb drugs from the bloodstream.

_____   **2.** Abuse potential comes from a drug's ability to give pleasure or relieve pain.

_____   **3.** An addictive personality does not put an individual at risk.

_____   **4.** "Bazuko" is taken into a person's system by smoking.

_____   **5.** Cold turkey is most commonly linked with heroin.

APPLICATIONS

Application 1: Roots and Prefixes

A. Fill in each blank by using the **root word** that best fits the meaning of the sentence.

Root	Meaning
aqua	water
cap	head
ego	self
phobia	fear

1. Maxine has a _____ about flying and won't travel by airplane.

2. Be sure to put the _____ on the tube of toothpaste.

3. José has a big _____—he is always talking about himself.

4. The actress wore a beautiful _____ blue dress.

B. Study the following set of **prefixes** and **roots**:

Prefix	Meaning	Root	Meaning
dis-	apart	*sect*	cut
in-	in, into	*spect*	look
re-	back, again		

Using these prefixes and roots, create three words.

5. _____

6. _____

7. _____

Fill in each blank with a word from the box. Use each word once.

dissect	inspect	respect

8. We had to _____ a frog in science class today.

9. Children should _____ house rules.

10. The police officer needs to _____ the scene for evidence.

Application 2: Roots and Suffixes

A. Using the chart, fill in each blank with the word that best fits the meaning of the sentence.

Root	Meaning	Suffix	Meaning
dent	tooth	*-al*	of, like, related to, being
dynam	power	*-ic*	related to
log	speech, science, reason		

dental	dynamic	logic

1. My gums are sore from the _____ work Dr. White did on my teeth.

2. The energetic Robin Williams is an entertainer with a _____ personality.

3. The union president gave a speech explaining his _____ for threatening a strike.

B. Using the chart and the context of the sentences, fill in each blank with a word from the box. Use each word once.

Root	Meaning	Suffix	Meaning
psych	mind	*-ic*	related to
		-ist	person
		-logy	study of

psychiatric	psychiatrist	psychology

4. George is studying _____. He is learning about the mind and behavior.

5. George hopes to be a _____ who can help people understand the way they think and behave.

6. One day, George hopes to open a _____ clinic for homeless individuals who are suffering from mental illness.

Application 3: Using a Glossary and a Dictionary

A. Study this list of words from the glossary of a college sociology textbook. Then answer the questions that follow.

Textbook Skills

> **Glossary**
>
> **Group** people who think of themselves as belonging together and who interact with one another
> **In-group** a group toward which one feels loyalty
> **Out-group** a group toward which one feels antagonism
> **Primary group** a close, long-term, face-to-face group
> **Reference group** a group that we use as a standard to evaluate ourselves
> **Secondary group** a larger, short-term group based on some interest or activity
> **Social network** social ties radiating from the self that link people together

Based on the definition of each word and the context of each sentence, label the statements below either true (T) or false (F).

_____ **1.** Primary groups such as the family play a key role in the development of the self.

_____ **2.** To the gang known as the Crips, the rival gang known as the Bloods is an in-group.

_____ **3.** The American Medical Association is an example of a reference group.

_____ **4.** The international convention called Comic Con is a secondary group that brings together fans of comic books and science fiction.

_____ **5.** Facebook and MySpace are examples of reference groups.

B. Study the excerpt based on *Merriam-Webster's Collegiate Dictionary, Eleventh Edition*. Then answer the questions that follow.

[1]**ag·gre·gate** \\'a-gri-gət\\ *adj* [ME *aggregat,* fr. L. *aggregatus,* pp. of *aggregare* to add to, fr. *ad-* + *greg-, grex* flock] (15c) : formed by the collection of units or particles into a body, mass, or amount : COLLECTIVE: as **a (1)** : clustered in a dense mass or head <an ~ flower> **(2)** : formed from several separate ovaries of a single flower <~ fruit> **b** : composed of mineral crystals of one or more kinds or of mineral rock fragments **c** : taking all units as a whole <~ sales> — **ag·gre·gate·ly** *adv* — **ag·gre·gate·ness** *n*
[2]**ag·gre·gate** \\-,gāt\\ *vt* **-gat·ed; -gat·ing** (15c) **1** : to collect or gather into a mass or whole **2** : to amount in the aggregate to : TOTAL
[3]**ag·gre·gate** \\-gət\\ *n* (15c) **1** : a mass or body of units or parts somewhat loosely associated with one another **2** : the whole sum or amount : SUM TOTAL **3 a** : an aggregate rock **b** : any of several hard inert materials (as sand, gravel, or slag) used for mixing with a cementing material to form concrete, mortar, or plaster **c** : a clustered mass of individual soil particles varied in shape, ranging in size from a microscopic granule to a small crumb, and considered the basic structural unit of soil **4** : SET 21 **5** : MONETARY AGGREGATE — **in the aggregate** : considered as a whole: COLLECTIVELY <dividends for the year amounted *in the aggregate* to 25 million dollars>
ag·gre·ga·tion \\,a-gri-'gā-shən\\ *n* (1547) **1** : a group, body, or mass composed of many distinct parts or individuals **2 a** : the collecting of units or parts into a mass or whole **b** : the condition of being so collected — **ag·gre·ga·tion·al** \\-shnəl, -shə-nᵊl\\ *adj*
ag·gre·ga·tive \\'a-gri-,gā-tiv\\ *adj* (1644) **1** : of or relating to an aggregate **2** : tending to aggregate — **ag·gre·ga·tive·ly** *adv*

Source: By permission. From *Merriam-Webster's Collegiate® Dictionary,* 11th Edition © 2010 by Merriam-Webster, Incorporated (www.Merriam-Webster.com).

_____ **6.** How many parts of speech does the word "aggregate" have?
a. one   c. three
b. two   d. four

_____ **7.** What does the root "greg, grex" mean?
a. to add   c. whole
b. to divide   d. flock

_____ **8.** Which of the following words is a noun?
  a. aggregation
  b. aggregatively
  c. aggregational
  d. aggregrating

Based on the definition of the words in the dictionary and the context of each sentence, fill in the blank with the word that best fits the sentence.

9. An _____ consists of individuals who temporarily share the same physical space but who do not see themselves as belonging together.

10. In the natural world, the _____ response is the tendency for consumers to spend most of their feeding time in areas with the most prey.

REVIEW TEST 1

Score (number correct) _____ × 10 = _____%

Vocabulary-Building Skills

A. Using the chart and the context of each sentence, select the word from the box that best fits the meaning of the sentence. Use each word once.

Prefix	Meaning	Root	Meaning	Suffix	Meaning
hypo-	under	*derm*	skin	*-ic*	of, like, related to, being
hyper-	excessive	*errat*	wander	*-logy*	study of
				-ally	in that manner

dermatology	erratic	hyperactive	hypodermic

1. Eric is afraid of _____ needles.

2. By the time we noticed the dog's _____ behavior, it was too late to cure his case of rabies.

3. Some brands of cough medicine make Lana _____.

4. _____ is the study of the skin.

B. Look over the following entry from *Merriam-Webster's Collegiate Dictionary, Eleventh Edition.* Then mark each statement **T** (true) or **F** (false), based on the entry.

innards • in-process

in·no·vate \'i-nə-,vāt\ *vb* -**vat·ed;**   -**vat·ing** [L *innovatus,* pp. of *innovare,* fr. *in-* + *novus* new — more at NEW] *vt* (1548) **1** : to introduce as or as if new **2** : *archaic* : to effect a change in <the dictates of my father were . . . not to be altered, *innovated,* or even discussed —Sir Walter Scott> ~ *vi* : to make changes : do something in a new way — **in·no·va·tor** \-,vā-tər\ *n* — **in·no·va·to·ry** \'i-nə-və-,tōr-ē, -,tȯr-; 'i-nə-,vā-tə-rē\ *adj*

Source: By permission. From *Merriam-Webster's Collegiate® Dictionary,* 11th Edition © 2010 by Merriam-Webster, Incorporated (www.Merriam-Webster.com).

_____ **5.** The word *innovate* comes from a Latin word that means "new."

_____ **6.** The date the word *innovate* was first recorded in English is not known.

_____ **7.** The word *innovate* has four syllables.

_____ **8.** The word *inside* would be found on this page of the dictionary.

C. Look over the terms from the glossary of the textbook *Government in America.* Based on the definition of each term and the context of the sentence, write the term that best fits the meaning of each of the sentences that follow the list.

Textbook
Skills

Glossary

affirmative action A policy designed to give attention to members of a group that had been deprived up to that time.
arms race A tense relationship beginning in the 1950s between the Soviet Union and the United States. One side's advance in weapons caused the other side to develop more weapons, and so on.

—Adapted from Edwards, Wattenberg, & Lineberry, *Government in America: People, Politics, and Policy,* 5th ed., Brief Version, p. 490.

9. The Soviet Union and the United States began an _____ in the 1950s.

10. Several minority groups have benefited from _____.

REVIEW TEST 2

Score (number correct) _____ × 10 = _____%

Vocabulary-Building Skills

A. Using the chart and the context of each sentence, select the word from the box that best fits the meaning of the sentence. Use each word once.

Prefix	Meaning	Root	Meaning	Suffix	Meaning
re-	back, again	*fluct*	flow	*-ation*	action, state of, like, related
		pater	father	*-al*	to, being
				-ity	quality

fluctuation	paternal	paternity	reflux

1. Heartburn is caused by a _____ of stomach acid.

2. Graham demanded a _____ test to determine if he was the child's father.

3. Arthur has strong _____ feelings for his nieces and nephews.

4. Seasons of flood and drought cause a _____ in the water supply.

B. Look over the following entry for *chop suey* from *Merriam-Webster's Collegiate Dictionary, Eleventh Edition.* Then mark each statement **T** (true) or **F** (false), based on the entry.

chopper • chowder

chop su·ey \,chäp-'sü-ē\ *n, pl* **chop sueys** [Chin (Guangdong) *jaahp-seui* odds and ends, fr. *jaahp* miscellaneous + *seui* bits] (1888) **:** a dish prepared chiefly from bean sprouts, bamboo shoots, water chestnuts, onions, mushrooms, and meat or fish and served with rice and soy sauce

Source: By permission. From *Merriam-Webster's Collegiate® Dictionary,* 11th Edition © 2010 by Merriam-Webster, Incorporated (www.Merriam-Webster.com).

_____ **5.** *Chop suey* is a term that had its origin in China.

_____ **6.** The word *suey* means "pig."

_____ **7.** The word *chorus* would be found on this page of the dictionary.

C. Look over the list of words from the glossary of the textbook *The Family.* Based on the definition of each word and the context of the sentence, write the word that best fits the meaning of each sentence that follows the list.

Textbook
Skills

> **Glossary**
>
> **Gender** A term that refers to being male or female.
> **Gender role** The expected behaviors of a gender that are assigned by a given culture.
> **Househusband** A husband who stays at home and performs the domestic tasks and takes care of the children while his wife is employed full time.

—Adapted from Eshleman, *The Family*, 9th ed., p. 558.

8. Being a _____ is a new role for many men.

9. Giving toy cars to boys and dolls to girls is seen by some people as a way to teach children their proper _____.

10. New medical breakthroughs with DNA promise future parents the ability to choose their child's _____.

REVIEW TEST 3

Score (number correct) _____ × 10 = _____%

Vocabulary-Building Skills

A. Using the chart and the context of each sentence, select the word from the box that best fits the meaning of the sentence. Use each word once.

Prefix	Meaning	Root	Meaning	Suffix	Meaning
in-	into	*quir, quis*	question	*-tion*	action, state
				-ive	of, like, related to, being
				-or	one who

inquire	inquisition	inquisitive	inquisitor

1. You can _____ at the window about your food order.

2. A 2-year-old child is naturally _____ about the world around her.

3. The grand jury is conducting an _____ about the missing woman.

4. The defense attorney took on the role of _____ in an attempt to prove that the witness was lying.

B. Look over the following words from *Merriam-Webster's Collegiate Dictionary, Eleventh Edition*. Then mark each statement **T** (true) or **F** (false), based on the entry.

IQ • ironness

¹**irk** \'ərk\ *vt* [ME] (15c) **:** to make weary, irritated, or bored   *syn* see ANNOY
²**irk** *n* (ca. 1570)   **1 :** the fact of being annoying   **2 :** a source of annoyance
irk·some \'ərk-səm\ *adj* (15c) **:** tending to irk **:** TEDIOUS <an ~ task>
— **irk·some·ly** *adv* — **irk·some·ness** *n*

Source: By permission. From *Merriam-Webster's Collegiate® Dictionary,* 11th Edition © 2010 by Merriam-Webster, Incorporated (www.Merriam-Webster.com).

_____ **5.** The word *irk* can be used as both a verb and a noun.

_____ **6.** Another word for *irksome* is *tedious*.

_____ **7.** The noun form of *irksome* is *irksomely*.

C. Look over the words from the glossary of the textbook *Psychology: The Brain, the Person, the World*. Based on the definition of each word and the context of the sentence, select the word that best fits the meaning of each sentence that follows the list.

Textbook
Skills

Glossary

Social loafing The tendency to work less hard when responsibility for the result is spread among a group's members.
Social phobia A fear of public embarrassment and the desire to avoid social situations.
Social psychology The study of how people think about other people, relationships, and groups.

—Adapted from Kosslyn/Rosenberg, *Psychology: The Brain, the Person, the World*, p. 691 © 2001 Allyn and Bacon. Reproduced by permission of Pearson Education, Inc.

8. Researchers who study how people flirt and make dates work in the field of _____.

9. Randy is seldom selected by his peers for group projects; he is known for his _____.

10. Emma never leaves her apartment because of her _____.

WHAT DO YOU THINK?

Have you ever heard of the terms "social loafing" or "social phobia"? Have you ever known anyone to be a social loafer or to have a social phobia? Assume you are taking a college psychology course, and you have completed a group project. Your professor has asked you to evaluate the members in your group based on their performances. One member consistently missed group meetings and deadlines. Write a paragraph or two that evaluates your classmate. In your evaluation use the term and definition (social loafing or social phobia) that best explains his or her performance.

REVIEW TEST 4   **Score** (number correct) _____ × 10 = _____%

Vocabulary-Building Skills

Read the passage from the online magazine *American Chronicle* by Bart Bagget. Then, using the glossary and the context of the sentences, answer the questions that follow.

Glossary

apparently that which seems to be true may not actually be true

astute clever, shrewd, showing good judgment, especially for personal benefit

determine to decide, limit, influence, or end something

hazardous harmful, very dangerous to living beings or the environment

imitate to follow the example of somebody or something, to be or look like something

internal located within or affecting the inside of something, especially the inside of the body

literally strictly adhering to basic meaning, shows that a statement is actually true and not exaggerated

Who Else Wants to Get Rid of Toxic Vocabulary to Learn the Language Patterns That Imitate Success?

1   The language patterns you use **determine** your behavior, your future and your success. The correct language pattern directs your brain towards your goals and targets and vice versa.

2   The most **hazardous** language pattern that can spoil your future is the word 'TRY'. If you tell your brain you will "give it a try," you are actually telling your brain to fail. If you "try" and do something, your **unconscious** mind has permission not to succeed. Try is a language pattern that doesn't give a command to your brain that you have to succeed rather it gives a choice to your brain to be successful or not.

3   I remember my dad teaching me the power of language patterns at a very young age. Not only did my dad understand that language patterns are the specific words that affect our mental pictures, but he understood words are a powerful programming factor in lifelong success.

scamper to run quickly or playfully

unconscious the part of the mind containing memories, thoughts, feelings, and ideas that the person is not generally aware of but are revealed in dreams and disconnected acts

toxic deadly, contaminated, poisonous

4   One particularly interesting event occurred when I was eight. As a kid, I was always climbing trees, poles, and **literally** hanging around upside down from the rafters of our lake house. So, it came as no surprise to my dad to find me at the top of a 30-foot tree, swinging back and forth. My little eight-year-old brain didn't realize the tree could break or I could get hurt. I just thought it was fun to be up so high.

5   My older cousin, Tammy, was also in the same tree. She was hanging on the first big limb, about ten feet below me. Tammy's mother also noticed us at the exact same time my dad did. About that time a huge gust of wind came over the tree. I could hear the leaves start to rattle and the tree begin to sway. I remember my dad's voice over the wind yell, "Bart, Hold on tightly." So I did. The next thing I know, I heard Tammy screaming at the top of her lungs, laying flat on the ground. She had fallen out of the tree.

6   I **scampered** down the tree to safety. My dad later told me why she fell and I did not. **Apparently,** Tammy's mother was not as an **astute** student of language patterns as my father. When Tammy's mother felt the gust of wind, she yelled out, "Tammy, don't fall!" And Tammy did . . . fall.

7   My dad then explained to me that the mind has a very difficult time processing a negative image. In fact, people who rely on **internal** pictures cannot see a negative at all. In order for Tammy to process the command of not falling, her nine-year-old brain had to first imagine falling, then try to tell the brain not to do what it just imagined. Whereas, my eight-year-old brain instantly had an internal image of me hanging on tightly. (The language pattern made this difference.)

8   This is why people who try to stop smoking struggle with the act of stopping smoking. They are running pictures all day of themselves smoking. Smokers are rarely taught to see themselves breathing fresh air and feeling great. The language pattern they use becomes one barrier to success.

9   Who else wants to get rid of **toxic** vocabulary to learn the language patterns that imitate success?

—Bart Baggett*, "Who Else Wants to Get Rid of Toxic Vocabulary to Learn the Language Patterns That Imitate Success?" *American Chronicle*. 19 Nov. 2007. http://www.americanchronicle.com/articles/view/43338.

---

*Bart Baggett is the most well known handwriting analyst in the world. Bart has appeared on over 1500 TV and radio shows including CNN's Larry King, Fox News, and NPR. Bart is the director of Handwriting University, the world's leading handwriting training institute. His books are translated and distributed worldwide including in India and China.

_____ **1.** What is the best definition for the word **imitate** in the title of the selection?
  a. look like
  b. make fun of
  c. are
  d. follow the example of

_____ **2.** What is the best synonym for the word **determine** in paragraph 1?
  a. end
  b. enhance
  c. limit
  d. support

_____ **3.** What is the best synonym of the word **hazardous** in paragraph 2?
  a. harmful
  b. rude
  c. safe
  d. fulfilling

_____ **4.** What is the best synonym of the word **unconscious** in paragraph 2?
  a. lifeless
  b. unaware
  c. ignorant
  d. known

_____ **5.** What is the best synonym of the word **literally** in paragraph 4?
  a. exaggerated
  b. easily
  c. plainly
  d. naturally

_____ **6.** What is the best meaning of the word **scampered** in paragraph 6?
  a. hurried
  b. climbed
  c. played
  d. fell

_____ **7.** What is the best synonym for the word **apparently** in paragraph 6?
  a. actually
  b. inwardly
  c. truly
  d. seemingly

_____ **8.** What is the best meaning of the word **astute** in paragraph 6?
  a. ignorant
  b. wise
  c. selfish
  d. generous

_____ **9.** What is the best meaning of the word **internal** in paragraph 7?
  a. mental
  b. visible
  c. spoken
  d. real

_____ **10.** What is the best synonym of the word **toxic** in paragraph 9?
  a. hazardous
  b. lethal
  c. harmful
  d. beneficial

WHAT DO YOU THINK?

Do you or someone you know use toxic vocabulary? In a short essay, identify the toxic phrases you use or someone you know uses on a daily basis. Explain the effect of these toxic phrases. Rewrite each toxic phrase into a positive statement. Be sure to explain the positive effect of revising toxic words.

After Reading About Vocabulary-Building Skills

Now that you have read and studied vocabulary-building skills, take time to reflect on what you have learned before you begin the Mastery Tests. Think about your learning and performance by answering the following questions. Write your answers in your notebook.

- How has my knowledge base or prior knowledge about vocabulary-building skills changed?
- Based on my studies, how do I think I will perform on the Mastery Test(s)? Why do I think my scores will be above average, average, or below average?
- Would I recommend this chapter to other students who want to learn more about vocabulary-building skills? Why or why not?

Test your understanding of what you have learned about Vocabulary-Building Skills by completing the Chapter 3 Review Card on the insert near the end of your text.

CONNECT TO **myreadinglab**

To check your progress in meeting Chapter 3's learning outcomes, log in to **www.myreadinglab.com**, and try the following activities.

- The "Vocabulary" section of MyReadingLab introduces several vocabulary-building tools, such as using a dictionary and understanding roots, prefixes, suffixes, and word origins. This module provides an overview, a model, flash animations, practices, and tests. To access this resource, click on the "Study Plan" tab. Then click on "Vocabulary."
- MyReadingLab offers several additional resources for learning content or subject area words such as study tips, lists of academic and college vocabulary, quizzes, Internet exercises, and web resources. To access one

resource, go to "Other Resources" on the Home page of MyReadingLab. Under the heading "Course Resources," click on the link labeled "Vocabulary Website." Under the heading, "Explore Other Vocabulary Resources," click on each of the following links:

- Academic Vocabulary
- Campus Vocabulary
- Links to More Vocabulary Resources

To access another resource, go to the "Other Resources" on the Home page of MyReadingLab. Under the heading "Course Resources," click on the link labeled "Study Skills Website." Under the heading "Reading and Writing," click on the link labeled "Vocabulary."

To measure your mastery of the content of this chapter, complete the tests in the "Vocabulary" section of MyReadingLab and click on Gradebook to find your results.

Read the following passage, adapted from the textbook *Social Psychology*. Then, using the glossary and the context of the sentences, answer the questions that follow it.

Textbook Skills

Intrinsic versus Extrinsic Motivation

Glossary

extrinsic motivation the desire to engage in an activity for outside rewards or pressures

intrinsic motivation the desire to engage in an activity for pleasure

overjustification effect placing too much emphasis on extrinsic reasons to explain behavior

performance-contingent rewards rewards given for how well a task is done

task-contingent rewards rewards given for performing a task, regardless of how well the task is done

[1]Say you love to play the piano. [2]We would say that your interest in playing the piano stems from **intrinsic motivation**. [3]Your reasons for engaging in the activity have to do with you—the enjoyment and pleasure you feel when playing the piano. [4]In other words, playing the piano is play, not work. [5]Now let's say your parents get the brilliant idea of rewarding you with money for playing the piano. [6]They figure this will make you practice even harder. [7]Your playing now stems from **extrinsic motivation** as well. [8]According to self-perception theory, extrinsic rewards can hurt intrinsic motivation. [9]Whereas before you played the piano because you love it, now you are playing it so that you'll get the reward. [10]What was once play is now work. [11]Replacing intrinsic motivation with extrinsic motivation makes most people lose interest in the activity they originally enjoyed. [12]This result is called the **overjustification effect**. [13]The results of overjustification studies are distressing, given the wide use of rewards and incentives by parents, educators, and employers. [14]However, certain types of rewards can have a positive impact. [15]So far we have been discussing **task-contingent rewards**. [16]In contrast, **performance-contingent rewards** are used to recognize how well people perform the task. [17]This type of reward is less likely to decrease interest in a task—and may even increase interest—because it conveys the message that you are good at a task.

—Adapted from Aronson, Wilson, & Akert, *Social Psychology*, 4th ed., pp. 155–157.

Read each sentence, and mark the statement that follows it **T** (true) or **F** (false).

1. We would say that your interest in playing the piano stems from **intrinsic motivation**. (*sentence 2*)

   _____ Intrinsic motivations come from within a person.

2. Your playing now stems from **extrinsic motivation** as well. (*sentence 7*)

   _____ An athlete competing for a trophy is an example of an extrinsic motivation.

3. The results of **overjustification** studies are distressing, given the wide use of rewards and incentives by parents, educators, and employers. (*sentence 13*)

   _____ Overjustification is used by parents, educators, and employers to encourage hard work.

4. So far we have been discussing **task-contingent rewards**. (*sentence 15*)

   _____ Getting extra credit for class attendance is an example of a task-contingent reward.

5. In contrast, **performance-contingent rewards** are used to recognize how well people perform the task. (*sentence 16*)

   _____ Receiving a certificate for completing a training program is an example of a performance-contingent reward.

Name _____ Section _____

Date _____ **Score** (number correct) _____ × 20 = _____%

Read the following passage. Then, using the glossary and the context of the sentences, answer the questions that follow it.

**Textbook
Skills**

Glossary

impending looming, approaching, coming

inhibitory a person, thing, or substance that holds something back or restrains something

receptors receiver

stimulus cause, reason

transmit send out

Pain

[1]Despite the discomfort, even the agony, pain brings, the inability to feel pain is even worse in the long run than the inability to smell odors. [2]One researcher described children who could not feel pain normally. [3]As a result, they picked off their nostrils and bit off their fingers because they didn't notice what they were doing. [4]Pain serves to warn us of **impending** danger, and it is crucial to survival.

[5]The sensation of pain arises when three different kinds of nerves are stimulated. [6]These nerves differ in size and in the speed with which they **transmit** impulses. [7]Thus, we can feel double pain: the first phase, of sharp pain, occurs at the time of the injury; it is followed by a dull pain. [8]The two kinds of pain arise from different fibers sending their messages at different speeds.

[9]One of the ways we deal with pain is by producing substances in our brains, called endorphins, which have painkilling effects. [10]Some drugs, such as morphine, bind to the same **receptors** that accept endorphins. [11]This explains how those drugs can act as painkillers. [12]However, pain involves more than simple bottom-up processing. [13]Top-down processing can directly inhibit the inter-neurons that regulate the input of pain signals to the brain. [14]This gate control mechanism may explain how hypnosis can control pain. [15]Indeed, hypnosis can selectively alter our experience of the unpleasantness of pain without affecting how intense it feels. [16]Hypnosis thus may alter processing in only some of the brain areas that register pain. [17]**Inhibitory** impulses from the brain to neurons also send signals from the body. [18]Thus, pain is reduced by a *counter-irritant,* a painful **stimulus** elsewhere in the body. [19]Such effects may explain how acupuncture, the placing of small needles to treat pain, works. [20]People differ widely in the amount of pain they can stand.

—Adapted from Kosslyn/Rosenberg, *Psychology: The Brain, the Person, the World,* p. 123 © 2001 Allyn and Bacon. Reproduced by permission of Pearson Education, Inc.

Read the sentences, and mark the statements that follow them **T** (true) or **F** (false).

1. Pain serves to warn us of **impending** danger, and it is crucial to survival. (*sentence 4*)

   _____ Pain signals a problem that could get worse if not corrected.

2. These nerves differ in size and in the speed with which they **transmit** impulses. (*sentence 6*)

   _____ Nerves carry messages from the various parts of the body to the brain.

3. Some drugs, such as morphine, bind to the same **receptors** that accept endorphins. (*sentence 10*)

   _____ Nerve endings are not receptors.

4. **Inhibitory** impulses from the brain to neurons also send signals from the body. (*sentence 17*)

   _____ Acupuncture is a type of inhibitory impulse.

5. Thus, pain is reduced by a *counter-irritant,* a painful **stimulus** elsewhere in the body. (*sentence 18*)

   _____ A stimulus is the result of pain.

Textbook Skills

Read the following passage, adapted from the textbook *Understanding Parenting*. Then, using the glossary and the context of the sentences, answer the questions that follow it.

Glossary

authority command, power

departure a going out, going away, separation

image-making making pictures in the mind, using the imagination

interdependent sharing a reliance on or trust in other people

interpretative explaining

nurturing supplying with nourishment, educating

[1]The main challenge of adulthood is learning to care for others and future generations. [2]Experts describe six stages that parents go through before, during and after they raise their children.

[3]During the first or **image-making** stage, expectant couples face several tasks; the major task is getting ready for birth and parenthood. [4]Before the birth of their child, all parents have to go on are "images." [5]These expectant parents imagine what their child and their new family will be like.

[6]The next stage is the **nurturing** stage. [7]During this stage, parents learn to love and accept the child. [8]This may seem like it should come naturally. [9]However, many parents struggle when the images they had before the birth of the child are different from the actual baby.

[10]The third or **authority** stage spans the preschool years. [11]During this stage, parents must learn how to assert their authority. [12]In the authority stage, parents are learning to use power. [13]Out of the use of power, self-concepts are being shaped—for both parent and child.

[14]The fourth or **interpretative** stage occurs during the elementary school years. [15]In this stage, parents explain and teach their children skills and values that help shape their self-image.

[16]The fifth or **interdependent** stage spans adolescence. [17]Authority and communication issues arise again. [18]As the child grows, the old issues must be updated to keep up with the changing needs of the child.

[19]The final or **departure** stage occurs when grown children leave home. [20]Parents are wise to prepare for a child's departure. [21]When the last child leaves home, the parents must redefine their own life's role. [22]This means that parents have to think differently about themselves as a couple and as individuals.

—Adapted from Jaffe, *Understanding Parenting*, excerpts from pp. 36–38 © 1997 Allyn and Bacon. Reproduced by permission of Pearson Education, Inc.

Read each sentence, and mark the statement that follows it **T** (true) or **F** (false).

1. During the first or **image-making** stage, expectant couples face several tasks; the major task is getting ready for birth and parenthood. (*sentence 3*)

   _____ Expectant couples think about the baby and the changes it will bring long before the baby is born.

2. The third or **authority** stage spans the preschool years. (*sentence 10*)

   _____ Children fight their parents for control during the third stage of growth.

3. The fourth or **interpretative** stage occurs during the elementary school years. (*sentence 14*)

   _____ In the fourth stage, the parents' main purpose is to teach their child.

4. The fifth or **interdependent** stage spans adolescence. (*sentence 16*)

   _____ Parents and children rely on each other in the fifth stage.

5. The final or **departure** stage occurs when grown children leave home. (*sentence 19*)

   _____ Parents should pack their children's belongings when the children leave home.

Read the following passage about multitasking. Answer the questions that follow.

The Limits of Multitasking

[1]So you think you can juggle several tasks at once with ease? [2]Think again! [3]Research suggests that we humans are not made to handle two complex tasks at one time. [4]That doesn't mean we can't walk and talk at the same time, but it does means we can't drive and send text messages at the same time. [5]And we certainly can't add eating or putting on makeup to the mix—not if we want to get where we are going without causing harm to ourselves or others.

[6]Why can't we multitask? [7]The human brain has two lobes that divide the responsibility equally when two tasks are being carried out at the same time. [8]When we humans pursue two goals (such as driving and talking on a cell phone) concurrently, the two frontal lobes divide the work to focus on each of the two goals and related actions simultaneously. [9]The anterior most part of the frontal lobes, the executive control region of our brain, enables us to switch back and forth between the two goals. [10]We can execute one goal while we put the other goal on hold. [11]Therefore, our cognition is dual in nature so we can easily switch back and forth between two fairly simple tasks. [12]Even so, the effort to switch between two tasks requires time and effort and lowers our ability to perform either task as efficiently as we could if we concentrated on one task at a time. [13]Importantly, switching between two tasks is very different from performing two tasks at the same time. [14]And adding a third task overwhelms the ability of the frontal lobes to function.

[15]Although we may think we can drive and text at the same time, our brains actually cannot carry out these two complex functions at the same time. [16]This fact has implications for the classroom and work place as well. [17]Multitasking adversely affects memory and efficiency. [18]Multitasking may keep us busy and make us feel productive. [19]However, activity doesn't always mean productivity.

[20]We must understand the difference between task switching, something we can do, and multitasking, something we simply are not geared to do.

Using the chart and the context of the passage, select the word from the box that best completes each entry in the glossary. Then complete the summary of the passage by filling in each blank with the appropriate word from the glossary.

Prefix	Meaning	Root	Meaning	Suffix	Meaning
ad-	to	*currere*	to run	*-ior, -ive*	of, like, related to
ante-	before	*sequi*	follow, carry out	*-ly*	the quality of
co-, con-	together	*gnoscrere*	to know	*-tion*	action, process
ex-	out of, from	*vertere*	turn (against)		

adversely	anterior	cognition	concurrently	executive

1. _____ description of something suited for carrying out plans, duties, or functions

2. _____ actions that are unfavorable, undesirable, or harmful

3. _____ taking place, existing, or running parallel at the same time

4. _____ at, near, or from the front of something

5. _____ the thought process and the acquiring of knowledge

Summary: Multitasking requires the **(6)** _____ region of the brain in the **(7)** _____ frontal cortex to manage two or more tasks **(8)** _____. However, because our **(9)** _____ is dual in nature, multitasking **(10)** _____ affects our ability to efficiently carry out two or more complex tasks at the same time.

Topics and Main Ideas

4

After studying this chapter you should be able to do the following:

1. Distinguish between general and specific ideas.
2. Define the following terms: *topic*, *main idea*, *topic sentence*, and *supporting details*.
3. Identify the topic of a reading selection.
4. Distinguish between a topic, a main idea, and supporting details.
5. Assess your comprehension of topics and main ideas.
6. Evaluate the importance of what you have learned.
7. Use topics and main ideas to comprehend an author's meaning.

 Before Reading About Topics and Main Ideas

Skilled use of the reading process relies on developing questions about the material that will guide you as you read. Look over the learning outcomes. Next, skim the chapter and note the key terms highlighted in boxes. Based on these ideas, create at least five questions that you can answer as you study the chapter. Write your questions in the following spaces:

_____?

_____?

_____?

_____?

_____?

Compare the questions you created with the following questions. Then write the ones that seem the most helpful in your notebook, leaving enough space between each question to record the answers as you read and study the chapter.

What is a topic? What is the difference between general and specific ideas? What is a main idea? What is a topic sentence? How are the main idea and a topic sentence related? What are supporting details? How are supporting details related to the main idea? What is the difference between the central idea and a topic sentence?

 ## Topics

Question: *Why read?* Answer: *For entertainment, for escape, for emotional release, and for information about topics.* Think about it. Without reading and writing, we would not know the cures for diseases. Reading allows us to explore the effects of violence, examine the lives of influential men and women, and learn ways to stay healthy. Without reading, we would not be able to build new ideas based on older ones. Instead, we would have to keep rediscovering the same information.

Reading passages contain information about countless important **topics**.

> The **topic** is the general subject matter of a reading passage. The topic is who or what the passage is about. The topic can be stated in one word or just a few words.

EXAMPLE Read the following paragraph. Then write down the topic of the paragraph.

Bacteria are single-celled "living" microorganisms. They are some of the smallest of living beings. They reproduce by dividing. Although bacteria come in several shapes, their most common shape is like a rod. Most bacteria can grow on nonliving surfaces. For example, you can find bacteria on countertops and doorknobs. However, not all bacteria are harmful. Some are even helpful to your health. For example, the good bacteria in yogurt help you digest your food. These helpful bacteria are also called probiotics (for life). But when harmful bacteria enter your body, they can make you sick. Harmful bacteria make toxins. And they can damage the cells they invade. Some bacterial infections are contagious. For example, strep throat and tuberculosis can be passed by contact.

Topic: _____

EXPLANATION As you read, it becomes clear that every statement in the paragraph has to do with bacteria. In fact, the word *bacteria* appears nine times in fifteen sentences. Often, an author repeats the topic throughout the paragraph.

Repeating the topic ties the details in the paragraph to the topic. The details in this paragraph describe the traits of bacteria. Therefore, if you guessed the topic of the paragraph to be "traits of bacteria," you were right.

To identify the topic of a paragraph, just ask yourself, "Who or what is the paragraph about?" You should be able to answer this question in just a few words.

PRACTICE 1

Read the following paragraph. Then write down the topic of the paragraph.

> In contrast to bacteria, viruses are not "living" organisms. Instead they are capsules of genetic material. Viruses are much smaller than bacteria. And viruses come in a wide variety of shapes. Most importantly, viruses must have living hosts to multiply. Hosts for viruses include people, plants, or animals. Without a host, a virus can't survive. Overall, viruses do not have a helpful purpose. Their sole mission is to create more viruses. When a virus enters your body, it invades some of your cells and takes over the cell machinery, redirecting it to produce the virus. The virus may eventually kill the host cells. Some viral infections are contagious. For example, influenza and HIV can be spread through contact.

Topic: _____

A topic is the general idea of a reading passage. Reading passages also include specific ideas.

VISUAL VOCABULARY

An HIV _____ fuses with a host T-Cell in the human body.

  a. bacteria
  b. virus

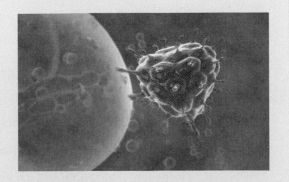

General and Specific Ideas

The ability to identify the topic of a paragraph or passage is closely tied to the ability to see the differences between general ideas and specific ideas. In a reading passage, the **general idea** must be broad enough to include all the **specific ideas** that are used to explain or support it.

> A **general idea** is a broad subject that needs specific ideas to support or explain it.
> A **specific idea** is a point used to support or explain a general idea.

EXAMPLE The following list is made up of one general idea and several specific ideas. Write the letter **G** in front of the general idea and the letter **S** in front of each specific idea.

___sunscreen   ___towels   ___items for the beach

___surfboard   ___beach chairs   ___beach umbrella

EXPLANATION If you wrote **G** next to "items for the beach," you were correct, for it is the only idea general enough to include all the other ideas. Sunscreen, towels, surfboard, beach chairs, and beach umbrella are all examples of items someone might take to the beach. In a reading passage, each specific idea relates to and supports the general idea.

PRACTICE 2

A. Each of the following items is made up of one general idea and four specific ideas. Write the letter **G** in front of the general idea and the letter **S** in front of each specific idea.

1. ___hurricane   ___rain   ___wind   ___flooding   ___warnings

2. ___hamburger   ___lamb   ___meats   ___chicken   ___turkey

3. ___basketball   ___sports   ___soccer   ___football   ___baseball

4. ___coins   ___dimes   ___nickels   ___quarters   ___pennies

5. ___water   ___soda   ___coffee   ___drinks   ___wine

6. ___peach   ___apple   ___fruit   ___banana   ___kiwi

7. ___starfish   ___sea life   ___whale   ___dolphin   ___mackerel

8. ___emotions   ___anger   ___joy   ___sadness   ___love

9. ___chair   ___couch   ___furniture   ___table   ___bookshelf

10. ___Prius   ___Lexus   ___Mustang   ___cars   ___Malibu

B. For each of the following general ideas, list two additional specific ideas.

11. *General idea:*   exercise

    Specific ideas: walking   _____   _____

12. *General idea:*   soft drinks

    Specific ideas: Pepsi   _____   _____

13. *General idea:*   flowers

    Specific ideas: daisy   _____   _____

14. *General idea:*   hand

    Specific ideas: forefinger   _____   _____

15. *General idea:*   clothes

    Specific ideas: shirt   _____   _____

16. *General idea:*   dogs

    Specific ideas: poodle   _____   _____

17. *General idea:*   fast-food restaurants

    Specific ideas: Burger King   _____   _____

18. *General idea:*   seasons

    Specific ideas: spring   _____   _____

19. *General idea:*   bodies of water

    Specific ideas: lakes   _____   _____

20. *General idea:*   extended family

    Specific ideas: cousin   _____   _____

C. The following items are made up of specific ideas. Write a general idea that covers all the specific ideas. The first one is done as an example.

21. *Specific ideas:* rake leaves   mow lawn   trim hedges   water garden

 General idea: _____

22. *Specific ideas:* strings   pick   frets   neck   bridge

 General idea: _____

23. *Specific ideas:* stove   oven   grill   microwave

 General idea: _____

24. *Specific ideas:* nail   print   cuticle   knuckle

 General idea: _____

25. *Specific ideas:* books   desks   students   teachers

 General idea: _____

VISUAL VOCABULARY

The best caption that states the topic of this photograph is

_____.

a. "Preparing for Hurricane Frances"
b. "Repairing the damage after Hurricane Frances"

Identifying the Topic of a Paragraph

Remember that a broad subject needs specific ideas to support or explain it. However, no single paragraph can discuss all the specific ideas linked to a broad idea. So an author narrows the broad subject to a topic that needs fewer specific ideas to support it. The topic "fast-food restaurants" is an example of a general idea that has been narrowed. (See item 17 of Practice 2.) The very broad subject "restaurants" had been narrowed to "fast-food restaurants." In fact, you might have listed a very different set of specific ideas if the topic had remained as broad as "restaurants." The narrower topic of "fast-food restaurants" demanded a very specific list of ideas to support it. Study the diagram below for a better understanding of the flow from broad to specific ideas.

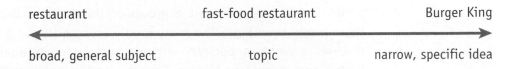

The challenge in reading a passage or paragraph is to pick the topic out of statements that range from broad and general to narrow and specific ideas.

EXAMPLE Read the following paragraph, and determine the topic.

Hip-Hop is a form of popular music believed to have originated in the Bronx. Hip-Hop has four basic elements. Two main aspects of Hip-Hop are mc'ing, also known as rapping, and dj'ing. The other two elements are graffiti and breakdancing. Although Hip-Hop has evolved into big business, the music is often criticized for disrespecting women and glorifying violence. Hip-Hop has probably encountered more problems with censorship than any other form of popular music in recent years, due to the use of expletives.

_____ Topic
a. rapping
b. music
c. Hip-Hop

EXPLANATION "Rapping" (a) is too narrow, for the paragraph lists rapping as one of the traits of Hip-Hop music. "Music" (b) is too broad, for music includes all types from country to classical. "Hip-Hop" (c) is the topic of this paragraph.

PRACTICE 3

Each of the following paragraphs is followed by three ideas. One idea is too general to be the topic. Another idea is too specific. Identify the idea that correctly states the topic.

_____ **1.**   Vitiligo (pronounced vit-ill-EYE-go) is a skin disorder. The cells that make pigment in the skin are destroyed. As a result, white patches appear on the skin in different parts of the body. Similar patches also appear on the tissues that line the inside of the mouth and nose and the inner layer of the eyeball. The hair that grows on areas affected by vitiligo sometimes turns white. The cause of vitiligo is not known. But there is strong evidence that people with vitiligo inherit a group of three genes that make them prone to vitiligo. The most widely accepted view is this is a disease in which a person's immune system reacts against the body's own organs or tissues. People's bodies produce proteins called cytokines. And cytokines alter their pigment-producing cells and cause these cells to die. Another view is that cells that produce the dark brown or black pigments destroy themselves. Michael Jackson suffered from vitiligo.

—"Vitiligo." National Institute of Arthritis and Musculoskeletal and Skin Diseases. 16 Sept. 2009. http://www.niams.nih.gov/Health_Info/Vitiligo/default.asp.

a. causes of vitiligo
b. Michael Jackson and vitiligo
c. definition of vitiligo

_____ **2.**   Pain can be controlled by several methods. First, proper breathing can aid in pain control. For example, many women use breathing to manage pain during labor. Second, use of a focal point helps a person endure or even reduce pain. Often before an injection, a nurse will direct a patient to look at a picture or an object nearby. This keeps the patient from tensing up. A third method is, of course, the use of pain relievers. A large variety of medicines are available when the pain becomes unbearable.

a. pain control through proper breathing
b. pain control methods
c. pain

_____ **3.**   Dog bites are very common. One insurance expert states that of all injury claims filed, at least one-third are related to dog bites. Any dog may be capable of biting. Even the well-loved family dog can suddenly turn into a biter for no known reason. The most common breeds to bite are chows, cocker spaniels, pit bulls, and Rottweilers. The most common victim is a child. Experts believe dogs go after children because of their size.

a. dog bites
b. dogs
c. dog breeds that bite

 ## Main Ideas

A skilled reader must be able to determine the author's main idea. The **main idea** of a paragraph is the author's controlling point about the topic.

Every piece of writing has a main idea. However, it is important to note here that some types of passages do not put the main idea directly into words. For example, novels, short stories, and poems do not directly state their main ideas. Chapter 6, *Implied Main Ideas,* teaches the skills needed to identify main ideas that are not stated.

Most of the paragraphs in college textbooks directly state the author's main idea. In fact, the main idea is usually stated in a single sentence called the **topic sentence.**

To identify the main idea, ask yourself, "What is the author's controlling point about the topic?" You should be able to answer this question in one sentence.

To be sure you have selected the correct statement as the topic sentence, ask yourself, "Do all the specific details in the paragraph support this statement?"

> The **main idea** is the author's controlling point about the topic.
> The **topic sentence** is a single sentence in a paragraph that states the author's main idea.

A paragraph is like a well-planned house of ideas. The *topic* or general subject matter is the roof. The roof covers all the rooms of the house. The *main idea* is the frame of the house, and the supporting details are the different rooms. The following diagram shows these relationships:

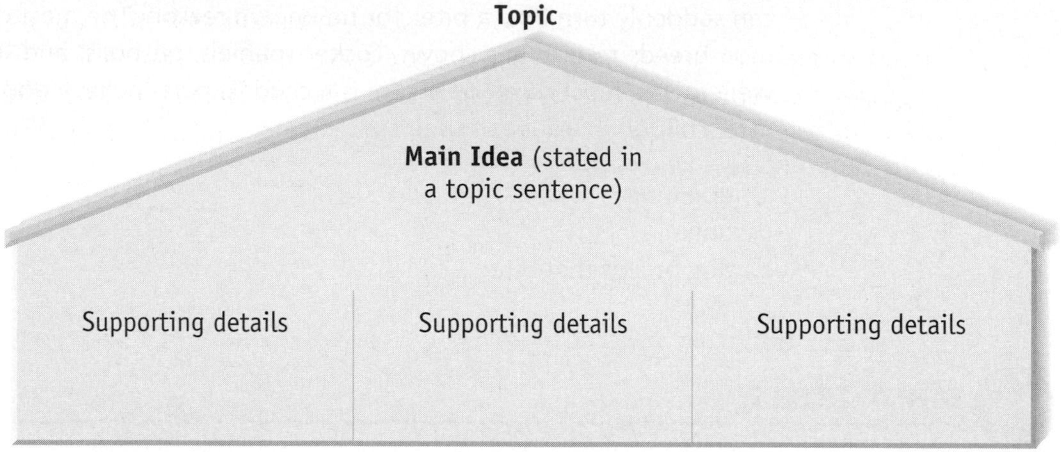

Topic

Main Idea (stated in
a topic sentence)

| Supporting details | Supporting details | Supporting details |

EXAMPLE Here is a list that includes a topic, a main idea (stated in a topic sentence), and supporting details. Finish the following diagram by writing in the main idea.

Topic	Lack of sleep
Main idea (stated in *topic sentence*)	Lack of sleep can lead to serious health consequences and can jeopardize safety.
Supporting detail	Lack of sleep leads to an increase in body mass index.
Supporting detail	Lack of sleep increases risk of diabetes and heart problems.
Supporting detail	Lack of sleep increases risk of motor vehicle accidents.

Topic: Lack of Sleep

Main Idea (stated in
a topic sentence):

_____

Supporting Details:

| Leads to an increase in body mass index | Increases risk of diabetes and heart problems | Increases risk of motor vehicle accidents |

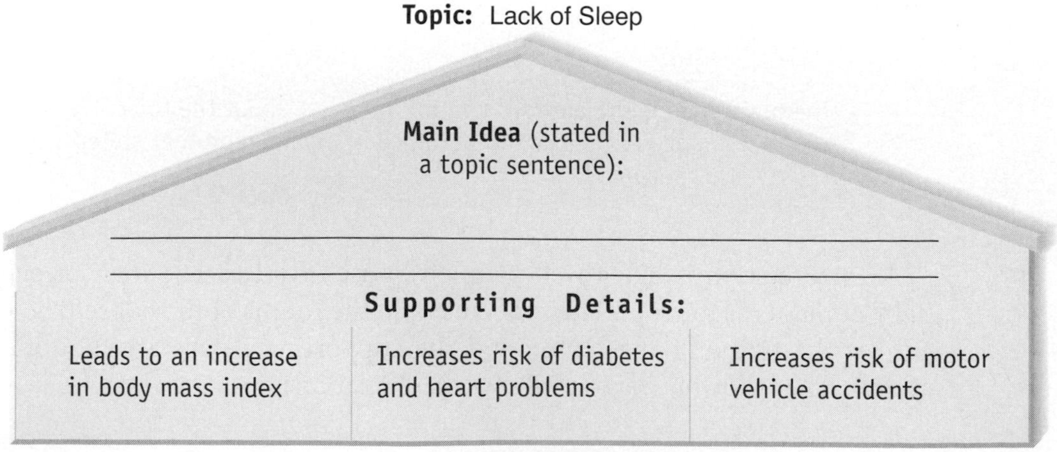

EXPLANATION If you wrote, "Lack of sleep can lead to serious health consequences and can jeopardize safety," you are correct. All the supporting details explain this main idea about lack of sleep. Remember: The main idea is general enough to cover all the supporting details and can be stated in one sentence (the topic sentence).

PRACTICE 4

A. Finish the following diagram by writing in the topic and main idea from the following paragraph.

- To find the **topic**, ask: "Who or what is the one thing the author is writing about in this paragraph?"
- To find the **main idea**, ask: "What is the controlling point the author is making about the topic?"
- To find the topic sentence, ask: "Does this sentence contain the topic and main idea, and does it cover all the other sentences in the paragraph?"

Many heroes are everyday people who simply rely on courage and hope. The father who gives one of his kidneys to his young daughter is just one instance of such a hero. Another inspiring example is the young person who refuses to let a friend drink and drive or the teacher who chooses to teach in a high-crime neighborhood. Even the young man who lost his arm in an accident yet learns to be a top-notch motorcycle technician is a living model of an everyday hero.

Topic: 1. _____

Main Idea (stated in a topic sentence):

2. _____

Supporting Details:

Father who gives a kidney to his young daughter	Young person who won't let a friend drive drunk	Teacher in a high-crime area	Young man who lost his arm and learned to be a technician

B. Read the paragraph. Identify the topic and main idea by answering the questions that follow it.

> [1]An aspect of Native American life that alternately intrigued, perplexed, and sometimes alarmed European and European-American observers, most of whom were male, during the 17th and 18th centuries, was the influential role of women. [2]In many cases they hold pivotal positions in Native political systems. [3]Iroquois women, for example, nominate men to positions of leadership and can "dehorn," or impeach, them for misconduct. [4]Women often have veto power over men's plans for war. [5]In a matrilineal society—and nearly all the confederacies that bordered the colonies were matrilineal—women owned all household goods except the men's clothes, weapons, and hunting implements. [6]They also were the primary conduits of culture from generation to generation."
>
> —http://www.america.gov/st/peopleplace-english/2009/June/20090617110824wrybakcuh0.5986096.html

_____ **3.** Which of the following best states the topic of the paragraph?
   a. the Iroquois
   b. cultural differences between Native Americans and European settlers
   c. Native political systems
   d. the influential role of Iroquois women in their society

_____ **4.** Identify the sentence that states the main idea in a topic sentence.
   a. sentence 1   c. sentence 4
   b. sentence 2   d. sentence 9

VISUAL VOCABULARY

These protestors consider animal testing a _____ act.

   a. barbaric
   b. reverent

C. Read the paragraph. Identify the topic and main idea or controlling point by answering the questions that follow it.

> Road rage is a dangerous problem caused by fear and anger. The fast pace of our lives creates a strong sense of anxiety for many people. The person who is worried about getting somewhere on time may become frustrated and angry at slow-moving traffic. This anger sometimes intensifies if other drivers make careless mistakes, such as turning without signaling or stopping too quickly. The angry driver may try to get even by tailgating or passing and cutting in too quickly. Sometimes the angry driver even chooses to get out of the car for a face-to-face confrontation. Too many times, these kinds of situations have led to fistfights or shootings.

5. What is the author's topic? _____

6. What is the author's main idea or controlling point? _____

_____

 ## Supporting Details

Most paragraphs have three essential parts:

- A topic (the general idea or subject)
- A main idea, often stated in a topic sentence (the author's controlling point about the topic)
- Supporting details (the specific ideas to support the main idea)

> **Supporting details** are specific ideas that *develop, explain, support,* or *illustrate* the main idea or controlling point.

Think again of the house of ideas that a writer builds. You will recall that the roof is the *general idea* that covers all the rooms' *specific ideas*. Think about all the different rooms of a house: kitchen, bedroom, bathroom, living room, and so on. Each room is a different part of the same house and serves a different purpose. Yet all the rooms are covered by the same roof.

The same is true for a paragraph. The supporting details of a paragraph are framed by the topic sentence and serve to explain or support the author's view of the topic.

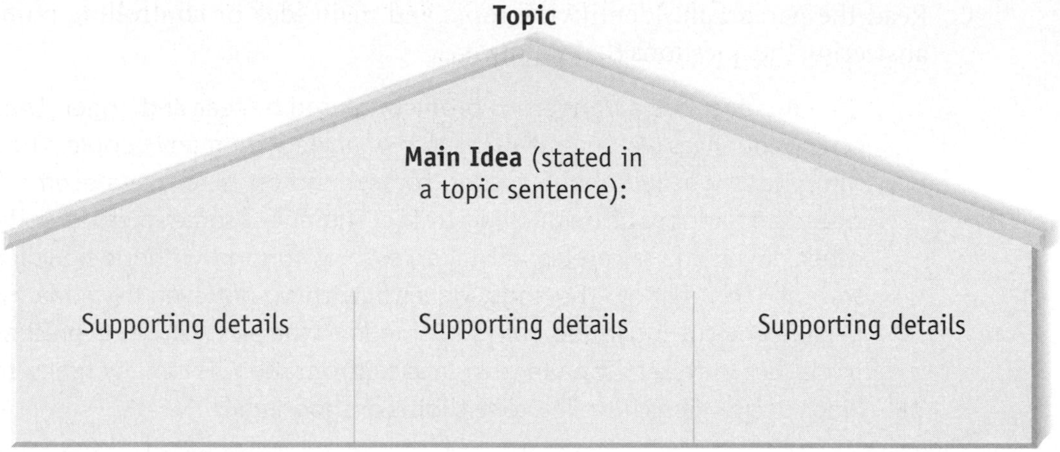

Topic

Main Idea (stated in
a topic sentence):

| Supporting details | Supporting details | Supporting details |

Now look again at the information about lack of sleep. First review the information; then study how it fits into the diagram below.

Lack of sleep can lead to serious health consequences and can jeopardize safety. First, lack of sleep leads to an increase in body mass index. In addition, lack of sleep increases risk of diabetes and heart problems. Finally, lack of sleep increases risk of motor vehicle accidents.

Topic: Lack of Sleep

Main Idea (stated in
a topic sentence):

Lack of sleep can lead to serious health consequences and can
jeopardize safety.

Supporting Details:

| Leads to an increase in body mass index | Increases risk of diabetes and heart problems | Increases risk of motor vehicle accidents |

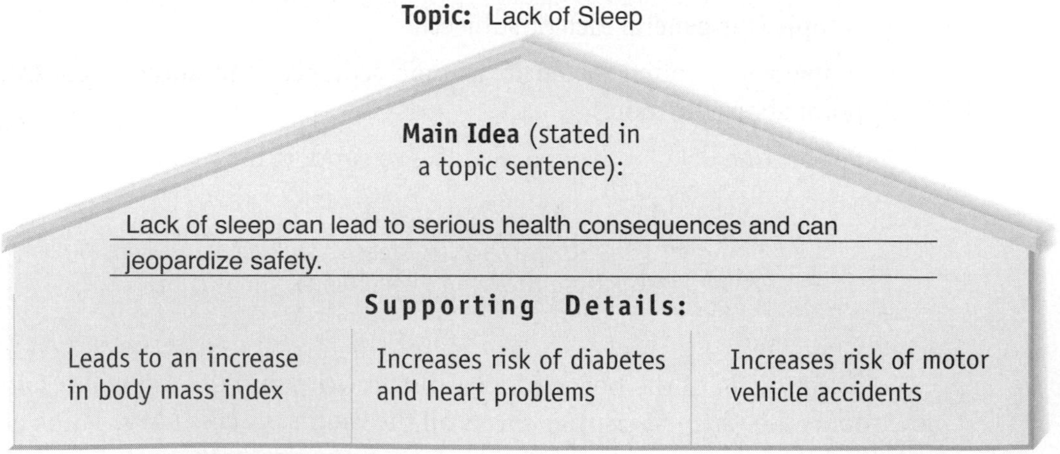

As a skilled reader, you will see that every paragraph has a topic, a main idea or controlling point, and supporting details. It is much easier to tell the difference between these three parts of a paragraph once you understand how each part works.

EXAMPLE Read the following list of ideas. Answer the questions that follow.

A. Beauty takes effort, time, and money.

B. For many women, a typical weekly visit to a beauty salon can take three hours and average about $150.

C. Additional services such as a pedicure and manicure can triple the cost and double the time.

_____ **1.** Which of the following best states the topic for the list of ideas?
  a. additional services
  b. beauty
  c. a typical visit to a beauty salon
  d. the cost of beauty

_____ **2.** Sentence A states
  a. the main idea.
  b. a supporting detail.

_____ **3.** Sentence B states
  a. the main idea.
  b. a supporting detail.

_____ **4.** Sentence C states
  a. the main idca.
  b. a supporting detail.

EXPLANATION The topic of the ideas is (d) the cost of beauty. Notice that the topic is very general and is stated in a phrase, not in a complete sentence. Sentence A is the main idea stated in a topic sentence. Sentence B gives two details that support the main idea. Sentence C gives another supporting detail.

PRACTICE 5

A. Read each of the following groups of ideas. Answer the questions that follow each group.

Group 1

a. Effects of stress
b. Stress can cause loss of appetite and loss of sleep.
c. Many people toss and turn in bed for hours worrying about the mistakes they think they made that day.

_____ **1.** The first idea states
  a. the topic.
  b. the main idea.
  c. a supporting detail.

_____ **2.** The second idea states
  a. the topic.
  b. the main idea.
  c. a supporting detail.

_____ **3.** The third idea states
    a. the topic.
    b. the main idea.
                                   c. a supporting detail.

Group 2

a. At the football game last weekend, the crowd around my 9-year-old daughter and me became drunk and used foul language.
b. Some people's behavior makes it impossible to enjoy attending live events.
c. Improper public behavior

_____ **4.** The first idea states
    a. the topic.   c. a supporting detail.
    b. the main idea.

_____ **5.** The second idea states
    a. the topic.   c. a supporting detail.
    b. the main idea.

_____ **6.** The third idea states
    a. the topic.   c. a supporting detail.
    b. the main idea.

Group 3

a. Women must realize that drinking alcohol may raise their chances of developing breast cancer.
b. Alcohol and breast cancer
c. A woman who drinks four glasses of wine a week may be more likely to get breast cancer than a woman who does not drink alcohol.

_____ **7.** The first idea states
    a. the topic.   c. a supporting detail.
    b. the main idea.

_____ **8.** The second idea states
    a. the topic.   c. a supporting detail.
    b. the main idea.

_____ **9.** The third idea states
    a. the topic.   c. a supporting detail.
    b. the main idea.

Group 4

a. The Public Broadcasting System (PBS)

b. For example, those people who love history enjoy the story of the Civil War as told through the actual photographs and letters of the soldiers who fought and died.

c. PBS offers high-quality programs for viewers of all interests.

_____ **10.** The first idea states
a. the topic.   c. a supporting detail.
b. the main idea.

_____ **11.** The second idea states
a. the topic.   c. a supporting detail.
b. the main idea.

_____ **12.** The third idea states
a. the topic.   c. a supporting detail.
b. the main idea.

B. Read the paragraph. Identify the topic and main idea by answering the questions that follow it.

> ¹Coffee brings flavor and zest to life. ²For countless people, coffee is the drink of choice. ³First, coffee comes in a wide variety of flavors. ⁴Some people drink only the heavy, thick Colombian brew; others love a sweeter French vanilla taste. ⁵Still others love their coffee tinged with chocolate or mint or some other exotic flavor. ⁶Second, even when coffee drinkers disagree on the choice of flavor, most agree on the need for its jolt of energy. ⁷Nothing seems to open the eyes wider than coffee's caffeine.

_____ **13.** Which of the following best states the topic of the paragraph?
a. the attraction of coffee   c. the zest of coffee
b. the taste of coffee

_____ **14.** Which sentence states the author's main idea in a topic sentence?

Textbook
Skills

Topics in Headings

Textbook authors often state the topic of a paragraph or passage in a heading. Identifying the topic in a heading makes it easier for you to see the main idea and supporting details. Remember, though, that headings and titles are *not* topic sentences.

EXAMPLE Read the following paragraph from the college textbook *Introduction to Geography: People, Places, and Environment*. Then answer the questions that follow it.

Tornadoes

[1]Tornadoes have the highest wind speeds known to occur on earth and cause near total but localized damage. [2]Tornadoes are intense columns of rising air, usually connected with thunderstorms. [3]As the air rises, it creates a partial vacuum (an area of low pressure). [4]This vacuum draws air in toward it. [5]As this air is drawn in, it creates a swirling vortex, much like the swirling motion of water as it drains out of a sink. [6]As the air swirls in, it gains tremendous speed, sometimes exceeding 185 miles per hour. [7]This vortex usually moves horizontally. [8]Sometimes it touches the ground, and sometimes it rises above it. [9]It leaves an erratic and usually very narrow path of destruction. [10]The south-central United States has the greatest frequency of tornadoes of any place in the world.

—Bergman & Renwick, *Introduction to Geography: People, Places, and Environment*, 4th ed., p. 66.

1. The topic of the paragraph is _____.

_____ **2.** Sentence 1 states
    a. the main idea.   b. a supporting detail

_____ **3.** Sentence 2 states
    a. the main idea.   b. a supporting detail.

EXPLANATION The topic of the paragraph is tornadoes; it is stated in the heading. Sentence 1 is the main idea, and sentence 2 is a supporting detail. (In fact, sentences 2–10 are all supporting details.)

PRACTICE 6

Read the following paragraph from a college history textbook. Then answer the questions that follow.

Religious Beliefs in Egyptian Civilization

[1]Egyptians believed that many gods controlled their destinies. [2]Ra, the sun god, was one of their most important gods. [3]Ra embodied the power of Heaven and Earth. [4]He created the universe and everything in

it. [5]He traveled across the sky every day in a boat, rested at night, and returned in the morning to resume his eternal journey. [6]The rising and setting of the sun stood as a symbol of the order and harmony that Ra created. [7]Evil, however, always threatened the order of the universe in the form of Apopis. [8]Apopis was a serpent god whose coils could trap Ra's boat like a reef in the Nile. [9]Ra's journey could only continue if proper worship and justice existed among humans. [10]To make this possible, Ra created Egyptian kings. [11]These kings shared in his divine nature and ruled as his representatives on Earth. [12]Egyptians also worshiped Osiris. [13]Osiris was the son of the sky and the Earth and the god of the dead. [14]According to Egyptian belief, Osiris was murdered by his brother Seth, god of chaos, after Osiris married their sister Isis, goddess of fertility. [15]Seth cut Osiris into pieces and scattered them over the Earth. [16]But Isis gathered the pieces and restored Osiris to life. [17]Osiris then became king of the underworld where he judged the dead.

—Adapted from Levack, Muir, Veldman, & Mass, *The West: Encounters & Transformations*, 2nd ed., pp. 23–24.

1. The topic of the paragraph is _____

____ 2. Sentence 1 states
    a. the main idea.   b. a supporting detail.

____ 3. Sentence 2 states
    a. the main idea.   b. a supporting detail.

____ 4. Sentence 10 states
    a. the main idea.   b. a supporting detail.

____ 5. Sentence 11 states
    a. the main idea.   b. a supporting detail.

APPLICATIONS

Application 1: General and Specific Ideas

A. Each of the following items is made up of one general idea and four specific ideas. Write the letter G in front of the general idea in each item.

1. ___court ___hoop ___basketball game ___foul ___free throw

2. ___tickets ___movies ___previews ___popcorn ___movie theater

3. —Ellen DeGeneres   —Stephen Colbert   —Jon Stewart
    —Conan O'Brien   —comedians

4. —nurse   —exam room   —exam table   —doctor's office
    —stethoscope

5. —keyboard   —computer   —mouse   —CD   —software

6. —shoes   —sandals   —loafers   —high heels   —running shoes

B. For each of the following general ideas, list two additional specific ideas.

7. *General idea:*   female movie stars
    Specific ideas: Meg Ryan   _____   _____

8. *General idea:*   college courses
    Specific ideas: Freshman English   _____   _____

9. *General idea:*   small kitchen appliances
    Specific ideas: blender   _____   _____

10. *General idea:*   hair products
    Specific ideas: shampoo   _____   _____

Application 2: Identifying Topics

Each paragraph is followed by three ideas. One idea is too general to be the topic. Another idea is too specific. Identify the idea that correctly states the topic.

> Oprah Winfrey surmounted many barriers and became a great success. Oprah is an African American woman who was born in the South, out of wedlock and into poverty. Yet in 1998, America voted her one of the two most admired women in the country. By then, her talk show had earned 30 Daytime Emmy Awards. Later that same year, Oprah, only 44 years old, received a lifetime achievement award at the Emmys. Some 20 million people in the United States watch Oprah every day. And countless numbers of people from 132 other countries watch her afternoon show.

_____ **1.** The topic of the paragraph is
   a. Oprah Winfrey.
   b. Oprah Winfrey and her awards.
   c. Oprah Winfrey's overcoming barriers to become a great success.

Lower-back pain has several causes. First, weak stomach muscles can cause the lower back to ache. The muscles of the lower back and the stomach work together and need each other to support the body's frame. If the stomach muscles are weak, the lower back muscles feel the strain. Also, the lower back may hurt due to poor posture. Slouching the shoulders forward throws the whole back out of whack and places great pressure on the lower back. Finally, a common cause of lower-back pain is injury. Trying to lift heavy objects without proper support strains the lower-back muscles.

_____ **2.** The topic of the paragraph is
   a. lower-back pain caused by weak stomach muscles.
   b. lower-back pain.
   c. causes of lower-back pain.

Textbook
Skills

Loneliness puts a person at risk for other problems. Research shows that loneliness and poor health often go together. Older women who live alone on small pensions may find themselves in poor health. In addition, they are isolated from others and become lonely. Isolation and loneliness can lead to physical and mental breakdowns. These breakdowns can lead to more problems, such as increased risk of drug and alcohol abuse.

—Novak, *Issues in Aging: An Introduction to Gerontology*, p. 143.

_____ **3.** The topic of the paragraph is
   a. risks associated with loneliness.
   b. loneliness.
   c. loneliness leading to increased risk of drug and alcohol abuse.

Textbook
Skills

All life on Earth is carbon-based. What this means is that all living creatures are made up of complex molecules based on the framework of carbon atoms. The carbon atom is able to bond readily with other carbon atoms. As they bond, they form long, complex carbon-based molecules. The carbon needed to build these molecules comes from various sources. Humans, like all other animals, get their carbon by consuming plant and animal materials. However, the chief source of carbon is carbon dioxide in the atmosphere.

—Smith & Smith, *Elements of Ecology*, 4th ed., p. 21.

_____ **4.** The topic of the paragraph is
   a. life on earth.
   b. carbon-based life on earth.
   c. the carbon atom's ability to bond with other carbon atoms.

Application 3: Topics, Main Ideas, and Supporting Details

Read the following passage from a college history textbook. Then answer the questions that follow.

Textbook Skills

The Pyramids

[1]With their emphasis on the afterlife, Egyptians took great pains to provide proper housing for the dead. [2]Many tombs were built as monuments to the dead person's wealth and social status. [3]These tombs were a resting place for the corpse and an entryway to the next life. [4]Members of the elite were buried in expensive tombs filled with ivory furniture and other luxurious goods. [5]But kings had the grandest tombs of all.

[6]Burial customs in the Old Kingdom grew ever more elaborate. [7]For the first several centuries of the Old Kingdom, kings built their tombs in the city of Abydos. [8]Abydos was the homeland of the first kings. [9]The tombs were an underground room with a special room for the royal corpse. [10]The king's treasures filled nearby underground rooms. [11]Above the ground sat a small palace with courtyards and halls suitable for a royal afterlife. [12]The earliest of these tombs dates to about 2800 B.C.E. [13]And they contain the bones of animals and people sacrificed to go with the ruler into the next world.

[14]About 2680 B.C.E., architects began building a new kind of royal tomb. [15]The defining feature was a great four-sided monument of stone in the shape of a pyramid. [16]Elaborate temples in which priests worshiped statues of the king surrounded the monument. [17]The structure also had rooms where the king could dwell in the afterlife in the same luxury he enjoyed during his life on Earth. [18]King Djoser, the founder of the Old Kingdom, built the first pyramid complex at Saqqara near Memphis. [19]Known today as the Step Pyramid, this structure rests above Djoser's burial place. [20]It rises high into the air in six steps. [21]The Step Pyramid represents a ladder to Heaven.

[22]For the next 2,000 years, kings continued building pyramids for themselves and smaller ones for their queens. [23]Each tomb became more architecturally sophisticated. [24]The walls grew taller and steeper. [25]They also contained hidden burial chambers and treasure rooms. [26]The Great Pyramid at Giza, built around 2600 B.C.E. by King Khufu (or Cheops), stood as the largest human-made structure in the ancient world. [27]It is made of more than two million stones. [28]Each stone weighs an average of two and a half tons each. [29]Covering thirteen acres, it reaches over 480 feet into the sky.

—Adapted from Levack, Muir, Veldman, & Maas, *The West: Encounters & Transformations*, 2nd ed., p. 24.

1. The topic of the passage is _____

_____ **2.** In paragraph 1, which sentence states the main idea?
a. sentence 1   c. sentence 3
b. sentence 2   d. sentence 4

_____ **3.** In paragraph 2, which sentence states the main idea?
a. sentence 6   c. sentence 8
b. sentence 7   d. sentence 12

_____ **4.** In paragraph 3, which sentence states the main idea?
a. sentence 14   c. sentence 16
b. sentence 15   d. sentence 21

_____ **5.** In paragraph 4, which sentence states the main idea?
a. sentence 22   c. sentence 24
b. sentence 23   d. sentence 26

REVIEW TEST 1

Score (number correct) _____ × 5 = _____%

General and Specific Ideas

A. Each of the following items is made up of one general idea and four specific ideas. Write the letter **G** in front of the general idea in each item.

1. ___hot   ___temperatures   ___cold   ___warm   ___freezing

2. ___remote control   ___surround sound   ___entertainment system
___plasma screen

3. ___wasp   ___insects   ___spider   ___ant   ___bee

4. ___chapter   ___index   ___glossary   ___textbook   ___table of contents

5. ___rodents   ___mice   ___rats   ___gerbils   ___squirrels

6. ___broccoli   ___carrots   ___squash   ___zucchini   ___vegetables

7. ___sewing   ___thread   ___needle   ___cloth   ___pins

8. ___fever   ___chills   ___nausea   ___flu symptoms   ___aching muscles

9. __joke   __humor   __cartoon   __laughter   __prank

10. __server   __chef   __entrée   __menu   __restaurant

B. The following items are made up of specific ideas. For each space, write a general idea that covers all the specific ideas.

11. *Specific ideas:*   beef   veal   pork

    General idea: _____

12. *Specific ideas:*   orange   grapefruit   tangerine

    General idea: _____

13. *Specific ideas:*   weights   treadmill   personal   trainer

    General idea: _____

14. *Specific ideas:*   knuckle   kneecap   elbow

    General idea: _____

15. *Specific ideas:*   surround sound   big-screen TV   DVD player

    General idea: _____

C. For each of the following general ideas, list two additional specific ideas.

16. *General idea:*   allergy symptoms

    Specific ideas: runny nose   _____   _____

17. *General idea:*   fire safety

    Specific ideas: fire extinguisher   _____   _____

18. *General idea:*   bees

    Specific ideas: stingers   _____   _____

19. *General idea:*   tobacco products

    Specific ideas: snuff   _____   _____

20. *General idea:*   résumé

    Specific ideas: job experience   _____   _____

REVIEW TEST 2

Score (number correct) _____ × 10 = _____%

Identifying the Topic of a Paragraph

A. Each of the following paragraphs is followed by three ideas. Identify the idea that correctly states the topic.

Yosemite National Park is located in central California along the western edge of the Sierra Nevada mountain range. Yosemite offers beautiful views of deep valleys and spectacular mountains. At the center of the park is a valley 2,750 feet deep.

_____ **1.** The topic of the paragraph is
a. national parks.
b. Yosemite National Park.
c. beautiful views of deep valleys.

The word *pueblo* is Spanish for "town." It is also the name of a group of Native American Indians. The Pueblos live in Arizona and New Mexico. Some of these Pueblo Indians still carry out age-old rituals and customs. The Pueblos were too out-of-the-way to be controlled by the government.

_____ **2.** The topic of the paragraph is
a. lack of control of the Pueblos.
b. Native American Indians.
c. Pueblo Indians.

Charles "Chuck" Berry is an African American musician who greatly affected the development of rock music. Berry's rock music brought together blues and country music styles. His songs told stories about young love, fast cars, and disappointment, set to a catchy beat.

_____ **3.** The topic of the paragraph is
a. a mixture of blues and country music styles.
b. Chuck Berry and his music.
c. rock music.

Brainwashing techniques force confessions of wrongdoing and replace lowered self-esteem with new beliefs. Confessions can be forced through lack of sleep and food. Kept awake for days without food, the person is told of his or her shortcomings and is forced to admit to them. The brainwashed person is also cut off from family and friends so that no one can contradict the new beliefs.

_____ 4. The topic of the paragraph is
   a. two ways to brainwash a person.
   b. lack of sleep and food.
   c. brainwashing techniques.

B. In each pair, one idea is general and the other is specific. The general idea includes the specific idea. Do two things:

- Circle the idea in each pair that is *more general.*
- Then write one more specific idea that is covered by the general idea you circled.

5–6. light bulb   lamp   _____

7–8. money   dollar   _____

9–10. Johnny Depp   actors   _____

REVIEW TEST 3

Score (number correct) _____ × 10 = _____%

Topics, Main Ideas, and Supporting Details

A. Read the following paragraph from a communications textbook. Then fill in the house diagram with the topic, main idea, and supporting details from the passage.

Textbook
Skills

The Importance of Rules in a Family

Family rules are important for several reasons. First, rules define the family as a unit. Through rules, families establish roles for each member. Second, rules help members within the family relate to one another. Third, rules contribute to a family's sense of stability.

—Adapted from Galvin & Brommel, *Family Communication: Cohesion and Change,* 5th ed., p. 88.

Topic: 1. _____

Main Idea (stated in
a topic sentence):

2. _____

Supporting Details:

3. _____   4. _____   5. _____
   _____   _____   _____
   _____   _____   _____
   _____   _____   _____

B. Read the following paragraph from a college science textbook. Then answer the questions that follow it.

Textbook
Skills

Reducing Fat in Your Diet

[1]Three basic steps will help you reduce fat in your diet. [2]First, know what you are putting in your mouth; read food labels. [3]Second, choose lean meats, fish, or chicken. [4]Third, choose nonfat dairy products such as skim milk whenever possible.

—Adapted from Donatelle, *Access to Health*,
7th ed., pp. 229–230.

6. The topic of the paragraph is _____.

_____ **7.** Sentence 1 states
    a. the main idea.   b. a supporting detail.

_____ **8.** Sentence 2 states
    a. the main idea.   b. a supporting detail.

_____ **9.** Sentence 3 states
    a. the main idea.   b. a supporting detail.

_____ **10.** Sentence 4 states
    a. the main idea.   b. a supporting detail.

WHAT DO YOU THINK?

Do you agree with the statement "Family rules are important for several reasons"? Why or why not? Assume your family is going to host an international student. For the student's smooth transition into your family life, write an email or letter that explains a few important family rules.

REVIEW TEST 4

Score (number correct) _____ × 10 = _____%

Topics and Main Ideas

Read the following passage from a government website. Answer the questions that follow.

Avoiding Credit and Charge Card Fraud

[1]*A thief goes through trash to find discarded receipts, and then uses your account numbers illegally.*

[2]*A dishonest clerk makes an extra imprint from your credit or charge card and uses it to make personal charges.*

[3]*You respond to a mailing asking you to call a long distance number for a free trip or bargain-priced travel package.* [4]*You're told you must join a travel club first and you're asked for your account number so you can be billed.* [5]*The catch!* [6]*Charges you didn't make are added to your bill, and you never get your trip.*

[7]Credit and charge card fraud costs cardholders and issuers hundreds of millions of dollars each year. [8]While theft is the most obvious form of fraud, it can occur in other ways. [9]For example, someone may use your card number without your knowledge.

[10]It's not always possible to prevent credit or charge card fraud from happening. [11]But there are a few steps you can take to make it more difficult for a crook to capture your card or card numbers and minimize the possibility.

Guarding Against Fraud

[12]Here are some tips to help protect yourself from credit and charge card fraud.

Do

- [13]Sign your cards as soon as they arrive.
- [14]Carry your cards separately from your wallet, in a zippered compartment, a business card holder, or another small pouch.
- [15]Keep a record of your account numbers, their **expiration** dates, and the phone number and address of each company in a secure place.
- [16]Keep an eye on your card during the **transaction,** and get it back as quickly as possible.
- [17]Void incorrect receipts.
- [18]Save receipts to compare with billing statements.
- [19]Open bills promptly and reconcile accounts monthly, just as you would your checking account.
- [20]Report any questionable charges promptly and in writing to the card issuer.
- [21]Notify card companies in advance of a change in address.

Don't

- [22]Lend your card(s) to anyone.
- [23]Leave cards or receipts lying around.
- [24]Sign a blank receipt. [25]When you sign a receipt, draw a line through any blank spaces above the total.
- [26]Write your account number on a postcard or the outside of an envelope.
- [27]Give out your account number over the phone unless you're making the call to a company you know is reputable. [28]If you have questions about a company, check it out with your local **consumer** protection office or Better Business Bureau.

Reporting Losses and Fraud

[29]If you lose your credit or charge cards or if you realize they've been lost or stolen, immediately call the issuer(s). [30]Many companies have toll-free numbers and 24-hour service to deal with such emergencies. [31]By law, once you report the loss or theft, you have no further responsibility for **unauthorized** charges. [32]In any event, your maximum **liability** under federal law is $50 per card. [33]If you suspect fraud, you may be asked to sign a statement under oath that you did not make the purchase(s) in question.

—"Avoiding Credit and Charge Card Fraud." Federal Trade Commission. 18 Sept. 2009. http://www.ftc.gov/bcp/edu/pubs/consumer/credit/cre07.shtm.

Vocabulary in Context

_____ **1.** The best meaning of **expiration** in sentence 15 is
   a. breathing out.   c. end.
   b. death.   d. due.

_____ **2.** The best meaning of **transaction** in sentence 16 is
   a. exchange.   c. contract.
   b. event.   d. record.

_____ **3.** The best meaning of **consumer** in sentence 28 is
   a. provider.   c. seller.
   b. buyer.   d. hunter.

_____ **4.** The best meaning of **unauthorized** in sentence 31 is
   a. approved.   c. unwritten.
   b. secret.   d. without permission.

_____ **5.** The best meaning of **liability** in sentence 32 is
   a. danger.   c. problem.
   b. responsibility.   d. asset.

Topics and Main Ideas

_____ **6.** What is the topic of the passage?
   a. Guarding Against Fraud
   b. Do and Don't Tips About Fraud
   c. Reporting Losses and Fraud
   d. Avoiding Credit and Charge Card Fraud

_____ **7.** How many subtopics did the author identify in the passage?
   a. 5   c. 3
   b. 4   d. 2

_____ **8.** Which of the following sentences states the most general idea in
        paragraph 4 (sentences 7–9)?
   a. sentence 7   c. sentence 9
   b. sentence 8

_____ **9.** Sentence 13 states
   a. a general idea.   b. a specific idea.

_____ **10.** Which sentence states the main idea of the last paragraph in the passage (sentences 29–33)?

a. sentence 29
b. sentence 30
c. sentence 31
d. sentence 33

WHAT DO YOU THINK?

Credit card fraud is just one of the dangers of having a credit card. What other concerns should a credit card holder think about? Assume you are a mentor for a young adult who is going to apply for a credit card for the first time. Write a letter of advice about the wise use of a credit card. Although you should feel free to include information about credit card fraud, also discuss other common sense tips for wise use of a credit card.

 After Reading About Topics and Main Ideas

Before you move on to the Mastery Tests on topics and main ideas, take time to reflect on your learning and performance by answering the following questions. Write your answers in your notebook.

- How has my knowledge base or prior knowledge about topics and main ideas changed?

- Based on my studies, how do I think I will perform on the Mastery Test(s)? Why do I think my scores will be above average, average, or below average?

- Would I recommend this chapter to other students who want to learn more about topics and main ideas? Why or why not?

Test your understanding of what you have learned about Topics and Main Ideas by completing the Chapter 4 Review Card on the insert near the end of your text.

CONNECT TO myreadinglab

To check your progress in meeting Chapter 4's learning outcomes, log in to **www.myreadinglab.com**, and try the following activities.

- The "Main Idea" section of MyReadingLab provides review materials, practices, and tests about topics and main ideas. To access this resource, click on the "Study Plan" tab. Then click on "Main Idea." Then click on the following links as needed: "Overview," "Model," "Practice," and "Tests."

- To measure your mastery of the content in this chapter, complete the tests in the "Main Idea" section and click on Gradebook to find your results.

A. Each of the following items is made up of one general idea and four specific ideas. Write the letter **G** in front of the general idea in each item.

1. ___senators ___balcony ___ Senate chamber ___leaders ___desks

2. ___oak ___palm ___trees ___maple ___pine

3. ___black snake ___rattlesnake ___cobra ___python ___snakes

4. ___flight attendant ___pilot ___passenger ___air transportation ___baggage

B. Read each of the following paragraphs. Answer the questions.

A speedy court trial is a basic right for a citizen of the United States of America. The accused has a right to be judged innocent or guilty by a jury. A jury is usually made up of 12 people who swear to reach a verdict based on the evidence and the law. The accused, also known as the defendant, has a right to a lawyer as well. If the defendant cannot afford a lawyer, the judge will appoint one to defend him or her. Tax dollars pay for the court-appointed defense lawyer.

_____ **5.** The topic of the paragraph is
    a. a speedy court trial.
    b. basic rights for citizens.
    c. the right to a jury trial.

Snakes, which are cold-blooded reptiles, come in a great many varieties. Most, such as the black snake, are harmless. Others, such as water moccasins, are quite dangerous because of their venom. A snake's venom breaks down its prey's tissues, making them easier for the snake to digest. The rattlesnake injects its venom by a bite. In contrast, the cobra can spray its venom as far as 6 feet.

_____ **6.** The topic of the paragraph is
    a. harmless black snakes.
    b. varieties of snakes and their venom.
    c. cold-blooded reptiles.

When you travel by air and use a carry-on bag, remember 3-1-1. All liquids, gels and aerosols must be in 3 ounce or smaller containers. Containers must be placed in a 1 quart-size, clear, plastic, zip-top bag. They must be removed from your carry-on and placed in the security bin. Only one zip-top bag is permitted per traveler. Larger liquids can be placed in checked baggage.

_____ **7.** The topic of the paragraph is
    a. airport security.
    b. air travel and 3-1-1.
    c. carry-on luggage.

C. Read the following groups of ideas. Write MI next to the main idea of the group.

8. _____ Conserving energy can become a good habit.

    _____ Saving energy

    _____ Always turn off the lights when you leave a room.

    _____ Set the air conditioner at 78 degrees.

9. _____ A steeplechase course can include low walls, water hazards, and fences.

    _____ A steeplechase is a race that tests balancing, hurdling, and running.

    _____ The race is for horses or people.

    _____ A steeplechase race

10. _____ The powwow is held to unite the minds and spirits of the people for the common good.

    _____ During a powwow, songs, dance, prayer, and gift-giving take place.

    _____ A North American Indian celebration known as a powwow

    _____ Powwows are held to celebrate manhood, as well as on other occasions.

Name _____ Section _____

Date _____ **Score** (number correct) _____ × 10 = _____%

A. Each of the following items is made up of one general idea and four specific ideas. Write the letter **G** in front of the general idea in each item.

1. ___Bart Simpson ___Bugs Bunny ___cartoon characters

___Daffy Duck ___Scooby Doo

2. ___saddle ___bridle ___horseshoe ___blacksmith ___horses

3. ___notebooks ___dictionary ___school tools ___textbooks

___highlighters

4. ___knee pads ___roller skating ___helmet ___elbow pads ___skates

5. ___fishing ___sinker ___hook ___bait ___pole

B. Read each of the following paragraphs. Answer the questions.

Textbook Skills

Earth has two main motions—rotation and revolution. **Rotation** is the spinning of the Earth on its axis. The axis is the imaginary line running through the poles. Our planet rotates every 24 hours. This rotation creates the daily cycle of daylight and darkness. At any moment, half of the Earth experiences daylight, and the other half darkness. The line separating the dark half from the lighted half is called the **circle of illumination**. **Revolution** is the movement of the Earth in its orbit around the Sun.

—Adapted from Lutgens & Tarbuck, *Foundations of Earth Science*, 5th ed., p. 300.

_____ **6.** The topic of the paragraph is
   a. Earth's rotation.
   b. Earth's revolution.
   c. Earth's motions.
   d. circle of illumination.

Textbook Skills

Handsome and outgoing, Franklin D. Roosevelt seemed to have a bright political future. Then disaster struck. In 1921, he was stricken with polio. It left him paralyzed from the waist down and in a wheelchair for the rest of his life. Instead of retiring, Roosevelt returned to public life. "If you had spent two years in bed trying to wiggle your toe," he later declared, "after that anything would seem easy."

—Martin et al., *America and Its Peoples: A Mosaic in the Making*, 3rd ed., p. 830.

_____ **7.** The topic of the paragraph is
  a. handsome Franklin D. Roosevelt.
  b. Franklin D. Roosevelt.
  c. Franklin D. Roosevelt and polio.

Textbook Skills

Emotions are the feelings you have. For example, you have feelings of anger, sorrow, guilt, depression, happiness and so on. *Emotional expression,* on the other hand, is the way you share these feelings. Experts do not agree over whether you can choose the emotions you feel. Some argue that you can; others argue you cannot. You are, however, clearly in control of the ways you express your emotions. You do not have to express what you feel.

—Adapted from DeVito, *Messages: Building Interpersonal Communication Skills*, p. 176 © 1999. Reproduced by permission of Pearson Education, Inc.

_____ **8.** The topic of the paragraph is
  a. emotional expression.
  b. emotions.
  c. anger, sorrow, guilt, depression, and happiness.

C.   Read each of the following groups of ideas. Then answer the questions that follow.

Group 1

A. A day at Walt Disney World may cost a family a month's salary.
B. The ticket to get in for just one person for one day is $79.00.
C. A typical family may spend another couple of hundred dollars on food and souvenirs.
D. Walt Disney World

_____ **9.** The topic is found in
  a. item A.   c. item C.
  b. item B.   d. item D.

Group 2

A. Small learning groups
B. In small groups, students become responsible for their own learning.
C. In small groups, students learn to listen to one another to solve problems.
D. Small learning groups teach students to be responsible and work together.

_____ **10.** A supporting detail is found in
  a. item A.   c. item C.
  b. item B.   d. item D.

Name _____ Section _____

Date _____ **Score** (number correct) _____ × 10 = _____%

A. Read the following group of ideas. Then answer the questions.

    A. In addition, the Internet allows you to do research for school projects.

    B. The Internet can offer helpful resources.

    C. The Internet

    D. The Internet allows access to friends and family through e-mail and chat rooms.

_____ **1.** The topic is found in

    a. item A.   c. item C.

    b. item B.   d. item D.

_____ **2.** The main idea is found in

    a. item A.   c. item C.

    b. item B.   d. item D.

_____ **3.** A supporting detail is found in

    a. item A.   c. item C.

    b. item B.   d. item D.

_____ **4.** A supporting detail is found in

    a. item A.   c. item C.

    b. item B.   d. item D.

B. Read each paragraph. Then answer the questions that follow it.

[1]Legendary heroes fought courageously against slavery during the 19th century. [2]A runaway slave, Harriet Tubman was a courageous and selfless leader in this fight. [3]Tubman was born a slave in Dorchester County, Maryland, in 1821. [4]At the age of 25, fearing she was about to be sold, she ran away. [5]She made her escape to freedom by following the North Star. [6]During the 1850s, Tubman made twenty successful trips back to the South. [7]During these trips, she led more than 300 others to freedom by using a series of safe houses and routes known as the Underground Railroad. [8]She often forced panicked or exhausted runaways ahead by threatening them with a loaded pistol. [9]Tubman never lost one life. [10]She became known as the "Moses" of her people.

    —Adapted from *Harriet Tubman*. Meet Amazing Americans: Activists & Reformers. *America's Story from America's Library*. Lib. of Congress. 21 Sept. 2009. http://www.americaslibrary.gov/cgi-bin/page.cgi/aa/activists/tubman.

_____ **5.** Who or what is the topic of this paragraph?

    a. legendary heroes   c. Harriet Tubman

    b. a runaway slave   d. the Underground Railroad

_____ **6.** Which sentence states the main idea of this paragraph?
  a. sentence 1   c. sentence 3
  b. sentence 2   d. sentence 4

[1]Cherokee women had many rights and were highly valued by their communities. [2]Not only could they speak at their town's yearly Grand Council, but they had their own council, too. [3]A *ghigau*, or "Beloved Woman," led the women's council. [4]Also, the Cherokee woman chose her husband, and he was expected to build her a house or live with her in her mother's house. [5]Cherokee women owned the house, property, and children. [6]Women planted crops, tended livestock, made clothes, and wove baskets. [7]Some women were even warriors.

_____ **7.** What is the topic of this paragraph?
  a. the "Beloved Woman"   c. Cherokee women
  b. Cherokee men   d. Cherokee children

_____ **8.** Which sentence states the main idea of the paragraph?
  a. sentence 6   c. sentence 4
  b. sentence 1   d. sentence 5

[1]One small room in the shuttle serves as the bathroom for astronauts in space. [2]The main item inside this 29-inch-wide area is the Waste Collection System, which is the Shuttle's toilet with all its accessories. [3]Its door is open, but two curtains, attached to the top and the side of the door, provide privacy. [4]Astronauts use two foot restraints and two body restraints (bars positioned over the thighs) to position and hold themselves on the commode's seat. [5]Body waste enters the commode through the 4-inch-diameter seat opening. [6]Then it is drawn in by air flowing through holes under the seat. [7]This downward rush of air substitutes for gravity in collecting and keeping the waste material in the commode. [8]The urinal is just a flexible hose with attachable funnels. [9]Each astronaut has a personal funnel. [10]The funnels are shaped differently for men and women. [11]The urinal can be used in a "standing" position or while the astronaut is "sitting" on the commode.

—Adapted from "Waste Collection System." *NASA*. Homepage. 7 April 2002. 21 Sept. 2009.

_____ **9.** What is the topic of this paragraph?
  a. the stress of being an astronaut
  b. traveling through space
  c. funnels and restraints
  d. the space shuttle's waste collection system

_____ **10.** Which sentence states the main idea of this paragraph?
  a. sentence 2   c. sentence 4
  b. sentence 10   d. sentence 9

Read the following passage from a college communication textbook. Answer the questions that follow.

Attack Your Self-Destructive Beliefs

[1]Being as honest with yourself as you can, ask yourself if you hold beliefs such as these:

1. [2]The drive to be *perfect:* Do you try to perform at unrealistically high levels at work, school, and home? [3]Do you act as if anything short of perfection is unacceptable?
2. [4]The drive to be *strong:* Do you believe that weakness is wrong? [5]Do you believe emotions like sadness, compassion, or loneliness are wrong?
3. [6]The drive to *please:* Do you seek approval from others? [7]Do you believe that if you gain the approval of others, then you're a worthy and deserving person? [8]Do you believe that if others disapprove of you, then you're worthless and undeserving?
4. [9]The drive to *hurry up:* Do you do things quickly? [10]Do you try to do more than can be reasonably expected in any given amount of time?
5. [11]The drive to try *hard:* Do you take on more responsibilities than any one person can be expected to handle?

[12]As you can see, these beliefs are unrealistic. [13]While it would be nice to be perfect, it is not a logical or realistic goal. [14]Similarly, it would be nice to be emotionally strong or to please others, but it is not always possible.

[15]These kinds of beliefs set up unattainable and unrealistic goals. [16]They lead you to fail and can damage your self-esteem. [17]And they prevent you from building meaningful and positive relationships.

[18]Recognizing that you may have internalized self-destructive beliefs is a first step toward eliminating them. [19]A second step involves recognizing that these beliefs are unrealistic and self-defeating. [20]Psychotherapist Albert Ellis and other cognitive therapists would argue that you can accomplish this through cognitive restructuring. [21]Understand why these beliefs are unrealistic and substitute more realistic ones. [22]A third step is giving yourself permission to fail, to be less than perfect, to be normal.

[23]Do recognize that it's the unrealistic nature of these "drivers" that creates problems. [24]Drivers are unrealistic beliefs that may motivate you

to act in ways that are self-defeating. [25]Certainly, trying hard and being strong are not unhealthy when they're realistic. [26]It's only when they become absolute—when you try to be everything to everyone—that they become impossible to achieve and create problems.

—Adapted from DeVito, *The Interpersonal Communication Book*, pp. 61–63 © 2007 by Pearson Education, Inc. Reproduced by permission of Pearson Education, Inc.

_____   **1.** The topic of the passage is
    a. honesty.
    b. self-destructive beliefs.
    c. cognitive restructuring.

_____   **2.** The main idea of sentences 1 through 14 is stated in
    a. sentence 1.   c. sentence 13.
    b. sentence 12.   d. sentence 14.

_____   **3.** The topic of sentences 18 through 22 is
    a. self-destructive beliefs.
    b. steps to eliminate self-destructive beliefs.
    c. psychotherapist Albert Ellis.
    d. permission to fail.

_____   **4.** Which of the following sentences states the central idea of the passage?
    a. sentence 1   c. sentence 18
    b. sentence 12   d. sentence 24

VISUAL VOCABULARY

When we have _____ negative beliefs about ourselves, we damage our self-esteem.

  a. reconstructed
  b. internalized

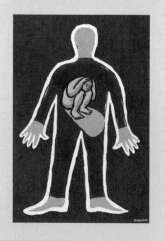

Locating Stated Main Ideas

LEARNING OUTCOMES

After studying this chapter you should be able to do the following:

1. Distinguish the movement of ideas from general to specific.
2. Define the following terms: *central idea* and *thesis statement*.
3. Locate the sentence that states the main idea.
4. Assess your comprehension of locating stated main ideas.
5. Evaluate the importance of locating stated main ideas.
6. Apply locating stated main ideas to improve comprehension.

Before Reading About Locating Stated Main Ideas

In Chapter 4, "Topics and Main Ideas," you learned several skills that will help you as you study how to locate main ideas. Review what you have already learned by stating in your own words the meaning of the following terms:

Main idea _____

Topic sentence _____

_____

Supporting details _____

Now, read the Chapter 5 learning outcomes and create at least two questions that you can answer as you study the chapter. Write your questions in the following spaces:

_____?

_____?

Compare the questions you created based on the learning outcomes with the following questions. Then write them in your notebook, leaving enough space between each question to record the answers as you read and study the chapter.

How does the flow of ideas affect the placement of the topic sentence? What is a central idea? What is a thesis statement?

The Flow of Ideas and Placement of Topic Sentences

So far, many of the passages you have worked with in this textbook have placed the main idea as the first sentence in the paragraph. When the topic sentence comes first in a paragraph, the three parts of the paragraph move from general to specific: the topic, the main idea stated in a topic sentence, and the supporting details. However, not all paragraphs put the main idea first. In fact, a topic sentence—that is, the sentence that states the main idea—can be placed at or near the **beginning** of a paragraph, in the **middle** of a paragraph, or at the **end** of a paragraph. The placement of the topic sentence controls the flow of ideas. In a sense, when a writer builds a house of ideas, the floor plan—the flow of ideas—changes based on the location of the topic sentence. Finding the main idea is one of the most important steps in the reading process. Therefore, one of the first things a skilled reader looks for is the location of the topic sentence.

> The **topic sentence** states the main idea of a paragraph.

It is important to note that, while all paragraphs have a main idea, not all paragraphs state the main idea in a topic sentence; sometimes, the main idea is implied. You will learn more about implied main ideas in Chapter 6.

Topic Sentence at the Beginning of a Paragraph

The topic sentence is the one sentence that is general enough to include all the ideas in the passage. So a topic sentence that begins a paragraph signals a move from general ideas to specific ideas. This flow from general to specific is often used in **deductive** thinking. When using deductive thinking, the author first states the main idea. Then the author offers specific reasons and supporting details to explain his or her line of thought. Editorials often use the deductive flow of ideas. The following diagram shows this flow from general to specific ideas:

Main idea: Topic sentence
Supporting detail
Supporting detail
Supporting detail

EXAMPLE Read the following paragraph, and identify its topic sentence. In the space provided, write the number of the sentence you chose.

Body Language

[1]Body language is a visible sign of our emotions. [2]For example, a man who is embarrassed about gaining weight may pull at the skin under his chin. [3]Likewise, a woman who is embarrassed by her weight may smooth down her dress or slacks. [4]When we feel afraid or defensive, we may fold our arms across our chests. [5]Hands on our knees shows our readiness to act. [6]Hands on our hips reveals our impatience. [7]Locked hands behind the back indicates self-control. [8]And hands locked behind the head indicates self-confidence. [9]Of course, the meanings of our gestures vary from culture to culture.

Topic sentence: _____1_____

EXPLANATION The topic sentence of this paragraph is sentence 1: "Body language is a visible sign of our emotions." All the other sentences state examples. Each example reveals a specific emotion. Notice how the paragraph presents the general idea of body language first. Then the details list and explain the examples.

Topic Sentence Within a Paragraph

Topic sentences within a paragraph can be near the beginning or in the middle of the paragraph.

Near the Beginning

A paragraph does not always start with the topic sentence. Instead, it may begin with a sentence or two that give a general overview of the topic. These introductory sentences are used to get the reader interested in the topic. They also lead the reader to the topic sentence. Sometimes the introductory sentences tell how the ideas in one paragraph tie into the ideas that came before it. At other times, the introductory sentences give background information about the topic.

This flow of ideas is also an example of deductive thinking. The flow of ideas is from general ideas (the introduction) and main idea (topic sentence) to specific ideas (supporting details). Authors often rely on this flow of ideas to write human interest stories in magazines and newspapers. In addition, this flow is often used to write academic papers and speeches. The following diagram shows this flow from general to specific ideas:

Introductory sentence(s)
Main idea: Topic sentence
Supporting detail
Supporting detail
Supporting detail

EXAMPLE Read the following paragraph, and identify its topic sentence. Remember to ask, "Does this sentence cover all the ideas in the paragraph?"

^{1}Bad habits are easy to form but hard to break. ^{2}Cursing is an example of a bad habit that is especially difficult for many to break. ^{3}However, strong will and self-awareness can break the habit of cursing. ^{4}First of all, a strong will is needed to stop the habit of swearing. ^{5}Many people yell out a profanity when they are under some kind of stress. ^{6}The stress may be caused by an argument or a stubbed toe. ^{7}Either case is likely to bring out a string of four-letter words. ^{8}Only a strong-willed person can choose another set of words in the moment of stress. ^{9}Next, self-awareness is needed to break this habit. ^{10}Often people who are in the habit of cursing do not listen to how they sound. ^{11}In fact, many times, they are not even aware of how often they swear or how many offensive words they use. ^{12}Thus to break this habit, a person needs to listen to what he or she is saying.

Topic sentence: _____

EXPLANATION Sentence 3 is the topic sentence of this paragraph. Sentence 1 offers a simple but true statement about the topic. The purpose of this sentence is to get the reader's attention. Sentence 2 introduces the topic. Sentences 4–12 are the supporting details that explain the topic sentence.

PRACTICE 1

Identify the topic sentences of each of the following paragraphs. Remember to ask, "Does this sentence cover all the ideas in the paragraph?"

¹Everyone wants a good friend. ²The best way to get a friend is to be a friend. ³However, few people know how to be a good friend. ⁴Being a friend requires time, patience, and honesty. ⁵First, being a friend takes time. ⁶Even when a busy life means no free time, a friend finds time to run errands, go to a movie, or just hang out. ⁷Even when money is tight, a friend gives when there is a need. ⁸Second, being a friend demands patience. ⁹Even when advice isn't wanted, a friend listens to unsolvable problems. ¹⁰Finally, being a friend requires honesty. ¹¹When advice is wanted, a friend gently tells the truth.

1. Topic sentence: _____

¹Binge eating may be a result of high stress. ²Long workdays, important deadlines, and family demands take their toll. ³Feelings of anxiety settle in the stomach. ⁴That feeling of unease may be mistaken for hunger, and the eating begins. ⁵Ice cream, cookies, and bread, for some reason, give comfort. ⁶A full stomach slows the body down and may even cause sleepiness. ⁷As the demands of a hectic lifestyle build, so does the urge to eat.

2. Topic sentence: _____

In the Middle

At times, an author will begin a paragraph with a few attention-grabbing details. These details are placed first to stir the reader's interest in the topic. The flow of ideas no longer follows the deductive pattern of thinking. The flow of ideas now moves from specific ideas (supporting details) to general ideas (the topic sentence) to specific ideas (additional supporting details). Creative essays and special-interest stories, in which authors strive to excite readers' interest, may take this approach. For example, often television news stories begin with shocking details to hook the viewer and prevent channel surfing. The following diagram shows this flow of ideas:

Supporting detail
Supporting detail
Main idea: Topic sentence
Supporting detail
Supporting detail

EXAMPLE Read the following paragraph, and identify its topic sentence. Remember to ask, "Does this sentence cover all the ideas in the paragraph?"

¹A dozen bats made of black construction paper hung from the ceiling of the front porch. ²Four pumpkins with fierce faces of triangle eyes and jagged teeth glowed by the front door. ³Spindly cobwebs covered the bushes. ⁴Spooky music filled the air. ⁵A tall witch with green hair held out a piece of candy. ⁶But the children were too afraid to take the candy. ⁷One little girl dressed as a princess stood on the sidewalk and refused to go anywhere near the witch. ⁸A little boy dressed as Harry Potter screamed as his big brother dragged him up the steps. ⁹Two sisters, twin ballerinas, held hands as they started and stopped three times before they finally ran away.

Topic sentence: _____

EXPLANATION Sentences 1, 2, 3, and 4 are all details that describe the spooky Halloween decorations. Sentence 5 describes a scary witch. Sentence 6 is the topic sentence. The reader is able to see why the children were afraid because of the opening details. The topic sentence also states that the children were too afraid to get their candy. Sentences 7–9 show the unwillingness of several children.

Topic Sentence at the End of a Paragraph

Sometimes an author waits until the end of the paragraph to state the main idea. This approach can be very effective, for it allows the details to build up to the main idea. This flow of ideas is known as **inductive**. The ideas move from specific (supporting details) to general (the topic sentence). When a topic sentence is at the end of a paragraph, it is usually a summary statement or a conclusion. Inductive thinking is used in math and science to build a theory or to explore how details connect with one other. In addition, inductive thinking is often used to argue a point. Politicians and advertisers use this approach. They want to convince people to agree with their ideas or to buy their products. If a politician begins with a main idea such as "Taxes must be raised," the audience may strongly disagree. Then the audience may not listen to the specific reasons why taxes must be raised. However, if the politician begins with the details and leads up to the main idea, people are more likely to listen. For example, people are more likely to agree that schools need to be improved. Once they hear the specific details, then they may agree to raise taxes. This flow from specific to general also works well in creative writing. Inductive thinking is the process of arriving at a general understanding based on specific details. The following diagram shows the ideas moving from specific to general:

Supporting detail
Supporting detail
Supporting detail
Supporting detail
Main idea: Topic sentence

EXAMPLE Read the following paragraph, and identify its topic sentence. Remember to ask, "Does this sentence cover all the ideas in the paragraph?"

[1]Ashleigh had been trying to write her essay for three days. [2]First, she tried to write about her summer vacation, but it seemed too boring. [3]Next, she tried to write about breaking up with her boyfriend. [4]She was able to write two full pages but knew she couldn't share the ideas with a teacher for a grade. [5]Her third and final try brought nothing but a page full of doodles. [6]Desperate, for the essay was due in the morning, Ashleigh turned on her computer. [7]"Maybe I can find something to write about on the Internet," she said to herself. [8]She typed in the words "essay ideas" and hit the search button. [9]Several sites had essays already written for free. [10]Quickly, she found an essay about soccer; she recopied it in her own handwriting, put her name on it, and turned it in. [11]By cheating, Ashleigh joined the ranks of countless other students who cheat themselves out of an education. [12]Cheating can be easier than learning.

Topic sentence: _____

EXPLANATION Sentences 1–10 tell the story of Ashleigh struggling to do the assignment and then deciding to cheat. Sentence 11 makes a judgment about Ashleigh's actions and other students who choose to cheat. Sentence 12 is the topic sentence. It clearly states the point the author is making, and it sums up the details of the story. Starting the paragraph with the details of Ashleigh's story makes the idea much more interesting. Ending the paragraph with a main idea that draws a conclusion or makes a judgment is very powerful.

PRACTICE 2

Identify the topic sentence of each of the following paragraphs. Remember to ask, "Does this sentence cover all the ideas in the paragraph?"

¹On April 11, 2009, Susan Boyle walked onto the national stage of *Britain's Got Talent*. ²Her chances for stardom did not appear good. ³Her gold lace dress made her look frumpy. ⁴Her frizzy hair, unkempt and graying, made her look dowdy. ⁵The judges of the talent competition scoffed at her answers to their questions. ⁶Simon Cowell asked, "Who do you want to be most like?" ⁷Boyle replied, "Elaine Paige." ⁸The audience laughed and rolled their eyes. ⁹How could this ugly duck aspire to be like the reigning queen of British musical theatre? ¹⁰Then Susan Boyle sang "I Have a Dream," and her rich, powerful voice brought the audience to its feet in joyous disbelief. ¹¹Susan Boyle defied stereotypes and fulfilled her dream of becoming a professional singer. ¹²Her performance from that night in April has been viewed by over 100 million people on YouTube. ¹³And her debut album "I Dreamed a Dream" became a best seller on Amazon.com before it was even released. ¹⁴She is beloved by fans worldwide.

1. Topic sentence: _____

¹"It's 10 P.M. Do you know where your children are?" ²Remember that phrase from your own childhood? ³It's still a valid question, but now, it comes with a twist: "Do you know where your kids are—and who they're chatting with online?" ⁴Social networking allows people to exchange information about themselves. ⁵However, many young people aren't aware of the dangers of social networks. ⁶Here are safety tips you can use to reduce the risks. ⁷Help your children understand what information should be private. ⁸Remind them that once they post information online, they can't take it back. ⁹Talk to them about avoiding sex talk online. ¹⁰Tell them to trust their gut if they have suspicions. ¹¹Finally, use privacy settings to restrict access to your child's website.

2. Topic sentence: _____

Topic Sentences at the Beginning and the End of a Paragraph

A paragraph may start and end by stating one main idea in two different sentences. Even though these two sentences state the same main idea, they word the idea in different ways. A topic sentence presents the main idea at or near the beginning of the paragraph. Then, at the end of the paragraph, the main idea is stated again, but with different words. The following diagram shows this flow of ideas.

> Main idea: Topic sentence
> Supporting detail
> Supporting detail
> Supporting detail
> Supporting detail
> Supporting detail
> Supporting detail
> Main idea: Topic sentence

EXAMPLE   Read the following paragraph, and identify its topic sentences. Remember to ask, "Do these sentences cover all the ideas in the paragraph?"

[1]Walking is a healthy, safe, and easy method of exercising. [2]Walking builds muscles in the legs, buttocks, torso, and arms. [3]The whole body is used when walking. [4]A brisk walk raises the heart rate, making the heart work harder, and become stronger. [5]Walking also helps keep weight within healthy guidelines. [6]Not only is walking healthy, but walking is also safe. [7]Unlike jogging, which can cause damage to ligaments and joints, walking is easy on the body. [8]Finally, walking is easy to do. [9]No special equipment, clothes, or training are needed. [10]All anyone needs for a good walk is desire and time. [11]Safe and easy, walking improves overall health.

Topic sentences: _____

EXPLANATION   Sentences 1 and 11 both state the main idea of the paragraph: Walking is healthy, safe, and easy. Notice how the wording changes at the end of the paragraph. Repeating the main idea makes the point much stronger and more likely to be remembered. Remember: Even though the paragraph has two topic sentences, it only has *one* main idea.

PRACTICE 3

Identify the topic sentence(s) in each of the following paragraphs.

Types of Cyclones

[1]A hurricane is a type of tropical cyclone. [2]A tropical cyclone is the name for all circulating weather systems that turn counterclockwise in the Northern Hemisphere. [3]Three types of tropical cyclones exist. [4]The first type of tropical cyclone is a tropical depression. [5]A tropical depression is an organized system of clouds and thunderstorms. [6]A tropical depression has a defined circulation, and it has sustained winds of 38 mph or less. [7]The second type of tropical cyclone is a tropical storm. [8]A tropical storm is an organized system of strong thunderstorms. [9]This storm has a defined circulation, and it has sustained winds of 39 to 73 mph. [10]The third type of tropical cyclone is a hurricane. [11]A hurricane has a well-defined circulation, and it has sustained winds of 74 mph or higher.

—Adapted from "Hurricane and Natural Disaster Brochures."
National Weather Service. 31 August 2004.

1. **Topic sentence(s):** _____

Stress at Work

[1]Teresa shared the following information with a friend as they sat in her doctor's waiting room. [2]"In my new job, the computer routes the calls, and they never stop. [3]I even have to schedule my bathroom breaks. [4]All I hear the whole day are complaints from unhappy customers. [5]I try to be helpful and sympathetic, but I can't promise anything without getting my boss's approval. [6]Most of the time I'm caught between what the customer wants and company policy. [7]I'm not sure who I'm supposed to keep happy. [8]The other reps are so uptight and tense they don't even talk to one another. [9]We all go to our own little cubicles and stay there until quitting time. [10]To make matters worse, my mother's health is deteriorating. [11]If only I could use some of my sick time to look after her. [12]No wonder I'm in here with migraine headaches and high blood pressure. [13]A lot of the reps are seeing the employee assistance counselor and taking stress management classes, which seem to help. [14]But sooner or later, someone will have to make some changes in the way the place is run." [15]Teresa's story is unfortunate but not unusual. [16]Job stress has become a common and costly problem in the American workplace.

—Adapted from "Stress at Work." National Institute for
Occupational Safety and Health. 7 January 1999.

2. **Topic sentence(s):** _____

Weather, Work, and Stress

[1]The hurricane had just left a messy trail a short two weeks earlier. [2]Now another hurricane threatens the area with 140 mph winds. [3]We all watch as the new storm moves steadily closer. [4]At work, we log online to Internet weather channels and gather in hallways to talk about our plans. [5]No one can concentrate on work; we all yearn to dash to our homes, gather our belongings, secure our property, and flee. [6]Yet we feel obligated to wait until management gives the official release from work. [7]A hurricane causes great stress at the work place. [8]Most of us know that after the hurricane hits, we may not be able to return to work for days. [9]So we want to stay on the job as long as possible, hoping our businesses are still standing when we return. [10]Experience has taught us that we will lose electricity for days. [11]Incoming and outgoing mail will be delayed. [12]Cell phones won't work. [13]Tension and anxiety does not end with the storm. [14]In its path, a hurricane leaves a wake of on-the-job stress.

3. Topic sentence(s): _____

Choose the Colors of Health

[1]Eating 5 or more servings of colorful fruits and vegetables a day is an important part of a plan for healthier living. [2]Deeply hued fruits and vegetables provide a wide range of vitamins, minerals, fiber, and phytochemicals. [3]Your body needs each of these to maintain good health and energy levels. [4]Colorful fruits and vegetables protect against the effects of aging and reduce the risk of cancer and heart disease. [5]It's all about color—blue/purple, green, white, yellow/orange, and red: the power of colorful fruits and vegetables to promote good health. [6]So when you're grocery shopping, planning your meals, or dining out, think color. [7]Eat 5 or more servings of colorful fruits and vegetables a day and stay healthy.

—Adapted from "5 a Day, The Color Way." 5aday.org 1 Sept. 2004
http://www.5aday.com/html/colorway/colorway_home.php

4. Topic sentence(s): _____

Textbook
Skills

The Central Idea and the Thesis Statement

Many paragraphs state the main idea in a topic sentence. Longer passages in articles, essays, and textbooks have **central ideas**, which can be thought of as the passage's main idea. Often the author will state the central idea in a single sentence called the **thesis statement**.

> The **central idea** is the main idea of a passage made up of two
>   or more paragraphs.
> The **thesis statement** is a sentence that states a longer
>   passage's central idea.

You identify the central idea of a longer passage the same way you identify
the topic sentence of a paragraph. The thesis statement is one sentence that is
general enough to include all the ideas in the passage. In longer reading selections, each paragraph will have a topic sentence in addition to the central idea.

EXAMPLE   Read the following passage. In the space provided, write the number of the sentence that states the central idea.

The Dangers of Marijuana Use

¹Marijuana has significant short- and long-term effects. ²The obvious
short-term effects are increased heart rate, dry mouth, and dry, red eyes.
³The red eyes result from the dilation, or widening, of the blood vessels in
the eyes. ⁴This dilation occurs throughout the body, increases the flow of
blood, and causes a drop in blood pressure. ⁵The drop in blood pressure
makes some people dizzy. ⁶Use of this drug also affects balance, coordination, and the ability to judge distances. ⁷Research has shown that a majority of marijuana users failed roadside sobriety tests an hour and a half after
smoking. ⁸One study found that one-third of a group of reckless teenage
drivers who had been tested for drugs on the scene had used marijuana.

⁹Marijuana may also have dangerous long-term effects. ¹⁰First of all,
marijuana smoke has over 150 ingredients that can cause cancer. ¹¹And
smoking one marijuana joint is the same as smoking five tobacco cigarettes. ¹²Thus five marijuana joints could do as much damage to the lungs
as 25 cigarettes. ¹³In addition, the marijuana smoke emits five times as
much carbon monoxide into the blood and three times as much tar into
the lungs. ¹⁴Users may lower their immunity to diseases. ¹⁵The body depends on white blood cells to fight off illness. ¹⁶White blood cells attack
and destroy germs and bacteria. ¹⁷THC, a chemical found in marijuana,
stops the growth of white blood cells. ¹⁸Therefore, marijuana users are
more prone to chest colds and coughs than nonusers. ¹⁹Users are more
likely to suffer from cancer of the throat, tongue, and sinuses.

Central idea: _____

EXPLANATION   The central idea of the passage is stated in sentence 1,
"Marijuana has significant short- and long-term effects." The first paragraph
discusses the drug's short-term effects, and the second paragraph discusses its

long-term effects. Thus the first sentence is the only sentence broad enough to cover all the details in both paragraphs.

PRACTICE 4

Identify the central idea of the following passage.

Textbook
Skills

Cross-Cultural Sensitivity

[1]Professional ice hockey players are tough. [2]They shoot the puck and throw body checks. [3]Sometimes some of them drop their gloves and fight with their bare fists. [4]They are not joking around. [5]The fights are for real. [6]So are the injuries they may inflict on each other. [7]What is the maximum penalty for fighting? [8]Five minutes on a penalty bench. [9]And then the player is back in the game. [10]If you are hit, you hit back. [11]Do not complain. [12]Physical fighting is a part of ice hockey.

[13]However, some words that you say on the ice rink are more painful than cuts and bruises. [14]We are not talking about sexual profanities—if you watch any U.S. professional game from the stands you know that these obscenities are thrown in every game and basically are left unnoticed by sports officials and the public. [15]We are talking about ethnic and racial slurs—disparaging and extremely offensive remarks about or related to one's ethnicity, religion, or race (origin). [16]The National Hockey League has established "zero tolerance" for racial and ethnic slurs on the ice. [17]Moreover, the league severely punishes some players for using such slurs during the game. [18]Apparently, words can hurt more than fists.

—Shiraev & Levy, *Cross-Cultural Psychology: Critical Thinking and Contemporary Applications*, 3rd ed., p. 312.

Central idea: _____

APPLICATIONS

Application 1: Identifying the Topic Sentence

Identify the topic sentence in each paragraph. One paragraph will have two topic sentences: one at the beginning and one at the end.

1.   [1]Thirty minutes of walking three or four times a week can improve both fitness and attitude. [2]Walking tones muscles and strengthens the heart. [3]Well-developed muscles and a strong heart can lengthen a person's life. [4]Walking also allows time for personal thoughts and works out stress. [5]Taking personal time and relieving stress lead to feelings of peace and well-being.

Topic sentence(s): _____

2.   [1]AIDS is a devastating disease caused by the HIV virus. [2]So far, over a quarter of a million Americans have died from this disease. [3]The best safeguard against getting AIDS is becoming educated about it. [4]Knowing how it is passed from one person to another is the first step. [5]One way HIV can be passed is by having sex with an infected person. [6]A second way it can be passed is by sharing a dirty needle, such as during heroin use.

Topic sentence(s): _____

3.   [1]Rosa Parks was an African American woman who worked hard as a seamstress in a department store in the early 1960s. [2]One day, tired from work, she refused to give up her seat on a bus in Montgomery, Alabama, and became a national hero. [3]She was arrested and placed in jail for her refusal to move to the back of the bus, where African Americans were forced to sit in those days. [4]The way she was treated garnered national attention. [5]Some people say her refusal to give up her seat launched the civil rights movement. [6]Rosa Parks proved that one brave person can make a difference.

Topic sentence(s): _____

4.   [1]Knowing the slang, or street words, used in the drug culture may help parents and teachers prevent the use of illegal drugs. [2]By learning the street language, adults show that they care enough to be involved. [3]It is also likely that young people will respect and listen to the advice of adults who know what they are talking about. [4]For example, "dope" used to be the name used for hard drugs like narcotics; now it refers to all drugs. [5]And a "dealer" usually only sells soft drugs like marijuana; a "pusher" sells hard drugs like heroin. [6]Knowing these terms gives adults a way to talk to young people about preventing drug use.

Topic sentence(s): _____

Application 2: Identifying the Thesis Statement

Read the following passage, and identify the thesis statement.

Textbook
Skills

Toys and Gender Roles

[1]Children will eagerly tell you about their favorite toy or about a "cool" new toy they would like to have. [2]Toys are without a doubt a major concern of most children because, as any child will tell you, they're fun. [3]However, toys not only entertain children; they also teach children. [4]Playing with toys teaches skills and allows children to try on different roles they may one day occupy as adults. [5]Some believe that there are significant differences between the toys girls and boys play with, and

these different types of toys train girls and boys for separate roles as adults.

[6]More than twenty years ago, two researchers went into middle-class homes and studied the toys found in children's rooms. [7]Their comparison of the boys' and girls' rooms is a study of contrasts. [8]Girls' rooms contained a large number of dolls, dollhouses, and small appliances such as toy stoves. [9]In contrast, the boys' rooms contained military-type toys and athletic equipment. [10]Boys also had building and motor toys such as cars, trucks, and wagons. [11]In fact, boys had more toys overall, as well as more types of toys, including those considered educational. [12]The only items girls were as likely to have as boys were musical instruments and books.

—Adapted from Renzetti/Curran, *Women, Men, and Society*, p. 73 © 1999 Pearson Education, Inc. Reproduced by permission of Pearson Education, Inc.

Thesis statement: _____

VISUAL VOCABULARY

Some believe that a child's **gender** affects his or her choice of toys.
The best meaning of gender is

_____.

a. sex.
b. role.
c. attitude.

REVIEW TEST 1

Score (number correct) _____ × 25 = _____ %

Identifying the Topic Sentence

Identify the topic sentence in each paragraph. One paragraph has two topic sentences: one at the beginning and one at the end.

1. [1]Many of our cities have survived horrible natural disasters. [2]One city that has faced and survived natural disaster is San Francisco,

California. ³At 5:12 A.M. on April 18, 1906, a terrible earthquake shattered San Francisco. ⁴Fires broke out throughout the city due to broken gas pipes. ⁵Three thousand people were killed, and 200,000 were left homeless. ⁶In spite of the widespread damage, the city rebuilt.

Topic sentence(s): _____

2.   ¹In the past 200 years, bird and animal species have vanished from the earth as cities and towns have replaced the natural landscape. ²Only a small fraction of America's original forests remain. ³Sadly, more than the forest has been lost. ⁴Hunters killed off the last of the eastern bison in 1825 and the eastern elk in 1855. ⁵Millions of passenger pigeons once lived in the forest near the Great Plains. ⁶The last such pigeon died in a zoo in 1914. ⁷Many people have called these losses "progress."

Topic sentence(s): _____

Basic Emotions

Textbook Skills

3.   ¹Charles Darwin believed that we are born with many emotional behaviors—actions that come from emotions. ²He noticed that people from many races and cultures use the same facial expressions to show the same emotions. ³Likewise, blind people also use those very expressions, even if they never have had the chance to see the way others look. ⁴Are we all born with a built-in set of emotions? ⁵If so, these emotions would be a basic part of what we call "human nature." ⁶Some experts believe that surprise, happiness, anger, fear, disgust, and sadness are basic emotions. ⁷**Basic emotions** are those feelings that are innate (born within us) and shared by all humans. ⁸Other experts list surprise, interest, joy, rage, fear, disgust, shame, and anguish. ⁹The differences may be a simple matter of word choice. ¹⁰Joy and happiness, for example, may be different words for the same emotion. ¹¹Although the exact number of basic emotions is debated, most agree that humans do have a set of built-in emotions.

—Adapted from Kosslyn/Rosenberg, *Psychology: The Brain, the Person, the World*, pp. 312–314 © 2001 Allyn and Bacon. Reproduced by permission of Pearson Education, Inc.

Topic sentence(s): _____

Boundaries

Textbook Skills

4.   ¹Boundaries are the limits placed on behavior. ²Boundaries may be clear in some families and not as clear in others. ³**Rigid boundaries** are firmly set and difficult to break through. ⁴Rigid boundaries create a different situation than **diffuse boundaries**. ⁵Diffuse boundaries change often

and are easily crossed. [6]For instance, the mother and father in a family may set themselves apart from the rest of the family by making their bedroom off limits to other members of the family. [7]By doing this, they show that they expect to be respected as a couple. [8]In their case, the boundary or limit is rigid or clear. [9]Another couple may not have defined their boundary as a couple as clearly. [10]They may not have shown other members of the family that they must be respected as a couple. [11]Therefore, they may allow their children to interrupt their conversations and arguments. [12]In summary, boundaries affect the way a family functions.

—Adapted from Yerby, Buerkel-Rothfuss, & Bochner,
Understanding Family Communication, 2nd ed., p. 62.

Topic sentence(s): _____

VISUAL VOCABULARY

The parents are setting

_____ boundaries.

a. diffuse
b. rigid

REVIEW TEST 2

Score (number correct) _____ × 25 = _____%

Identifying the Topic Sentence

Identify the topic sentence for each paragraph. One paragraph has two topic sentences: one at the beginning and one at the end.

1.   [1]There is no such thing as a routine space flight, for the dangers are great. [2]Four flights have proved that the risks and tragedies of space

flight are ever present. [3]A fire aboard the spacecraft *Apollo 1* on the ground in Cape Kennedy, Florida, killed three astronauts in 1967. [4]On April 13, 1970, a major power failure crippled *Apollo 13.* [5]The astronauts had to use the frail lunar landing craft to get back to earth. [6]On January 28, 1986, the space shuttle *Challenger* exploded and killed all seven of its crew. [7]And on February 1, 2003, the space shuttle *Columbia* broke apart on its return to earth, costing another seven lives.

Topic sentence(s): _____

2.   [1]Ray Charles is a famous singer and musician who also happens to be blind. [2]As a young person, this remarkable man worked hard to overcome the constraints of his blindness. [3]Charles taught his ears to do what his eyes could not do. [4]He would stand in a hallway and throw a golf ball and listen to the sounds it made. [5]Then, as he listened, he would try to catch the ball as it came back to him. [6]By working hard, he learned how to live with being blind.

Topic sentence(s): _____

3.   [1]Reggae music is a complex mix of message and style. [2]Originating in Jamaica in the 1960s, reggae evolved from folk music that protested racism and corruption. [3]Reggae also has a religious side that is based on the Bible from the view of black culture. [4]Some critics say that the serious messages of reggae are easier to accept because of its powerful dance beat.

Topic sentence(s): _____

The Role of Antioxidants

Textbook Skills

4.   [1]Although large doses of vitamins may be harmful, research has revealed a new role for some vitamins. [2]Some vitamins protect the body's cells by working as antioxidants. [3]Vitamins A, E, and C are a few of the vitamins that act as antioxidants. [4]Antioxidants stop a harmful kind of oxygen (called *oxygen free radicals*) from hurting the cells. [5]The body is always making free radicals. [6]If too many of these build up, diseases may occur. [7]Free radicals may be linked to cancer, lung disease, heart disease, and even the aging process. [8]Exercise may cause a rise in free radicals. [9]The question is, Do active people need to take in more antioxidants? [10]Some studies show that extra vitamin E may help fight against the damage caused by free radicals.

—Adapted from Powers & Dodd, *Total Fitness: Exercise, Nutrition, and Wellness,* 2nd ed., pp. 178–79.

Topic sentence(s): _____

REVIEW TEST 3

Score (number correct) _____ × 20 = _____%

Locating Central Ideas

How Can You Work Effectively with Others?

[1]In the past, you could have lived your entire lifetime surrounded by people from your own culture. [2]Not anymore. [3]The United States is made up of people from a wide range of countries and cultures. [4]And now technology links us to people from cultures around the world like never before. [5]Now, your success depends upon your ability to work as a team with a wide variety of people. [6]Your ability to grasp and value diversity is key to your success.

Value Diversity

[7]Diversity means differences among people. [8]On one level, diversity refers to the differences between you and others. [9]It's the differences between the group you belong to and the ones you don't. [10]Many differences are obvious. [11]For example, clear differences include gender, age, race, or physical traits and abilities. [12]Other differences are less clear such as education or family background. [13]On another level, diversity is the differences within a person. [14]These factors include personality, learning styles, strengths, weaknesses, natural talents, interests, and abilities.

[15]In college, the work place, and your everyday life, you come in contact with people from a wide variety of groups, as in the following examples:

- [16]People who are biracial or multiracial
- [17]Non-native English speakers who have come from outside the United States
- [18]Persons who live with various kinds of disabilities
- [19]People who have other religious beliefs
- [20]People who have different lifestyles—as seen in their dress, interests, or recreation

Develop Personal and Social Skills

[21]In a diverse world, you need more than just the basic career skills. [22]To work well with others, you also need to develop personal and social skills. [23]Personal skills give you self-control. [24]Personal skills allow you to

know yourself and what motivates you. [25]Personal skills allow you to master your feelings and get along with others. [26]In fact, personal skills affect social skills, and social skills help you handle your relationships with others. [27]Social skills help you sense the needs and feelings of others. [28]And social skills help you understand the way the social world works. [29]Active listening is a key social skill.

[30]You can increase your personal and social skills by developing the following traits.

- [31]*Self-Awareness*: Know your emotions and how they affect you. [32]Understand your strengths and limits. [33]Be confident in your abilities. [34]Be open to improvement.
- [35]*Self-Management*: Control your emotions and impulses. [36]Delay gratification when there is something more important to be gained. [37]Be trustworthy. [38]Adapt to change and new ideas. [39]Persist and overcome obstacles.
- [40]*Social Awareness*: Sense the feelings and views of others. [41]Help others improve themselves. [42]Know how to relate to people from different cultures. [43]Sense how to serve the needs of others.
- [44]*Social Skills:* Know how to work in a team. [45]Inspire people to act. [46]Understand how to lead a group. [47]Know how to persuade people. [48]Make positive change happen.

Know How to Work with Others in a Group

[49]A real-world application of diversity in action is likely to occur in the college study group setting. [50]Students taking the same course may form a study group that meets one or more times a week or right before exams. [51]Instructors sometimes set up student study groups, known as *peer-assisted study sessions* or *supplemental instruction*.

[52]When you study with one or more people you gain benefits. [53]You share and gain knowledge. [54]You increase your motivation. [55]You gain the ability to work as a team member. [56]You increase your awareness and value of diversity.

[57]Every study group is unique. [58]The way a group operates depends the personalities of the members, the subject you study, the location of the group, and the size of the group. [59]However, a few general strategies apply to all groups:

- [60]**Set long-term and short term goals**. [61]Know what the group wants to accomplish. [62]At the start of each meeting, have one person compile a list of questions to address.

- [63]**Determine a regular schedule and rotate leaders**. [64]Try to meet weekly or, at least, every other week. [65]Rotating leadership among members helps everyone take responsibility.
- [66]**Create study materials for one another and help one another learn**. [67]Assign each member a task. [68]Have group members teach pieces of information, create quizzes, or go through flashcards together.
- [69]**Share the workload and pool your note-taking resources**. [70]Compare notes and fill in information you don't have.
- [71]**Know how to be an effective leader**. [72]Know how to define projects, assign work, set schedules, set a positive tone, keep people moving, ahead, and evaluate results.
- [73]**Know how to be an effective team member**. [74]Be organized and willing to discuss. [75]Fulfill the tasks you promise to do.

—Carter, et al., *Keys to Success: Building Analytical, Creative, and Practical Skills*, pp. 19-23 © 2009. Reproduced by permission of Pearson Education, Inc.

_____ **1.** What is the topic of the passage?
   a. diversity
   b. personal skills
   c. social skills
   d. working with others

_____ **2.** What is the thesis statement of the passage?
   a. sentence 1
   b. sentence 2
   c. sentence 5
   d. sentence 7

_____ **3.** Which sentence states the central point of paragraphs 2–3 (sentences 7–20)?
   a. sentence 7
   b. sentence 8
   c. sentence 13
   d. sentence 14

_____ **4.** Which sentence states the central point of paragraphs 4–5 (sentences 21–48)?
   a. sentence 21
   b. sentence 22
   c. sentence 28
   d. sentence 30

_____ **5.** Which sentence states the central point of paragraphs 6–8 (sentences 49–75)?
   a. sentence 49
   b. sentence 52
   c. sentence 57
   d. sentence 59

VISUAL VOCABULARY

The ability to persist is an important social skill.
The best meaning of *persist* is

_____.

a. continue.
b. suffer.

WHAT DO YOU THINK?

On a scale of one to five, how would you rate the diversity of your college campus (1 = no diversity; 5 = great diversity). Do you think students on your college campus would benefit from diversity training? Why or why not? Assume you are a member of the Student Government Association, which is sponsoring a diversity workshop. Using the information from the passage create a power point presentation about personal and social skills, along with a few strategies for working with diverse groups.

REVIEW TEST 4

Score (number correct) _____ × 20 = _____ %

Identifying the Central Idea

Read the following passage from the website KidsHealth, from Nemours, one of the largest nonprofit organizations devoted to children's health. Answer the questions that follow.

Prescription Drug Abuse

¹Angie overheard her parents talking about how her brother's medicine for attention **deficit hyperactivity** disorder (ADHD) was making him less hungry. ²Because Angie was worried about her weight, she started sneaking one of her brother's pills every few days. ³To keep her parents from finding out, she asked a friend to give her some of his ADHD medicine as well.

⁴Todd found an old bottle of painkillers that had been left over from his dad's operation. ⁵He decided to try them. ⁶Because a doctor had prescribed the pills, Todd figured that meant they'd be OK to try.

[7]Both Todd and Angie are taking risks, though. [8]Prescription painkillers and other medications help lots of people live more productive lives. [9]Prescribed drugs free them from the symptoms of medical conditions like depression or ADHD. [10]But that's only when they're given for a specific individual to treat a specific condition.

[11]Taking prescription drugs in a way that hasn't been recommended by a doctor can be more dangerous than people think. [12]In fact, it's drug abuse. [13]And it's just as illegal as taking street drugs.

Why Do Some People Abuse Prescription Drugs?

[14]Some people experiment with prescription drugs because they think that the drugs will help them have more fun, lose weight, fit in, and even study more effectively. [15]Prescription drugs can be easier to get than street drugs. [16]Family members or friends could have a prescription. [17]But prescription drugs are also sometimes sold on the street like other illegal drugs. [18]A 2006 National Survey on Drug Use and Health showed that among all youths aged 12 to 17, 6% had tried prescription drugs for **recreational** use in the last month.

[19]Why? [20]Some people think that prescription drugs are safer and less addictive than street drugs. [21]After all, these are drugs that moms, dads, and even kid brothers and sisters use. [22]To Angie, taking her brother's ADHD medicine felt like a good way to keep her appetite in check. [23]She'd heard how bad diet pills can be. [24]And she wrongly thought that the ADHD drugs would be safer.

[25]But prescription drugs are only safe for the individuals who actually have prescriptions for them. [26]That's because a doctor has examined these people and prescribed the right dose of medication for a specific medical condition. [27]The doctor has also told them exactly how they should take the medicine. [28]The doctor has warned them about things to avoid while taking the drug—such as drinking alcohol, smoking, or taking other medications. [29]Doctors also are aware of possible dangerous side effects. [30]And they can monitor patients closely for these.

[31]Other people who try prescription drugs are like Todd. [32]They think they're not doing anything illegal because these drugs are prescribed by doctors. [33]Both Angie and Todd are wrong. [34]Taking drugs without a prescription—or sharing a prescription drug with friends—is actually dangerous and illegal.

—Adapted from "Prescription Drug Abuse." © 2010 The Nemours Foundation/
KidsHealth. Reprinted with permission. http://kidshealth.org/teen/
drug_alcohol/drugs/prescription_drug_abuse.html.

Vocabulary in Context

_____ 1. The best synonym for the word **deficit** in sentence 1 is
   a. debt.
   b. shortage.
   c. excess.
   d. balance.

_____ 2. The best meaning of the word **hyperactivity** in sentence 1 is
   a. restlessness.
   b. forcefulness.
   c. laziness.
   d. rebellious.

_____ 3. The best meaning of **recreational** in sentence 18 is
   a. healing.
   b. safe.
   c. free.
   d. leisure.

Main Ideas

_____ 4. Which sentence states the central idea of paragraphs 1 through 4 (sentences 1–13)?
   a. sentence 1
   b. sentence 4
   c. sentence 7
   d. sentence 13

_____ 5. Which sentence states the central idea of the passage?
   a. sentence 13
   b. sentence 14
   c. sentence 25
   d. sentence 34

WHAT DO YOU THINK?

Do you think that taking drugs prescribed for another person is wrong or dangerous? Is there ever a time when taking a drug prescribed for another person is okay? Assume that you are enrolled in a college speech class, and you have decided to take a stand on this issue. Write a draft of your speech. Clearly state your view about using drugs that have been prescribed for someone else. Support your point with examples.

After Reading About Locating Stated Main Ideas

Before you move on to the Mastery Tests on locating stated main ideas, take time to reflect on your learning and performance by answering the following questions. Write your answers in your notebook.

- How has my knowledge base or prior knowledge about locating stated main ideas changed?

- Based on my studies, how do I think I will perform on the Mastery Test(s)? Why do I think my scores will be above average, average, or below average?

- Would I recommend this chapter to other students who want to learn more about stated main ideas? Why or why not?

Test your understanding of what you have learned about Locating Stated Main Ideas by completing the Chapter 5 Review Card on the insert near the end of your text.

CONNECT TO myreadinglab

To check your progress in meeting Chapter 5's learning outcomes, log in to **www.myreadinglab.com**, and try the following activities.

- The "Main Idea" section of MyReadingLab provides review materials, practice activities, and tests about topics and main ideas. To access this resource, click on the "Study Plan" tab. Then click on "Main Idea." Then click on the following links as needed: "Overview," "Model," "Practice," and "Tests."

- To measure your mastery of the content in this chapter, complete the tests in the "Main Idea" section and click on Gradebook to find your results.

A. Identify the topic sentence of each paragraph. One paragraph has two topic sentences.

1.   [1]Alzheimer's disease is a serious and growing problem for millions of the elderly. [2]In 2002, some 4 million Americans suffered from this dreadful disease. [3]Alzheimer's affects the brain as people age. [4]The disease causes a loss of memory, personality, and eventually all logical thought. [5]Unfortunately, this disease could affect 20 million Americans by the year 2050.

Topic sentence(s): _____

2.   [1]Few of us become as skilled in our chosen field as LeBron James is in his. [2]This talented athlete reached the top of his profession through determined hard work. [3]To stay competitive in the game, LeBron spends countless hours practicing his basketball skills. [4]More of us should be as determined to succeed as LeBron James is.

Topic sentence(s): _____

3.   [1]Today, students of all ages fill college classrooms. [2]In fact, 28 is the average age of a current community college student. [3]Many of these students are returning to the classroom after years on the job and away from the books. [4]Returning students often face many stresses. [5]The first problem many face is the college system. [6]Dealing with admissions and financial aid, transferring credits, and registering for classes can be a stressful process. [7]Once classes begin, these students often find balancing classwork, family life, and jobs challenging and tiring. [8]Finally, many of these older students feel the pressure to keep up with other college students. [9]Despite these stressors, returning students are often the most successful students in their classes.

Topic sentence(s): _____

Textbook
Skills

4.   [1]Sickle cell disease is a disorder that affects oxygen-carrying red blood cells. [2]Red blood cells are normally round. [3]In sickle cell anemia, the red blood cells are elongated and crescent-shaped (looking like a sickle shape). [4]This makes the blood thicker, which harms the blood cells' ability to carry oxygen to the body's tissues. [5]Sickled cells are unable to pass through the body's tiny capillaries. [6]The disease can cause

fatigue, pain, damage to vital organs, and death in early childhood. [7]When blood vessels in the hands and feet get clogged, for instance, the hands and feet become painful and swollen. [8]When blood flow is blocked to vital organs like the kidneys, lungs, or brain, serious damage can occur.

> —Adapted from Nakamura, *Health in America:*
> *A Multicultural Perspective*, pp. 197–198.

Topic sentence(s): _____

B. Read the following passage. Write the number of the sentence that states the central idea in the space provided.

5.

Textbook
Skills

Memory and Learning

[1]One of the most remarkable discoveries in the study of memory is that it doesn't matter how hard you try to remember. [2]How well you understand and organize what you remember matters most. [3]One study asked a group of people to form mental pictures connected to each pair of words in a list. [4]For example, they paired *car* and *desk* by thinking of a desk strapped to the roof of a car. [5]In one part of the study, the members were told to use the image to memorize the pairs of words. [6]This kind of learning, in which you try to learn something, is called **intentional learning**.

[7]In another part of the study, the members were told simply to rate the vividness of each image and did not try to learn the pairs of words. [8]Learning that occurs without intention is called **incidental learning**. [9]The interesting finding was that the members in the incidental learning part did as well as those who were told to memorize the words. [10]The effort that went into organizing the objects into an image appears to have helped them learn, even without specific instruction.

> —Adapted from Kosslyn/Rosenberg, *Psychology: The Brain,*
> *the Person, the World*, p. 214 © 2001 Allyn and Bacon.
> Reproduced by permission of Pearson Education, Inc.

Central idea: _____

Name _____ Section _____

Date _____ Score (number correct) _____ × 25 = _____%

A. The following selections have topic sentences that may appear at the beginning of, within, at the end of, or in two places in the paragraph. Write the number(s) of the topic sentence(s) of each paragraph in the space provided.

1. Chunking Information

Textbook
Skills

[1]One way to keep ideas in short-term memory is called chunking. [2]Most people can rehearse and remember up to seven different pieces of information. [3]Once your short-term memory is "full," no extra data can get in. [4]Chunking is a method of grouping items so you have fewer units to remember. [5]If, for example, you had to recall 15 different tasks, you might find it hard to keep repeating all 15 items one at a time. [6]Using chunking, you would group the items into small numbers of units. [7]Thus instead of repeating 15 items one at a time, you chunk the list into five groups with three items in each group. [8]It is much easier to remember a large body of information if you break it into smaller groups.

—Adapted from Brownell, *Listening*, p. 149 © 2002 by Pearson Education, Inc. Reproduced by permission of Pearson Education, Inc.

Topic sentence(s): _____

2. Birth Order

Textbook
Skills

[1]Birth order (sibling position) has a major influence on a wide variety of behaviors and attitudes. [2]Those who are firstborn tend to be intellectual achievers and have high levels of self-esteem. [3]Females who are firstborn share particular traits. [4]For example, they tend to be religious, and they are often old-fashioned about sex and their role in the family. [5]Female firstborns are more likely to be found in the company of adults. [6]Lastborn, or youngest, children, like only children, tend to be more open about sex and their role in the family. [7]These children like to engage in social activities, so they are more likely to visit with friends. [8]They are also more likely to make use of media. [9]Middle children are different from firstborns and lastborns. [10]Middle-born children have less self-esteem than either firstborn or lastborn children. [11]Middle-born children do not have the special place of being their parents' first or last child.

—Adapted from Eshleman, *The Family*, 9th ed., pp. 376–377.

Topic sentence(s): _____

B. Identify the sentence that states the central idea of the passage.

3.   ¹Depression can be bad for your heart and should not be ignored. ²Recent studies indicate that people who are depressed are three times more likely to die of heart disease than those who are not depressed. ³It seems that depression can raise the level of stress in the body. ⁴And stress triggers an increase in heart rate and blood pressure. ⁵In addition, if you are depressed, you are less likely to exercise or eat right than people who are not depressed. ⁶Because depression can be harmful to your heart, it is important to pay attention to your emotional health.

Topic sentence(s): _____

Textbook
Skills

4.   **Taste Buds**

¹Human taste buds, unlike the taste buds of other species, are sensitive sensing receptors located solely in the mouth. ²Taste buds are microscopic structures on the sides of the little bumps you can see on your tongue in the mirror. ³You have taste buds in other places in your mouth as well, such as the back of your throat and cheeks. ⁴Your taste buds die and are replaced about every ten days.

⁵Humans have more taste buds than some other species. ⁶Chickens have fewer than we do, but fish have taste buds spread all over their skin. ⁷Children have more sensitive taste buds than adults, so flavors are much stronger for them than for adults. ⁸This may account for children's strong likes and dislikes of foods. ⁹However, adults can also be very sensitive to slight differences in taste. ¹⁰President Calvin Coolidge could tell that chickens raised in the White House yard didn't taste quite right. ¹¹As it happened, they ate their feed on the ground that was once Teddy Roosevelt's mint garden. ¹²So the flavor of the mint made its way into their meat. ¹³When wine tasters speak of wine as having a flavor of mushrooms or cloves, they may be speaking the truth. ¹⁴Based on the soil in which the vines grow, grapes' taste differs.

—Adapted from Kosslyn/Rosenberg, *Psychology: The Brain, the Person, the World*, p. 121 © 2001 Allyn and Bacon. Reproduced by permission of Pearson Education, Inc.

Central idea: _____

Name _____   Section _____

Date _____   **Score** (number correct) _____ × 20 = _____%

Read the passage, posted on the Lifestyle web page of MSN. Answer the questions that follow.

Clutter-Busting in 5 Minutes a Day*

[1]Help keep your home clutter-free in five minutes with these five simple steps—from *It's All Too Much: An Easy Plan for Living a Richer Life with Less Stuff* by Peter Walsh, professional organizer from TLC's hit series *Clean Sweep*.

Daily Purging

[2]You'd be amazed at how much you can accomplish in ten minutes. [3]Every day, take five minutes to straighten up and five minutes to focus on cleaning out the clutter in a drawer or on a shelf or flat space, and your house will always be in order. [4]Think about it—if you do this five days out of every week, you'll have purged 260 small areas in your home at the end of a year. [5]Those small projects really add up.

[6]It's best to use the same time slot every day. [7]If you're a stay-at-home mom, do it when the kids nap or leave for school. [8]If you're a morning person who either works from home or never has trouble getting to work on time, then make it part of your morning ritual. [9]If you're always in a rush in the morning, pick a time when you get home—as soon as you walk in the door, or after dinner, or after the kids are in bed—whatever makes the most sense for you. [10]One of my clients likes to straighten up in the morning so she comes home to a clean house. [11]She saves her purge for the evening so that she can be sure to finish up. [12]These small steps really make a difference!

The Five-Minute Purge

[13]Here's what the five-minute purge looks like:

1. [14]Set the kitchen timer for five minutes.

2. [15]Grab a medium-size garbage bag. [16]You'll use this bag to throw things away or to drop them off at your charity of your choice, whichever makes more sense for the items you're purging.

3. [17]Pick your target. [18]Make sure to keep it small so you can be thorough. [19]It's one drawer in the kitchen, one shelf of video tapes, the floor of the coat closet, etc.

4. [20]Clear out anything you haven't used for the last six months to a year. [21]Remember? [22]You were supposed to have done this when you first cleaned

Source: *Adapted with the permission of The Free Press, a Division of Simon & Schuster, Inc., from It's All Too Much: An Easy Plan for Living a Richer Life with Less Stuff by Peter Walsh. Copyright © 2007 by Peter Walsh. All rights reserved.

your home. [23]But a home is a living thing and what you felt you needed to keep yesterday, you may be able to let go of today. [24]Now be ruthless. [25]The more you get rid of, the longer you can wait before you revisit this area.

5. [26]When the timer goes off, stop. [27]If the bag is full, put it in the garbage (or in your car trunk so you can drop it off the next time you drive past a Goodwill or other charity). [28]If the bag isn't full, put it with the garbage or recycling in preparation for tomorrow, when you'll surely fill it up in your next purge.

_____ **1.** What is the topic of the passage?
    a. daily purging   c. getting rid of clutter in five minutes a day
    b. the five-minute purge.   d. getting rid of clutter

_____ **2.** What is the thesis statement of the passage?
    a. sentence 1   c. sentence 13
    b. sentence 2   d. sentence 28

_____ **3.** What is the topic sentence of the third paragraph (sentences 6–12)?
    a. sentence 6   c. sentence 7
    b. sentence 9   d. sentence 12

_____ **4.** Which sentence states the central point of sentences 13–28?
    a. sentence 13   c. sentence 23
    b. sentence 14   d. sentence 28

_____ **5.** What type of thinking (or flow of information) did the author use to organize his ideas?
    a. deductive   b. inductive

VISUAL VOCABULARY

To keep your house clutter-free, make cleaning a daily _____.
  a. purge.
  b. ritual.

Read the passage; then answer the questions that follow it.

Emotion: "I Feel; Therefore, I Am"

Textbook
Skills

[1]After facing off a mugger, John felt an odd mixture of emotions as he hurried to the restaurant to meet Barbara. [2]He had no thought of what might happen later in the evening; his romantic after-dinner plans were no longer on his mind. [3]Instead, he was trembling with fear. [4]Now he felt nervous when he passed an alley, even though the mugger who attacked him was surely far away. [5]Also, he was surprised at the strength of his feelings when he was grabbed by the mugger and after the horrifying event was over. [6]When he saw Barbara, he was **overwhelmed** with intense feelings of warmth and relief.

[7]An emotion is a positive or negative effect of a seen or remembered object, event, or situation. [8]Emotions come with **subjective** (personal) feelings. [9]Emotions not only help guide us to move toward some things and move away from others, but they also give visible cues. [10]These cues help other people know key qualities of our thoughts and wishes.

[11]Understanding the difference between emotions is interesting, but it doesn't tell us what emotion is for or why an emotion arises when it does. [12]Why did John feel fear after the mugger had left? [13]Two major **theories** of emotion try to answer this question.

[14]Over 100 years ago, William James argued that you feel emotions after your body reacts. [15]For example, if you come across someone who begins acting like a mugger, James believes that you would first run and then feel afraid, not the other way around. [16]The emotion of fear arises because you sense your body as you flee. [17]You sense your heart speeding up and your breathing increase. [18]This theory says that emotions come from different sets of bodily reactions. [19]This theory is the "body-emotion theory."

[20]Walter Cannon did not agree with James's theory. [21]Instead, he claimed the brain itself is all that matters. [22]When you see a mugger, the brain gets the body ready to flee or fight *at the same time* as an emotion rises up. [23]This theory is the "brain-emotion theory."

—Adapted from Kosslyn/Rosenberg, *Psychology: The Brain, the Person, the World*, pp. 315–316
© 2001 Allyn and Bacon. Reproduced by permission of Pearson Education, Inc.

_____ **1.** Write the number of the sentence that is the topic sentence of the first paragraph (sentences 1–6).

_____ **2.** Write the number of the sentence that is the topic sentence of the second paragraph (sentences 7–11).

_____ **3.** Write the number of the sentence that is the topic sentence of the fourth paragraph (sentences 14–19).

_____ **4.** Write the number of the sentence that is the topic sentence of the fifth paragraph (sentences 20–23).

_____ **5.** Write the number of the sentence that states the central idea of the passage.

Implied Main Ideas

LEARNING OUTCOMES

After studying this chapter you should be able to do the following:

1. Define the term *implied main idea*.
2. Analyze supporting details to identify and state a topic of a passage.
3. Determine an implied main idea of a passage based on the topic, supporting details, and thought patterns of a passage.
4. Apply annotations to a passage to determine the implied main idea.
5. Create a topic sentence that states the implied main idea of a passage.
6. Evaluate the importance of stating implied main ideas.

Before Reading About Implied Main Ideas

Take a moment to study the learning outcomes. Underline key words that refer to ideas you have already studied in previous chapters.

Circle terms that you need to know more about. Then complete the following chart:

What I Know and What I Need to Learn About Implied Main Ideas	
What I already know that will help me master implied main ideas	
What I need to learn to master implied main ideas	

An Introduction to Implied Main Ideas

Often an author will create a paragraph that does not include a topic sentence or a stated main idea. Even though the main idea is not stated in a single sentence, the paragraph still has a main idea. In these cases, the details clearly suggest or **imply** the author's main idea. When the main idea is not stated, you must figure out the author's point based on the facts, examples, descriptions, and explanations given. Learning how to develop a main idea based on the details will help you develop several skills. You will learn how to study information, value the meaning of supporting details, and use your own words to express an implied main idea.

> An **implied main idea** is a main idea that is not stated directly but is strongly suggested by the supporting details in the passage.

Many different types of reading materials use implied main ideas. For example, you will often need to formulate the implied main idea when you read literature. Short stories, novels, poems, and plays rely heavily on vivid details to suggest the author's point. In addition, many paragraphs in college textbooks do not provide a topic sentence. In these paragraphs, the author uses supporting details to imply the main idea.

When a main idea is not stated but **implied**, you must figure out the main idea on your own. For example, read the following paragraph.

> Employees with burnout feel tired all the time, and they often show symptoms of depression. The likelihood of burnout is increased if they feel trapped in the job. Burnout can also occur if the job demands an overload of work. Ongoing lack of social support, rigid rules, and unkind bosses also lead to burnout.

Did you notice that every sentence in this paragraph is a supporting detail? In the paragraph, no single sentence covers all the other ideas. Ask the following questions to figure out the implied main idea:

> **Questions for Determining the Implied Main Idea**
>
> 1. What is the topic, or subject, of the paragraph?
> 2. What are the major supporting details?
> 3. What is the author's controlling point?

Apply these three questions to the paragraph you just read by writing your responses to each question in the blanks.

1. What is the topic of the paragraph? _____

Each of the sentences in the paragraph uses the word *burnout*.

2. What are the major supporting details? List four supporting details:

a. _____

b. _____

c. _____

d. _____

All the examples listed deal with burnout at work. The supporting details make up a list of a few causes of burnout at work.

3. What is the author's controlling point? _____

_____

By identifying the topic and supporting details used, it is easy to find the main idea of this paragraph.

EXAMPLE Read the following paragraph. Then answer the questions that follow it.

^{1}Glen painfully jogged 3 of the 6 miles he runs every morning. ^{2}For several weeks, his right knee had become increasingly sore. ^{3}Suddenly, he yelped in pain and came to a full stop. ^{4}He tried to take a step, but the sharp pain in his knee made it impossible. ^{5}He had to sit helplessly on the curb while his wife ran back to their house to get the car. ^{6}At the doctor's office, Glen learned that a small piece of bone had broken off right above the kneecap. ^{7}The doctor said that over time, the punishing impact of running had cut off blood to the bone, making it weak. ^{8}Like many runners, Glen had to face surgery and give up running.

_____ **1.** The topic of this paragraph is
   a. exercising.   c. Glen's injury from running.
   b. Glen's knee surgery.   d. the pain Glen experienced.

_____ **2.** The supporting details include
   a. a list of reasons why people shouldn't run.
   b. one runner's story about a serious and painful injury.

_____ **3.** The implied main idea for this paragraph is
   a. running can cause a broken bone.
   b. running can have serious and painful effects.
   c. Glen's injury occurred over time.
   d. people should not run for exercise.

1. The topic of the paragraph is (c) "Glen's injury from running." Choice (a) is too broad; the paragraph focuses on a running injury and does not mention other kinds of exercise. Choice (b) is too specific because only one sentence deals with Glen's surgery. Choice (d) is too general because many sentences describe Glen's pain, but sentences 5, 6, and 7 do not mention pain.

2. The supporting details include (b) "one runner's story about a serious and painful injury."

3. The implied main idea for the paragraph is (b) "Running can have serious and painful effects." The last sentence (8) gives a good clue to the author's main point. "Like many runners" suggests that the author used Glen's story as an example of how serious and painful running injuries can be. Choice (a) is too specific in that a broken bone is only one kind of injury that runners may experience. Choice (c) is also too specific; it is a supporting detail. Choice (d) is too general because not all runners suffer serious and painful injuries.

Searching for an implied main idea is much like a treasure hunt. You must carefully read the clues provided by the author. This kind of careful reading is a skill that improves dramatically with practice. The following examples and practices are designed to strengthen this important skill.

Studying Supporting Details to Identify and State the Topic

A topic is a general subject to which specific details belong. Thus, specific details suggest a specific topic. You can study the details to determine the topic that the details develop.

Following is a list of specific details. Read the list. Then determine the topic that best covers all the specific details.

Specific details: brushes, chalk, pens, inks, paints

_____ The **topic** is
a. art.
b. art supplies.
c. painting supplies.

The topic of art includes many ideas that are not listed here. So (a) is too general. Item (c) is too specific, for it does not cover chalk, pens, and inks. Thus (b) is the correct choice, for all the specific details belong to the topic of art supplies. Look for the flow of ideas from general to specific. The flow of ideas will help you find the topic for a specific set of details. For example, study the following diagram. The diagram shows the flow from general to specific ideas.

art	art supplies	painting supplies	paint brushes
broad, general topic	more specific topic than "art"	more specific topic than "art supplies"	more specific topic than "painting supplies"

In the diagram, the topics become more and more specific. And each specific topic suggests a specific set of supporting details. The following diagram shows the flow of ideas. The diagram shows how ideas move from a general topic to a more specific topic, to a specific set of supporting details.

art	art supplies	painting supplies	paint brushes
drawing painting sculpting	brushes chalk pens inks paints	brushes paints	oil paint brushes watercolor brushes

Each topic generates a unique list of details. The topic "art supplies" is the only topic that matches this list of details: brushes, chalk, pens, inks, and paints. To identify topics suggested by specific details ask the following questions:

Is this topic *too specific?* Does it cover *all* the given details?

Is this topic *too general?* Does it suggest *more* details than the ones that are given?

Once you identify the topic based on a set of details, these questions will also help you state the topic. Following is a list of specific details. Study the details. Determine the topic based on the details. Then state the topic by filling in the blank with your own words.

Specific details: lightning strikes, tornadoes, hurricanes, floods, mudslides

Topic: _____

This list of details is a list of events that occur in nature. Wording may vary, but one possible way to state this topic is "acts of nature." You must be able to study a set of specific details and find your own accurate label for the topic.

EXAMPLES

A. Read the following lists of specific details. In the space provided, write the letter of the best topic for each list.

Specific details: Wendy's, Taco Bell, McDonald's, Burger King

_____ **1.** The **topic** is
  a. fast food.
  b. fast-food restaurants.
  c. fast-food restaurants that sell hamburgers.

Specific details: toothbrush, toothpaste, dental floss, mouthwash

_____ **2.** The **topic** is
  a. items for cleaning the teeth and mouth.
  b. items for brushing teeth.
  c. items for flossing teeth.

B. Read the following list of specific details. Then write a word or phrase that best states the topic. Remember: not too specific; not too general; find that perfect fit!

Specific details: printer, monitor, keyboard, mouse, processor

Topic: _____

EXPLANATIONS

A. **1.** Item (a) is too broad. "Fast food" covers specific details not listed. Item (c) is too narrow, for Taco Bell does not sell hamburgers. So (b) is correct. All the places listed are fast-food restaurants.

  2. Item (b) is too narrow. "Items for brushing teeth" does not include dental floss or mouthwash. Item (c) is also too narrow, because toothbrushes, toothpaste, and mouthwash are not used to floss teeth. So (a) is correct, for it includes all the items in the list.

B. Each of these objects is a specific part of a personal computer. Thus a personal computer is the topic suggested by the details.

PRACTICE 1

A. Read each group of specific details. In the space provided, write the letter of the best topic for each group.

Specific details: beds, a couch, easy chairs, a dining table, televisions

_____ **1.** The **topic** is
    a. furniture.
    b. furniture for a house.
    c. furniture for a living room.

Specific details: Georgia, Alabama, Mississippi

_____ **2.** The **topic** is
    a. geographical regions.
    b. states in the United States of America.
    c. southern states in the United States of America.

Specific details: pancakes, waffles, eggs, salad, roasted pork, green beans, carrot cake

_____ **3.** The **topic** is
    a. foods.
    b. foods found on a menu.
    c. foods found on a restaurant dinner menu.

Specific details: Mountain Dew, Coca-Cola, Pepsi, Dr Pepper

_____ **4.** The **topic** is
    a. drinks.
    b. soft drinks.
    c. soft drinks with caffeine.

Specific details: driving too slowly, tailgating, leaving a turn signal on for miles and miles, cutting in too close while changing lanes

_____ **5.** The **topic** is
    a. driving.
    b. driving habits.
    c. annoying driving habits.

B. Read each group of specific details. Then, in the space provided, using your own words, write the topic for the group. (Clues are given for Questions 1–5.)

1. **Topic:** types of _____ questions

   Specific details: multiple-choice, matching, fill-in-the-blank

2. **Topic:** recent _____ of the United States

   Specific details: Bill Clinton, George W. Bush, Barack Obama

3. **Topic:** items served at a _____ restaurant

   Specific details: shrimp, lobster, crab cakes, fried catfish, broiled trout

4. **Topic:** types of _____

   Specific details: sales, property, state, federal income

5. **Topic:** types of _____

   Specific details: love, hate, jealousy, anger, sorrow

Using Topics, Supporting Details, and Thought Patterns to Determine the Implied Main Idea

Remember that an implied topic is suggested by a set of specific details. Similarly, specific details given in a series of sentences suggest the **implied main idea**. The implied main idea cannot be so general that it suggests details not given; nor can it be so specific that some of the given details are not covered. Instead, the implied main idea must cover *all* the details given.

The skill of identifying a stated main idea will also help you grasp the implied main idea. You learned in Chapter 4 that the stated main idea (the topic sentence) has two parts. A main idea is made up of the topic and the author's controlling point about the topic. One trait of the controlling point is the author's opinion or bias. A second trait is the author's thought pattern, the way an author organizes ideas. Consider, for example, the topic sentence "Running can have serious and painful effects." The topic of this sentence is "running." The words "serious and painful" state the author's opinion (bias). And the word "effects" states the thought pattern. By using the word "effect," the author limits the details to those that explain or show results of running. So supporting details in a selection offer important clues about the implied main idea.

When you read material that implies the main idea, you should mentally create a topic sentence based on the types of details in the material.

EXAMPLE Read the following list of supporting details. Circle the topic as it recurs throughout the list of details. Underline transition words and biased words. Then choose the statement that best expresses the author's controlling point about the topic.

Typically, icebergs are ice made of freshwater that float in the sea.

Icebergs are classified by size and shape.

For example small icebergs are 3 feet by 16 feet.

Large icebergs can be over 240 feet by 670 feet.

Two common shapes for icebergs are the dome and wedge.

For ships, the most dangerous trait of an iceberg is that it floats very low in the water.

Most of an iceberg remains unseen below water.

_____ The **implied main idea** is
a. icebergs are dangerous.
b. icebergs vary in size and shape.
c. icebergs are formed on land but float in the sea.
d. icebergs have several distinct traits.

VISUAL VOCABULARY

Icebergs are created when large pieces **calve** from the front of a glacier when it reaches a water body.

The best meaning of the word

calve is _____.

a. gash.
b. split.
c. merge.

EXPLANATION The topic that recurs throughout the list is icebergs. Words that indicate the types of details include *typically*, *classified*, and *trait*. So the author provides details that describe the traits of icebergs such as *small, 3 feet by 16 feet, large, 240 feet by 670 feet, two common shapes, dome, wedge, most*

dangerous, *floats very low in the water*, and *most, unseen below water*. Thus the sentence that best states the implied main idea based on the topic, thought pattern, and details is (d) "Icebergs have several distinct traits." Choice (a) is too broad, and choices (b) and (c) are too narrow.

PRACTICE 2

Read each group of information. Circle the topic and underline words that reveal the author's bias and type of details. Then choose the best statement of the main idea. Share and explain your answers with a peer or small group of classmates.

Group 1

- Influenza (the flu) is a contagious respiratory illness.
- It spreads from person to person and can cause mild to severe illness.
- In some cases, the flu can cause death.
- The best way to prevent the flu is by getting a flu vaccination each year.

_____ The **implied main idea** is
   a. influenza can cause serious health problems.
   b. influenza can be prevented.
   c. a yearly vaccination can prevent influenza from causing serious health problems.

Group 2

- One step to take when you have the flu is to cover your nose and mouth with a tissue when you cough or sneeze.
- Always throw the flu-infected tissue in the trash after you use it.
- Another step is to wash your hands often with soap and water to keep them free from flu germs.
- Don't skip this step if soap and water are not available; instead use an alcohol-based hand rub.
- A key step is to avoid touching your eyes, nose, or mouth; flu viruses spread this way.
- Also, try to avoid close contact with people who are sick with the flu.
- A final step to take if you are sick with flu-like illness is to stay home for at least 24 hours after your fever is gone except to get medical care or for other necessities.

_____ The **implied main idea** is
   a. flu viruses are spread mainly from person to person through coughing or sneezing by people with influenza.
   b. take these everyday steps to help prevent the spread of germs that cause influenza.
   c. people who have the flu should stay home until they are free of fever.

Group 3

- One challenge faced by many campers is pitching a tent.
- Some campers find figuring out how to thread the poles through the canvas tent a challenging puzzle.
- And sinking the tent's stakes can be a test of strength.
- Another challenge while camping is keeping the food away from wildlife such as raccoons and bears.
- And at some camping locations, many find themselves in a contest against mosquitoes or other pesky bugs.
- Camping does offer fun activities such as swimming, hiking, and canoeing.
- For many, the most fun part of camping occurs around a roaring fire where everyone gathers in the evening and shares tall tales or scary stories.

_____ The **implied main idea** is
   a. camping is a challenging activity.
   b. camping can be a challenging yet fun experience.
   c. camping is not for everyone.

Group 4

Textbook
Skills

- At the intimacy stage of a relationship, you commit yourself deeply to the other person.
- One phase of intimacy is the interpersonal commitment phase.
- In this phase, you commit yourselves to each other in a kind of private way.
- The second phase is the social bonding phase.
- In this phase, the commitment is made public—perhaps to family and friends, or perhaps to the public at large through a formal marriage.
- In this phase of intimacy, the two of you become a unit, a pair.

—Adapted from DeVito, *Messages: Building Interpersonal Communication Skills,*
p. 264 © 1999. Reproduced by permission of Pearson Education, Inc.

_____ The **implied main idea** is

a. intimacy is a deep commitment by one person to another person.

b. intimacy can lead to marriage.

c. the intimacy stage of a relationship has two phases of commitment.

VISUAL VOCABULARY

One phase of intimacy is the interpersonal commitment phase.

The best synonym **interpersonal** is _____.

a. individual.

b. social.

c. group.

Annotating the Paragraph to Determine the Implied Main Idea

So far, you have found the implied main idea from the specific details in a group of sentences. In this next step, the sentences will form a paragraph, but the skill of determining the implied main idea is exactly the same. The implied main idea of a paragraph must not be too general or too specific. In the last section, you learned to annotate or mark ideas. You circled the topic and underlined words that revealed the author's thought pattern and bias. Annotating a paragraph in the same way is a helpful tool in determining its implied main idea.

EXAMPLE Read and annotate the following paragraph. Circle the topic and underline words that reveal thought patterns and bias. Then choose the best statement of the implied main idea.

¹Argus was a mythical giant guard with 100 eyes. ²According to the Greek myth, Argus was created by Hera, queen of the Greek gods, to keep her husband, Zeus, away from his mistress. ³It was difficult to slip past Argus's hundred eyes, but another god, Hermes, was able to lull Argus to sleep with music and then behead him. ⁴Myth has it that Hera

put Argus's eyes on the tail of a peacock. [5]Today, a highly watchful and prepared person can be described as "Argus-eyed."

_____ The **implied main idea** is
  a. Greek myths have had a powerful impact on our society.
  b. Argus was a tragic Greek character.
  c. the story of Argus is one example of current sayings that came from Greek myths.

EXPLANATION *Argus* is the obvious topic of this paragraph. However, several clues point to a more general topic. For example, the words *mythical, Greek myth*, and *myth* appear often enough to suggest that Greek myths are also part of the topic. In addition, sentence 5 suggests that the story of Argus, one of many Greek myths, has had an effect on us *today*. However, the first choice is too broad. There are many other ways in which Greek myths have affected our society. This paragraph just gives one specific way. The second choice is too narrow. Argus is just an example of the implied main idea. The correct answer is (c), for it includes the idea in sentence 5.

PRACTICE 3

Read and annotate the following paragraphs. Then choose the best statement of the implied main idea for each paragraph.

_____ **1.** [1]**Regenerative braking** is one energy-saving feature of a hybrid car. In a hybrid car, the electric motor applies resistance to the drive train. [2]This resistance slows down the wheels. [3]In return, the energy from the wheels turns the motor. [4]This energy-saving system is a source of energy. [5]Thus, the hybrid car takes energy usually wasted during coasting and braking. [6]This saved energy turns it into electricity. [7]This energy is stored in a battery until it is needed by the electric motor. [8]The **automatic start/shutoff** feature is another energy-saving feature of hybrid cars. [9]This feature automatically shuts off the engine when the vehicle comes to a stop. [10]The feature also restarts the hybrid when the accelerator is pressed. [11]This feature stops the waste of energy when a hybrid car idles, like at a stop light.

—Adapted from U. S. Dept. of Energy. "How Hybrids Work." *FuelEconomy.com*
25 Sept. 2009. http://www.fueleconomy.gov/feg/hybridtech.shtml.

a. Everyone should buy a hybrid car.
b. Hybrid cars have two energy-saving features.
c. Hybrid cars use wasted energy.

VISUAL VOCABULARY

A starfish regenerates its lost arm. Likewise, a hybrid car uses regenerative brakes to save energy.

The best synonym for

regenerative is _____ .

a. retaining.
b. renewing.

_____ 2.   [1]The members of today's gangs are younger and more active than gang members in the 1970s. [2]Gangs now rise up in wealthier and more suburban communities than they used to. [3]Gangs are more likely to include girls and people of different races. [4]The use of drugs and alcohol has increased in today's gangs, and so has violence. [5]In fact, many newer gangs show no regard for human life and cause senseless deaths. [6]Some make large amounts of money from prostitution and the sale of illegal drugs. [7]These new gangs use cell phones, beepers, automatic weapons, and guerrilla warfare tactics.

a. Gangs are violent.
b. Today, gangs rise up in wealthier and more suburban communities.
c. Today's gangs are different from gangs of the past.

Textbook
Skills

_____ 3.   [1]One aspect of self-concept is self-image. [2]*Self-image* is the sort of person you believe yourself to be. [3]It is made up of physical and attitudinal descriptions of the self and the roles you play. [4]Another aspect of self-concept is self-esteem. [5]*Self-esteem* is a measure of the value you place on the images you have of your-self. [6]It includes your attitudes and feelings about yourself. [7]It is your judgment of how you are doing in life compared to how you think you should be doing. [8]A number of social forces come together to help create and feed your self-concept.

—Adapted from Gamble & Gamble, *The Gender Communication Connection,* p. 44.

a. The self-concept is sometimes broken in two components: self-image and self-esteem.
b. Self-image is an important aspect of self-concept.
c. Self-concept is the result of many forces.

_____ **4.**   [1]Most Chinese immigrants entered California through the port of San Francisco. [2]They came by the thousands looking for better jobs and freedom from oppression. [3]Sadly, Chinese settlers faced bigotry immediately upon arrival in California. [4]In the 1850s, the United States reserved the right of citizenship for white immigrants to this country. [5]Thus, Chinese immigrants lived at the whim of local governments. [6]Some were allowed to be-come citizens, but most were not. [7]Without this right, they had difficulty earning a living. [8]For example, they were unable to own land or file mining claims. [9]Also in the 1850s, California passed a law taxing all foreign miners. [10]And in 1885, the citizens of Tucson, Arizona, created a petition to force Chinese to live in Chinatowns. [11]During this time, many Chinese chose to live in Chinatowns. [12]One Chinatown grew in the middle of San Francisco. [13]They called it *Dai Fou* or "Big City." [14]It remains one of the largest Chinatowns in the country.

—Adapted from "Topical Overview: Essays & Galleries: Chinese and Westward Expansion." Special presentation. *The Chinese in California, 1850-1925. American Memory.* Lib. of Congress. 28 March 2003. 12 July 2007. http://memory.loc.gov/ammem/award99/cubhtml/theme1.html.

a. Thousands of Chinese immigrated into San Francisco.
b. Chinese Americans fled China due to bigotry.
c. Chinese Americans faced many obstacles when they immi-grated to America during the nineteenth century.

Creating a Topic Sentence from Supporting Details

In this chapter so far, you have developed the skill of figuring out main ideas that are not directly stated. This ability to reason from specific details to main ideas will serve you well throughout college.

One further step will also prove helpful in your reading and studying: the ability to state the implied main idea in your own words. The statement you come up with must be a complete sentence. It must not be too specific, for it must cover all the details in the paragraph, and it must not be too general or go beyond the supporting details.

The one-sentence statement of the implied main idea is a one-sentence summary of all the details given in the paragraph, or a topic sentence. Your topic sentence should state the topic and the author's controlling point about the topic. Remember, the controlling point has two traits. First, the controlling point is made up of the author's opinion about the topic. Second, the controlling point often states the author's thought pattern. You have learned to annotate the topic, thought pattern, and biased details. Once you have marked these ideas in the paragraph, you can then blend them into a topic sentence using your own words.

EXAMPLE   Read and annotate the following paragraph. Circle the topic as it recurs throughout the paragraph. Underline words that reveal the author's thought pattern and bias. Use your own words to state the implied main idea.

> [1]According to government figures, over 16,000 gangs are active in this country, and at least half a million gang members commit more than 600,000 crimes each year. [2]Many members are young people who come from unhappy homes. [3]They feel neglected or are abused by their parents. [4]In addition, their parents may be gang members themselves. [5]Also, gang members often have a history of poor performance in school, and they have trouble making and keeping friends. [6]Sometimes they feel threatened by peers or the violence in their neighborhoods. [7]Others live in poor neighborhoods with few resources.

Implied main idea: _____

_____

EXPLANATION   To come up with the implied main idea, it is important to review all the supporting details. The first sentence points out that half a million young people join gangs and commit crimes. Sentences 2–6 give the reasons they join these gangs. You should have annotated the following words. The words *gangs, members,* and *gang members* should have been circled as the topic. The words *more,* *young, unhappy, neglected, abused, often, poor, trouble, threatened,* and *few* should have been underlined as biased words. The words *come from* signal the cause-and-effect thought pattern. The transitions *in addition, also, often,* and *sometimes* add to the list of reasons that young people join gangs. The following statement puts those ideas into one sentence: *Young people become gang members for many reasons.*

PRACTICE 4

Read the following paragraphs. Circle the topic as it recurs throughout the paragraph. Underline words that reveal the author's thought pattern and bias. Use your own words to state the implied main idea for each paragraph.

1.   [1]No one knows for sure how Valentine's Day came to be. [2]In ancient Rome, Juno, queen of the Roman gods and goddesses, was also the goddess of women and marriage. [3]February 14 was set aside as a holiday to honor Juno. [4]On the following day, February 15, the Feast of Lupercalia began. [5]It was customary to keep young boys and girls apart as they were growing up. [6]However, on the night before the festival of Lupercalia, the names of Roman girls were written on slips of paper and placed in jars. [7]Each young man would draw a girl's name from the jar; then for the rest of the festival, they would be partners. [8]Sometimes the couple would stay a pair for the year. [9]And often they fell in love and got married when they were grown.

Implied main idea: _____

2.   [1]A Doctor of Osteopathy (DO) is held to the same standards as a Doctor of Medicine (MD). [2]They both attend four years of medical school. [3]They both complete their training in residency programs. [4]Both a DO and MD take the same test to become board certified surgeons. [5]There are some differences in training and views between the two types of doctors. [6]A DO has been specially trained to perform osteopathic manipulations on patients. [7]Osteopathic Medical Treatment (OMT) uses the hands to treat the body—like what is done by chiropractors. [8]Unlike most medical doctors, a DO views the patient as a total person. [9]A DO focuses on preventive care. [10]A DO views the whole body rather than treat specific symptoms or illness. [11]For example, think of a patient who suffers from chronic headaches. [12]An MD will likely run a series of tests to find medical reasons for a headache. [13]In contrast, a DO may manipulate the neck to assess the patient.

Implied main idea: _____

_____

3.

[1]More than 2 million Native Americans live in the United States. [2]More than one-third live on reservations, on lands placed in trust for them, or in other areas set aside as Native American. [3]One of every three lives in poverty. [4]Sixteen percent of Native American homes do not have a telephone. [5]This number is alarming when compared to the fact that 6 percent of non–Native American homes do not have phones. [6]In some places, the state of affairs is much worse. [7]For example, on the Navaho Reservation, phone lines are available to less than 20 percent of the people; this means that 80 percent of the Navahos cannot have telephone service. [8]On reservations where phones are offered, the average person pays $100 for basic monthly service. [9]Calls off the reservation are billed as long distance. [10]Thus, an average phone bill can soar quickly past $200 a month.

—Adapted from Folkerts & Lacy, *The Media in Your Life: An Introduction to Mass Media*, 2nd ed., p. 288.

Implied main idea: _____

_____

4.

[1]One type of natural disaster is an earthquake. [2]Earthquakes strike suddenly and violently at any time of the day or night. [3]A second type of natural disaster is the wildfire. [4]Wildfires occur during dry conditions at various times of the year and in various parts of the United States. [5]A third type of natural disaster is a flood. [6]Floods are one of the most common hazards in the United States. [7]Some floods develop slowly, sometimes over a period of days. [8]Flash floods develop quickly. [9]Sometimes floods occur in just a few minutes and without any visible signs of rain. [10]A fourth type of natural disaster is the tornado. [11]Tornadoes are nature's most violent storms. [12]The FEMA website lists five other natural disasters for which we should be prepared.

Implied main idea: _____

_____

5.

[1]Speeding is a factor in almost one-third of all crashes involving young drivers. [2]For example, on his way to the beach, which was 90 miles from his house, Marcus averaged around 80 mph instead of the posted 65 mph speed limit. [3]When confronted with a car going the limit in front of him, Marcus hugged the car's bumper. [4]Often he passed other cars when he did not have the room to do so by flooring the gas pedal. [5]His girlfriend constantly asked

Textbook Skills

him to slow down and to stop tailgating. ⁶Marcus replied, "Don't worry; I know what I am doing." ⁷Suddenly, Marcus noticed the traffic in front of him had slowed significantly. ⁸He tried to brake, but the pressure of the brakes at high speed spun his car out of his lane and off the road.

Implied main idea: _____

_____

Textbook
Skills

Pictures as Details

Textbook authors often use pictures, drawings, or graphs to make the relationship between the main ideas and supporting details clear.

EXAMPLE Study the figure, and read the caption beside it. Put the main idea suggested by the details into a sentence.

Textbook
Skills

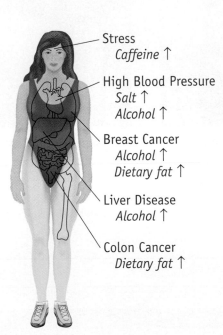

Stress
Caffeine ↑

High Blood Pressure
Salt ↑
Alcohol ↑

Breast Cancer
Alcohol ↑
Dietary fat ↑

Liver Disease
Alcohol ↑

Colon Cancer
Dietary fat ↑

◀ Possible health problems linked to poor diet habits. The upward arrow indicates excessive intake.

M. Williams, *Nutrition for Fitness and Sport* 4/e, © 1995. Reprinted by permission of The McGraw-Hill Companies, Inc.

Implied main idea: _____

_____

EXPLANATION   The figure clearly shows that taking in too much caffeine, salt, alcohol, and fat leads to stress, high blood pressure, breast cancer, liver disease, and colon cancer. Thus the implied main idea is "Poor eating habits can lead to serious health problems."

PRACTICE 5

Study the photographs, and read the caption. Put the main idea suggested by the details into a sentence.

▲ Which version of the picture do you find more attractive? If you are male, you probably find the one with the larger pupils (left) "more feminine," "soft," or "pretty," whereas the one with the small pupils (right) may appear "hard," "selfish," or "cold" (Hess, 1975).

—From Kosslyn & Rosenberg, *Psychology,* p. 95.

Implied main idea: _____

_____

APPLICATIONS

Application 1: Determine the Topic

Read each group of specific details. In the space provided, write the letter of the best topic for each group.

Specific details: osprey, eagles, falcons, vultures

_____ **1.** The **implied topic** is
   a. birds.   c. winged creatures.
   b. birds of prey.

Specific details: shells, driftwood, seaweed, sea turtles, sand

_____ **2.** The **implied topic** is
   a. nature.
   b. wildlife at the beach.
   c. nature at the beach.

Specific details: credit card, debit card, money order, check

_____ **3.** The **implied topic** is
   a. ways to spend money.
   b. money.
   c. ways to use credit to spend money.

Specific details: greenish black clouds, a loud roaring noise, whirling wind, flying debris

_____ **4.** The **implied topic** is
   a. dangerous weather.
   b. traits of a tornado.
   c. sounds of a tornado.

Application 2: Identify and State Topics

Read each group of specific details. Then use your own words to state the topic.

1. **Specific details:** canoe, kayak, sail boat, raft, barge, surfboard

   Topic: _____

2. **Specific details:** fruits, oils, cereal, protein, dairy

   Topic: _____

3. **Specific details:** Biology 101, Intro to Chemistry, Earth Science, Physics

   Topic: _____

4. **Specific details:** disgust, fear, anger, sadness, anxiety

   Topic: _____

Application 3: Study to Determine the Implied Main Idea

Read the following lists of information. Annotate the text using circles and underlines. Then choose the best statement of the implied main idea for each list.

_____ **1.** Some parents and politicians think that video games encourage violent behavior in young people.

For example, *Doom 3, Crime Life: Gang Wars*, and *Killer 7*, violent, shoot-'em-up games full of blood and gore, may make some young people more aggressive.

These games seem to send the message that violence is fun and does not have serious effects.

In addition, certain television shows have raised the same concerns.

During the first six seasons of *South Park,* one of the show's main characters was killed off in each episode, only to come back in the next episode.

   a. Video games lead to murder.
   b. Hollywood has a negative effect on young people.
   c. Violence in the media may have a negative effect on some young people.

Textbook
Skills

_____ **2.** Every year, nearly half a million Americans are newly diagnosed with skin cancer.

Skin cancer is mainly found in people who are most often exposed to the sun.

Ultraviolet rays from the sun often are the cause.

Repeated exposure to the sun has an increased effect.

—Nakamura, Health in America: A Multicultural Perspective, p. 189.

   a. Skin cancer is a growing problem.
   b. Exposure to the sun causes skin cancer.
   c. Everyone is in danger of getting skin cancer.

Application 4: Study to Determine the Implied Main Idea in a Paragraph

Read the following paragraphs. Annotate the text using circles and underlines. Then choose the best statement of the implied main idea for each paragraph.

Sunglasses

[1]Do you see sunglasses as an accessory or as a necessity? [2]Sunglasses protect you from the damage caused by the sun. [3]Sunglasses protect your eyes from two types of sun rays that reach the Earth's surface. [4]First, sunglasses protect you against UVA rays, which cause premature aging of the eyes. [5]Second, sunglasses also protect you against UVB rays, which cause snow blindness, cataracts, and eye cancer. [6]You should wear sunglasses year round and even on cloudy days because UV rays are always present. [7]Not all sunglasses protect your eyes. [8]For example, many designer sunglasses may look good, but they don't block out damaging sun rays.

_____ **1.** The best statement of the **implied main idea** of the paragraph is
   a. sunglasses protect your eyes against sun damage.
   b. choose and wear sunglasses that protect your eyes from the sun.
   c. two types of sun rays damage your eyes.

Why Use YouTube

[1]YouTube is an online site. [2]YouTube connects you to the public. [3]On YouTube you can post or view a video. [4]One reason to use YouTube is to sell a product. [5]For example, a local gym can post videos that show workouts and success stories of their members. [6]A famous example of YouTube's power to reach an audience is Susan Boyle's success. [7]The YouTube video of Susan Boyle on _Britain's Got Talent_ was viewed by millions of people within days of being posted. [8]And now she is a best-selling artist with fans around the world. [9]Another reason to use YouTube is to learn more about a topic. [10]Thousands of video lessons have been posted by experts, teachers, colleges, and organizations. [11]Three final reasons to use YouTube are because it's easy, free, and fun.

_____ **2.** The best statement of the implied main idea of the paragraph is
   a. YouTube is a popular online site.
   b. YouTube offers videos for business and education.
   c. you should use YouTube for several reasons.

Application 5: Create Topic Sentences

Read the following paragraphs. Annotate the text. Use your own words to state the implied main idea in a topic sentence for each paragraph.

Going Public

[1] By law, people who want to make their private lives public have every right to do so. [2] However, it is illegal to videotape or record another person's image without that person's consent. [3] A camera hidden by a landlord for the purpose of taping the tenant's private life is illegal. [4] Recording is a crime if its purpose is sexual arousal. [5] In these cases, the crime could be a misdemeanor, and the guilty party could be fined as much as $2,000 in some states. [6] If, however, the recording is distributed to others without the agreement of the subject, the crime becomes a felony. [7] The guilty party could serve up to five years in jail and be fined up to $5,000.

1. Write a topic sentence that states the **implied main idea** for the paragraph:

_____

Cramming

[1] Like many high school students, 16-year-old Sandy pulled a "late-nighter." [2] As usual, she had not studied ahead of time for her history midterm, scheduled for first period the next day. [3] So she stayed up cramming and listening to music until 3 A.M. [4] She had gotten no more than two hours' sleep when her alarm rang. [5] During the exam, she was so tired that she became confused and forgot most of what she had studied the night before. [6] Like many of her peers who pull late-night cram sessions, Sandy failed her exam.

2. Write a topic sentence that states the **implied main idea** for the paragraph:

_____

REVIEW TEST 1   Score (number correct) _____ × 20 = _____ %

Determining Topics from Specific Details

A. Read each group of specific details. In the space provided, write the letter of the best topic for each group.

Specific Details: first-born, middle-born, last-born, only child

_____   **1.** The **topic** is

    a. family.

    b. siblings.

    c. birth order.

Specific Details: 3-day water supply; 3-day non-perishable food supply; first-aid kit; battery-powered radio; flashlight, batteries, cash

_____   **2.** The **topic** is

    a. items for the kitchen.

    b. items for an emergency.

    c. items to give to charity.

Specific Details: Tylenol, Bayer Aspirin, Aleve, Advil, Motrin

_____   **3.** The **topic** is

    a. over-the-counter pain relievers.

    b. pain relievers.

    c. medicine for headaches.

B. Read the following lists of information. In space provided, write the best statement of the implied main idea for each list. (Hint: Annotate the text.)

List A

- Dogs were used in World War I to kill rats in the trenches.
- 10,000 dogs were used in World War II to act as sentries, scouts, messengers, and mine detectors.
- Hundreds of dogs serve with U. S. forces in Afghanistan and Iraq as patrol dogs and explosive and drug detectors.
- One soldier who served in Vietnam tells the story about how a dog saved his life.
- The K-9 unit alerted the soldiers about an ambush they were about to walk into while they were on patrol.
- The dogs saved all their lives.

_____   **4.** The **implied main idea** for this list is

    a. dogs are brave and loyal.

    b. dogs save lives.

    c. dogs have served the United States in major wars.

The **implied main idea** for this list is

a. people struggle to fit in.
b. most students in public schools likely belonged to one of three peer groups.
c. in most public schools, the group of kids who could be called the "rulers" occupied the top of the social ladder.

_____ **10.** Signs of pauses and uneven pressure in handwriting may be the result of pain.

The handwriting of stroke victims is often weak and slants downward.

Downward slopes in handwriting may also indicate depression.

Upward slopes in handwriting may show hopefulness.

The **implied main idea** for this list is

a. physical problems and mental states may be revealed by handwriting.
b. handwriting reveals emotions.
c. handwriting provides interesting information.

REVIEW TEST 3

Score (number correct) _____ × 25 = _____ %

Determining Implied Main Ideas

Read the following passage from "The American I," by the critically acclaimed author Richard Rodriquez. Answer the questions that follow.

[1]I am the observer.
[2]Every American comes upon the "I," awakens to it. [3]The prow of the ship. [4]The top of the tree. [5]The hilt of the sword. [6]The animate eye. [7]The quick. [8]The reader of the card pertaining to the sword. [9]Very interesting, but now I need to go to the bathroom. [10]The American I. [11]As in, *I believe, I take Jesus Christ as my personal savior.* [12]*I am sorry for the earthquake victims.*[13]*I will have tuna on rye.* [14]*I love you.* [15]The I does not impose solitude, though it is lonely; the I is alive. [16]The I may be an instrument of connection, but even as such it is an assertion of will. [17]I have my rights.
[18]As so often happens in America, the I attached to me at school:
[19]You!
[20]Who? [21]I was no longer my brother's brother, my sister's brother, my mother's son, my father's son, my backyard's potentate. [22]I was alone.
[23]I...I had to go to the bathroom, what should I do?

^{24}Go to college, become a man different from your father. ^{25}It's up to you. ^{26}Don't go to college, become a man different from your father.

^{27}The American I is as old as the Boston Tea Party, as old as the document of Constitution: "We the People..."

^{28}We? But I am a royalist. ^{29}As the son of immigrants, I do not remember America seeming like a choice, though Americans were always and everywhere talking about choices.

^{30}They talked about black beans or refried. ^{31}Presbyterian or Methodist. ^{32}Ford or Chevrolet. ^{33}Cinema One or Cinema Two. ^{34}Gay or straight. ^{35}CBS or NBC. ^{36}Paper or plastic. ^{37}Diet or regular. ^{38}Regular or decaf. ^{39}Plain or buttered. ^{40}White or whole wheat or sourdough or English muffin. ^{41}Every lighted window, every court, every slug of type, every knuckle of America strained to accomplish my assertion: I am innocent.

^{42}I may be unwise, I may be mistaken, I may be guilty. ^{43}But the essence of the American I is that I am irreducible.

^{44}I can be punished for my crime, in other words. ^{45}Isn't that odd? ^{46}My body can bear the weight of punishment for a crime weighed in the apprehension of others who did not see, who do not know what I know.

^{47}Americans are so individualistic, they do not realize their individualism is a communally derived value. ^{48}The American I is deconstructed for me by Paolo, an architect who was raised in Bologna: "You Americans are not truly individualistic, you merely are lonely. ^{49}In order to be individualistic, one must have a strong sense of oneself within a group." ^{50}(The "we" is a precondition for saying "I.") ^{51}Americans spend all their lives looking for a community: a chatroom, a church, a support group, a fetish magazine, a book club, a class-action suit.

^{52}But illusions become real when we think they are real and act accordingly. ^{53}Because Americans thought themselves free of plural pronouns, they began to act as free agents, thus to recreate history. ^{54}Individuals drifted away from tribe or color or 'hood or hometown or card of explanation, where everyone knew who they were. ^{55}That's Victoria and Leo's son, isn't it? ^{56}Americans thus extended the American community by acting so individualistically, so anonymously.

—"Peter's Avocado," from *Brown: The Last Discovery of America* by Richard Rodriguez, copyright © 2002 by Richard Rodriguez. Used by permission of Viking Penguin, a division of Penguin Group (USA) Inc.

_____ **1.** What is the topic of the passage?
   a. Richard Rodriquez   c. American individuality
   b. America   d. American immigrants

_____ **2.** What is the implied main idea of the sixth paragraph (sentences 24–26)?

    a. People want to grow up to be like their parents.

    b. People should grow up to be different than their parents.

    c. Parents influence their children.

    d. We all become like our parents no matter what we do.

_____ **3.** Which sentence best states the main idea of paragraph 12 (sentences 47–51)?

    a. sentence 47

    b. sentence 48

    c. sentence 49

    d. sentence 50

_____ **4.** The implied main idea of the passage is

    a. Americans hold a false belief in individualism.

    b. American individualism is to be admired.

    c. Americans are lonely.

    d. American individualism has destroyed American families and communities.

VISUAL VOCABULARY

Workers deconstruct the Berlin Wall. The best meaning of the word **deconstruct** is

_____.

    a. build.

    b. demolish.

    c. examine.

WHAT DO YOU THINK?

Do you think Americans are too focused on personal values and goals? Do you think Americans have a strong sense of community? How does American culture encourage a person to become a strong individual? How does American culture encourage a strong sense of community? Assume you are writing an essay for a contest sponsored by a local civic group, and the author of the winning essay will receive a $100 prize. In your essay, explain the link between an American individual and the American community.

REVIEW TEST 4

Score (number correct) _____ × 20 = _____ %

Implied Main Ideas

Before you read, skim the passage and answer the Before Reading questions. Read the essay. Then answer the After Reading questions.

Textbook
Skills

Power Plays

[1]Power plays are patterns of communication that take unfair advantage of another person. [2]Power plays aim to rob us of our right to make our own choices. [3]Power plays bully through **intimidation** and call for specific responses.

[4]For example, in the power play *Nobody Upstairs,* another person will not recognize your request, no matter how or how many times you make it. [5]One common form of this power play is the refusal to take no for an answer. [6]Sometimes *Nobody Upstairs* takes the form of pleading ignorance of unspoken rules. [7]These common rules include knocking when you enter someone's room or asking permission before opening another person's mail or wallet. [8]This person says, "I didn't know you didn't want me to look in your wallet" or "Do you want me to knock the next time I come into your room?"

[9]Another power play is *You Owe Me*. [10]Here others do something for you and then demand something in return. [11]They remind you of what they did for you and use this to get you to do what they want. [12]In the *You've Got to Be Kidding* power play, one person attacks the other by saying "you've got to be kidding" or some similar phrase: "You can't be serious," "You can't mean that," "You didn't say what I thought you said, did you?" [13]The purpose here is to show utter disbelief in the other's statement. [14]This disbelief is supposed to make the statement and the person seem stupid.

[15]These power plays are just examples. [16]There are, of course, many others that you've no doubt encountered on occasion. [17]What do you do when you see such a power play? [18]One common response is to

ignore the power play and allow the other person to take control. [19]Another response is to treat the power play as just one incident and object to it. [20]For example, you might say, "Please don't come into my room without knocking first" or "Please don't look in my wallet without asking me first."

[21]In a **cooperative** response, you state your feelings, describe the behavior that you don't like, and state a response you both can live with. [22]A cooperative response to *Nobody Upstairs* might go something like this: "I'm angry [statement of feelings] that you keep opening my mail. [23]You have opened my mail four times this past week alone [description of behavior]. [24]I want you to allow me to open my own mail. [25]If there is anything in it that concerns you, I will let you know" [statement of cooperative response].

—DeVito, *Messages: Building Interpersonal Communication Skills*, pp. 333-334
© 1999. Reproduced by permission of Pearson Education, Inc.

Before Reading

Vocabulary in Context

_____   **1.** The word **intimidation** in sentence 3 means
    a. lies.   c. threats.
    b. anger.   d. love.

_____   **2.** The word **cooperative** in sentence 21 means
    a. one-sided.   c. caring.
    b. for shared benefit.   d. angry.

After Reading

Central Idea and Main Idea

_____   **3.** What is the central idea of the passage?
    a. sentence 1   c. sentence 3
    b. sentence 2   d. sentence 15

Implied Main Idea

_____   **4.** What is the best statement of the implied main idea for the second paragraph (sentences 4–8)?
    a. Walking into someone's room without asking is unfair.

b. Someone playing *Nobody Upstairs* will not take no for an answer.

c. One type of power play is called *Nobody Upstairs*.

d. A person playing *Nobody Upstairs* pleads ignorance of unspoken rules.

_____ **5.** What is the best statement of the implied main idea for the third paragraph (sentences 9–14)?

a. *You Owe Me* and *You've Got to Be Kidding* are two additional examples of power plays.

b. In *You Owe Me*, a person demands something in return for a favor.

c. A person playing *You've Got to Be Kidding* tries to make the other person seem stupid.

d. Power plays attack other people.

WHAT DO YOU THINK?

Do you or someone you know use power plays? Why do you think people resort to power plays? Assume you are writing a report for a college psychology class. Write a short essay that explains why people use power plays and why power plays are so effective. Also discuss how to best respond to specific power plays.

 ## After Reading About Implied Main Ideas

Before you move on to the Mastery Tests on implied main ideas, take time to reflect on your learning and performance by answering the following questions. Write your answers in your notebook.

- How has my knowledge base or prior knowledge about implied main ideas changed?

- Based on my studies, how do I think I will perform on the Mastery Test(s)? Why do I think my scores will be above average, average, or below average?

- Would I recommend this chapter to other students who want to learn more about implied main ideas? Why or why not?

Test your understanding of what you have learned about Implied Main Ideas by completing the Chapter 6 Review Card on the insert near the end of the text.

CONNECT TO **myreadinglab**

To check your progress in meeting Chapter 6's learning outcomes, log in to **www.myreadinglab.com**, and try the following activities.

■ The "Main Idea" section of MyReadingLab provides review materials, practice activities, and tests about topics and main ideas. To access this resource, click on the "Study Plan" tab. Then click on "Main Idea." Then click on the following links as needed: "Overview," "Model," "Practice," and "Tests."

■ To measure your mastery of the content in this chapter, complete the tests in the "Main Ideas" section and click on Gradebook to find your results.

A. Read each group of specific details. Then choose the best topic for each group.

Specific details: crossword puzzles, dictionary, thesaurus, Scrabble

_____ **1.** The **topic** is
   a. games.
   b. reference tools.
   c. resources to build word skills.

Specific details: Honda Civic, Nissan Altima, Toyota Prius, Dodge Charger, Chevrolet Equinox

_____ **2.** The **topic** is
   a. names of cars.
   b. names of wildlife.
   c. names of trucks.

B. Read the following lists of information. Then choose the best statement of the implied main idea for each list.

_____ **3.** Comfortable chairs make it easy to linger over coffee and dessert.
   Good food is presented with elegance.
   Fresh flowers on the table add a special touch.
   Linen tablecloths and napkins, soft lighting, and excellent service round out the fine dining experience.

   The **implied main idea** for this list is
   a. atmosphere and good food are important in fine dining.
   b. places of fine dining use cloth table linens.
   c. fine dining is fun.

_____ **4.** Hypnosis is often used to help hard-core smokers kick their habit.
   Nicotine chewing gum also helps many people quit smoking.
   A number of smokers have found relief in nicotine patches.
   Good old-fashioned willpower is often needed.

   The **implied main idea** for this list is
   a. giving up smoking is hard for many people.
   b. smoking becomes a habit because of a lack of willpower.
   c. several methods can help smokers quit smoking.

C. Read the following paragraph. Then choose the best statement of its implied main idea.

_____ **5.** ¹Basketball is fast-paced and requires the body to run, turn, twist, pass, jump, aim, and shoot, all at high speeds and for long periods of time. ²Football is a slower-moving game and brings together a team of players who have specialized skills. ³Each type of player requires a different kind of physical skill. ⁴Quarterbacks must be able to aim, throw, run short distances, and fall without getting hurt. ⁵Centers must be able to hand off the ball, block, and tackle. ⁶Running backs must be able to run, jump, catch, and fall without getting hurt. ⁷Golf moves slowly and requires the ability to concentrate, aim, swing, putt, and walk.

The **implied main idea** for the paragraph is

a. different sports move at different paces and require different sets of skills.

b. football is more complicated than other sports.

c. people who participate in sports have amazing athletic abilities.

Name _____ Section _____

Date _____ **Score** (number correct) _____ × 10 = _____%

A. Read each group of specific details. Then use your own words to state the topic of each group.

1. **Specific details:** toothpaste, deodorant, toothbrush, floss, shampoo, fingernail clippers, makeup

   Topic: _____

2. **Specific details:** spatulas, wooden spoons, knives, measuring cups, measuring spoons

   Topic: _____

3. **Specific details:** Jenny Craig, Weight Watchers, the Atkins Plan

   Topic: _____

4. **Specific details:** Congressional, Presidential, and Judicial

   Topic: _____

5. **Specific details:** New Year's Day, Christmas, Thanksgiving, President's Day, Independence Day, Labor Day

   Topic: _____

6. **Specific details:** stock car racing, drag racing, sports car racing, off-road racing

   Topic: _____

7. **Specific details:** Buffalo Bills, Pittsburg Steelers, Houston Texans, Denver Broncos, Dallas Cowboys, Seattle Seahawks

   Topic: _____

8. **Specific details:** Serena Williams, Roger Federer, Deion Sanders, Kobe Bryant, Danica Patrick

   Topic: _____

B. Read the following paragraphs. Then choose the best statement of the implied main idea for each paragraph.

_____ 9.

Yesterday's Homemaking

¹Many of our great-grandmothers learned to cook on a woodstove and draw water out of a well. ²To fix a meal, many had to kill the chicken or clean the fish. ³They also had to pick the vegetables from the family garden. ⁴Women worked hard in the hot months canning food for the winter months. ⁵Without running water, laundry and bathing called for heating water on the woodstove or over open fires. ⁶Large families were common, and laundry was done on washboards or with wringer washers. ⁷Ironing clothes meant heating a heavy wedge of iron with an attached handle on the woodstove or in the fireplace.

The **implied main idea** for the paragraph is
a. homemaking tasks at one time demanded much physical labor.
b. homemaking led to early death for women.
c. homemaking meant tending the family's livestock.

Wind and Waves

Textbook
Skills

¹The drag caused by the friction of the wind on the surface of smooth water ripples the water. ²As the wind continues to blow, it applies more pressure to the steep side of the ripple, and wave size begins to grow. ³As the wind becomes stronger, short, choppy waves of all sizes appear; and as these waves absorb more energy, they continue to grow. ⁴When the waves reach a point at which the energy supplied by the wind is equal to the energy lost by breaking waves, they become whitecaps. ⁵Up to a certain point, the stronger the wind, the higher the waves.

—Smith & Smith, _Elements of Ecology_, 4th ed., p. 489.

_____ **10.** The **implied main idea** for the paragraph is
a. a strong wind means high waves.
b. wind creates waves.
c. wind creates friction.

A. Read each group of specific details. Use your own words to state the topic for each group.

Textbook Skills

1. **Specific details:** toast, eggs, jelly, hash browns, pancakes, cereal

   Topic: _____

2. **Specific details:** moss, birds, squirrels, bark, leaves

   Topic: _____

3. **Specific details:** north, south, east, west

   Topic: _____

B. Read the following paragraphs. Using your own words, write a one-sentence summary that states the implied main idea for each paragraph.

4.

Textbook Skills

Seventeen Readers

[1]*Seventeen* magazine caters to teenage females. [2]Every few years, the magazine's audience "ages out," and *Seventeen* has to find new readers. [3]The magazine does not target a set of specific women, but rather an age group. [4]And the wants and needs of this age group are always changing. [5]Since readers change, so do the topics that grab their interest. [6]Today's *Seventeen* includes stories that were not considered interesting or proper 10 or 20 years ago. [7]Chances are that gun violence in the schools and beepers for staying in touch would not have concerned an editor in the 1970s or 1980s. [8]Even if your older sister or aunt read *Seventeen* when she was a high school student, she most likely read a very different magazine than teenagers read today.

—Adapted from Folkerts & Lacy, *The Media in Your Life: An Introduction to Mass Media*, 2nd ed., pp. 132–133.

Implied main idea: _____

_____

Textbook
Skills

5.

Layers of the Rain Forest

[1]The uppermost layer of a tropical rain forest is made up of emergent trees. [2]These trees are over 40 to 80 meters and have deep crowns that billow above the rest of the forest. [3]Their canopy is uneven. [4]The second layer is made up of mop-crowned trees, and their canopy is also uneven. [5]It is hard to tell these two layers apart from each other and together they form one unbroken canopy. [6]The third level of a tropical rain forest is the lowest level of trees. [7]These trees have conelike crowns, and their canopy is unbroken, deep, and well defined. [8]The fourth layer, usually poorly developed in deep shade, is made up of shrubs, young trees, tall herbs, and ferns. [9]The fifth level is the ground layer of tree seedlings and low-growing plants and ferns.

—Adapted from Smith & Smith, *Elements of Ecology*,
4th ed., pp. 444–445.

VISUAL VOCABULARY

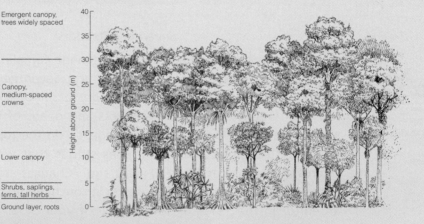

Figure 31.3 Vertical stratification of a tropical rain forest.

▲ Vertical Stratification of a Tropical Rain Forest

Source: Smith & Smith, *Elements of Ecology*, 4th ed. Update. Benjamin Cummings, 2000, p. 444. Reprinted by permission of Pearson Education, Inc., Glenview, IL.

Implied main idea: _____

The fifth and lowest level of a rain forest is the _____.

    a. ground layer.
    b. shrubs and saplings.

Name _____ Section _____

Date _____ Score (number correct) _____ × 20 = _____%

A. Read the following paragraphs. Then choose the best statement of the implied main idea for each paragraph. (Hint: Annotate the text.)

_____ **1.**   [1]Andrea was frustrated. [2]When she arrived at work, her phone was blinking with three messages from unhappy customers. [3]At midmorning, she discovered that the assistant store manager had not completed an order in time for the big sale that was to begin the next day. [4]Then the home office called to announce a surprise audit and demanded a monthly sales report by the end of the day. [5]The last blow came when two key workers on the afternoon shift called in sick. [6]Andrea's head throbbed. [7]She felt like screaming at someone or hitting something. [8]So she left work three hours early.

The **implied main idea** for the paragraph is
a. all managers face stress.
b. Andrea walked off the job.
c. high work stress can lead to worker absenteeism.

_____ **2.**   [1]Steven drove around aimlessly trying to gain control of his anger. [2]He noticed the entrance to River End Park, and he pulled in. [3]He parked under a tree facing the Tomoka River and rolled down his car windows. [4]A gentle breeze brought the smell of water and freshly mowed grass into the car. [5]A few thin, white clouds slowly moved across a deep blue sky. [6]The sun glistened on the water's surface. [7]The soft sounds of small waves lapping against the pier drifted into range. [8]Slowly, he began to relax. [9]An osprey flew low above the water in search of a catch. [10]The sound of a small boat puttered in the distance. [11]Steven breathed deeply and lingered by the river for a little while. [12]Finally, he felt ready to go back home and make up with his wife.

The **implied main idea** for the paragraph is
a. driving is good for stress.
b. nature has a positive impact on Steven's emotions.
c. anger can be controlled only by noticing nature.

B. Read the following paragraphs. Using your own words, write a topic sentence that states the implied main idea for each paragraph. (Hint: Annotate the text.)

3.   [1]Many men are choosing to stay home and let their wives support the family. [2]According to government records, the number of men working or looking for work fell to a record low in the early part of 2002. [3]The number of men who now choose not to work may be as high as one in ten. [4]One reason may be because of the growing success of women in the workforce. [5]Second, men are leaving the workforce because companies are eliminating their jobs. [6]Finally, technology has replaced many of the hard-labor jobs. [7]Jobs that call for strength and muscle no longer exist in the numbers that they once did.

The **implied main idea** for the paragraph is

_____

4.   [1]They were the kids who just didn't fit in. [2]Perhaps they looked or dressed in an offbeat or creative fashion. [3]Sometimes physical traits, such as severe acne or obesity, marked them as undesirable. [4]Too often, gifted youngsters who loved to study and learn found themselves at odds with most of their peers. [5]Interestingly, not fitting in is most often a short-term problem. [6]Multimillionaire computer wizard Bill Gates is a good example. [7]In a graduation speech he once gave, he said, "Be nice to the geeks; they will be your boss one day."

The **implied main idea** for the paragraph is

_____

_____ 5.   [1]A local youth baseball, football, or soccer league may charge as much as $50 for registration and a shirt. [2]Shoes, gloves, and protective gear can run as high as $150. [3]In addition, parents are often expected to bring refreshments once or twice during the season, which can add an extra $40 in expenses. [4]Then there is the cost of transportation. [5]The total cost can run over $200, and that is just for one child. [6]Some parents simply cannot afford the cost.

The **implied main idea** for the paragraph is

_____

Supporting Details

7

LEARNING OUTCOMES

After studying this chapter you should be able to do the following:

1. Define the terms *major supporting details, minor supporting details,* and *summary.*
2. Create questions to locate supporting details.
3. Distinguish between major and minor supporting details.
4. Complete a simple chart that outlines the topic, main idea, and supporting details of a passage.
5. Create a summary of a passage.
6. Evaluate the importance of supporting details.
7. Apply the use of supporting details to improve comprehension.

Before Reading About Supporting Details

In Chapters 4, 5, and 6, you learned several important ideas that will help you as you work through this chapter. Use the following questions to call up your prior knowledge about supporting details.

What is a main idea? (Refer to page 129.) _____

_____

_____.

What are the three parts of most paragraphs? (Refer to page 133.) _____,

_____, and _____

Define supporting details: (Refer to page 133.) _____

_____.

What are the different locations of topic sentences? (Refer to page 162.) ____

_____

_____

What is a central idea? (Refer to page 172.) _____

_____ .

Questions for Locating Supporting Details

Look at the following main idea:

Main idea: Laughter speeds recovery from an illness and lengthens the life span.

This main idea raises two major questions: "How does laughter speed recovery?" and "How does laughter lengthen the life span?" Supporting details answer these questions, for the role of supporting details is to explain a main idea.

Supporting details hold up a main idea by giving reasons, examples, steps, evidence, or any other kind of needed information.

> **Supporting details** explain, develop, and illustrate the main idea.

To identify supporting details, a skilled reader turns the main idea into a question. This question asks one of the reporter's questions: *Who, What, When, Where, Why,* or *How.* Supporting details answer the question, and the answer will yield a specific set of supporting details. For example, the question *why* is often answered by listing and explaining reasons or causes. The question *how* is answered by explaining a process. The answer to the question *when* is based on time order. An author strives to answer some or all of these questions with the details in the paragraph. You may want to try out several of the reporter's questions as you turn the main idea into a question. Experiment to discover which question is best answered by the details.

Take the topic "the value of hard work." An author might choose to write about the people who have taught her the value of hard work. The main idea of such a paragraph might read as follows:

Main idea: Other people have taught me the value of hard work.

Using the word *who* turns the main idea into the following question: "Who has taught her the value of hard work?" Read the following paragraph for the details that directly answer this question.

The Value of Hard Work

¹Other people have taught me the value of hard work. ²First, my grandmother taught me the joy of hard work by her example. ³The mother of a farming family of nine children, she lovingly grew the vegetables, harvested

the crops, and cooked three meals a day. [4]Her recipes for food and love still feed the family legacy. [5]Next, my sister taught me the importance of hard work by coaching me through high school. [6]When I wanted to goof off and ignore my studies, she coaxed me to study with her. [7]When I came across a discouraging problem, she helped me understand and praised my effort. [8]Finally, my first boss taught me the rewards of hard work. [9]He noticed my efforts by giving me a raise and offering me a college scholarship. [10]He said my willingness to work hard would take me far in life.

The supporting details for this main idea answer the question "who?" by listing three people who taught the author the value of hard work. Then the paragraph discusses what each person taught her. A simple outline chart shows the relationship between the main idea and its supporting details.

Topic: The Value of Hard Work

Main idea: Other people have taught me the value of hard work.
Question based on main idea:
        Who has taught her the value of hard work?

Supporting detail:
        1. Grandmother taught the joy of hard work.
Supporting detail:
        2. Sister taught the importance of hard work.
Supporting detail:
        3. First boss taught the rewards of hard work.

EXAMPLE Read the following paragraph. Turn the main idea into a question. Then finish the simple outline that follows with a few words that state three details that directly answer the question based on the main idea. The first detail has been filled in for you.

How to Communicate Equality

Textbook
Skills

[1]In communication, the term *equality* refers to an attitude or approach. [2]Equality treats each person as an important and vital part of the process. [3]The following four suggestions will help you express equality in any situation. [4]First, avoid "should" and "ought" statements. [5]Two examples are "You really ought to call your mother more often" or "You should learn to speak up." [6]These statements put the listener down. [7]Second, make requests (be polite) and avoid

demands (don't be rude). ^{8}Third, avoid interrupting. ^{9}This signals an unequal relationship. ^{10}It also implies that what you have to say is more important than what the other person is saying. ^{11}Finally, acknowledge the other person's view before stating your own. ^{12}Say "I see," "I understand," or "That's right." ^{13}These statements let the other person know you're listening and understanding.

—Adapted from DeVito, *The Interpersonal Communication Book,* p. 291 © 2007 by Pearson Education, Inc. Reproduced by permission of Pearson Education, Inc.

Topic: How to Communicate Equality

Main idea: The following four suggestions will help you express equality in any situation.

Question based on main idea:
What are the four suggestions that will help me express equality in any situation?

Supporting details:
1. Avoid "should" and "ought" statements.
2. _____
3. _____
4. _____

EXPLANATION   Four supporting details directly answer the question about the main idea. Thus the simple outline chart should look as follows.

Topic: How to Communicate Equality

Main idea: The following four suggestions will help you express equality in any situation.

Question based on main idea:
What are the four suggestions that will help me express equality in any situation?

Supporting details:
1. Avoid "should" and "ought" statements.
2. Make requests and avoid demands.
3. Avoid interrupting.
4. Acknowledge the other person's view.

PRACTICE 1

Read the following paragraph. Turn the main idea into a question. Then use a few words to state two details that directly support the main idea.

Volcanic Hazards

Textbook Skills

[1]Volcanoes pose a wide variety of hazards. [2]These hazards can kill people and wildlife, as well as, destroy property. [3]Perhaps the greatest threats to life are pyroclastic flows. [4]These hot mixtures of gas, ash, and pumice sometimes exceed 1500^0F. [5]The speeds of these flows down the flanks of volcanoes give people little chance of surviving. [6]The next most dangerous volcanic hazard may be Lahars. [7]Lahars can occur even when a volcano is not erupting. [8]These mud flows of volcanic debris and water can race down a valley at speeds that may exceed 62 miles per hour. [9]Other obvious hazards include explosive eruptions. [10]Such eruptions put in danger people and property at great distances from a volcano. [11]During the past 15 years, at least 80 commercial jets have been damaged by unknowingly flying into clouds of volcanic ash.

—Adapted from Lutgens & Tarbuck, *Foundations of Earth Science*, 5th ed., p. 218.

Topic: Volcanic Hazards

Main idea: Volcanoes pose a wide variety of hazards.
Question based on main idea:
_____

Supporting details:
1. _____
   _____

2. _____
   _____

3. _____
   _____

Major and Minor Details

A supporting detail will always be one of two types:

A **major detail** explains, develops, or supports the *main idea*.
A **minor detail** explains, develops, or supports a *major detail*.

A **major detail** is directly tied to the main idea. Without the major details, the author's main idea would not be clear.

In contrast, a **minor detail** explains the major detail. The minor details could be left out, and the main idea would still be clear. Thus minor details are not as important as major details. Most often, minor details are used to add interest. To better understand the flow of ideas, study the chart:

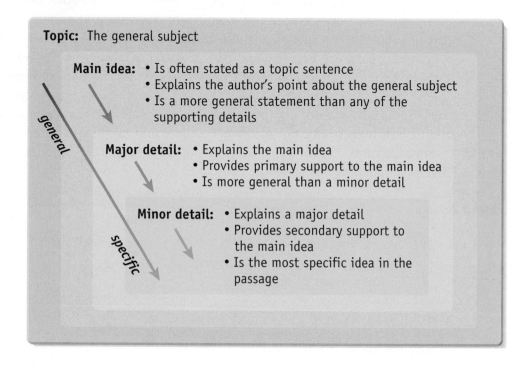

Topic: The general subject

Main idea:
- Is often stated as a topic sentence
- Explains the author's point about the general subject
- Is a more general statement than any of the supporting details

general

Major detail:
- Explains the main idea
- Provides primary support to the main idea
- Is more general than a minor detail

Minor detail:
- Explains a major detail
- Provides secondary support to the main idea
- Is the most specific idea in the passage

specific

EXAMPLE See if you can tell the difference between major and minor details. Read the following paragraph. The first sentence states the main idea. Turn the main idea into a question. Then complete the outline chart that follows.

The Three Stages of Alcoholism

[1]Alcoholism can be divided into three stages. [2]The first stage, *initiation,* happens as a harmless social event. [3]For many young people, the initiation into alcoholism begins at weekend parties where beer is served as the drink of choice. [4]Most think of these weekend binges as nothing more than fun. [5]However, the habit of seeking fun through drinking leads to the next phase. [6]The second stage is the *developing* phase of alcoholism. [7]A developing alcoholic turns to beer, wine, or hard liquor not only to have fun but also to relieve stress. [8]During this stage, few drinkers realize the

extent of their problem and rarely find help until the final stage. [9]The last stage of alcoholism is the *chronic* stage. [10]This stage comes as the result of years of habitual drinking. [11]During this phase, the alcoholic will put family, job, property, and even safety at risk for the sake of a drink.

Topic: The Three Stages of Alcoholism

Main idea: Alcoholism can be divided into three stages.
Question based on main idea:

_____

Major supporting detail:
   1. _____

     Minor supporting details:
      a. _____
      b. _____
      c. leads to the next phase

Major supporting detail:
   2. _____

     Minor supporting details:
      a. _____
      b. _____

Major supporting detail:
   3. Last stage, the chronic phase

     Minor supporting details:
      a. result of years of habitual drinking
      b. _____

       _____

EXPLANATION The word *what* turns the topic sentence into a question that the major details answer. Compare your answers to the following outline chart:

Creating a Summary

Textbook
Skills

Textbook authors often use headings that show the flow from general ideas to specific ideas. For example, textbook authors often use headings at the beginning of a passage. A heading at the beginning of a passage states the general topic. In addition, textbook authors also use headings within a passage to point out important ideas. In longer passages, headings signal the central idea of a section. In shorter passages, the headings may signal major supporting details. Usually, headings are in **bold** or *italic* type. A skilled reader can use headings, main ideas, and major supporting details to create a summary of the text. Creating a summary is an effective activity to do after reading.

> A **summary** is a brief, clear restatement of the most important points of a paragraph or passage.

Creating a Summary: Stated Main Ideas

Annotating or marking your text during reading will help you create a summary after you read. First, locate and underline the main idea. Then, create a question based on the main idea. Write this question in the margin of your textbook. Next, as you read, assign a number or letter to each heading or major detail that directly answers the question based on the main idea. Finally, to create a summary after you read, restate the ideas you marked in a few brief sentences. Often you will want to paraphrase or restate the ideas in your own words. You can use your annotations and summary to study the material. For example, cover up the passage. Next, use the question in the margin to test your memory of the material. Then, check your memory against your summary.

EXAMPLE Read the following passage from the textbook *Communication@ Work*. Complete each activity as directed.

A. As you read, annotate or mark the passage. Locate and underline the main idea. Write a question based on the main idea in the margin next to the passage. Number each detail that answers the question.

Use Academic Settings to Build Listening Strength

[1]Like training for athletic competition, listening training takes commitment, dedication, and endurance. [2]Ironically, some of the most effective behaviors are common sense, and yet they require the most effort.

³Use the following six practices to become an "Olympic listener."

- ⁴Let the other person talk.
- ⁵Ignore distractions.
- ⁶Seek the speaker's picture.
- ⁷Take time to listen.
- ⁸Empathize with the speaker.
- ⁹Note what you learn.

Get Active

¹⁰To become an Olympic listener, you must get active. ¹¹Be physically prepared to actively listen—rested, nourished, and alert. ¹²For that "ears flapping forward" feeling, pretend that there will be a pop quiz at the end of class. ¹³Don't let words flow through your ears and out through pens without registering the message in memory. ¹⁴Instead of waiting to become interested, listen immediately and expect interesting ideas. ¹⁵That is, *quit other tasks, quickly attend,* and quietly listen.

—Kelly, *Communication@Work*, pp. 97–98.

B. Fill in the blanks with the **second** major detail and its minor supporting details.

Topic: Use Academic Settings to Build Listening Strength

Main Idea: Like training for athletic competition, listening training takes commitment, dedication, and endurance.

First Major Detail: Follow the six practices to become an Olympic listener.

Second Major Detail: _____

_____

Minor Details: _____

_____

_____

_____

C. Create a summary. Paraphrase the ideas you marked as you read into a one- or two-sentence summary. Wording will vary.

_____

_____

EXPLANATION

A. You should have underlined sentence 1 "Like training for athletic competition, listening training takes commitment, dedication, and endurance." You should have a question based on the central idea similar to the following: "How do you build listening strength?" Finally, the sentences that answer the question based on the central idea are sentences 4 through 9, and sentence 15.

B. The flow of ideas is from general to specific. The author states the general topic in the heading. The thesis statement is at the beginning of the passage. The main idea explains how to build strong listening skills. The first major support asserts that six practices can build listening skills, and the minor supports state the six practices. The **second** major support states the need to be active to become an Olympic listener. The minor details give hints about how to quit other tasks, quickly attend, and quietly listen.

C. Compare the summary you created with the following wording: Listening training takes commitment, dedication, and endurance. You can become an Olympic listener, but you must practice six steps and be active throughout the process.

Creating a Summary: Implied Main Ideas

At times, a textbook author may choose to imply a main idea instead of directly stating it. As you learned in Chapter 6, you can use supporting details to create a topic sentence or thesis statement when the main idea or central point is implied. Annotating your text will also help you create a summary for passages with an implied main idea.

First, identify the topic of the passage. Underline recurring words or phrases. Locate each heading or major supporting detail in the passage. (Remember, minor details explain or support major details. Thus, to create a summary, you can ignore these minor details.) Assign a number or letter to each of the headings or major details you identified. Next, for each piece of information you have marked, ask the question "What controlling point or opinion about the topic does this detail reveal?" Often, a main heading can be turned into a question that will help you determine the implied main idea. Then, write a brief answer to each question in the margin next to the detail you marked. Next, after you finish reading, create a topic sentence or thesis statement for the passage. Finally, use only a few brief sentences to create the entire summary.

EXAMPLE Read the following passage taken from a college health textbook. As you read, complete the following steps. Then create a summary of the passage in the space provided after the passage.

Step 1:   Annotate the text: Underline the recurring key terms or phrases and label the major supporting details with a number or letter.

Step 2:   Turn the main heading into a question to determine the implied main idea. If needed, turn major details into questions that reveal the author's controlling point.

Step 3:   Answer each question in your own words.

Step 4:   Create a thesis statement based on the main heading and/or supporting details.

Step 5:   Write a summary that combines the thesis statement and the major supporting details in one or a few brief sentences.

Strategies for Anger Control

[1]**Calm** yourself. [2]There are many relaxation techniques. [3]Find one that works for you and bring yourself back to a level feeling.

[4]**Change your thoughts about the situation**. [5]When angry, many people act out in verbally abusive or other dramatic ways. [6]Instead of screeching and yelling, tell yourself that you are justified in being angry and that you have a right to be upset, but don't act overtly. [7]Remember that the "get it all out of your system" impulse is really not productive. [8]It only makes you feel good for a bit, and then you realize that you have hurt others and said much more than you should have—and in the end, nothing is changed. [9]Avoid thoughts or statements such as "never" or "always." [10]Stay in the present.

[11]**Improve your communication with the person who has made you angry or frustrated**. [12]Talk with them when you are calm. [13]Be direct and assertive. [14]Let them know how you feel without being aggressive or attacking them. [15]If you can't express it immediately, try writing down your feelings and thoughts in a journal and describe what you'd like to see changed. [16]Be clear when you talk with the person and try to keep your comments to "I" rather than "you" statements (e.g., "I feel like I have been insulted in some way," rather than "You insulted me"). [17]Don't fight back. [18]Instead of reacting with anger, listen to what the person is saying, ask clarifying questions, and keep your cool. [19]When the person has finished talking, acknowledge that you have heard and then express your own feelings.

[20]**Use humor if possible**. [21]Sometimes, the sheer volatility of a situation requires a bit of defusing, similar to the comic relief that accompanies a

long dramatic passage in a movie or play. [22]Try to defuse the situation if possible, and don't allow it to escalate. [23]However, this doesn't mean sitting there with a smirk on your face or laughing at the other person or being sarcastic. [24]Try to get the other person to laugh with you.

[25]**Recognize that certain situations may cause little things to blow out of proportion**. [26]Drinking, not enough sleep, responses to loss, and other situations may make people short fused. [27]Avoid conflict when you are tired or too drained to respond appropriately, and respect these needs in others.

[28]**Seek help**. [29]If you feel about yourself or have others telling you that you are a chronically hostile or angry person, seek help. [30]Your school has counselors who are able to help you. [31]Talk with them or someone else you trust.

—Adapted from Donatelle, *Access to Health*, 10th ed., p. 96.

Summary: _____

_____

_____

EXPLANATION   In this passage, the heading of the passage gives a great clue about the implied main idea. Think about the following question based on the heading, "How many strategies are there to control anger?" To answer this question, you have to number the major supporting details. And the bold print makes locating and numbering these details quite easy. So, very quickly you can answer the question based on the heading: "The following six strategies can help you control your anger." This answer states the central point of the passage. By using your own words to combine the thesis statement and the major supporting details, you create your summary.

PRACTICE 3

Textbook
Skills

Read the following passage, adapted from the textbook *The Dynamics of Drug Abuse*. As you read, complete each activity as directed.

A. As you read, annotate or mark the paragraph. Locate and underline the main idea. Write a question based on the main idea in the margin next to the passage. Number each detail that answers the question.

Drug Dependence

[1]Drug dependence is what most experts refer to as the final stage of drug use. [2]The onset of drug dependency is seen when users are no longer in control of their drug-taking behavior. [3]Three traits mark drug dependence:

[4]*Overwhelming need:* The user has a chemical need for the drug. [5]His or her strong desire to use means that efforts to stop are unsuccessful. [6]In addition, the user spends a great deal of time getting drugs.

[7]*Tolerance:* Larger doses are needed over time to produce the same original effect of a smaller dose. [8]The user becomes less responsive to the effects of the drug.

[9]*Withdrawal:* Withdrawal symptoms occur when drug use comes to an end. [10]Often withdrawal includes symptoms that are opposite to the effect produced by the drug. [11]For example, a person who has taken sleeping pills for a period of time and ends their use will feel unusually restless.

—Adapted from Fishbein/Pease, *The Dynamics of Drug Abuse*, pp. 64–67 © 1996 Allyn and Bacon. Reproduced by permission of Pearson Education, Inc.

B. Note the flow from general to specific. Fill in the blanks with the main idea, the major supporting details, and their minor details from the passage.

Topic: Drug dependence

Topic sentence: _____

    Major details: _____

    Minor details: _____

_____

_____

C. Create a summary. Paraphrase the ideas you marked as you read into a one- or two-sentence summary.

_____

_____

_____

_____

more than ever. [27]Finally, more voters may now distrust the government. [28]More and more people state that they lack confidence in their leaders. **Weak Political Parties.** [29]Political parties today are no longer as strong as they once were. [30]In the past, political parties rallied voters, made sure they were registered, and got them to the polls. [31]The parties once were grassroots organizations. [32]They forged strong party-group links with their supporters. [33]Today these bonds have been stretched to the breaking point for many. [34]Now campaigns are focused on the candidate. [35]The growth of huge party systems has resulted in a more distant party. [36]Most people do not identify very strongly with these large, distant parties.

—Adapted from O'Connor & Sabato, *American Government: Continuity and Change*, pp. 496–498.

B. Create a summary of the passage you just read. Paraphrase the ideas you marked as you read into a one- or two-sentence summary. Wording of answers will vary.

_____

_____

_____

_____

_____

Application 3: Implied Central Idea, Supporting Details, and a Summary

Read the following passage from a college communication textbook. Create questions as necessary. Annotate the text. Then work together with a peer or in a small group of classmates. Create a thesis statement that states the implied main idea. Then, write a summary for the passage.

Friendship

Textbook Skills

[1]What is friendship? [2]What are the types of friendship? [3]What purposes does friendship serve? [4]How does friendship differ in different cultures and between men and women?

- [5]Friendship is a relationship between two persons. [6]It is mutually productive. [7]It is marked by mutual positive regard.

- [8]Three types of friendship are:
  - [9]*Reciprocity*, marked by loyalty, self-sacrifice, mutual affection, and generosity.
  - [10]*Receptivity*, marked by a comfortable and positive imbalance in the giving and receiving of rewards. [11]Each person's needs are satisfied by the exchange.
  - [12]*Association*, a passing relationship, more like a friendly relationship than a true friendship.
- [13]Friendships serve a variety of needs. [14]They give us a variety of values. [15]These values include utility, affirmation, ego support, stimulation, and security.
- [16]Friendship demands vary among cultures. [17]For example, members of a culture that value individuals tend to look out for Number One. [18]In contrast, members of a culture that value collective groups, tend to have closer friendships based on cooperation.
- [19]Friendships vary based on gender. [20]Women share more. [21]And they are more intimate with same-sex friends than men are. [22]Men's friendships are often built around shared activities such as sports.

—Adapted from DeVito, *The Interpersonal Communication Book*, pp. 282–283 © 2007 by Pearson Education, Inc. Reproduced by permission of Pearson Education, Inc.

Thesis statement: _____

Summary: _____

_____

_____

REVIEW TEST 1   Score (number correct) _____ × 20 = _____ %

Main Ideas and Major Supporting Details

Read the paragraph. Complete the diagram by filling in the blanks with the topic, the main idea, a question based on the main idea, and two major supporting details from the paragraph.

Two Brave African-American Women

[1]African-American women have a tradition of independence and leadership dating back to the times of slavery. [2]In spite of great danger, black women took leading roles in the struggle for abolition. [3]Two strong leaders against slavery were Sojourner Truth and Harriet Tubman. [4]Sojourner Truth was a powerful speaker against slavery. [5]A heckler once called out, "Old woman . . . I don't care any more for your talk than I do for the bite of a flea." [6]Truth replied, "Perhaps not, but the good Lord willing, I'll keep you scratching." [7]Another strong leader, Harriet Tubman bravely attained her own freedom and then risked her life to lead many others to theirs. [8]Tubman declared, "I had a *right* to liberty or death; if I could not have one I would have another." [9]Despite a reward of $40,000 for her capture, pistol-packing Tubman returned to the South many times. [10]She led more than 300 slaves to their freedom via the "Underground Railway." [11]She served with Union forces during the Civil War and acted as a scout behind enemy lines.

—Adapted from "Work Among Our Women." *The Progress of a People.*
African-American Perspectives: Pamphlets from the Daniel A. P. Murray
Collection, 1818–1907. American Memory. Library of Congress.

Topic: 1. _____

Main idea: 2. _____
_____

Question based on main idea:
3. _____
_____

Major supporting detail:
4. _____
_____

Major supporting detail:
5. _____
_____
_____

REVIEW TEST 2

Score (number correct) _____ × 25 = _____%

Main Ideas, Major and Minor Supporting Details

Read the paragraph from a college history textbook. Answer the questions.

The Long and Rich History of Utah's Rugged Terrain

Textbook
Skills

[1]One thousand years ago, the Fremont Indians created a string of thriving villages nestled along Range Creek in the high-desert Book Cliff region of Utah. [2]There they built homes made of round stones and covered with roofs of pine boughs. [3]They also built stone walls, granaries, and silos for corn and beans. [4]They made baskets woven of grass and willow. [5]They also made pottery, tools, and beads. [6]In the early 1940s, a young cowboy named Waldo Wilcox came across the ruins of these villages. [7]The dry climate had kept many buildings and objects intact. [8]Since the Fremont Indians made their home in central Utah, humans have used the land for a variety of purposes. [9]Coal mining, a major activity in the state, was particularly dangerous. [10]In the 1900 Winter Quarters disaster, coal dust caused an underground explosion. [11] 200 people lost their lives. [12]The mountains of Utah are a popular cultural and tourist destination. [13]In 2000, Salt Lake City welcomed the Winter Olympics. [14]Park City hosts the annual Sundance Film Festival. [15]This event is the largest independent-film festival in the United States. [16]Utah's rugged terrain has a long and rich history of supporting human life.

—Adapted from Wood, Borstelmann, May & Ruiz, *Created Equal: A Social and Political History of the United States, Vol.1 to 1877*, 2nd ed., p. 520.

_____ **1.** Sentence 1 is a
   a. main idea.
   b. major supporting detail.
   c. minor supporting detail.

_____ **2.** Sentence 2 is a
   a. main idea.
   b. major supporting detail.
   c. minor supporting detail.

_____ **3.** Sentence 8 is a
   a. main idea.
   b. major supporting detail.
   c. minor supporting detail.

_____ **4.** Sentence 16 is a
   a. main idea.
   b. major supporting detail.
   c. minor supporting detail.

REVIEW TEST 3

Score (number correct) _____ × 10 = _____%

Main Ideas, Supporting Details, and Summarizing

A. Read the following passage from a government website. Annotate the text to determine the implied main idea and to complete a summary. Then complete the activities that follow.

Plastics: Facts and Processes

¹Plastics play an important role in almost every part of daily life. ²Plastics are used to manufacture everyday products. ³Plastic beverage containers, household items, and furniture just are a few examples. ⁴The widespread use of this material has created the need to manage a large amount of used plastics. ⁵And used plastics are a large part of the municipal solid waste (MSW) stream.

Just the Facts

⁶In 2008, the United States generated about 13 million tons of plastics in the MSW stream made up of containers and packaging. ⁷Almost 7 million tons were nondurable goods. ⁸And almost 11 million tons were durable goods.

⁹The total amount of plastics in MSW was about 30 million tons. ¹⁰That number was 12.0 percent of total MSW generation in 2008.

¹¹The amount of plastics in MSW has increased from less than 1 percent in 1960 to 12.0 percent in 2008.

¹²Plastics are a rapidly growing industry. ¹³The largest category of plastics are found in containers and packaging. ¹⁴This includes items like soft drink bottles, lids, and shampoo bottles. ¹⁵But they also are found in durable goods such as appliances and furniture. ¹⁶And they are found in nondurable goods like diapers, trash bags, cups and utensils, and medical devices.

¹⁷Plastics also are found in automobiles. ¹⁸But recycling of these materials is counted separately from the MSW recycling rate.

How Plastics Are Made

¹⁹Plastics are polymers. ²⁰The simplest definition of a polymer is something made up of many units. ²¹Polymers are chains of molecules. ²²Each link of the chain is usually made of carbon, hydrogen, oxygen, and/or silicon. ²³To make the chain, many links are hooked, or polymerized, together.

[24]To create polymers, petroleum and other products are heated under controlled conditions. [25]Then they are broken down into smaller molecules. [26]These molecules are called monomers. [27]These monomers are the building blocks for polymers. [28]Different combinations of monomers produce different types of plastic resins. [29]For example, resins can vary in strength or molding capability. [30]Plastics are divided into two major types. [31]They are either thermosets or thermoplastics.

- [32]A thermoset is a polymer that solidifies or "sets" for all time when heated. [33]They are useful for their durability and strength. [34]Therefore, they are used mainly in automobiles and construction applications. [35]Other uses are adhesives, inks, and coatings.
- [36]A thermoplastic is a polymer in which the molecules are held together by weak bonds. [37]These weak bonds create plastics that soften when exposed to heat. [38]They also return to their original condition at room temperature. [39]Thermoplastics can easily be shaped. [40]Thus they are molded into products such as milk jugs, floor coverings, credit cards, and carpet fibers.

[41]Plastic resins are processed in several ways. [42]These processes include extrusion, injection molding, blow molding, and rotational molding. [43]All of these processes involve using heat and/or pressure. [44]The plastic resin is formed into useful products, such as containers or plastic film.

How Plastics Are Recycled

[45]According to the American Plastics Council (APC), more than 1,800 U.S. businesses handle or reclaim post-consumer plastics. [46]Plastics from MSW are usually collected from curbside recycling bins or drop-off sites. [47]Then, they go to a material recovery facility. [48]There they are sorted either mechanically or manually from other recyclables. [49]The resulting mixed plastics are sorted by plastic type, baled, and sent to a reclaimer. [50]At the reclaiming facility, the scrap plastic is passed across a shaker screen. [51]This step removes trash and dirt. [52]Then the scraps are washed and ground into small flakes. [53]A flotation tank then further separates contaminants, based on their different densities. [54]Flakes are then dried, melted, filtered, and formed into pellets. [55]The pellets are shipped to product manufacturing plants. [56]There they are made into new plastic products.

—Adapted from U. S. Environmental Protection Agency. "Plastics." Wastes-Resource
Conversation-Common Wastes & Materials. 23 Nov. 2009. 7 June 2010.
http://www.epa.gov/wastes/conserve/materials/plastics.htm.

A. Create a question based on the topic: (**1**) _____

_____

B. Write a thesis statement of the implied main idea: (**2**) _____

_____

_____

C. Complete the following summary notes with details from the passage:

The Facts: In 2008, The total amount of plastics in MSW was about 30 million tons. And plastics are rapidly growing.

How Plastics Are Made: Plastics are (**3**) _____. Polymers are heated and broken down into (**4**) _____. Different combinations of monomers produce different types of plastic. A (**5**) _____ is a polymer that solidifies or "sets" for all time when heated. A (**6**) _____ is a polymer in which the molecules are held together by weak bonds that soften when exposed to heat.

How Plastics Are Recycled: Plastics are usually collected from curbside (**7**) _____ or drop-off sites and taken to a (**8**) _____. There they are sorted by plastic type, baled, and sent to a (**9**) _____. There the plastic scraps are cleaned, washed, and ground into small flakes. Flakes are then dried, melted, filtered, and formed into pellets. The pellets are shipped to product (**10**) _____. There they are made into new plastic products.

WHAT DO YOU THINK?

What are the benefits of using plastic? What are the drawbacks to using plastic? Assume you are planning to open your own business such as a car wash, beauty salon, gym, computer repair store, etc. To get a license to operate your business, the city has asked you to submit a recycling plan. Write a report to the city that answers the following questions: What types of plastic will your business require? How will you recycle used plastic goods?

REVIEW TEST 4

Score (number correct) _____ × 10 = _____%

Main Ideas and Major and Minor Supporting Details

Textbook
Skills

Before you read the following passage from a college communications text-book, skim the material and answer the Before Reading questions. Read the passage. Then answer the After Reading questions.

Vocabulary Preview

oration (1) speech

interred (1) buried

obvious (4) under-standable, known

appreciation (17) approval, admiration, understanding

inferences (27) guesses, conclusions

communicate (30) to exchange ideas

relational (31) of or based on dealings with people

Surface and Depth Listening

[1]In Shakespeare's *Julius Caesar,* Marc Antony, in giving the funeral **oration** for Caesar, says: "I come to bury Caesar, not to praise him. / The evil that men do lives after them; / The good is oft **interred** with their bones." [2]And later: "For Brutus is an honourable man; / So are they all, all honourable men." [3]But Antony, as we know, did come to praise Caesar and to convince the crowd that Brutus was not an honorable man.

[4]In most messages there's an **obvious** meaning. [5]You arrive at this clear meaning from a **literal** reading of the words and sentences. [6]But there's often another level of meaning. [7]Sometimes, as in *Julius Caesar*, it's the opposite of the literal meaning. [8]At other times, it seems totally unrelated. [9]In reality, most messages have more than one level of meaning. [10]Consider some often heard messages. [11]Carol asks you how you like her new haircut. [12]On one level, the meaning is clear. [13]Do you like the haircut? [14]But there's also another, perhaps more important, level. [15]Carol is asking you to say something positive about her appearance. [16]The same is true for the parent who complains about working hard at the office or in the home. [17]The parent, on a deeper level, may be asking for an expression of **appreciation**. [18]The child who talks about the unfairness of the other children in the playground may be asking for comfort and love. [19]To grasp these other meanings you need to engage in depth listening.

²⁰If you respond only to the surface-level message, you miss making meaningful contact with the other person's feelings and needs. ²¹If you say to the parent, "You're always complaining. ²²I bet you really love working so hard," you fail to respond to his or her real need. ²³You have ignored his or her need for support and encouragement. ²⁴To adjust your surface and depth listening, think about the following guidelines:

²⁵*Focus on both verbal and nonverbal messages.* ²⁶Look for both **consistent** and inconsistent "packages" of messages. ²⁷Use these as guides for drawing **inferences** about the speaker's meaning. ²⁸Ask questions when in doubt. ²⁹Listen also to what is omitted. ³⁰Remember, speakers **communicate** by what they don't say as well as by what they do say.

³¹*Listen for both content and **relational** messages.* ³²For example, take the student who always challenges the teacher. ³³On one level, this student may be disagreeing with the content. ³⁴Yet, on another level, the student may be confronting the teacher's authority. ³⁵The teacher needs to listen and respond to both types of messages.

³⁶*Make special note of statements that refer back to the speaker.* ³⁷People usually talk about themselves. ³⁸Whatever a person says is, in part, a result of who that person is. ³⁹So listen carefully to those personal messages.

⁴⁰*Don't ignore the literal meaning of a message in trying to find the hidden meaning.* ⁴¹Balance your listening. ⁴²Reply to the different levels of meaning in the messages of others, just as you would like others to respond to you. ⁴³Be sensitive. ⁴⁴Listen carefully, but don't be too eager to uncover hidden messages.

—Adapted from DeVito, *The Interpersonal Communication Book*, pp. 111–112 © 2007 by Pearson Education, Inc. Reproduced by permission of Pearson Education, Inc.

Before Reading

Vocabulary in Context

_____ **1.** In sentence 5 of the passage, the word **literal** means
  a. hidden.   c. natural.
  b. factual.   d. focused.

_____ **2.** In sentence 26 of the passage, the word **consistent** means
  a. conflicting.   c. subtle.
  b. clear.   d. reliable.

After Reading

Central Idea and Main Idea

_____ **3.** Which sentence states the central idea of the passage?
    a. sentence 1   c. sentence 19
    b. sentence 4   d. sentence 20

_____ **4.** Which sentence states the main idea of paragraph 3?
    a. sentence 20   c. sentence 22
    b. sentence 21   d. sentence 23

Supporting Details

_____ **5.** Sentence 32 is a _____ in its paragraph.
    a. major supporting detail
    b. minor supporting detail

_____ **6.** Sentence 34 is a _____ in its paragraph.
    a. major supporting detail
    b. minor supporting detail

7–10. Complete the summary with information from the passage.

Listening at a (**7**)_____level, a person reacts to a literal message.
(**8**)_____ listening responds to hidden meanings based on the feelings and needs of the speaker. Several (**9**)_____help one listen on both levels. First, listen to messages that are verbal (what is said) and (**10**) _____(what is not said). Next, listen to messages about content and relationships. Also, listen to statements that may be about the speaker. Finally, don't ignore clear meanings in the hunt for hidden meanings.

WHAT DO YOU THINK?

Do you think that our ability to listen is affected by our gender? Do you think one gender is more likely to listen at a surface level or a depth level? Which of the guidelines seem most helpful? Do the guidelines apply to both males and females? Assume you are a mentor for a young person who is in conflict with an authority person such as a teacher or parent of the opposite sex. For example, a teenage girl doesn't feel as if her father trusts her. Or a senior in high school wants to improve his history class grade, but doesn't know how to approach his teacher, Ms. Gomez, for help. Write a letter of advice to this young person. Explain how she or he can use depth listening to improve communication.

After Reading About Supporting Details

Before you move on to the Mastery Tests on supporting details, take time to reflect on your learning and performance by answering the following questions. Write your answers in your notebook.

- How has my knowledge base or prior knowledge about supporting details changed?
- Based on my studies, how do I think I will perform on the Mastery Test(s)? Why do I think my scores will be above average, average, or below average?
- Would I recommend this chapter to other students who want to learn more about supporting details? Why or why not?

Test your understanding of what you have learned about supporting details by completing the Chapter 7 Review Card on the insert near the end of the text.

CONNECT TO **myreadinglab**

To check your progress in meeting Chapter 7's learning outcomes, log in to **www.myreadinglab.com**, and try the following activities.

- The "Supporting Details" section of MyReadingLab offers more information about supporting details. You will find an overview, model, review materials, practice activities, and tests. To access this resource, click on the "Study Plan" tab. Then click on "Supporting Details." Then click on the following links as needed: "Overview," "Model," "Practice," and "Tests."
- The "Outlining and Summarizing" section of MyReadingLab gives an overview about memory and active reading. This section also provides a model for summarizing. You will find practice activities and tests. To access this resource, click on the "Study Plan" tab. Then click on "Outlining and Summarizing." Then click on the following links as needed: "Overview," "Model: Summarizing," "Practice," and "Tests."
- To measure your mastery of the content of this chapter, complete the tests in the "Supporting Details" section and click on Gradebook to find your results.

A. Read the paragraph, then complete the simple outline. In the chart below, fill in the blanks with the main idea, a question based on the main idea, and three major supporting details from the paragraph.

Creative People Are Daring

Textbook Skills

[1]For the creative, thinking is an adventure. [2]Three traits reveal the daring nature of creative people. [3]First, creative people are fairly free of pre-set ideas and biased views. [4]Therefore, they are not as quick to accept existing views. [5]They are less narrow in their views. [6]And they are less likely to conform with the thinking of those around them. [7]Second, they are bold in their thinking. [8]They are willing to think about unpopular ideas. [9]They also consider seemingly unlikely possibilities. [10]Therefore, like Galileo and Columbus, Edison and the Wright brothers, they are more open than others to creative ideas. [11]Their daring has an additional benefit. [12]It makes them less prone to face-saving than others. [13]As a result, they are willing to face unpleasant experiences. [14]They apply their curiosity. [15]Then they learn from those experiences. [16]Thus, they are less likely than others to repeat the same failure over and over.

—Adapted from Ruggiero, *The Art of Thinking: A Guide to Critical and Creative Thought*, 7th ed., p. 84.

Topic: The Daring Nature of Creative People

Main idea: 1. _____
Question based on main idea:
    2. _____
        _____

    Major supporting detail:
        3. _____
            _____

    Major supporting detail:
        4. _____
    Major supporting detail:
        5. _____

B. Read the paragraph, then answer the questions.

Space Fun

¹Astronauts need a break from their busy schedules when they are orbiting Earth. ²Days or even months of straight work cause stress among space workers. ³Not only do astronauts have time to unwind, they also have many activities that help them relax and have fun. ⁴First, free time is built into their routine. ⁵They are given time every day to relax and exercise. ⁶Like most people who work full time, they also get weekends off. ⁷Second, space workers have a choice of fun and relaxing activities. ⁸One popular pastime while orbiting the Earth is looking out the window. ⁹Astronauts onboard the space shuttle can look out the cockpit windows. ¹⁰They can watch the Earth below or the deep blackness of space. ¹¹Inside the International Space Station, crewmembers have many windows they can look out. ¹²They often talk about their awe as they look at the Earth spin beneath them with its many shades and textures. ¹³Stunning sunsets and sunrises occur every 45 minutes above the Earth's atmosphere. ¹⁴In addition, space workers can watch movies, read books, play cards, and talk to their families. ¹⁵They also have an exercise bike, a treadmill, and other equipment to keep their bodies in shape.

—Adapted from "Space Fun." NASA. 7 Oct. 2009.

_____ **6.** Which sentence is the topic sentence of the paragraph?
   a. sentence 1   c. sentence 3
   b. sentence 2

_____ **7.** Sentence 4 is a
   a. major supporting detail.   b. minor supporting detail.

_____ **8.** Sentence 6 is a
   a. major supporting detail.   b. minor supporting detail.

_____ **9.** Sentence 7 is a
   a. major supporting detail.   b. minor supporting detail.

_____ **10.** Sentence 13 is a
   a. major supporting detail.   b. minor supporting detail.

Read the paragraph from a college history textbook. Then, complete the simple outline. Fill in the blanks with the main idea, a question based on the main idea, and two major supporting details from the paragraph.

The Two Brilliant Ideas of Henry Ford

Textbook Skills

¹Henry Ford was the person most responsible for the growth of the automobile industry. ²Ford was a self-taught mechanic from Greenfield, Michigan. ³He was not a great inventor, nor was he one of the true automobile pioneers. ⁴He was not even the first person to manufacture a good low-priced car. ⁵Ransom E. Olds, producer of the "Merry Oldsmobile" was the first to do that. ⁶Ford had two brilliant insights that made him successful. ⁷The first was, in his words, "get the prices down to the buying power." ⁸Through mass production, cars could be made cheaply enough to put them within reach of the ordinary citizen. ⁹In 1908, he designed the Model T Ford, a simple, tough box on wheels. ¹⁰In a year, he proved his point by selling 11,000 Model T's. ¹¹He relentlessly cut costs and increased efficiency by using the assembly-line system. ¹²He expanded production at an unbelievable rate. ¹³By 1925, he was turning out more than 9000 cars a day, one approximately every 10 seconds. ¹⁴And the price of the Model T had been reduced to below $300. ¹⁵His second insight was the link between high wages and selling more automobiles. ¹⁶High wages led to more output. ¹⁷The assembly line made work simple, boring, and more tiring. ¹⁸Workers often missed work, and turnover was high. ¹⁹To combat this problem, Ford paid workers $5 a day. ²⁰This was a $2 raise over existing wages. ²¹The rate of turnover in his plants dropped by 90 percent. ²²Later, he raised the minimum wage to $6 a day and then to $7 a day.

—Adapted from Garraty & Carnes, *The American Nation: A History of the United States*, 10th ed., p. 712.

Topic: Two Brilliant Ideas of Henry Ford

Main idea: 1. _____

_____

Question based on main idea:

2. _____

_____

Major supporting detail:

3. _____

Major supporting detail:

4. _____

VISUAL VOCABULARY

Robot arms assemble truck bodies in the fully automated Ford truck plant in Dearborn, Michigan. Robot automation has improved **efficiency**. But it has reduced the number of human workers needed.
The best meaning of **efficiency** is 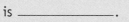.

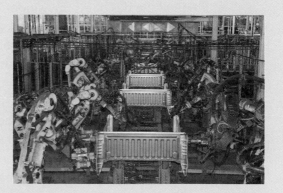

   a. productivity.
   b. profit.
   c. failure.

A. As you read, annotate this passage from a government website. (**1**) Locate and underline the central idea. (**2**) Write a question based on the central idea in the margin next to the passage. (**3–7**) Number the five major details that answer the question.

Ratings for Video Games

Question based on the central idea: (**2**)

_____

_____

_____

_____

[1]Media ratings systems are a way for children and parents to control what they buy and view. [2]Ratings are sources of information to help protect children from violence in movies, games, and music. [3]Video games are rated based on five levels, and each level is based on age and content.

[4]**EC** stands for early childhood. [5]The content of these videos is suitable for children age 3 and older.

[6]**E** stands for everyone. [7]The content of these videos is suitable for those 6 and older. [8]The game may contain minimal violence, some comic mischief, or some mild language.

[9]**T** stands for teen. [10]The content is suitable for those 13 and older. [11]The game may contain violent content. [12]It may also use mild or strong language and suggestive themes.

[13]**M** stands for mature. [14]The content is suitable for those 17 and older. [15]The game may include more intense violence or language than games rated T. [16]It may include mature sexual themes.

[17]**AO** stands for adults only. [18]The content is suitable only for adults. [19]The game may include graphic sex and/or violence. [20]Games rated AO are not intended to be sold or rented to anyone under the age of 18.

[21]The Entertainment Software Rating Board assigns content descriptions to video games. [22]You will find these on the back of the video game packages. [23]Some descriptions you might see are Animated Blood, Blood, Blood and Gore, Cartoon Violence, Comic Mischief, Fantasy Violence, Intense Violence, Mild Violence, Sexual Violence, and Violence.

—Adapted from "Entertainment Ratings: Pocket Guide."
Federal Trade Commission. July 2004.

B. Complete the following summary with the ideas you marked as you read.

The rating system for (**8**) _____ includes five levels based on (**9**) _____ and (**10**) _____. The labels for the ratings include (**11**) _____ for (**12**) _____, (**13**) _____ for (**14**) _____, (**15**) _____ for (**16**) Teen, (**17**) _____ for (**18**) _____, and (**19**) _____ for (**20**) _____.

Adolescents play a round of first-person shooter *Halo 3* on XBox 360. This video game has been rated

_____

by the Entertainment Software Rating Board.

a. E
b. EC
c. M

Name _____ Section _____

Date _____ **Score** (number correct) _____ × 10 = _____%

A. As you read, annotate this passage taken from a government website. (**1**) Locate and underline the central idea. (**2**) Write a question based on the central idea in the margin next to the passage. (**3–5**) Number the three major details that answer the question.

Textbook
Skills

Question based on
the central idea: (**2**)

_____

_____

_____

_____

_____

The Symptoms of Attention Deficit Hyperactivity Disorder

[1]Attention Deficit Hyperactivity Disorder (ADHD) occurs in some children in the preschool and early school years. [2]It is hard for these children to control their behavior or pay attention. [3]Children who have ADHD usually display one or more of the following traits.

Hyperactivity. [4]Children who are hyperactive always seem to be "on the go" or constantly in motion. [5]They dash around touching or playing with whatever is in sight, or they talk incessantly. [6]Sitting still at dinner or during a school lesson or story can be a difficult task. [7]They squirm and fidget in their seats or roam around the room. [8]Or they may wiggle their feet, touch everything, or noisily tap their pencil. [9]Hyperactive teenagers or adults may feel internally restless. [10]They often report needing to stay busy and may try to do several things at once.

Impulsivity. [11]Children who are impulsive seem unable to curb their immediate reactions. [12]They do not think before they act. [13]They will often blurt out inappropriate comments, display their emotions without restraint, and act without regard for the later consequences of their conduct. [14]It is hard for them to wait for things they want or to take their turn in games. [15]They may grab a toy from another child or hit when they're upset. [16]Even as teenagers or adults, they may impulsively choose to do things that have an immediate but small payoff. [17]They have trouble with activities that may take more effort yet provide much greater but delayed rewards.

Inattention. [18]Children who are inattentive have a hard time keeping their minds on any one thing. [19]They may get bored with a task after only a few minutes. [20]If they are doing something they really enjoy, they have no trouble paying attention. [21]But focusing deliberate, conscious attention to organizing and completing a task or learning something new is difficult. [22]Homework is difficult for these children. [23]They will forget to write down an assignment, or leave it at school. [24]They will forget to bring a book home, or they will bring the wrong one. [25]The homework, if finally finished, is full of errors and erasures. [26]Homework is often frustrating for both parent and child.

—Adapted from "Attention Deficit Hyperactivity Disorder
(ADHD)." National Institute of Mental Health.

B. Paraphrase the ideas you marked as you read to complete the following summary. Wording of some answers may vary.

Children who have (**6**) _____ may have
one or more of three (**7**) _____. First, (**8**) _____
_____. Second, (**9**) _____
_____. Third, (**10**) _____
_____.

Outlines and Concept Maps

8

After studying this chapter you should be able to do the following:

1. Define the terms *outline* and *concept map*.
2. Create an outline.
3. Create a concept map.
4. Evaluate the importance of outlines and concept maps.
5. Apply outlines and concept maps to passages to improve comprehension.

 ## Before Reading About Outlines and Concept Maps

In Chapter 7, you learned several important ideas that will help you effectively use outlines and concept maps. Review the diagram about the flow of ideas on page 242 in Chapter 7. Next, skim this chapter for key ideas in boxes about outlines, concept maps, and the table of contents in a textbook. Refer to the diagram and boxes, and create at least three questions that you can answer as you read the chapter. Write your questions in the following spaces (record the page number for the key term in each question):

_____

_____? (page_____)

_____

_____? (page_____)

_____

_____? (page_____)

Compare the questions you created with the following questions. Then write the ones that seem most helpful in your notebook, leaving enough space between each question to record the answers as you read and study the chapter.

What words signal the topic sentence or central idea? What words signal each new idea in a passage? What is a concept map? Where are main ideas placed in an outline, concept map, and table of contents? Where are major supporting details placed in an outline, concept map, and table of contents? Where are minor supporting details placed in an outline, concept map, and table of contents? What is the difference between a formal outline and an informal outline?

Outlines

An outline shows how a paragraph or passage moves from a main idea to specific supporting details; thus it helps you make sense of the ways ideas relate to one another. A skilled reader uses an outline to see the relationships among the main idea, major supporting details, and minor supporting details.

> An **outline** shows the relationships among the main idea, major supporting details, and minor supporting details of a paragraph or passage.

An author often uses signal words and phrases to indicate that a supporting detail or a series of supporting details is coming. Signal words are sometimes called *transitional words*.

Signal words that indicate a series of details are frequently located in the stated main idea, so they can serve as a clue that the sentence is likely to be a topic sentence of a paragraph or the central idea of a passage.

Words That Signal the Topic Sentence or Central Idea		
a few causes	a few steps	several advantages
a few effects	a number of	several kinds of
a few factors	a series of	several steps
a few reasons	among the results	

Signal or transition words are also frequently used to introduce each new detail in a paragraph or passage.

Words That Signal Each New Detail in a Paragraph or Passage		
additionally	first of all	moreover
also	for example	next
another	furthermore	one
finally	in addition	second
first	last	third

EXAMPLE   Read the following paragraph. Fill in the details to complete the outline. Then answer the questions that follow.

> ¹Jeremy tried a number of ways to get rid of his hiccups. ²First, he tried holding his breath and counting to 10 very slowly. ³However, he was never able to count any higher than 6 before an unstoppable string of hiccups would take over. ⁴Next, he tried breathing into a paper bag. ⁵While he was breathing out into the bag, the hiccups would erupt loudly and painfully. ⁶By this time, Jeremy's stomach had begun to hurt. ⁷Finally, he tried scaring his hiccups away. ⁸He asked his sister to help; several times she ran up behind him, when he least expected it, and screamed at the top of her voice. ⁹For a time, the scare tactic would seem to help, but then, without fail, the hiccups returned. ¹⁰Each time, they seemed louder and more frequent. ¹¹Jeremy suffered the whole day with his stubborn hiccups.

Main idea: Jeremy tried a number of ways to get rid of his hiccups.

Question: In what ways did Jeremy try to get rid of his hiccups?

1. **Major supporting details**

   a. _____

   _____

   b. _____

   _____

   c. _____

   _____

2. **Signal words for supporting details**

   a. What words in the main idea signal that a list of details will follow?

   _____

   b. What words introduce the three major details?

   Major detail 1: _____

   Major detail 2: _____

   Major detail 3: _____

EXPLANATION Compare your answers with the following outline.

Main idea: Jeremy tried a number of ways to get rid of his hiccups.

Question: In what ways did Jeremy try to get rid of his hiccups?

1. **Major supporting details**

   a. tried holding his breath and counting to 10

   b. tried breathing into a paper bag

   c. tried scaring his hiccups away

2. **Signal words for supporting details**

   a. Signal words in the main idea: a number of

   b. Major detail 1: First

   Major detail 2: Next

   Major detail 3: Finally

Notice that even without the minor supporting details, the main idea and the major supporting details make sense. You do not need the minor details to understand the main point the author is trying to make. However, the minor details do make the passage more interesting to read and deepen the author's ideas.

   The outlines you have worked with so far are informal outlines. Often, a traditional or formal outline is used to see the relationships between ideas in a longer passage of several paragraphs. A traditional outline uses the central idea as a heading and Roman numerals to indicate the topic sentence of each paragraph, capital letters to indicate the major details of each paragraph, and Arabic numbers to indicate the minor details of each paragraph. If you were to use a traditional outline to show the relationships among the main idea, the major supporting details, and the minor details in the paragraph about Jeremy, it would look like the following outline:

Main Idea: Jeremy tried a number of ways to get rid of his hiccups.

   I. He tried holding his breath and counting to 10.

      A. He was never able to count higher than 6.

      B. An unstoppable string of hiccups would take over.

   II. He tried breathing into a paper bag.

      A. While he was breathing out into the bag, the hiccups would erupt loudly and painfully.

      B. Jeremy's stomach began to hurt.

III. He tried scaring his hiccups away.

    A. He asked his sister to help.

    B. She ran up behind him, when he least expected it, and screamed.

    C. The scare tactic would seem to work.

    D. The hiccups returned.

    E. They seemed louder and more frequent.

    F. Jeremy suffered the whole day.

PRACTICE 1

Read the following paragraph from a college science textbook. Complete the outline with the major details from the paragraph. Then answer the questions that follow.

The Skeleton of the Hand

Textbook
Skills

[1]The skeleton of the hand consists of three sections. [2]First, the eight carpal bones, arranged in two irregular rows of four bones each, form the part of the hand carpus, or more commonly, the wrist. [3]The carpals are bound together by ligaments that restrict movements between them. [4]Next, the palm of the hand consists of the metacarpals. [5]The metacarpals are numbered 1 to 5 from the thumb side of the hand toward the little finger. [6]When the fist is clenched, the heads of the metacarpals become obvious as the "knuckles." [7]Finally, the phalanges are the bones of the fingers. [8]Each hand contains 14 phalanges. [9]There are three in each finger (proximal, middle, and distal), except in the thumb, which has only two (proximal and distal).

—Adapted from Marieb, *Essentials of Human Anatomy
& Physiology*, 9th ed., p. 162.

Main Idea: The skeleton of the hand consists of three sections.

Question: What are the three sections that make up the skeleton of the hand?

1. **Major supporting details:**

    a. _____

       _____

b. _____

c. _____

2. Signal words for supporting details:

a. What words in the topic sentence signal that a list of details will follow?

_____

b. What words introduce the three major details?

Major detail 1: _____

Major detail 2: _____

Major detail 3: _____

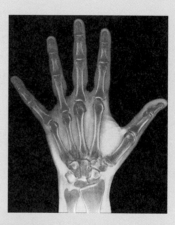

VISUAL VOCABULARY

The knuckles of the hand are made up
of the bones known as _____.

   a. carpals.
   b. metacarpals.
   c. phalanges.

Concept Maps

An outline is one way to see the details in a paragraph or passage. Another way to see details is through the use of a concept map. A **concept map** is a diagram that shows the flow of ideas from the main idea to the supporting details. Think of what you already know about a map. Someone can tell you how to get somewhere, but it is much easier to understand the directions if you can see how each road connects to other roads by studying a map. Likewise, a concept map shows how ideas connect to one another.

> A **concept map** is a diagram that shows the flow of ideas from the main idea to the supporting details.

To make a concept map, the skilled reader places the main idea in a box or circle as a heading and then places the major supporting details in boxes or circles beneath the main idea. Often arrows or lines are used to show the flow of ideas.

EXAMPLE Read the following paragraph. Then complete the concept map by adding the missing major supporting details from the paragraph.

[1]Instead of moping around without energy, overcome the "blahs" in two basic ways. [2]First, eat right. [3]A proper diet can help keep those lazy feelings of boredom away. [4]Avoid sweets, chips, and fast foods. [5]Instead, eat a balanced diet from the four food groups to give your body the fuel it needs. [6]Second, get active. [7]Moderate exercise burns away that sluggish feeling. [8]Instead of relying totally on cars and elevators, walk and take the stairs.

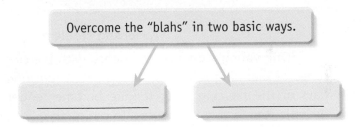

Overcome the "blahs" in two basic ways.

EXPLANATION The main idea is in the top box. The signal words *First* and *Second* indicate the major supporting details in the paragraph. Therefore, the missing details are "Eat right" and "Get active."

PRACTICE 2

Read each paragraph. Then complete the concept map for that paragraph.

American Idol

[1]*American Idol* is a one-of-a-kind reality television show that turns contestants into stars. [2]The first winner of *American Idol* was Kelly Clarkson, and she has had an amazing career. [3]Clarkson has won two Grammy Awards, four American Music Awards, and twelve Billboard Music Awards. [4]Her first album debuted at number one on the Billboard chart. [5]Since then, she has sold over ten million albums in the United States.

[6]The fourth season's winner was Carrie Underwood. [7]She has won five American Music Awards, fourteen Billboard Music Awards, and four Grammy awards. [8]She has sold over nine and a half million albums in the United States. [9]Even those who lose on *American Idol* can become stars. [10]In season five, Chris Daughtry only ended up in fourth place. [11]However, his first two albums have sold over five million copies in the United States alone. [12]In season eight, Adam Lambert had to settle for being the runner-up. [13]Despite the loss, his success seems sure. [14]In 2009, the pre-sales for his debut album put him at number one on the Amazon.com bestsellers list. [15]*American Idol* serves up the American dream for its talented contestants.

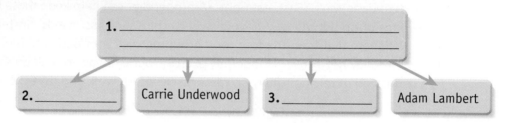

1. _____
   _____

2. _____   Carrie Underwood   3. _____   Adam Lambert

A Piercing Problem

[1]One young woman's experience with piercing her tongue led to a series of alarming health problems. [2]First, an infection occurred within days of the piercing. [3]Her tongue became tender and swollen, and it oozed a foul-tasting discharge. [4]To get some relief, she removed the jewelry she had inserted. [5]Within days, the hole closed up. [6]Then she began to have severe headaches, trouble with balance, nausea, and vomiting. [7]These symptoms appeared almost a month after the piercing occurred. [8]Doctors discovered an abscess in her cerebellum, the part of the brain that controls coordination. [9]When they drained the abscess, they found four types of oral bacteria in the fluid. [10]The doctors believe that bacteria found in the mouth entered her bloodstream through her pierced tongue. [11]Once in the bloodstream, the bacteria made their way to her brain.

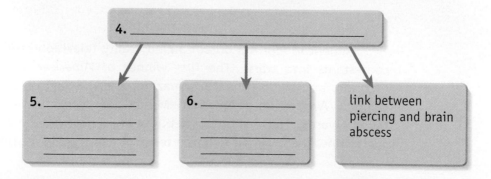

4. _____

5. _____   6. _____   link between
   _____   _____   piercing and brain
   _____   _____   abscess

Mattie's Heroic Story

¹Mattie Stepanek was a remarkable American writer and speaker. ²Before his death in 2004 at the age of 14, he had become a national hero for several reasons. ³First, Mattie modeled valor as he battled a horrible disease, muscular dystrophy. ⁴Mattie lived near death each day in a wheelchair hooked to a ventilator that supplied him with oxygen. ⁵Next, Mattie showed great talent and wisdom. ⁶He began writing poetry when he was three years old. ⁷By 2004, five volumes of his poems had been published. ⁸The titles are *Heartsongs*, *Journey Through Heartsongs*, *Hope Through Heartsongs*, *Celebrate Through Heartsongs*, and *Loving Through Heartsongs*. ⁹All five books became *New York Times'* Best Sellers. ¹⁰Mattie also modeled great leadership. ¹¹He never focused on his own suffering; instead, he brought peace and hope to others. ¹²His stirring message landed him on shows like *Oprah* and *Good Morning, America*. ¹³In 2009, Mattie's life story *Messenger: The Legacy of Mattie J.T. Stepanek and Heartsongs* was published. ¹⁴This book tells Mattie's life story through the eyes of his mother, Jeni Stepanek, with a Foreword by Maya Angelou.

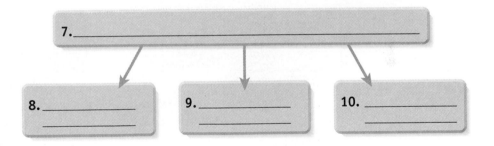

7. _____

8. _____   9. _____   10. _____
_____   _____   _____

Textbook
Skills

The Table of Contents in a Textbook

The table of contents of a textbook is a special kind of outline that is based on topics and subtopics. A **topic** is the *general subject,* so a **subtopic** is a *smaller part* of the topic. The general subject of the textbook is stated in the textbook's title. For example, the title *Health in America: A Multicultural Perspective* tells us that the book is about health concerns from the view of different cultures.

Textbooks divide the general subject into smaller sections or subtopics. These subtopics form the chapters of the textbook. Because a textbook looks deeply into the general subject, a large amount of information is found in each chapter. A chapter is further divided into smaller parts or subtopics, and each subtopic is labeled with a heading. The table of contents lists the general subjects and subtopics of each chapter.

Most textbooks provide a brief table of contents that divides the textbook into sections and lists the chapter titles for each section. A separate detailed table of contents may also be provided that lists the subtopics for each chapter.

A skilled reader examines the table of contents of a textbook to understand how the author has organized the information and where specific information can be found.

EXAMPLE   Survey, or look over, the following brief table of contents. Then answer the questions.

Sociology: A Down-to-Earth Approach, 9th ed.

Brief Contents

vi

—Henslin, *Sociology: A Down to Earth Approach*, "Table of Contents," © James M. Henslin. Reproduced by permission of Pearson Education, Inc.

1. What is the general topic of this textbook? _____

2. How many parts did the author use to divide the general topic? _____

3. How many chapters are in Part II? _____ What is the length of Chapter 3?

_____ pages.

4. Write a one-sentence summary using the topic and subtopics for Part IV.

_____

_____

The topic of this textbook is sociology. The book has six parts. Part II has three chapters. Plan your study time based on the length of a chapter. For example, Chapter 3 is 32 pages in length. How long do you think you need to read 32 pages? One way to get a general sense of a chapter or part is to write a summary based on the headings. Compare your summary of Part IV to the following. "Social institutions include the economy, politics, marriage and family, education, religion, and medicine and health."

PRACTICE 3

Study the following detailed table of contents for one section of Chapter 2 of *Sociology: A Down-to-Earth Approach*, 9th ed.

—Henslin, *Sociology: A Down to Earth Approach*, "Section of Ch. 2 detailed TOC"
© James M. Henslin. Reproduced by permission of Pearson Education, Inc.

1. What is the topic of this section of the chapter? _____

2. How many subtopics are listed for the section? _____

3. On what page does the discussion about the Hmong begin? _____

4. What are the two major supporting details of this chapter? _____

_____

APPLICATIONS

Textbook
Skills

Application 1: Supporting Details and Outlines

Read the paragraph. Then complete the outline and answer the questions following the paragraph.

The Stages of Syphilis

[1]Though curable, syphilis is a serious and even deadly sexually transmitted disease. [2]Passed only through sexual contact, syphilis has three stages. [3]The first stage occurs ten days to three months after infection. [4]A small sore develops on the mouth, vagina, penis, or anus, where the bacteria that cause syphilis first entered the body. [5]The open, oozing sore is not painful. [6]The second stage begins within weeks or months after the sore goes away. [7]In this stage, the infected person breaks out in a rash and has flulike symptoms. [8]The rash may cover any or all of the body, including hands, feet, and groin. [9]One doctor called syphilis the "reptilian disease" because of the ugly black scabs that may form during this stage. [10]During both the first and second stages, syphilis is highly contagious. [11]After the second stage ends, the disease can lie hidden in the blood for as long as 40 years. [12]When it returns in its third stage, syphilis can be deadly. [13]It attacks organs and the nervous system. [14]It can cause a heart attack, paralysis, or even insanity. [15]Syphilis is curable in any of the three stages, yet whatever damage the disease has caused cannot be undone.

Main idea: Syphilis has three stages.

1. _____

   a. A small sore develops

   b. Open, oozing sores not painful

2. Second stage

   a. _____

   b. First and second stages highly contagious

   c. Hidden in the blood

3. _____

   a. Attacks organs and the nervous system

   b. Causes heart attack, paralysis, or even insanity

4. What signal word introduces the first major detail? _____

5. What signal word introduces the second major detail? _____

Application 2: Concept Maps and Signal Words

Read the following paragraph. Then complete the concept map with information from the paragraph and answer the questions.

Sitting Bull

[1]Sitting Bull was a notable Native American for two reasons. [2]First, Sitting Bull, leader of a Sioux tribe, won a key victory during one of the wars against the white man. [3]Sitting Bull brought together nearly 11,000 Sioux, Arapaho, and Cheyenne warriors at the Little Big Horn River in Montana. [4]In a bloody fight against the United States Army, Sitting Bull's warriors wiped out all of General Custer's 264 men. [5]Second, later in his life, Sitting Bull became a star in Buffalo Bill's Wild West Show. [6]Buffalo Bill's show included roundups, stagecoach robberies, and Indian fights. [7]Sitting Bull drew huge crowds, for many people were eager to see the famous Sioux warrior.

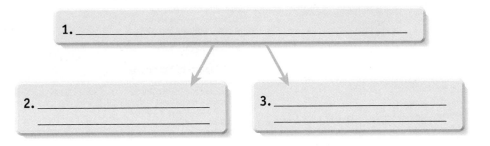

4. What signal word introduces the first major detail? _____

5. What signal word introduces the second major detail? _____

Application 3: A Textbook Table of Contents

Study the following detailed table of contents for Unit I of Kozier and Erb's *Fundamentals of Nursing: Concepts, Process, and Practice,* 8th ed. Then answer the questions.

1. What is the topic of Chapter 4? _____

2. How many subtopics are listed for Chapter 4? _____

3. On what page does the discussion about the legal responsibilities of students begin? _____

4. What are the major supporting details of Chapter 5? _____

_____

REVIEW TEST 1   Score (number correct) _____ × 10 = _____ %

Outlines, Concept Maps, and Supporting Details

A. Read the paragraph. Then state a question based on the main idea, list the major supporting details from the paragraph, and answer the question.

Malcolm X

[1]Malcolm X has become a hero for several reasons. [2]First of all, he rose from humble but proud beginnings. [3]Born the seventh of 11 children to a Baptist minister, Malcolm X, whose name at birth was Malcolm Little, came from a modest background. [4]His father preached self-respect and black independence. [5]Next, Malcolm and his family faced many tragedies. [6]The local Ku Klux Klan, a hate group, ran the Little family out of Omaha, Nebraska. [7]When they moved to Lansing, Michigan, another hate group set fire to their home. [8]Malcolm's father rebuilt their home; the same men later murdered him. [9]Six years old when his father died, Malcolm eventually dropped out of school and ended up serving time in prison. [10]Finally, he emerged as a national leader. [11]He became a Black Muslim, changed his last name from Little to X, and began to organize and educate African Americans.

Main idea: Malcolm X has become a hero for several reasons.

**Question based
on main idea:**   **1.** _____

Major supporting detail: **2.** _____

Major supporting detail: **3.** _____

Major supporting detail: **4.** _____

5. What signal word introduces the last major detail? _____

B. Read the following paragraph. Then complete the concept map with information from the paragraph and answer the question.

Information Processing and Three Types of Memory

[1]Information processing refers to how people use their long-term and short-term memory. [2]Experts have identified three types of memory used in information processing. [3]The first type is sensory memory. [4]Sensory memory briefly stores information until you can process it. [5]Sensory memory lasts for about one second for vision and two to four seconds of hearing. [6]To use sensory memory, pay careful attention to one task before moving on to another. [7]For example, take time to study a chart or graph until it makes sense to you. [8]The second type is working memory. [9]Working memory holds information while you process it. [10]To make the most of working memory, ask questions. [11]Also, work with information in both verbal and visual forms. [12]For example, create a time line of an important event in history. [13]The third type is long-term memory. [14]This is your

permanent store of information. [15]Working memory is limited to about seven items of information for a few seconds. [16]In contrast, long-term memory is vast. [17]And it may last for a lifetime. [18]To tap into long-term memory, connect new information to what you already know about a topic.

—Adapted from Parkay & Standord, *Becoming a Teacher*, pp. 350–351, © 2010 Pearson Education, Inc. Reproduced by permission of Pearson Education, Inc.

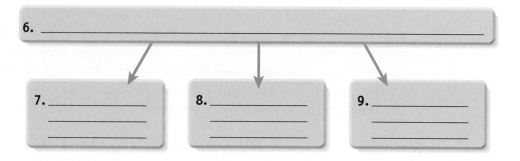

6. _____

7. _____

8. _____

9. _____

10. What signal word introduces the first major supporting detail? _____

_____

REVIEW TEST 2

Score (number correct) _____ × 10 = _____%

Supporting Details and Concept Maps

A. Read the following paragraph. Then complete the concept map by giving the main idea and the three major supporting details that are missing.

Stages of Grief

[1]Grief is a natural and healthy response to our loss of something or someone. [2]Elizabeth Kubler-Ross explains in her book *On Death and Dying* that grief occurs in stages, and understanding those stages helps us cope with our grief. [3]According to Kubler-Ross, grief has five stages. [4]The first stage of grief is *denial*. [5]At first, we tend to refuse to accept the reality of the loss. [6]Denial protects us from the shock of the loss until we are better able to cope. [7]The second stage is *anger.* [8]Anger results from feeling abandoned or helpless. [9]Sometimes resentment toward God or the one we lost takes first place in our emotions. [10] The third phase is the *bargaining* phase. [11]We may spend much time thinking about what we could have done differently to prevent the loss. [12]The fourth phase is *depression*.

¹³Once we realize the depth of the loss, we often find we have trouble sleeping and concentrating. ¹⁴Frequent crying jags and feelings of loneliness, emptiness, isolation, and self-pity often overtake us. ¹⁵The fifth and final stage of grief is *acceptance*. ¹⁶The sharp pain of grief lessens, and we begin to make plans for our future. ¹⁷We learn to accept the new and different life that lies before us.

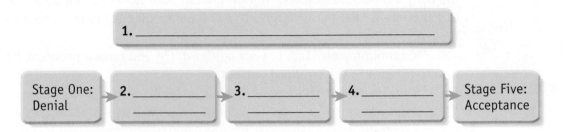

1. _____

| Stage One: Denial | → | 2. _____ _____ | → | 3. _____ _____ | → | 4. _____ _____ | → | Stage Five: Acceptance |

5. What signal words introduce the final major supporting detail? _____

_____

B. Read the following passage. Then complete the concept map using information from the passage.

Six Tips for Renters

¹From finding the right place to beating out others who want the place to getting along with the landlord, renting can be tricky. ²The following six tips should take some of the hassle out of finding and renting a home.

³*Be prepared!* ⁴Bring the following papers with you when you meet prospective landlords, and you will have an edge over others: a filled-out rental application; written references from landlords, employers, friends, and colleagues; and a current copy of your credit report.

⁵*Read before signing!* ⁶Carefully read the entire rental contract before you sign. ⁷Your lease may have terms that you just can't live with; for example, there may be limits on the guests or pets you can have or on changes you can make in decorating. ⁸Make sure you understand the security deposit refund policy.

⁹*Get everything in writing!* ¹⁰Avoid quarrels with your landlord by getting everything in writing. ¹¹Keep copies of any correspondence, and follow up decisions made in person or over the phone with a letter. ¹²For example, if you ask your landlord to make repairs, put your request in writing, and keep a copy for yourself. ¹³If the landlord agrees verbally, send a letter to document your understanding.

[14]*Know your rights!* [15]You have the right to privacy. [16]A landlord must give you notice before entering your premises. [17]You have a right to a livable rental unit. [18]You have the right to heat, water, and electricity. [19]You have the right to live in a clean and safe building. [20]If your place is not properly kept up, you can keep part of the rent to pay for repairs, or you can move out without having to pay for future rent. [21]Ask if the neighborhood is safe and, if it isn't, what your landlord will do about it. [22]If crime is likely, your landlord may have to take some steps to protect you.

[23]*Communicate!* [24]Talk to your landlord. [25]If you have a problem, be sure to bring it to the landlord's attention.

[26]*Get insurance!* [27]Purchase renter's insurance for your belongings. [28]Your landlord's insurance policy will not cover your losses. [29]Renter's insurance typically costs $350 a year for a $50,000 policy that covers loss due to theft or damage caused by other people or natural disasters.

[30]Taking heed of these six tips should aid in the renting process.

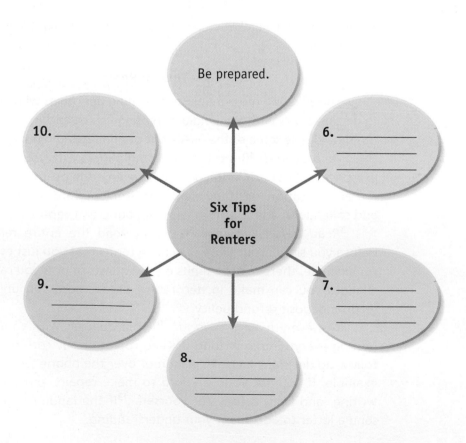

Be prepared.

10. _____

6. _____

Six Tips for Renters

9. _____

7. _____

8. _____

REVIEW TEST 3

Score (number correct) _____ × 10 = _____ %

Supporting Details and Outlines

Read the following article for the San Jose *Mercury News* by Ruben Navarrette, Jr. Then complete the activities that follow.

Civic Rules Shouldn't Be Just for Immigrants

[1]There was a huge response to a column listing 10 ways for immigrants—especially those from Mexico and Latin America—to improve their relationship with the United States. [2]The feedback was about 95 percent positive. [3]That was true even among self-identified Latinos, both immigrants and the native-born.

[4]But by far the most interesting reaction was from dozens of readers who suggested that the advice—don't feel entitled, don't play the victim, stress the value of education, etc.—should not be limited to immigrants. [5]The sermon, they said, should also be aimed at Americans, too many of whom have grown soft and have shed the values of their immigrant ancestors.

[6]Great idea. [7]I have no problem criticizing my own tribe—my fellow native-born Americans. [8]After all, it's the cohort I know best. [9]Besides, the criticisms apply to me too. [10]There are plenty of things I could learn from my Mexican immigrant grandfather, if only he were here to teach me.

[11]There are traps that I have to avoid, such as spoiling my kids. [12]Or buying too many things on credit; my grandfather paid cash for everything. [13]And let's just say I'm grateful I never had to put my work ethic up against his. [14]It would have been no contest.

[15]Americans can pay tribute to their immigrant ancestors, live up to their potential, and avoid getting passed up by the immigrants of today by adhering to some simple rules.

1. [16]Work hard, and teach your children to take summer and after-school jobs. [17]Don't treat any kind of work as beneath you. [18]Someone has to do it, and you're no better than they are.
2. [19]If you don't want Mexican immigrants to treat the United States like an enormous ATM, then resist the temptation to treat Mexico like a gigantic temp agency. [20]Do your own chores.
3. [21]Learn a new language—at any age. [22]It's embarrassing that some cabdrivers, maids and dishwashers in Europe can speak more languages than MBAs, lawyers and engineers in the United States.

4. [23]Don't play the victim. [24]Just because you didn't get into the university of your choice or get a promotion doesn't mean you can blame affirmative action or other forces beyond your control.

5. [25]Have dinner as a family every night. [26]Studies show that conferring over the dinner table is a great way to keep your child's grades up and prevent drug and alcohol abuse.

6. [27]Get used to the "new normal" of not overspending. [28]We already have too much stuff, and what is of greatest value—our health, family, etc.—can't be obtained with a credit card.

7. [29]Raise your kids to be confident but not narcissistic. [30]Our youth are intoxicated with cheap self-esteem, taught to believe that everyone in a race deserves a trophy just for showing up.

8. [31]Don't think of yourself as entitled to anything. [32]Just concentrate on doing what is necessary to earn what you want.

9. [33]Immerse yourself in the "foreign" cultures of fellow Americans. [34]You'll see there are similarities in what we think are differences. [35]What we're going through, someone else went through.

10. [36]Take off your blinders and show empathy for foreigners, remembering that many of your forefathers were likewise despised and suffered discrimination, even if they came legally.

[37]Living in this, the most diverse country in the world, means you're constantly exposed to cultural differences.

[38]This is a blessing, not a reason to panic. [39]So don't just tolerate different experiences and diverse points of view, celebrate them. [40]And stop keeping up with the Joneses.

[41]But, when it comes to optimism, entrepreneurship and hard work, it wouldn't hurt to try to keep up with recent immigrants. [42]They might even help remind you how lucky you are, and what a special place this is.

—Navarrette, "Civic Rules Shouldn't Be Just for
Immigrants." 3 Oct. 2009 MercuryNews.com.

Outline　Complete the outline with information from the passage.

Thesis statement: _____

_____

_____

　　I. _____

_____

II. _____

III. _____

IV. _____

V. Have dinner as a family every night.

VI. _____

VII. _____

VIII. _____

IX. _____

X. _____

VISUAL VOCABULARY

Narcissus was a figure from a Greek myth. He was cursed by the gods to fall in love with his own reflection in a pool of water. Unable to take his eyes off his own beauty, he died beside his reflection. A person who

is **narcissistic** is —————.

a. handsome.
b. conceited.
c. selfless.

WHAT DO YOU THINK?

Ruben Navarrette states several strong opinions in his article. A number of people may be offended by some of his ideas. Do you agree with his 10 simple rules for civic (public) behavior? Why or why not? Which rules do you think might offend someone? Why? Assume you came across this article in your daily browsing of the web, and you have decided to post a comment to the *Mercury News* in response to this article. Express your agreement or disagreement with Navarrette's 10 civic rules.

REVIEW TEST 4

Score (number correct) _____ × 10 = _____%

Supporting Details

Before reading, skim the passage, and answer the Before Reading questions. Read the passage. Then answer the After Reading questions.

Vocabulary Preview

exile (8) forced absence from a home country

pornographer (8) one who produces or sells sexually graphic pictures, writing, or other material whose primary purpose is to cause sexual arousal.

applicable (37) related, relevant

perspective (43) viewpoint, outlook

translates (52) turns, changes

Students, Get Out Phones

[1]Jennifer Gould ended her class announcements and told her students to take out their cell phones.

[2]"I need at least three people who can get a signal in here," Gould said to her advanced placement literature class. [3]"We're going to be studying the works of D.H. Lawrence, and I want you to find some things about him that you don't already know."

[4]Nearly everyone whipped out a phone and began tapping away. [5]Within moments, the teens were sharing their Internet discoveries.

[6]"He lived during World War I."

[7]"He had relationships with men and women."

[8]"He lived the second half of his life in **exile**, considered a **pornographer** who had wasted his talents."

[9]With each detail, Gould pulled her students deeper into a discussion about the author. [10]When the talk had run its course, the students set their phones down and turned their attention to another author.

[11]In a world where most high schools have adopted a "we see them, we take them" policy on cell phones, Pasco County's Wiregrass Ranch High School swims upstream.

[12]It lets kids text and call and go online whenever they're not in class. [13]That alone puts Wiregrass Ranch among a small group of Tampa area high schools with relaxed cell phone policies. [14]Others are Largo and St. Petersburg in Pinellas County and River Ridge and Gulf in Pasco County.

[15]But Wiregrass Ranch goes a step further.

[16]It encourages teachers to allow students to use their phones in classes for educational purposes. [17]Teens routinely use their phones to shoot pictures for projects, **calculate** math problems, check their teachers' blogs and even take lecture notes.

[18]"That doesn't mean we don't have students who misuse the privilege," said principal Ray Bonti, who this summer distributed some recommended classroom uses for cell phones to teachers. [19]"There are boundaries just like at every other high school. [20]Those boundaries are just defined a little differently at Wiregrass Ranch High School."

[21]If anyone's complaining, Bonti hasn't heard it. [22]Parents, staffers and students alike have praised the school's many efforts to be technologically savvy, including giving students permission to use their personal laptops on campus, too, he said.

[23]The school also has plenty of firewalls and filters in place.

[24]Kids know they have something most other schools don't offer. [25]And they love it.

[26]"I think it's a good policy, because we're all pretty much adults here," senior Katie Everett said. [27]"People are going to text no matter what. [28]So I think it's good that the principal and staff here are being open and letting us use it for educational purposes."

[29]Senior Eric LaGattuta, who attended Freedom High in Hillsborough before moving to Wiregrass Ranch, called his new school "ahead of the game."

[30]"They're just following the rest of the world. [31]It's going digital," he said, checking his phone for messages repeatedly during a short interview. [32]"Once you're 16 or 17, there's things you need to know throughout the day. [33]It was so inconvenient when I had to hide it all the time." [34]Many teachers agreed.

[35]"They all have them anyway, and they're all dying to use them in class," said Spanish teacher Ariana Leonard, who admitted that she stores her life in her cell phone and uses it for a variety of functions. [36]"If they're texting when they're supposed to be listening, I might tell them to put it away. [37]But you might teach them a way to use it that might be **applicable** to their learning."

[38]Students in her English for language learners class often use their phones to take pictures of items she says in English, to demonstrate they understood her.

[39]Chemistry teacher Peter Skoglund said he barely pays attention to texting teens anymore. [40]He expects students having cell phones out in his class to be using them for learning. [41]If not, that's their problem.

[42]Most don't abuse the right, he said, knowing they have plenty of time at lunch and in passing periods to take care of personal issues.

[43]Gould shared that **perspective**. [44]Last year, she said, trying to get kids to put away cell phones in class was a daily battle.

[45]"Now, no," she said. [46]"It doesn't **infringe** upon the education anymore."

[47]The new rules have opened up a new world, she said. [48]Teachers no longer have to wait for a school computer lab to get a quick research project done. [49]The few students who don't have phones share in small groups, or use alternative school equipment.

[50]One girl raised her hand in Gould's class during the D.H. Lawrence discussion and said, "As the only person in here without a phone, I have a question." [51]It quickly got answered.

[52]Allowing students to use their cell phones in class means things get done immediately, which **translates** into more efficient use of learning time. [53]Gould said: "It puts the education in their hands."

> —Solochek, "Some Tampa Bay High Schools Allow Cell Phones to Be Used in Class." Tampabay.com. *St. Petersburg Times*. 4 Oct. 2009. http://www .tampabay.com/news/education/k12/some-tampa-bay-high-schools- allow-cell-phones-to-be-used-in-class/1041399.

Before Reading

Vocabulary in Context

_____ **1.** The best synonym for **calculate** in sentence 17 is
   a. add.   c. count.
   b. judge.   d. work out.

_____ **2.** The best synonym for **infringe** in sentence 46 is
   a. assist.   c. disobey.
   b. intrude.   d. offend.

After Reading

Implied Main Idea

_____ **3.** Which sentence best states the implied main idea of the passage?
   a. Wiregrass High School in Tampa, Florida, allows students to use cell phones at school.
   b. Wiregrass High School in Tampa, Florida, is technologically savvy.
   c. Students at Wiregrass High School in Tampa, Florida, use cell phones to shoot pictures for projects, calculate math problems, check their teachers' blogs and even take lecture notes.
   d. Wiregrass High School in Tampa, Florida, encourages students to use cell phones for educational purposes.

Supporting Details

_____ **4.** Is sentence 8 a major detail or a minor detail?

    a. major   b. minor

_____ **5.** Is sentence 48 a major detail or a minor detail?

    a. major   b. minor

Outline

Turn the title of the article into a question. Then, complete the outline based on major details in the passage. Wording of answers may vary.

6. Question based on the title: _____

_____

    I. Jennifer Gould tells her students to use their cell phones to (**7**) _____

_____.

    II. Wiregrass High School encourages teachers to allow students to use their phones (**8**) _____.

    III. Parents, staffers, and students alike have praised the school's many efforts to be technologically savvy.

    IV. They all have them anyway, and they're all dying to use them in class.

    V. Most don't abuse the right.

    VI. Teachers no longer have to wait for (**9**) _____

_____.

    VII. "It puts (**10**) _____."

WHAT DO YOU THINK?

In the article, the author discusses several positive uses of cell phones for educational purposes. Can you think of additional ways students can use cell phones to study and learn? The article states "most don't abuse the right." What are some abuses of cell phones in classrooms? How could cell phones affect student cheating? Assume you are the president of your college's Student Government Association. Write an article for the college's newspaper that takes a stand for or against the use of cell phones during class.

After Reading About Outlines and Concept Maps

Before you move on to the Mastery Tests on outlines and concept maps, take time to reflect on your learning and performance by answering the following questions. Write your answers in your notebook.

- How has my knowledge base or prior knowledge about outlines and concept maps changed?

- Based on my studies, how do I think I will perform on the Mastery Test(s)? Why do I think my scores will be above average, average, or below average?

- Would I recommend this chapter to other students who want to learn more about outlines and concept maps? Why or why not?

- Test your understanding of what you have learned about Outlining and Summarizing by completing the Chapter 8 Review Card on the insert near the end of the text.

CONNECT TO PEARSON **myreadinglab**

To check your progress in meeting Chapter 8's learning outcomes, log in to **www.myreadinglab.com**, and try the following activities.

- The "Outlining and Summarizing" section of MyReadingLab gives an overview about memory and active reading. This section also provides a model for outlining and a model for mapping. You will also find practice activities and tests. To access this resource, click on the "Study Plan" tab. Then click on "Outlining and Summarizing." Then click on the following links as needed: "Overview," "Model: Outlining," "Model: Mapping," "Practice," and "Tests."

- To measure your mastery of the content in this chapter, complete the tests in the "Outlining and Summarizing" section and click on Gradebook to find your results.

Read the following paragraph. The main idea is underlined. Then complete the activities that follow the paragraph.

Kwanzaa: An African American Celebration

1Millions of African Americans celebrate Kwanzaa from December 26 until the first day of the new year. **2**Kwanzaa honors African roots, community, and family. **3**<u>The holiday has two main goals.</u> **4**First, the creator of the holiday, Ron Karenga, wanted American blacks to be proud of their African roots. **5**The word *Kwanzaa* is a term from Swahili (an East African language) that means "first" or "first fruits." **6**Many African villages set aside seven days of "first fruits" celebration to give thanks for a good harvest. **7**Just as the African holidays last seven days, so does Kwanzaa. **8**Second, each day of the holiday honors pride and service:

- **9**The first day teaches the value of unity. **10**African Americans come together in their family, community, nation, and race.
- **11**The second day is given to self-determination. **12**Self-determination teaches African Americans to know who they are and where they came from. **13**Then they can take control of their future.
- **14**The third day of Kwanzaa reminds people of collective work and responsibility. **15**By solving problems together, each and every person helps.
- **16**The fourth day teaches cooperative economics. **17**African American success comes by owning stores and businesses, and blacks must help one another succeed by shopping at these stores.
- **18**The fifth day teaches purpose. **19**The true purpose of each individual is to return black people to their greatness.

VISUAL VOCABULARY

The word "Kwanzaa" means

_____.

a. first fruits.
b. good harvest.

- [20]The sixth day teaches creativity. [21]Through creativity, humans can leave a place better than it was before.
- [22]The seventh day focuses on faith. [23]Kwanzaa teaches faith in black people: parents, teachers, and leaders. [24]Kwanzaa also teaches faith in the rightness and victory of the African American struggle.

Main idea: The holiday has two main goals.

Major supporting detail: _____

_____

Minor supporting details: a. _____

_____

                                b. Many African villages set aside seven days of "first fruits" celebrations to give thanks for a good harvest.
                                c. Just as the African holidays last seven days, so does Kwanzaa.

Major supporting detail: _____

Minor supporting details: a. The first day teaches the value of unity. African Americans come together in their family, community, nation, and race.

                                b. _____
Self-determination teaches African Americans to know who they are and where they came from. Then they can take control of their future.
                                c. The third day of Kwanzaa reminds people of collective work and responsibility. By solving problems together, each and every person helps.
                                d. The fourth day teaches cooperative economics. African American success comes by owning stores and businesses, and blacks must help one another succeed by shopping at these stores.
                                e. The fifth day teaches purpose. The true purpose of each individual is to return black people to their greatness.
                                f. The sixth day teaches creativity. Through creativity, humans can leave a place better than it was before.

                                g. _____
Kwanzaa teaches faith in black people: parents, teachers, and leaders. Kwanzaa also teaches faith in the rightness and victory of the African American struggle.

Read each textbook selection, and complete the activities that follow it.

Body Language

Textbook Skills

[1]Our bodies speak as loudly as our voices. [2]Bodily cues send messages about our openness, our likes and dislikes, and our sense of power. [3]First, openness is necessary to reach any kind of agreement. [4]Opening the hands, unbuttoning coats or loosening ties, and relaxing the body are all signs of openness. [5]In contrast, crossed arms and crossed legs are signs of being closed off, and the chances to reach agreement are slim. [6]Moreover, our bodies also let our likes and dislikes be known. [7]The need to be liked is common, and we tend to like those who like us. [8]Leaning forward, directly facing another person, keeping the body posture open, nodding the head, touching, smiling, and making eye contact are all signs of liking another person. [9]In contrast, not making eye contact, leaning away, and making an unpleasant face are signs of disliking another person. [10]In either case, we send out and pick up strong hints that affect our choices. [11]Finally, for many people, the need for power has a strong pull. [12]A relaxed body, precise gestures, steady and direct eye contact, touching, staring, and interrupting are all power cues. [13]In contrast, keeping the body tense, smiling too much, and making little or no eye contact signal weakness.

—Adapted from Leathers, *Successful Nonverbal Communication: Principles and Applications*, pp. 79–84.

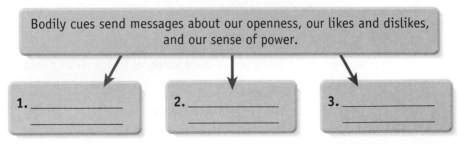

Bodily cues send messages about our openness, our likes and dislikes, and our sense of power.

1. _____

2. _____

3. _____

4. What signal words introduce the first major supporting detail? _____

5. What signal words introduce the last major supporting detail? _____

Good Friends

Textbook Skills

[1]Good friends—they can make a boring day fun, a cold day warm, or a gut-wrenching worry disappear. [2]They can make us feel that we belong, that we matter, and that we have the strength to get through just about anything. [3]They can also make us angry, disappoint us, or seriously jolt our own comfortable ideas about right and wrong. [4]No friendship is perfect, few are fault-free, and most need careful attention if they are to

301

remain stable over time. [5]We all know that friends enrich our lives. [6]Yet most people don't realize that real health benefits come from strong social bonds. [7]Social support has been shown to boost the immune system, improve the quality and possibly the length of life, and even reduce the risks of heart disease. [8]Good friends benefit us. [9]So it is important to recognize the traits of a good friend. [10]Beyond the fact that two people are in a relationship as equals, friendships include the following traits.

[11]*Enjoyment:* Friends enjoy each other's company most of the time. [12]Temporary states of anger, disappointment, or mutual annoyance may occur.

[13]*Acceptance:* Friends accept each other as they are, without trying to change or make the other into a different person.

[14]*Trust:* Friends share mutual trust. [15]Each assumes that the other will act in his or her friend's best interest.

[16]*Respect:* Friends respect each other in the sense that each assumes that the other exercises good judgment in making life choices.

[17]*Mutual assistance:* Friends are inclined to assist and support one another. [18]Specifically, they can count on each other in times of need, trouble, or personal distress.

[19]*Confiding:* Friends share experiences and feelings with each other that they don't share with other people.

[20]*Understanding:* Friends have a sense of what is important to each and why each behaves as he or she does. [21]Friends are not puzzled by each other's actions.

[22]According to psychologist Dan McAdams, most of us are fortunate to develop one or two lasting friendships in a lifetime.

—Adapted from Donatelle, *Access to Health*, 7th ed., p. 131.

_____ **6.** In general, the major details of this passage are
    a. the reasons we make friends.   c. a study about how to make friends.
    b. the traits of good friends.   d. examples of problems with friends.

_____ **7.** One of the health benefits of friendship is to
    a. prevent cancer.   c. boost the immune system.
    b. shorten life.   d. reduce the risk of Lyme disease.

_____ **8.** "Friends are not puzzled by each other's actions" (sentence 21) is a
    a. major supporting detail.   b. minor supporting detail.

_____ **9.** According to the passage, friends
    a. feel free to play roles and wear masks.
    b. try to help each other become better people.
    c. never get angry at each other.
    d. share experiences and feelings with each other that they don't share with other people.

10. The answer to Question 9 can be found in sentence _____.

A. Read the passage, adapted from the college textbook *America and Its Peoples.* Then answer the questions that follow it.

Textbook
Skills

Nancy Shippen

[1]Born in 1763, Nancy Shippen was to be admired for her beauty and her social graces rather than for her intellect. [2]She was an advantaged daughter in an upper-class family. [3]First and foremost, it was her duty to blossom into a charming woman. [4]Thus Nancy's schooling focused on skills that would please and entertain. [5]She learned how to dance, sing, play musical instruments, paint on fine china, and sew pretty pieces of needlework.

[6]In addition to being bound by duty, Nancy Shippen had two male tyrants in her life. [7]The first was her father, William, who in 1781 forced her to marry Henry Beekman Livingston, a man she did not love. [8]The man she did love wanted to know "for what reason in this free country a lady . . . must be married in a hurry and given up to a man she dislikes." [9]None of the Shippens answered him. [10]In truth, the answer was that Nancy legally belonged to her father until she became the property of her husband. [11]Her husband, Henry, was the second tyrant in her life. [12]The marriage was a disaster. [13]Henry was unfaithful. [14]Nancy took her baby daughter and moved back to her family. [15]She wanted full custody of the child, who by law was the property of her husband. [16]Henry made it clear that he would never give up his legal rights to his daughter, should Nancy embarrass him in public by seeking a divorce. [17]To keep her daughter, Nancy gave in. [18]Several years later, Henry changed his mind and arranged for a divorce, but by that time, Nancy's spirit was broken. [19]She lived unhappily, like a hermit, until her death in 1841. [20]The life of Nancy Shippen shows the fate that many women of her day faced.

—Adapted from Martin, et al., *America and Its Peoples: A Mosaic in the Making,* 3rd ed., p. 184.

_____ **1.** Sentence 20 is
   a. the main idea.
   b. a major supporting detail.
   c. a minor supporting detail.

2. How does the life of Nancy Shippen show the fate that many women of her day faced?

   a. _____

   b. _____

_____ **3.** According to the passage, Henry Beekman Livingston was
    a. Nancy Shippen's loving son.   c. Nancy Shippen's tyrant husband.
    b. Nancy Shippen's absent father.

_____ **4.** Sentence 5 is a
    a. major supporting detail.   b. minor supporting detail.

B. Read the paragraph, adapted from a health textbook. Create a map of the main idea and major supporting details by filling in the boxes. Then answer the questions that follow.

Abetting Addiction

Textbook
Skills
[1]The family and friends of an addict may suffer two main problems. [2]One major problem is codependency. [3]Codependence is a self-defeating relationship with the addict. [4]A person is "addicted to the addict." [5]Codependence is not a single event. [6]Instead it is a pattern of behavior. [7]Codependents assume responsibility for meeting the needs of others. [8]Often the need to help others is so strong that they lose sight of their own needs. [9]Their need to help goes far beyond being kind to another person. [10]Codependents feel less than human if they fail to respond to the needs of someone else, even when their help was not sought. [11]A second main problem is the risk of becoming an enabler. [12]Enablers are people who protect addicts from the natural outcomes of their behaviors. [13]Without the benefit of having to deal with the effects of their addiction, addicts are unable to see the harm in their behavior. [14]Thus they continue the harmful behavior. [15]Codependents are the main enablers of their addicted loved ones. [16]But anyone who has contact with an addict can be an enabler and thus aid the addict in continuing the addiction. [17]Enablers are usually unaware that their behavior has this effect.

—Adapted from Donatelle, _Access to Health_, 7th ed., pp. 321–322.

5. _____

6. _____   **7.** _____

_____ **8.** According to the paragraph, enablers are "addicted to the addict."
    a. true   b. false

9. What signal words introduce the first supporting major detail? _____

_____

10. What signal words introduce the second major supporting detail? _____

_____

Read each paragraph, and answer the questions that follow it.

Lies, Lies, Lies

¹Even the best of us find ourselves telling a lie. ²In fact, most of us have probably told at least one of three types of lies. ³One kind of lie we tell is the "white lie." ⁴We tell the white lie because we don't have faith in the person to whom we lie. ⁵We do not believe that the person can bear to hear the truth, so we spare feelings by lying. ⁶For example, when we tell a friend she looks good when she does not, we tell a white lie. ⁷Another kind of lie we tell is the "face-saving lie." ⁸The reason behind this lie is our need to look good to others and ourselves; low self-esteem leads us to think that others shouldn't know about our failure or that our best is not good enough. ⁹In reality, when we tell a lie to make ourselves look good, we lie to ourselves, and we may begin to believe our own lies. ¹⁰Exaggerating work experience on a résumé is one example of a face-saving lie. ¹¹A third kind of lie is the "do-no-harm lie." ¹²We tell this lie when the truth could cause devastating harm. ¹³The need to tell this lie arises during those rare times when the truth could cost a life or damage mental health. ¹⁴For example, during World War II, the lives of many Jews were saved by people who lied to the Nazis so that the Jews could escape.

What are the three types of lies we tell?

1. _____

2. _____

3. _____

The Warning Signs of Suicide

¹Many of our young people are deeply troubled, and teenage suicide is on the rise. ²To stop this tragic trend, we must be aware of the warning signs. ³First, notice the teen's situation. ⁴Stress can cause a young person with undeveloped coping skills to turn to thoughts of suicide. ⁵The loss of a loved one, fear of academic failure, increased responsibilities, or a serious illness all cause stress. ⁶Second, notice the teen's attitudes and emotions. ⁷Inexperienced youth often fall victim to the intensity of their feelings. ⁸Depression, guilt, rejection, and helplessness can seem never-ending, so suicide becomes a way to escape. ⁹Finally, notice any changes

in the teen's behavior. ¹⁰An abrupt change in behavior offers a clear clue. ¹¹A suicidal teen may give away treasured belongings, withdraw from family and friends, have trouble sleeping, and slip in school performance.

What are the warning signs of teenage suicide?

4. _____

5. _____

6. _____

Three Benefits of Exercise

¹Exercise benefits the aging mind, body, and spirit. ²First, exercise helps the mind stay active longer. ³Vigorous exercise three times a week lowers the risk of losing memory or developing Alzheimer's disease. ⁴Even mild exercise helps the flow of blood to the brain. ⁵The increase of blood flowing through the brain keeps brain cells alive and healthy. ⁶Furthermore, exercise helps the body work more effectively. ⁷Exercise makes the immune system stronger, increases the appetite, and keeps muscles toned and strong. ⁸Thus exercise will increase the chances of being healthy longer. ⁹Finally, exercise helps the spirit. ¹⁰Feeling and looking good add to a sense of well-being. ¹¹Remaining strong and independent makes life in the later years a true pleasure.

_____ 7. Which sentence contains the main idea?
- a. sentence 1
- b. sentence 2
- c. sentence 3
- d. sentence 4

_____ 8. Is sentence 5 a major detail or a minor detail?
- a. major detail
- b. minor detail

9. What signal word introduces the second major supporting detail? _____

_____

10. What signal word introduces the third major supporting detail? _____

_____

Transitions and Thought Patterns

9

LEARNING OUTCOMES

After studying this chapter you should be able to do the following:

1. Define the terms *transitions* and *thought patterns*.
2. Determine the relationships of ideas within a sentence.
3. Determine the relationships of ideas between sentences.
4. Determine the thought pattern used to organize a passage.
5. Evaluate the importance of transitions and thought patterns.
6. Apply transitions and thought patterns to passages to improve comprehension.

Before Reading About Transitions and Thought Patterns

Refer to the learning outcomes, and use the Reporter's Questions (such as What? and How?) to create at least three questions that you can answer as you study this chapter. Write your questions in the following spaces:

_____?

_____?

_____?

Now take a few minutes to skim the chapter for ideas and terms that you have studied in previous chapters. List those ideas in the following spaces:

_____

_____

Compare the questions you created based on the learning outcomes with the following questions. Then write the ones that seem the most helpful in your notebook, leaving enough space between each question to record the answers as you read and study the chapter.

What are transitions? What are thought patterns? What is the relationship between transition words and thought patterns? How do thought patterns use transition words?

On page 313, the terms *main idea, supporting details*, and *outlines* are discussed in relation to transitions and thought patterns. Consider the following study questions based on these ideas: How can transitions help me understand the author's main idea? How can transitions help me create an outline?

The Purpose of Transitions and Thought Patterns

Read the following set of ideas.

> Overuse of painkillers can hurt you. _____, taking too much Tylenol over a long period of time can damage your liver.

What word or phrase makes the relationship between these two ideas clear?

    a. Also
    b. However
    c. For example

The phrase that makes the relationship between these two ideas clear is (c) *For example.* The first sentence offers a general idea. The second sentence offers an example for the general idea. The transition *for example* signals that Tylenol is an example of a painkiller that can hurt you if it is overused.

Transitions are key pattern words and phrases that signal the logical relationships within and between sentences. **Transitions** help you make sense of an author's idea in two basic ways. First, transitions join ideas within a sentence. Second, transitions establish **thought patterns** so readers can understand the logical flow of ideas between sentences.

> **Transitions** are words and phrases that signal thought patterns by showing the logical relationships within a sentence and between sentences.
> **A thought pattern** is established by using transitions to show the logical relationship between ideas in a paragraph or passage.

Transition Words: Relationships Within a Sentence

Transitions show how the ideas *within a sentence* are linked. Read the following sentences. Which words make the relationship of ideas within the sentence clear?

_____ **1.** Jermaine has studied for weeks, _____ he still feels anxious about the exam.

    a. also   c. but

    b. when

_____ **2.** Jermaine's mind goes blank _____ he takes an exam.

    a. because   c. when

    b. for example

In the first sentence, the word that best states the relationship of ideas within the sentence is (c) *but*. The transition word *but* signals a contrast between the two ideas and helps us to understand that Jermaine is anxious in spite of the fact that he studied for the exam. In the second sentence, the word that best states the relationship of ideas within the sentence is (c) *when*. The transition word *when* tells us at what times these two events occur in relationship to each other. Notice that these transition words link two ideas expressed in a single sentence. Transitions serve a vital role in building ideas within a sentence.

EXAMPLE Complete the following ideas with a transition that shows the relationship within each sentence. Fill in each blank with a word from the box. Use each word once.

away	because	such as	than

1. Many students make lower scores on tests _____ they make on homework.

2. Test anxiety can have bodily effects _____ nausea, sweating, and headaches.

3. Aaron raised his test scores _____ he learned some simple test-taking strategies.

4. To stay focused on a test, Aaron chooses a seat _____ from the door, aisles, and other busy areas.

EXPLANATION

1. This sentence discusses the two topics, tests and homework, *in contrast* to each other. Many students perform differently on tests *than* on homework.

2. The transition *such as* indicates a list of examples. In this sentence, *such as* introduces a list of examples of *bodily effects of test anxiety*.

3. This sentence discusses two ideas: test scores and test-taking strategies. The relationship between these two ideas is *cause and effect*, and is indicated by the transition *because*. Aaron's use of test-taking strategies led to his higher test scores.

4. This sentence describes a test-taking strategy based on *space*. Aaron chose the best place in the room for taking a test. He chose a quiet place *away* from distractions.

PRACTICE 1

Complete the following ideas with a transition that shows the relationship within each sentence. Fill in each blank with a word from the box. Use each word once.

after	because	however	if	then

1. _____ you want to know the best time to do something, _____ you should read *Buy Ketchup in May and Fly at Noon*.

2. October may be the best time to buy a pair of jeans; _____, it is not the time to buy a vacuum cleaner.

3. The best time to learn math is the first 15 minutes _____ you attend class.

4. Taking a noon flight is best _____ you can avoid the airport rush hours.

Transitions reveal a variety of relationships between ideas. Therefore, you must look carefully at the meaning of each transitional word or phrase. Sometimes the same words can serve as two different types of transitions, depending on how they are used. For example, the word *since* can reveal time order, or it can signal a cause. Notice the difference in the following two sentences.

> **Since** *I got home from school, I have cleaned the apartment and completed my homework.*

> **Since** *the baby is finally asleep, I am going to get some rest too.*

The relationship between the ideas in the first sentence is based on time order. The relationship between the ideas in the second sentence is based on cause and effect.

Some transition words have the same meaning. For example, *also, too,* and *furthermore* all signal the same relationship of addition or listing. Skilled readers look for signal words, study their meaning in context, and use them as keys to unlock the author's message.

 # Thought Patterns: Relationships Between Sentences

Not only do transitions reveal the relationship of ideas *within* a sentence, but also they show the relationship of ideas *between* sentences. Read the following sentence and choose the word or phrase that best states the relationship between the sentences.

> Ancient Greece created important public spaces. For example, an acropolis served as a religious center from a high place "at the top of the city." _____, an agora served as a market place in the middle of the city.

>   a. In contrast   b. Also   c. For example

VISUAL VOCABULARY

The _____ in Athens overlooks the city.

  a. acropolis
  b. agora

In the example above, choice (a) *In contrast* best signals the relationship between the two sentences. Transitions of contrast signal how two or more ideas differ from each other. Choice (b) *Also* signals the addition of another idea. Choice (c) *For example* signals a specific detail that represents a more general idea.

In this chapter and Chapter 10, you will study the various ways in which authors use these and other transitions and thought patterns in paragraphs and passages. First, it is important to learn to read for the relationships **between** sentences.

EXAMPLE Complete each of the following items with a transition that makes the relationship between sentences clear. Fill in each blank with a word or phrase from the box. Use each word or phrase once.

another	as a result	first	for example

1. One basic human need is the need to be forgiven when we are sorry for our wrongs. _____ need is to forgive others who wrong us.

2. For your brain to function at its best, you should eat a variety of healthful foods. _____, your diet should include eggs, wheat, salmon, green leafy vegetables, apples, bananas, lean meats, and plenty of water.

3. A significant number of citizens of this country do not register to vote. _____, they do not have a voice in the democratic process.

4. You can improve your vocabulary in a two-step process. _____, notice new and difficult words as you read; then look up these words in a dictionary.

EXPLANATION

1. The relationship between sentences is addition. The word *one* indicates that the first of two or more ideas is going to be discussed. The word *another* signals the addition of a second need.

2. The first sentence states a general idea. The phrase *for example* signals that specific examples will follow.

3. The fact stated in the second sentence occurs because of the fact stated in the first sentence. The phrase *as a result* states the cause-and-effect relationship between the sentences.

4. The relationship between these sentences is based on time order. The first sentence states the idea that vocabulary can be improved in two steps. The second sentence states the two steps. The transition word *first* signals the first step.

 ## Thought Patterns: Organization of a Passage

You will recall that a paragraph is made up of a group of ideas. Major details support the main idea, and minor details support the major details. Transitions make the relationship between these three levels of ideas clear, smooth, and easy to follow.

Before beginning to write, an author must ask, "How should these ideas be organized so that the reader can follow and understand my point?" A **thought pattern** (also called a **pattern of organization**) allows the author to arrange the supporting details in a clear and smooth flow by using transition words.

> **Thought patterns** (or **patterns of organization**) are signaled by using transitions to show the logical relationship between ideas in a paragraph, passage, or textbook chapter.

Read the following heading taken from a college communications textbook:

Speaker Cues in Conversation

This heading clearly states the author's purpose: to explain the cues speakers use in conversations. Now read the following topic sentence about the topic "speaker cues in conversations."

A speaker controls the conversation with two cues.

A main idea (topic sentence) is made up of a topic and the author's controlling point about the topic. One way an author controls the topic is by using a specific thought pattern. This topic sentence clues the reader that the author is going to explain two cues a speaker uses to control conversation. A skilled reader can now skim ahead and look for the two cues. This sentence shows the close tie between an author's purpose, the topic, and the thought pattern, for this paragraph will list and explain the two cues. The thought pattern used here is listing. In this chapter we discuss four common thought patterns and the transition words and phrases used to signal each one:

- The time order pattern
- The space order pattern
- The listing pattern
- The classification pattern

Chapter 10 covers some additional common thought patterns.

The Time Order Pattern

The **time order** thought pattern generally shows a chain of events. The actions or events are listed in the order that they occur. This is called **chronological order**. Two types of chronological order are narration and process. An author uses narration to tell about the important events in the life of a famous person or during a significant event in history. The narration time order is also used to organize a piece of fiction. The second type of time or chronological order is process. Authors use process to give directions to a task using time order. In summary, there are two basic uses of time order: (1) narration: a chain of events and (2) process: steps, stages, or directions.

Narration: A Chain of Events

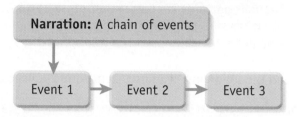

Transitions of **time** signal that the writer is describing when something occurred and in what order. The writer presents an event and then shows when each of the additional details or events flowed from the first event. Thus the details follow a logical order based on time.

Transitions Used in Narration: A Chain of Events				
after	eventually	later	over time	then
afterward	finally	meanwhile	previously	ultimately
as	first	next	second	until
before	in the end	now	since	when
currently	last	often	soon	while
during				

> Harriet Tubman, a runaway slave, led hundreds of slaves to freedom over the course of 10 years; later, during the Civil War, she was a spy for the federal forces in South Carolina as well as a nurse.

Notice that this sentence narrates a chain of events in the life of Harriet Tubman. Transition words and phrases (*over the course, later, during*) tell when each event occurred.

EXAMPLE Determine a logical order for the following three sentences. Write **1** by the sentence that should come first, **2** by the sentence that should come second, and **3** by the sentence that should come last. Circle the narration transition words.

_____ In the end, Althea lost her job, her husband, and her children, and due to years of drinking, she developed a liver disease that took her life.

_____ When Althea first began to drink, she just did not realize the risks she faced.

_____ Over time, her drinking slowly but surely took total control of her life.

EXPLANATION Compare your answers to the sentences arranged in the proper order in the following paragraph. The narration transition words are in **bold** print.

> **When** Althea **first** began to drink, she just did not realize the risks she faced. **Over time**, her drinking slowly but surely took total control of her life. **In the end**, Althea lost her job, her husband, and her children, and due to years of drinking, she developed a liver disease that took her life.

PRACTICE 2

Determine a logical order for the following four sentences. Write **1** by the sentence that should come first, **2** by the sentence that should come second, **3** by the sentence that should come third, and **4** by the sentence that should come fourth. Circle the time transition words.

_____ Moments before his fatal wreck at the Daytona Race Track, Dale Earnhardt was in third place.

_____ Ultimately, the head-on impact cost him his life.

_____ At that time, he was moving up and down the track to keep the cars behind him from passing.

_____ Then, suddenly, on the fourth turn, his car shot straight up the bank and into the wall.

Process: Steps, Stages, or Directions

The time order pattern for steps, stages, or directions shows actions that can be repeated at any time with similar results. This pattern is used to give directions.

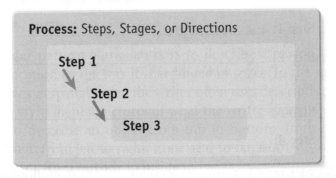

Process: Steps, Stages, or Directions

Step 1

Step 2

Step 3

Read the following topic sentences. Circle the words that signal process time order.

1. Follow five simple steps to create an online identity and password for your email account.

Transition words of **space order** signal that the details follow a logical order based on two elements: (1) how the object, place, or person is arranged in space, and (2) the starting point from which the author chooses to begin the description.

Transition Words Used in the Space Order Pattern

above	at the side	below	by	farther	left	right
across	at the top	beneath	center	front	middle	there
adjacent	back	beside	close to	here	nearby	under
around	back up	between	down	in	next to	underneath
at the bottom	behind	beyond	far away	inside	outside	within

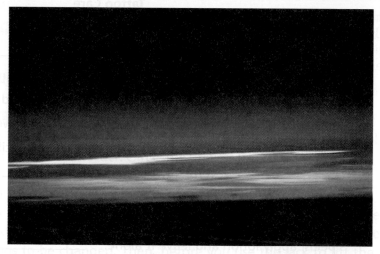

—Image courtesy of Earth Sciences and Image Analysis Laboratory, NASA Johnson Space Center. (ISS001:421:24) http://eol.jsc.nasa.gov.

EXAMPLE Study the picture. Then fill in each blank with the best word based on space order.

around	bottom	on	side
at	from	over	

Some of the most breathtaking views of Earth taken **(1)** _____ space are those that capture our planet's limb. When viewed from the **(2)** _____, the Earth looks like a flat circle, and the atmosphere appears like a halo **(3)** _____ it. This glowing halo is known as

the limb. This image shows the Earth's limb captured by astronauts
(4) _____ the International Space Station. This picture is a view
of the limb at sunset. The surface of the Earth appears as a dark area
(5) _____ the **(6)** _____ with the blackness of outer
space draped **(7)** _____ the limb.

EXPLANATION   Compare your answers to the completed paragraph.

Earth's Limb

Some of the most breathtaking views of Earth taken from space are
those that capture our planet's limb. When viewed from the side, the
Earth looks like a flat circle, and the atmosphere appears like a halo
around it. This glowing halo is known as the limb. This image shows the
Earth's limb captured by astronauts on the International Space Station.
This picture is a view of the limb at sunset. The surface of the Earth appears as a dark area at the bottom with the blackness of outer space
draped over the limb.

PRACTICE 4

Fill in each blank in the paragraph with the best word based on space order.
Choose your answers from the words in the box.

above	at the bottom	end	inland	over
at	away	in	middle	outlying

An earthquake **(1)** _____ of the ocean triggered a towering
tsunami. With waves rising **(2)** _____ 33 feet, the tsunami
gushed **(3)** _____ the island. The waves hit **(4)** _____
the **(5)** _____ of the harbor **(6)** _____ the island's capital.
Residents of **(7)** _____ villages on one **(8)** _____ of the
main island were cut off. The bridge connecting them to the main road
was washed **(9)** _____. Flood waters surged **(10)** _____
for miles.

The Listing Pattern

Often authors want to list a series or set of reasons, details, or points that support the main idea. Transitions of addition, such as *and, also,* and *furthermore,* are generally used to indicate a **listing pattern**.

Listing Pattern
Idea 1
Idea 2
Idea 3

Many people use the Internet to pay bills *and* shop for goods. *In addition,* people turn to the Internet as a source of information.

Notice that in these sentences, two transitions signal the addition of ideas: *and* and *in addition.* Transitions of addition signal that the writer is adding another idea to an earlier thought.

Addition Transitions Used in the Listing Pattern				
also	besides	first of all	last	one
and	final	for one thing	moreover	second
another	finally	furthermore	next	third
as well as	first	in addition		

EXAMPLE   Refer to the box of addition transitions used in the listing pattern. Complete the following paragraph with transitions that show the appropriate relationship between sentences. Some transitions may be used more than once.

Hispanics play important roles in American life. **(1)** _____, they are scientists **(2)** _____ explorers. Dr. Ellen Ochoa is a veteran of three NASA Space Shuttle flights. She has logged over 719 hours in space. **(3)** _____, she has traveled four million miles in one mission alone. On **(4)** _____ mission, she operated a robotic arm to transfer four tons of supplies from one spacecraft to the other. **(5)** _____, Hispanics are talented writers. Gary Soto is an award-winning Mexican-American author **(6)** _____ poet. Soto writes novels, plays, and memoirs, **(7)** _____ children's books. He has **(8)** _____ edited several literary anthologies. **(9)** _____, Hispanics are successful judges. Sonia Sotomayor was the first Puerto Rican woman to serve as a U.S. Circuit Court judge. **(10)** _____, she is the first Latina to serve on the Supreme Court.

EXPLANATION This paragraph began with a general idea. The three major details are introduced by the transitions of addition: (1) *First*, (5) *Next*, and (9) *Third*. Minor details are also signaled with transitions of addition: (2) *and*, (3) *Furthermore*, (4) *another*, (6) *and*, (7) *as well as*, (8) *also*, and (10) *In addition*.

PRACTICE 5

This paragraph uses the listing thought pattern. Complete the chart that follows it by giving the missing details in their proper order. Circle the addition transition words in the paragraph.

¹How many times have you heard the warning "You can't judge a book by its cover"? ²This saying is so overused that it has become just another one of thousands of clichés, and many clichés don't make a lick of sense. ³Some of the silliest clichés refer to animals. ⁴First, bugs are quite popular in senseless clichés. ⁵"Snug as a bug in a rug" is supposed to express comfort, and "Don't let the bedbugs bite" is a way of saying, "Sleep well." ⁶In addition, "crazy as a June bug" means crazy, but just how crazy is a June bug? ⁷Bulls are also used in some pretty silly clichés. ⁸To begin with, a "cock and bull story" is an untrue story, and "to shoot the bull" is to get together and talk. ⁹Finally, the saying "like a bull in a china shop" refers to someone who is vigorous but clumsy. ¹⁰When would anyone let a bull in a china shop? ¹¹It makes you wonder how these sayings got started.

Silly Animal Clichés

Bug clichés	Bull clichés
1. Snug as a bug in a rug	1. Cock and bull story
2. _____	2. _____
3. _____	3. _____

The Classification Pattern

Authors use the **classification pattern** to sort ideas into smaller groups and describe the traits of each group. Each smaller group, called a **subgroup**, is based on shared traits or characteristics. The author lists each subgroup and describes its traits.

Because groups and subgroups are listed, transitions of addition are used in this thought pattern. These transitions are coupled with words that indicate classes or groups. Examples of classification signal words are *first type*, *second kind*, and *another group*.

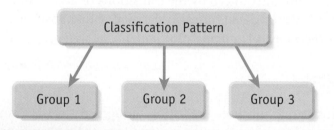

Transitions Used in the Classification Pattern	
another (group, kind, type)	first (group, kind, type)
categories	order
characteristics	second (group, kind, type)
class	traits

EXAMPLE   Determine a logical order for the following three sentences. Write **1** by the sentence that should come first, **2** by the sentence that should come second, and **3** by the sentence that should come last. Circle the addition and classification words.

_____ The second type of access is high-speed broadband through the TV cable line or high-speed DSL through fiber optic phone lines.

_____ The first type of access to the Internet is the old-fashioned phone line, which is quite slow.

_____ Most Internet users have two types of access choices for surfing the Web.

EXPLANATION   Compare your answers to the sentences arranged in the proper order in the following paragraph. The classification words are in **bold** print.

Most Internet users have **two types** of access choices for surfing the Web. The **first type** of access to the Internet is the old-fashioned phone line, which is quite slow. The **second type** of access is high-speed broadband through the TV cable line or high-speed DSL through fiber optic phone lines.

In the paragraph, transitions of addition combine with the classification signal word *type*. In this case, *first* and *second* set the order of discussion for the types listed.

PRACTICE 6

This paragraph uses the classification thought pattern. Complete the concept map that follows it by giving the missing details in their proper order. Circle the classification and addition transition words in the paragraph.

Offensive Players

[1]Several types of players make up the offense of a football team. [2]The offense is the unit of the team that moves the ball up the field to score points. [3]The first type is the center. [4]The center takes his place at the center of the offensive line. [5]As the first player to touch the football, he bends over the ball as it lies on the ground and snaps it to the quarterback. [6]The second type of player is the quarterback; he takes the ball from the center and can either pass, run, or hand the ball off to another player. [7]Most often, he works hard to get the ball into the hands of his offensive teammates. [8]Since he is the driving force of the offensive line, he is protected by the other players. [9]The third type of player on the offense is the guard. [10]There are two guards, one on either side of the center; their job is to keep the other team's players away from the quarterback so he can have time to pass or run with the ball. [11]The fourth type of offensive player is the tackle. [12]Tackles are two players who line up next to the guards. [13]Their main job is not really to tackle but to block for the quarterback or for any offensive player who has the ball. [14]A fifth type of offensive lineman is the tight end. [15]The two tight ends line up on each end of the offensive line. [16]A tight end not only blocks for other offensive players, but also is allowed to catch passes thrown by the quarterback. [17]A sixth type of offensive lineman is the wide receiver. [18]Wide receivers are placed on either side of the offensive line. [19]Wide receivers run down the field to catch the football when the quarterback throws to them and then run as far as they can without being tackled. [20]The final type of offensive player is the running back. [21]The two running backs line up in the back of the offensive line and carry the ball on most running plays; they are also allowed to receive passes. [22]When all eleven offensive players do each of their jobs well, football is exciting to watch.

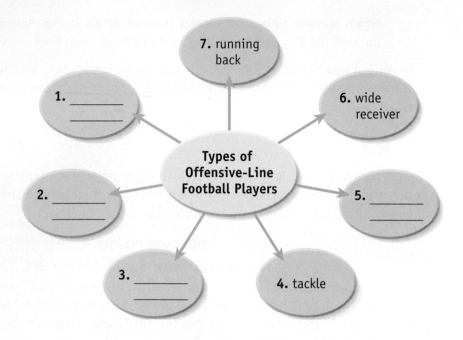

Textbook
Skills

Transitions and Clear Information

Textbook authors try to make information very clear and understandable. Often they use transitions to make relationships between ideas clear.

EXAMPLES   Read each of the following paragraphs, taken from college history, science, and social science textbooks. Circle the transitions used in each paragraph. Then identify the type of organizational thought pattern used in each paragraph.

Textbook
Skills

William Bradford, the First Pilgrim

Throughout his life, William Bradford (1590–1657) was a humble man. Early in life, he dedicated his life to serving the will of God. When he was a baby on a farm in England, his father died. After his mother re-married, his grandfather raised him to become a farmer. By the age of 12, William was an eager reader and focused his studies on the Bible. To his family's shame, he soon started worshiping with separatists in a nearby town. Later, in 1608, he was among the first Pilgrims who went to Holland in search of religious freedom.

—Adapted from Martin et al., *America and Its Peoples:*
A Mosaic in the Making, 3rd ed., p. 49.

_____ **1.** The thought pattern of the paragraph is
   a. time order.
   b. classification.
   c. listing.

Textbook
Skills

Two Types of Carbohydrates

There are two major types of carbohydrates: **simple sugars** and **complex carbohydrates**. The first type, simple sugars, is found mainly in fruits. The second type, complex carbohydrates, is found in several kinds of foods. One kind of complex carbohydrate is made up of grains and cereals. Another kind includes vegetables and fruits. Dark green leafy vegetables and yellow fruits and vegetables like carrots and yams are in this group. Most of us do not get enough complex carbohydrates in our diets. A typical diet contains large amounts of simple sugars.

—Donatelle, *Access to Health*, 10th ed., p. 249.

VISUAL VOCABULARY

This breakfast contains two types of carbohydrates. The oatmeal is a _____.
The berries are _____.
   a. simple sugars.
   b. complex carbohydrate.

_____ **2.** The thought pattern of the paragraph is
   a. time order.
   b. classification.
   c. listing.

How to Stay Young

Leroy "Satchel" Paige was the oldest baseball player, age 59. He pitched three scoreless innings in 1965 for the Kansas City Athletics. When asked about the secret of a good old age, Paige gave six rules for staying young. "First, avoid fried meats which angry up the blood. Second, if your stomach disputes you, lie down and pacify it with cool thoughts. Third, keep the juices flowing by jangling around gently as you move. Fourth, go very lightly on the vices, such as carrying on in society. The social ramble ain't restful. Fifth, avoid running at all times. And sixth, don't look back. Something might be gaining on you."

—Novak, *Issues in Aging: An Introduction to Gerontology,* p. 15.

_____ **3.** The thought pattern of the paragraph is
    a. time order.
    b. classification.
    c. listing.

EXPLANATIONS   Compare your answers to the ones that follow:

The paragraph in example 1 uses time order to relay biographical information about an historical figure, William Bradford. Notice the use of time order transitions such as "throughout," "when," and "later."

The paragraph in example 2 uses the classification thought pattern. The title uses one of the classification signal words, which is "types." The purpose of the paragraph is to describe the different types and traits of carbohydrates. Some of the classification transition phrases used include "first type," "another type," and "group."

The paragraph in example 3 uses the listing pattern to offer advice about staying young. The author suggests behaviors, but these behaviors do not have to be completed in a certain order or in a specific time frame, so the pattern of organization is not time order.

PRACTICE 7

Textbook
Skills

Read the following paragraph from a college social science textbook. Circle the transitions. Then identify the type of organizational thought pattern used in the paragraph.

Types of Economies

The oldest type of economy is the **subsistence economy**. People in subsistence economies meet their daily needs directly from nature. And they do not purchase or trade for most of the necessities of life. A second type is the **capitalist market economy**. In this system, buyers and sellers work together to find out which goods and services to produce. Buyers and sellers decide how much to produce. They also decide how to produce and deliver goods and services. A third type of economy is the **state socialist** economy. This system is a centrally planned economy. The government controls resources from the top-down. In reality, today's capitalist and socialist economies have borrowed much from one another. They have created a fourth type of economy known as a **mixed economy**.

—Adapted from Withgott & Brennan, *Essential Environment: The Science behind the Stories*, 3rd ed., p. 25.

_____ The thought pattern of the paragraph is
a. time order.
b. classification.
c. listing.

APPLICATIONS

Application 1: Identifying Transitions

Fill in each blank with a word or phrase from the box. Use each answer once.

also	and	eventually	in addition	next

1. Jonathan Moore is a good father. He is taking a full load of classes, works two jobs, _____ still manages to make all of his son's football games.

2. As toddlers, people fight to do things for themselves and begin to love the word *mine*. The _____ time they struggle with the same need for control and self-identity is when they are teenagers.

3. The fire ant is thought of as a painful pest, but some ants _____ eat insects and are used as helpful protectors of crops.

4. Smart phones and PDAs are two ways that workers stay closely connected to their customers and bosses; _____, e-mail has helped make the workday much more productive.

5. For a long time, Sarah believed that John Powers was the ideal man;

_____, she found out that he was greedy and self-centered.

Application 2: Identifying Thought Patterns

Identify the thought pattern suggested by each of the following topic sentences.

_____ **1.** Three kinds of parenting styles show a wide range of behaviors.
  a. classification b. time order

_____ **2.** A few simple steps can cut your cost of living and save you money.
  a. classification b. time order

_____ **3.** There are several reasons to include low-impact exercises in your daily routine.
  a. listing b. classification

_____ **4.** Mike Tyson rose from the streets to become a prize-winning boxer.
  a. time order b. listing

_____ **5.** Drivers should sit 10 to 12 inches from the steering wheel to allow the air bag to inflate toward the chest and away from the face and neck.
  a. space order b. classification

_____ **6.** The body of an insect has three distinct parts.
  a. listing b. time order

_____ **7.** Five simple steps can lead to effective communication.
  a. time order b. listing

_____ **8.** The Trail of Tears, the forced removal of Cherokees, began in Tennessee, Georgia, and North Carolina and ended in Oklahoma.
  a. space order b. time order

_____ **9.** Certain characteristics usually lead to student success in college.
  a. classification b. time order

_____ **10.** Understanding how the circulatory system works is a basic required unit of study in medical training programs.
  a. listing b. time order

Application 3: Thought Patterns: Organization of a Passage in a Textbook

Fill in each blank with a transition from the box that makes clear the relationship within or between sentences. Use each transition once.

as	beneath	from	on	onto	then	upward
at	during	in	once	over	third type	when
below	first type	into	one	second type	up	

Textbook Skills

Types of Fog and How They Form

Three common fogs form when air at Earth's surface is chilled **(1)** _____ its dew point. The **(2)** _____ is **advection fog**. When warm, moist air moves **(3)** _____ a cool surface, a blanket of fog called advection fog forms. **(4)** _____ example of advection fog affects Cape Disappointment, Washington. The fog **(5)** _____ this location, and other West Coast areas, is produced when warm, moist air **(6)** _____ the Pacific moves over the cold California Current and is **(7)** _____ carried **(8)** _____ shore by the prevailing winds. A **(9)** _____ of fog is **radiation fog**. As its name suggests, radiation fog forms **(10)** _____ cool, clear, calm nights **(11)** _____ Earth's surface cools rapidly by radiation. **(12)** _____ the night progresses, a thin layer of air in contact with the ground is cooled **(13)** _____ its dew point. As the air cools and becomes denser, it drains **(14)** _____ low areas and forms pockets of fog. The **(15)** _____ of fog is **upslope fog**. Upslope fog forms when relatively humid air moves **(16)** _____ a gradually sloping plain or up the steep slopes of a mountain. **(17)** _____ this **(18)** _____ movement, the air expands and cools. **(19)** _____ the dew point is reached, an extensive layer of fog may form. **(20)** _____ the United States, the Great Plains offers an excellent example of upslope fog.

—Adapted from Lutgens & Tarbuck, *Foundations of Earth Science*, 5th ed., pp. 337–339.

VISUAL VOCABULARY

_____ fog rolls in across the Golden Gate Bridge in the San Francisco Bay, California.

   a. Upslope
   b. Radiation
   c. Advection

REVIEW TEST 1

Score (number correct) _____ × 10 = _____%

Transition Words

Match each of the thought patterns to the appropriate group of transition words. Thought patterns will be used more than once.

   a. time order

   b. space order

   c. listing

   d. classification

_____ **1.** one kind, several groups, another type

_____ **2.** first, second, third, fourth

_____ **3.** before, after, while, during

_____ **4.** in, on, next to, over

_____ **5.** presently, as, ultimately

_____ **6.** in addition, as well, besides

_____ **7.** characteristics, traits, order

_____ **8.** below, nearby, within

_____ **9.** here, there

_____ **10.** and, also, for one thing

REVIEW TEST 2
Score (number correct) _____ × 10 = _____%

Transition Words

Read the passage. Some of the transition words are in **bold** print. Identify the relationship between ideas signaled by each transition word by filling in the blanks that follow the paragraph.

Capillary Action and the Physical Nature of Water

[1]Capillary action is important for moving water (and all of the things that are dissolved in it) around. [2]It is defined as the movement of water **within** the spaces of a porous material. [3]Capillary action is due to the forces of adhesion, cohesion, and surface tension.

[4]Capillary action occurs because water is sticky. [5]Water molecules stick to each other. [6]They also stick to other substances, such as glass, cloth, organic tissues, and soil. [7]Dip a paper towel into a glass of water and the water will "climb" onto the paper towel. [8]In fact, it will keep going up the towel **until** the pull of gravity is too much for it to overcome. [9]**When** you spill a glass of juice (which is, of course, mostly water) on the kitchen table, you rush to get a paper towel to wipe it up. [10]**First,** surface tension keeps the liquid in a nice puddle on the table. [11]**Next,** when you put the paper towel **onto** your mess the liquid attaches itself to the paper fibers.

[12]Plants and trees couldn't thrive without capillary action. [13]Plants put down roots into the soil. [14]Roots are capable of carrying water from the soil **up** into the plant. [15]Water, which contains dissolved nutrients, gets inside the roots and starts climbing up the plant tissue. [16]**As** the first water molecule starts climbing, it pulls along the water molecule **next** to it. [17]The second water molecule then drags up the water molecule **beside** it, and so on.

—Adapted from "Capillary Action." *Water Science for Schools*. USGS 27 September 2004. http://ga.water.usgs.gov/edu/waterproperties.html

Space (spatial) Order

1. _____

2. _____

3. _____

4. _____

5. _____

Time Order

6. _____

7. _____

8. _____

9. _____

10. _____

REVIEW TEST 3

Score (number correct) _____ × 10 = _____%

Transition Words and Thought Patterns

Read the following passage from a college business textbook. Answer the questions that follow.

Stages of Team Development

Textbook
Skills

[1]Teams don't form in a vacuum. [2]Like anything that grows and develops, the formation of a team occurs in stages, and these various stages occur throughout the life of the team. [3]The following is a five-stage model that identifies each stage of a team's development.

Stage 1: Forming. [4]This is the stage in which members first come together and get to know each other. [5]The ground rules of the group are established at this point.

[6]For example, several employees appointed to a professional development committee may come together for an initial team meeting. [7]Once the ice is broken and members understand their standing in the group, the forming stage is complete, and the group moves on to the next stage.

Stage 2: Storming. [8]In this stage, there is a large amount of conflict within the group. [9]Group members may not get along, or they may resist the leader's control.

[10]In the case of the professional development committee, members may disagree on the company's training needs or how to best conduct training. [11]If this behavior continues, the group could break up. [12]However, these conflicts may also make for a stronger team. [13]If the conflicts can be overcome, the group will move on to the next stage of development.

Stage 3: Norming. [14]This is when the group becomes more cohesive and the individual members begin to feel part of the team. [15]This is the best time to establish the team's vision or mission because the team is building toward a common purpose.

[16]In the professional development committee, close relationships develop among individual members, leading to a feeling of solidarity for the team.

Stage 4: Performing. [17]_____ a team has settled on a set of expectations and a process for getting things done, they're ready to move on to the performing stage. [18]All the growing pains of starting the team have been worked out, and the team is now ready to get to work. [19]Team members can now devote themselves to achieving their goals. [20]The performing stage is likely to last the longest since it constitutes the whole purpose of forming the team in the first place.

[21]For example, the professional development committee may begin to conduct specific company training.

Stage 5: Adjourning. [22]The fifth and final stage occurs only if the team has completed the mission it set out to do. [23]If there are no other tasks to accomplish, the team may decide to disband.

[24]For example, if the professional development committee has accomplished its goals, it may agree to disband.

[25]At each stage, leaders need to remain aware of what kind of upkeep and damage control may be required to maintain the team's efficiency and cohesion.

[26]Specific styles of leadership are also needed at different stages of team development. [27]And team leaders need to understand which style is most effective at each stage. [28]An autocratic style may be needed during the forming stage. [29]This type of leader can take charge and get things moving. [30]A democratic type of leader may be needed during the norming or performing stages. [31]This type of leader fosters feedback and cooperation. [32]An effective team leader can adjust his or her style of leadership.

—Van Syckle & Tietje, *Anybody's Business*, pp. 147–148.

_____ **1.** The overall thought pattern of the passage is
- a. listing.
- b. time order.
- c. classification.
- d. space order.

_____ **2.** The relationship within sentence 3 is
- a. addition.
- b. time order.
- c. classification.
- d. space order.

_____ **3.** The transition word that best indicates the relationship of ideas in sentence 17 is
- a. Then.
- b. Once.
- c. Next.
- d. In addition.

_____ **4.** The main thought pattern of paragraph 13 (sentences 26 through 32) is
- a. listing.
- b. time order.
- c. classification.
- d. space order.

_____ **5.** The relationship between sentence 26 and sentence 27 is
- a. addition.
- b. time order.
- c. classification.
- d. space order.

Concept Map Complete the following concept map with details from the passage.

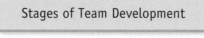

Stages of Team Development

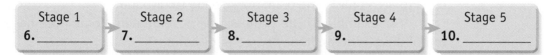

Stage 1	Stage 2	Stage 3	Stage 4	Stage 5
6._____	7._____	8._____	9._____	10._____

WHAT DO YOU THINK?

Have you ever worked on a group project for an academic class? If so, how well did the group work together? If the group worked well, why? If not, why not? Assume you have just completed a group project for your reading class, with a team that included two of your classmates. Your group was to look up information about an author of the group's choice, read a book written by that author, and give an oral report about the life of the author and a summary of the book. Now you must submit a peer evaluation of your teammates and their ability to work in a group. Write a brief summary of each teammate's contribution to the group's work. Organize your evaluation based on the five stages of team development.

REVIEW TEST 4   Score (number correct) _____ × 10 = _____%

Transition Words and Thought Patterns

Before you read, skim the following essay from a college psychology textbook. Answer the Before Reading questions. Then read the essay, and answer the After Reading questions.

Textbook
Skills

Vocabulary Preview

novel (5) new, original
potential (34) possible, likely
tactics (36) plans, strategies
modified (38) changed, adapted
genetic (38) inherited, inborn

Shyness

¹Surveys reveal that more than 50 percent of college students consider themselves to be "currently shy." ²Most of them say that shyness is an unwanted condition. ³In addition, they say it has negative personal and social effects. ⁴Another group of students say that they are "situationally shy." ⁵They

feel shy in certain situations that are **novel**, awkward, or intense. [6]For example, they feel shy on blind dates, at singles bars, or by being put on the spot. [7]Surprisingly, the "not shy" person is the rare, unusual breed in the United States and in every other country surveyed.

[8]Shyness has several traits. [9]First, it makes a person feel uncomfortable or **inhibited** in interpersonal situations. [10]Shyness also interferes with pursuing one's goals. [11]Shyness can be the mild **reticence** and social awkwardness many people feel in new situations. [12]Or it can worsen into a totally inhibiting fear of people. [13]Many shy people are also **introverted**. [14]They prefer solitary, nonsocial activities. [15]Others are "shy extraverts." [16]They are publicly outgoing, yet they are privately shy. [17]They prefer to engage in social activities, and they have the social skills to do so effectively. [18]Yet they doubt that others will really like or respect them.

[19]So why are some people shy and others are not? [20]One explanation may be nature. [21]Research suggests that about 10 percent of infants are "born shy." [22]From birth, these children are unusually cautious. [23]They are reserved when they interact with unfamiliar people or situations. [24]_____ explanation focuses on nurture. [25]Some children are ridiculed, laughed at, or singled out for public shame. [26]Others grow up in families that make "being loved" subject to success in appearance and performance. [27]A third explanation focuses on culture. [28]Among the nine countries studied, shyness is highest in some Asian countries, notably Japan and Taiwan. [29]And shyness is lowest in Israel. [30]A fourth explanation accounts, in part, for a recent rise in shyness in the United States. [31]Young people are very involved with technology. [32]They spend long hours, typically alone, watching TV, playing video games, surfing the Web, and doing e-mail. [33]These activities are socially isolating and reduce daily face-to-face contact. [34]Heavy use of the Internet has the **potential** to make people feel lonely, isolated, and shyer.

[35]As shyness gets more extreme, it intrudes on ever more aspects of one's life to minimize social pleasures and maximize social discomfort and isolation. [36]There are some simple concepts and **tactics** we suggest for shy students to think about and try out:

- [37]Realize that you are not alone in your shyness; every person you see is more like you than different from you in his or her shyness.
- [38]Shyness can be **modified**, even when there is a **genetic** component, but it takes dedication and a resolve to change, as with any long-standing habit you want to break.

- ^{39}Practice smiling and making eye contact with most people you meet.
- ^{40}Talk up; speak in a loud, clear voice, especially when giving your name or asking for information.
- ^{41}Be the first to ask a question or make a comment in a new social situation. ^{42}Be prepared with something interesting to say and say it first. ^{43}Everyone appreciates an "ice breaker."
- ^{44}Never put yourself down. ^{45}Instead, think about what you can do next time to gain the outcome you want.
- ^{46}Focus on making others feel comfortable, especially searching out those other shy people. ^{47}Doing so lowers your self-consciousness.

^{48}If you are shy, we hope you will adopt these suggestions. ^{49}Other students who have followed them have been released from the prison of shyness into a life filled with newfound liberties.

—Adapted from Gerrig/Zimbardo, *Psychology and Life*, p. 415 © 2010 Pearson Education, Inc. Reproduced by permission of Pearson Education, Inc.

Before Reading

Vocabulary in Context

_____ **1.** The word **inhibited** in sentence 9 means
    a. hindered.   c. open.
    b. guilty.   d. unique.

_____ **2.** The word **reticence** in sentence 11 means
    a. rejection.   c. boldness.
    b. confidence.   d. reserve.

_____ **3.** The word **introverted** in sentence 13 means
    a. outgoing.   c. social.
    b. withdrawn.   d. selfish.

Concept Maps

Finish the concept map by filling in the missing idea with information from the passage.

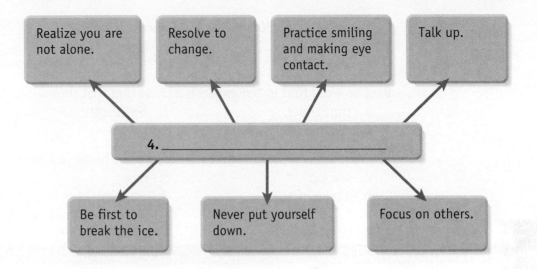

| Realize you are not alone. | Resolve to change. | Practice smiling and making eye contact. | Talk up. |

4. _____

| Be first to break the ice. | Never put yourself down. | Focus on others. |

After Reading

Implied Central Idea and Main Idea

_____ **5.** Which sentence best states the central idea or thesis statement of the passage?
a. People suffer from shyness for several reasons.
b. Shyness has several traits.
c. Once you recognize the traits of and reasons for shyness, you can develop tactics to overcome it.
d. You can liberate yourself from the prison of shyness and enjoy a life filled with newfound liberties.

Supporting Details

_____ **6.** Sentence 22 is what type of supporting detail?
a. major supporting detail
b. minor supporting detail

Transitions and Thought Patterns

_____ **7.** What is the thought pattern suggested by sentence 8?
a. time order   c. classification
b. space order

_____ **8.** What is the relationship between sentences 2 and 3?
    a. time order   c. classification
    b. addition

_____ **9.** The word **first** in sentence 9 is a transition that shows
    a. time order.   c. classification.
    b. addition.

_____ **10.** Choose the best transition word(s) for the blank in sentence 24.
    a. second   c. next
    b. a type of   d. another

WHAT DO YOU THINK?

Do you agree with the author's claim that most college students are shy? Why or why not? Assume that you and a classmate are reporters for your college newspaper. Together, conduct a survey to see how many fellow students in your classes are shy. Use information from the second paragraph of the article to create three or four questions for your survey. Then, write an article that contains the results of your survey and several suggestions to help shy people overcome their shyness.

After Reading About Transitions and Thought Patterns

Before you move on to the Mastery Tests on transitions and thought patterns, take time to reflect on your learning and performance by answering the following questions. Write your answers in your notebook.

- How has my knowledge base or prior knowledge about transitions and thought patterns changed?

- Based on my studies, how do I think I will perform on the Mastery Test(s)? Why do I think my scores will be above average, average, or below average?

- Would I recommend this chapter to other students who want to learn more about transitions and thought patterns? Why or why not?

Test your understanding of what you have learned about Transitions and Thought Patterns by completing the Chapter 9 Review Card on the insert near the end of the text.

CONNECT TO ^{PEARSON} myreadinglab

To check your progress in meeting Chapter 9's learning outcomes, log in to **www.myreadinglab.com**, and try the following activities.

- The "Patterns of Organization" section of MyReadingLab gives additional information about transitions and thought patterns. The section provides a model, practices, activities, and tests. To access this resource, click on the "Study Plan" tab. Then click on "Patterns of Organization." Then click on the following links as needed: "Overview," "Model," "Signal Words (Flash Animation)," "Other Patterns of Organization (Flash Animation)," "Practice," and "Tests."

- To measure your mastery of the content in this chapter, complete the tests in the "Patterns of Organization" section and click on Gradebook to find your results.

A. Read the paragraph. Some of the transition words are in **bold** print. Identify the relationship between ideas signaled by each transition word by filling in the blanks that follow the paragraph.

One Unsafe Place in a Tornado

[1]Stopping **under** a bridge to take shelter from a tornado is a very dangerous idea, for several reasons. [2]**First,** deadly flying debris can still be blasted into the spaces **between** the bridge and the grade. [3]Flying debris can impale any people hiding **there.** [4]**Second,** even when they strongly grip the girders (if they exist), people may be blown loose, out from under the bridge and into the open. [5]People can even be pulled well up **into** the tornado itself. [6]Chances for survival are not good **when** that happens. [7]**Third,** the bridge itself may fail. [8]It may peel apart and create large flying objects, or even collapse down onto people underneath. [9]The structural integrity of many bridges in tornado winds is unknown—even for those that look sturdy. [10]**Finally,** whether or not the tornado hits, parking on traffic lanes is illegal and dangerous to yourself and others. [11]You could create a potentially deadly hazard for others, who may plow into your vehicle at full highway speeds in the rain, hail, or dust. [12]**Also,** parking on traffic lanes can trap people in the storm's path against their will or block emergency vehicles from saving lives.

> —Adapted from Edwards, *The Online Tornado FAQ: Frequently Asked Questions about Tornados.* National Weather Service Storm Prediction Center. 29 Jan. 2009. http://spc.noaa.gov/faq/tornado/#f-scale1.

Space (spatial) Order	Addition (listing)	Time Order
1. _____	5. _____	10. _____
2. _____	6. _____	
3. _____	7. _____	
4. _____	8. _____	
	9. _____	

B. Read the following paragraph from the textbook *American Government: Continuity and Change*, and fill in the blanks with the correct transitions from the box. Use each expression once.

and	by	first	in addition	into

The 1850s: Changing Times

Textbook
Skills

(11) _____ 1850, much was changing in America. (12) _____, people were on the move. The Gold Rush had spurred westward migration. Cities grew as people were lured from their farms. Railroads and the telegraph increased mobility and communication. (13) _____, immigrants flooded (14) _____ the United States. Second, reformers called for change. The women's movement gained strength, (15) _____ slavery continued to tear the nation apart.

—O'Connor & Sabato, *American Government: Continuity and Change*, p. 179.

C. Read each of the following topic sentences taken from textbooks. Identify the thought pattern each one suggests.

_____ **16.** Stress has three types of symptoms.
    a. time order   b. classification

_____ **17.** Vision can be divided into three main phases.
    a. time order   b. classification

_____ **18.** There are a number of reasons that explain why we don't listen.
    a. time order   b. listing

_____ **19.** Animals can be divided into three groups based on physical traits.
    a. space order   b. classification

_____ **20.** The Navajo Nation's territory spans several states.
    a. space order   b. classification

Name _____ Section _____

Date _____ **Score** (number correct) _____ × 10 = _____%

A. Read the paragraph, and answer the questions that follow it.

The Five Phases of Conversation

[1]When experts discuss conversation, they divide the process into stages. [2]The **first** step is the opening or greeting that starts the conversation. [3]A message such as "Hello, this is Joe" establishes a connection between two people. [4]Openings can **also** be a nonverbal gesture such as a smile or kiss. [5]At the **second** step, you usually provide some kind of feedforward. [6]This step gives the other person a general idea about the topic of conversation. [7]"I'm really depressed and need to talk" is an example of feedforward that also sets the tone of the conversation. [8]The third step is the "business," the focus of the conversation. [9]All conversations are goal directed. [10]That is, you converse to fulfill one or several general purposes: to learn, influence, play, or help. [11]This is the longest part of the conversation. [12]The fourth step is feedback, the reverse of the second step. [13]Here you signal that the business is completed: "So you want to send Jack a get-well card?" [14]Of course the other person may not agree that the business has been completed and may counter with "But what hospital is he in?" [15]When this happens, you normally go back a step and complete the business. [16]The _____ and fifth step is the closing, the goodbye, which often reveals how satisfied the persons were with the conversation: "I hope you'll call soon" or "Don't call us, we'll call you." [17]When closings are vague, conversation becomes awkward; you're not sure if you should say goodbye or if you should wait for something else to be said.

—Adapted from DeVito, *The Interpersonal Communication Book*, pp. 194–196 © 2007 by Pearson Education, Inc. Reproduced by permission of Pearson Education, Inc.

VISUAL VOCABULARY

The situation in the photograph shows the

_____ phase of a

conversation.

a. opening
b. feedforward
c. business
d. feedback
e. closing

_____ **1.** The word **first** in sentence 2 is a transition that shows
    a. addition.   c. classification.
    b. time order.

_____ **2. Also** in sentence 4 shows
    a. addition.   c. classification.
    b. time order.

_____ **3. Second** in sentence 5 shows
    a. time order.   c. addition.
    b. classification.

_____ **4.** The best transition word for the blank in sentence 16 is
    a. since.   c. final.
    b. later.

_____ **5.** The thought pattern for this paragraph is
    a. classification.   c. time order.
    b. listing.

B. Fill in the blanks in the paragraph with transition words from the box. Use each expression once.

another type	kinds	one type	these kinds	two kinds

Laws That Protect Children

Unwanted infants are protected by **(6)** _____ of laws. Both **(7)** _____ deal with parents who are unable to cope with the pressures of parenthood. **(8)** _____ of law punishes neglect. Several states, such as Georgia and Massachusetts, will put parents in jail for several years if they leave or abandon a child. **(9)** _____ of law rewards parents for handing their unwanted children over to authorities. A number of states, such as South Carolina and California, have "safe haven" laws. **(10)** _____ of laws allow parents to leave the unwanted child at a church or hospital without being charged with a crime. These laws are supposed to lead to better treatment for the unwanted children.

A. The following topic sentences are taken from a college science textbook. Identify the thought pattern for each one.

Textbook
Skills

_____ **1.** There are two types of reproduction: asexual and sexual.
  a. classification   b. time order

_____ **2.** The formation of soil begins with the weathering of rocks and their minerals.
  a. classification   b. time order

_____ **3.** Animals can be divided into three groups, according to the way they maintain temperature.
  a. classification   b. time order

_____ **4.** In the United States in the early 1900s, a number of individuals began to make serious efforts to halt the destruction of wildlife.
  a. classification   b. listing

_____ **5.** There are two significant sources of atmospheric oxygen.
  a. time order   b. listing

B. Read the paragraph, and answer the questions that follow it.

Textbook
Skills

¹Geologists define three major types of rock. ²The first type, igneous rocks, is formed by the cooling of volcanic flows. ³The makeup of these rocks depends on the rate **and** temperature at which they form. ⁴The second type, sedimentary rocks, is formed from deposits of minerals (sediments). ⁵The makeup of sedimentary rocks depends on the type of sediment from which they are formed. ⁶Some sediments are of biological origin; for example, shells of sea life may fall **to** the ocean floor. ⁷The third type, metamorphic rocks, is either igneous or sedimentary rock that has been changed by heat and the pressure of overlying rock.

—Adapted from Smith & Smith, *Elements of Ecology*, 4th ed., p. 97.

_____ **6.** What thought pattern is suggested by the topic sentence (sentence 1)?
  a. classification   b. time order

_____ **7.** What relationship is suggested by the word **to** in sentence 6?
  a. space order   b. classification

C. Test your comprehension of the three types of rocks. Complete the following outline with information from the passage in part B.

Three Types of Rock

I. (**8**) _____

    A. Formed by cooling of volcanic flows

    B. Makeup depends on the rate and temperature at which they form

II. Sedimentary rocks

    A. Formed from deposits of (**9**) _____

    B. Makeup depends on type of sediment from which they are formed

III. Metamorphic rocks

    A. Existing rocks changed by heat and the pressure of overlying rock

        1. Igneous

        2. (**10**) _____

VISUAL VOCABULARY

Coquina is a (an)

_____ rock that contains numerous mollusk shells.

    a. igneous
    b. sedimentary
    c. metamorphic

A. Fill in each blank with a transition word from the box. Use each transition word once.

Textbook Skills

after	finally	first	second	third

Steps to Stop Sexual Harassment

Sexual harassment is defined as any form of unwanted sexual attention. Most companies now have sexual harassment policies in place. If you feel you are being harassed, there are several steps you can take. **(1)** _____, ask the harasser to stop. Be clear and direct. This may be the first time the person has ever been told such behavior is wrong. **(2)** _____, record the event. Having a record of exactly what occurred (and when and where) will be helpful in making your case. **(3)** _____, complain to a higher authority. Talk to your manager about what happened. **(4)** _____, remember that you have not done anything wrong. You will likely feel awful **(5)** _____ being harassed. However, you should feel proud that you are not keeping silent.

—Donatelle, *Access to Health*, 7th ed., pp. 109–110.

B. Read the passage and answer the questions that follow.

The 2010 Oil Spill in the Gulf of Mexico

[1]A Deepwater Horizon drilling rig was rocked by an explosion and fire on April 20, 2010, and sank into the Gulf of Mexico. [2]Eleven crew members died and 17 were injured. [3]The rig was drilling 42 miles southeast of Venice, Louisiana, beneath about 5,000 feet of water and 13,000 feet under the seabed. [4]A blowout preventer failed to stop the release of crude oil into the ocean. [5]On April 22, the Deepwater Horizon rig,

valued at more than $560 million, sank. [6]And a five-mile long oil slick could be seen. [7]By April 25, the Coast Guard said remote underwater cameras detected the well was leaking 1,000 barrels of crude oil per day.

[8]The Gulf of Mexico oil spill off the coast of Louisiana could not have occurred at a more critical place. [9]The vast estuary surrounding the river from New Orleans south is a breeding ground for every kind of fish from large-mouth bass and crappie to redfish and flounder. [10]Shrimp, too, thrive in the area. [11]Shrimping is a key industry. [12]In addition, the delicate marshes are vital to wildlife. [13]The marshes are critical habitats for hundreds of species of native birds. [14]The marshes also offer critical resting places for hundreds more species of migratory birds. [15]A huge offshore current called the Loop Current bends in near the delta. [16]This current brings everything from blue marlin to bluefin tuna to feed in the rich waters. [17]Now, unfortunately, the Loop may also bring death to wildlife in the form of balls of tar and slicks of oil from the spill.

Complete each statement with a term from the box. Some terms may be used more than once.

classification	listing	space order	time order

6. The main thought pattern for the first paragraph is _____.

7. The relationship of ideas within sentence 3 is _____.

8. The main thought pattern for the second paragraph is _____.

9. The thought pattern suggested by the phrase "every kind of fish" in sentence 9 is _____.

10. The relationship of ideas between sentences 13 and 14 is _____.

After studying this chapter you should be able to do the following:

1. Recognize the following relationships or thought patterns: *comparison, contrast, cause, effect, generalization and example, definition and example.*
2. Determine the relationships of ideas within a sentence.
3. Determine the relationships of ideas between sentences.
4. Determine the thought pattern used to organize a passage.
5. Evaluate the importance of transitions and thought patterns.
6. Apply thought patterns to passages to improve comprehension.

Before Reading About More Thought Patterns

In Chapter 9, you learned two important ideas that will help you as you work through this chapter. Use the following questions to call up your prior knowledge about transitions and thought patterns.

What are transitions? (Refer to page 308.) ⎯⎯⎯⎯⎯⎯⎯⎯⎯⎯⎯⎯⎯

⎯⎯⎯⎯⎯⎯⎯⎯⎯⎯⎯⎯⎯⎯⎯⎯⎯⎯⎯⎯⎯⎯⎯⎯⎯⎯⎯⎯⎯⎯⎯⎯

⎯⎯⎯⎯⎯⎯⎯⎯⎯⎯⎯⎯⎯⎯⎯⎯⎯⎯⎯⎯⎯⎯⎯⎯⎯⎯⎯⎯⎯⎯⎯⎯

What are thought patterns? (Refer to page 308.) ⎯⎯⎯⎯⎯⎯⎯⎯⎯⎯

⎯⎯⎯⎯⎯⎯⎯⎯⎯⎯⎯⎯⎯⎯⎯⎯⎯⎯⎯⎯⎯⎯⎯⎯⎯⎯⎯⎯⎯⎯⎯⎯

⎯⎯⎯⎯⎯⎯⎯⎯⎯⎯⎯⎯⎯⎯⎯⎯⎯⎯⎯⎯⎯⎯⎯⎯⎯⎯⎯⎯⎯⎯⎯⎯

Transitions and thought patterns show the relationships between ideas in sentences, paragraphs, and passages. You have studied four common types: time order, space order, listing, and classification. In this chapter, we will explore some other common thought patterns:

- the comparison-and-contrast pattern
- the cause-and-effect pattern

- the generalization-and-example pattern
- the definition-and-example pattern

 ## The Comparison-and-Contrast Patterns

Many ideas become clearer when they are considered in relation to one another. For example, comparing the prices different grocery stores charge makes us smarter shoppers. Likewise, noting the difference between loving and selfish behavior helps us choose partners in life. The comparison-and-contrast patterns enable us to see these relationships. This section discusses comparison and contrast, both individually and in combination.

The Comparison Pattern

Comparison points out the ways in which two or more ideas are alike. Sample signal words are *similar, like,* and *just as.*

Words and Phrases of Comparison				
alike	equally	in the same way	likewise	similar
as	in a similar fashion	just as	resemble	similarity
as well as	in a similar manner	just like	same	similarly
both	in like manner	like		

Here are some examples:

Our brains are capable of storing and getting information into and out of our memory. *Similarly,* computers have a memory bank in which they can store and get information.

Like a deer frozen in the headlights of a car, Justin could not move.

Jay Leno opens his late-night show with a stand-up comedy routine. *Likewise,* Jimmy Fallon begins his show with his own five minutes of comedy.

PRACTICE 1

Complete the following ideas with transitions that show comparison. Fill in each blank with a word or phrase from the "Words and Phrases of Comparison" box. Use each choice only once.

1. Standardized tests in the U.S. reveal that girls now score just

_____ boys in math.

2. Blood vessels are _____ highways in the body.

3. A human eye is _____ to a camera.

4. _____ a police force protects a community from crime, the immune system protects the body from infection.

5. Juanita and Angelo share biological _____. _____ inherited brown eyes and black hair from their father.

When comparison is used to organize an entire paragraph, the pattern looks like this:

Comparison Pattern		
Idea 1		**Idea 2**
Idea 1	*is like*	Idea 2
Idea 1	*is like*	Idea 2
Idea 1	*is like*	Idea 2

EXAMPLE Number the following four sentences to show their logical order. For example, write **1** by the sentence that should come first, **2** by the sentence that should come second, and so on until you have numbered all the sentences **1** through **4**. Then complete the chart based on the information in the paragraph.

_____ And just as in *InFamous*, players of *Prototype* have to make hard choices.

_____ The video game *InFamous* by PlayStation is exactly like the game *Prototype* by Radical Entertainment.

_____ First, both games are set in New York City during a terrorist attack.

_____ Finally, both games have a superhero who has to fight both the military and the bad guys.

Similarities Between the Video Games *InFamous* and *Prototype*

Traits of the Game	InFamous	Prototype
Set in NYC during a terrorist attack	yes	yes
_____	yes	yes
Superhero fights military and bad guys	yes	yes

EXPLANATION   Here are the sentences arranged in proper order. The organization and transition words are in **bold** print.

> The video game *InFamous* by PlayStation is exactly **like** the game *Prototype* by Radical Entertainment. **First, both** games are set in New York City during a terrorist attack. **And just as** in *InFamous*, players of *Prototype* have to make hard choices. **Finally, both** games have a superhero who has to fight both the military and the bad guys.

To fill in the blank, you should have written "Players have to make hard choices."

The Contrast Pattern

Contrast points out the ways in which two or more ideas are different. Sample signal words are *different*, *but*, and *yet*.

Words and Phrases of Contrast			
although	different	in spite of	rather than
as opposed to	different from	instead	still
at the same time	differently	nevertheless	to the contrary
but	even though	on the contrary	whereas
conversely	however	on the one hand	while
despite	in contrast	on the other hand	yet
difference			

Here are some examples:

Most television programs are geared for mindless enjoyment, *yet* good shows full of interesting information are becoming more common.

Janet and Rob reduced the amount of starchy foods they ate and began exercising three times a week. *Nevertheless,* they both gained 5 pounds in the next two months.

Despite having gone to the grocery store twice in the past three days, I need to go again today.

When contrast is used to organize an entire paragraph, the pattern looks like this:

Contrast Pattern		
Idea 1		**Idea 2**
Idea 1	*differs from*	Idea 2
Idea 1	*differs from*	Idea 2
Idea 1	*differs from*	Idea 2

Textbook
Skills

EXAMPLE Number the following five sentences from a college textbook to show their logical order. For example, write **1** by the sentence that should come first, **2** by the sentence that should come second, and so on until you have numbered all the sentences **1** through **5**. Then complete the chart based on the information in the paragraph.

_____ On the one hand, the front of the house is made up of anyone with guest contact.

_____ Restaurant operations are generally divided between what is commonly called the front of the house and the back of the house.

_____ In contrast to the front of the house, staff in the back of the house are the cooks or chefs, prep cooks, dishwashers, and bookkeepers.

_____ On the other hand, the back of the house refers to all the areas that guests do not typically come in contact with.

_____ The front of the house staff are the host or hostess, servers, bar workers, and the buspersons.

—Adapted from Walker, *Introduction to Hospitality Management*, 3rd ed., pp. 238, 247.

The Front of the House versus the Back of the House in Restaurant Operations

Front of the House	Back of the House
Made up of anyone with guest contact	All areas typically without guest contact
Host, hostess, servers, bar workers, buspersons	_____

EXPLANATION Here are the sentences arranged in their logical order. The transition words are in **bold** print.

Restaurant operations are generally **divided** between what is commonly called the front of the house and the back of the house. **On the one hand**, the front of the house is made up of anyone with guest contact. The front of the house staff are the host or hostess, servers, bar workers, and the buspersons. **On the other hand**, the back of the house refers to all the areas that guests do not typically come in contact with. **In contrast** to the front of the house, staff in the back of the house are the cooks or chefs, prep cooks, dishwashers, and bookkeepers.

To complete the chart you should have listed the staff for the back of the house: "Cooks, chefs, prep cooks, dishwashers, bookkeepers."

Complete the sentences with transitions that show contrast. Fill in each blank with a word or phrase from the "Words and Phrases of Contrast" box. Use each choice only once.

1. Mark Twain's novel *Huckleberry Finn* has often been banned from school

   libraries, _____ it remains popular with millions of young readers.

2. _____ Alkmal and Syreta have been married for over 30 years, they act like newlyweds.

3. _____ the risk for multiple births, many women who cannot become pregnant without medical help choose to take fertility drugs.

4. Resist honking your horn or cursing at annoying drivers; _____, give them room, leave them alone, and be thankful for your own driving skills.

The Comparison-and-Contrast Pattern

The **comparison-and-contrast pattern** shows how two things are similar, how they are different, or both.

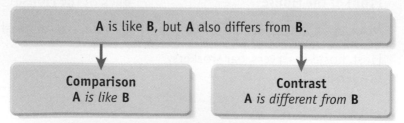

A is like B, but A also differs from B.

Comparison
A *is like* **B**

Contrast
A *is different from* **B**

Fast-food restaurants McDonald's and Subway are *similar* to each other, *but* not as much as one might think. The two fast-food chains do share obvious *similarities*. They *both* offer quick meals at low cost. They both also offer the choice of eat-in or take-out. *However*, there are striking *differences* between the two. McDonald's offers a menu that is filled with foods high in calories and fats, such as hamburgers and French fries. *Unlike* McDonald's fried hamburgers, Subway offers a very different and much healthier choice in lean meats such as turkey and chicken. Subway also *differs* from McDonald's by not offering the option of a drive-through window.

In the paragraph, the two things being compared and contrasted are the fast-food restaurants McDonald's and Subway. The author offers two similarities: quick, low-cost meals and the choice to eat in or take out. The author also offers two differences: the health factor in food choices and the lack of a drive-through window at Subway.

EXAMPLE   Read the following paragraph adapted from a college communications textbook. Circle the comparison-and-contrast words, and answer the questions that follow the paragraph.

Textbook
Skills

In the face of a mistake, one can offer either a good excuse or a bad excuse. Although good excuses and bad excuses share some similarities, their differences have deep meaning. Both good and bad excuses make it possible to take risks and be a part of an activity that may bring failure. They are also similar in their attempt to put a failure in the best possible light. Despite their similarities, good and bad excuses differ greatly in their effect. A good excuse helps one get out of a problem, while a bad excuse only makes matters worse. Good excuses avoid blaming others, especially those one works with; in contrast, a bad excuse avoids taking responsibility and blames others unfairly.

—Adapted from DeVito, *Messages: Building Interpersonal Communication Skills*, p. 214 © 1999. Reproduced by permission of Pearson Education, Inc.

1. What are the two ideas being compared and contrasted? _____

_____

2. List four different comparison-and-contrast words or expressions used in the paragraph. _____

_____

EXPLANATION The paragraph compares and contrasts good excuses and bad excuses. Nine different comparison-and-contrast words are used: *although, similarities, differences, both, similar, despite, differ, while,* and *in contrast.*

PRACTICE 3

Read the following paragraph from a college science textbook. Answer the questions that follow.

Textbook
Skills

Similarities and Differences of Objects in Space

¹Vast spaces separate the eight planets. ²Likewise, vast spaces extend to the outer reaches of the solar system. ³In these vast spaces are countless small chunks of debris. ⁴These chunks differ in size from several hundred kilometers in diameter down to tiny grains of dust. ⁵The objects found in this vast space include *asteroids, comets, meteoroids,* and *dwarf planets.* ⁶Asteroids and meteoroids are similar. ⁷Both are fragments of rocky and metallic material similar in structure to Earthlike planets. ⁸Yet they differ from each other on the basis of size. ⁹Those larger than 100 meters (330 feet) are asteroids, whereas anything smaller is a meteoroid. ¹⁰By contrast, comets are mostly ices. ¹¹Comets have only small amounts of rocky material. ¹²The newest class of solar-system objects is dwarf planets. ¹³Like planets, dwarf planets orbit the sun, have gravity, and are basically spherical in shape. ¹⁴Two dwarf planets are Ceres, the largest known asteroid, and Pluto, which is thought to have a nature similar to Neptune's icy moon, Triton.

—Adapted from Lutgens & Tarbuck, *Foundations of Earth Science,* 5th ed., p. 421.

_____ **1.** What is the relationship of ideas between sentence 1 and sentence 2?
   a. comparison   b. contrast

_____ **2.** What is the relationship of ideas within sentence 4?
   a. comparison   b. contrast

_____ **3.** What is the relationship of ideas within sentence 9?
   a. comparison   b. contrast

_____ **4.** What is the relationship of ideas between sentence 9 and sentence 10?
   a. comparison   b. contrast

_____ **5.** What relationship does the author establish between Pluto and Triton?
   a. comparison   b. contrast

VISUAL VOCABULARY

Dr. Fred Whipple uses a 500 pound snowball covered with dirt in his Harvard classroom to show how a _____ is like a dirty snowball.

a. asteroid
b. meteoroid
c. comet

The Cause-and-Effect Pattern

Sometimes an author talks about *why* something happened or *what* results came from an event. A **cause** states why something happens. An **effect** states a result or outcome. Sample signal words include *because* and *consequently*.

Cause-and-Effect Words			
accordingly	because of	leads to	so
as a result	consequently	results in	therefore
because	if . . . then	since	thus

Here are some examples:

George had run up his credit card bill to its limit. *As a result,* his monthly payments only covered the interest the bank charged.

Because peer pressure can be one of the greatest influences on a young person's life, we must teach our children to choose their friends wisely.

Dustin was always late for work, spent most of his time gossiping, and kept his home stocked with supplies from the office. *Consequently,* he was fired.

PRACTICE 4

Complete each sentence with a cause-and-effect word or phrase from the "Cause-and-Effect Words" box. Use each choice only once.

because	because of	leads to	result in	therefore

1. The bubonic plague is a horrible disease that _____ high fevers, muscle pain, vomiting, and delirium.

2. During the 14th century, _____ the bubonic plague, one third to one half of all the people in Europe died.

3. Lightning strikes may _____ more deaths than tornadoes and hurricanes.

4. _____ President John F. Kennedy backed the space program with great resolve, the space launch building located in Florida was re-named after him.

5. Opponents of the death penalty say that it is cruel, does not stop crime, and can result in innocent people being sentenced to die; _____, they sometimes hold candlelight vigils to protest an execution.

The writer using cause and effect introduces an idea or event and then provides supporting details to show how that event *results in* or *leads to* another event. Many times, the second event comes about because of the first event. Thus the first idea is the cause and the following ideas are the effects. If more than two ideas are discussed, the added ideas may show a chain reaction.

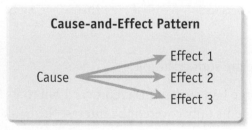

For example, read the following topic sentence:

Too much stress may *lead to* fatigue and anxiety.

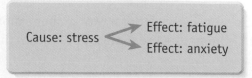

Often an author will begin with an effect and then give the causes.

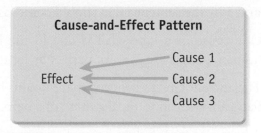

For example, read the following topic sentence:

The bone disease osteoporosis may be the result of poor diet and genetics.

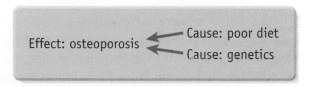

Sometimes the author may wish to emphasize a chain reaction.

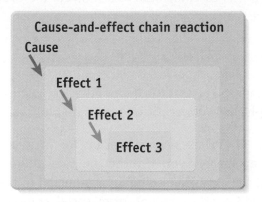

For example, read the following topic sentence.

Children spend more time using technology, and *thus* less time exercising; the less they exercise, the more likely they are to be overweight.

Cause-and-effect chain reaction
Cause: Children spend more time using technology. →
Effect: Children spend less time exercising. →
Effect: Children become overweight.

EXAMPLE Determine a logical order for the following three sentences. Write **1** by the sentence that should come first, **2** by the sentence that should come second, and **3** by the sentence that should come last.

_____ One cause of a hero's fall is due to the limits that come with being human; people are just not perfect by nature.

_____ The ancient Greeks believed that humans have two kinds of flaws; these flaws always lead to the downfall of a hero.

_____ A hero also faces failure because of extreme pride.

EXPLANATION Here are the sentences arranged in the proper order. The transition words are in **bold** print.

> The ancient Greeks believed that humans have two kinds of flaws; these flaws always **lead to** the downfall of a hero. **One cause** of a hero's fall is **due to** the limits that come with being human; people are just not perfect by nature. A hero **also** faces failure **because of** extreme pride.

In this paragraph, two addition words combine with the cause-and-effect signal words. In this case, *one* and *also* indicate the order in which these causes are discussed.

PRACTICE 5

This paragraph uses the cause-and-effect pattern of organization. Read the paragraph, and answer the questions that follow it.

Textbook
Skills

There are several reasons for your self-concept. One is the image others have of you. If those you love and respect think highly of you, you will see a positive self-image reflected in their behaviors. Another cause of self-concept comes from social comparisons. Comparing your test scores to your classmates' is a good example of a social comparison; if you do better than your peers, then you will most likely have a positive view of your abilities. Cultural teachings are another explanation for your self-concept. Parents, teachers, and the media instill a belief about success; when you fit in with these beliefs, you are likely to see yourself as successful.

—Adapted from DeVito, *Messages: Building Interpersonal Communication Skills*, pp. 38–40 © 1999. Reproduced by permission of Pearson Education, Inc.

1. What are the three causes discussed in the paragraph?

   a. _____

   b. _____

   c. _____

2. What is the effect of these causes? _____

3. What are the cause-and-effect signal words used in the paragraph?

   a. _____

   b. _____

   c. _____

 # The Generalization-and-Example Pattern

Going to a movie can be expensive. Two tickets may cost $20.

The first sentence is a general statement. This sentence suggests that it is only the high cost of tickets that makes going to a movie expensive. But expensive popcorn, candy, and drinks also help make moviegoing costly. Adding an **example word** makes it clear that the cost of tickets is only one part of the expense.

Going to a movie can be expensive. *For example,* two tickets may cost $20.

In the generalization-and-example thought pattern, the author makes a general statement and then offers an example or a series of examples to clarify the generalization.

The Generalization-and-Example Pattern
Statement of a general idea
Example
Example

Example words signal that a writer is giving an instance of a general idea.

Words and Phrases That Introduce Examples			
as an illustration	for instance	once	to illustrate
for example	including	such as	typically

EXAMPLE Read each of the following items and fill in the blanks with an appropriate example word or phrase.

1. Many classes teach worthwhile skills. _____, math teaches problem-solving skills.

2. Green plants living indoors help keep the air clean. _____, the corn plant absorbs many household chemicals.

3. More and more people have technology in the home, _____ a computer with access to the Internet, microwave ovens, remote controlled televisions, and cell phones.

EXPLANATION   Many words and phrases that introduce examples are easily interchanged. In the first two examples, you could have used any of these phrases: *for example*, *for instance*, or *as an illustration*. They all are similar in meaning. In the third example, the use of the transition phrase *such as* signals a list. Even though transition words have similar meanings, authors carefully choose transitions based on style and meaning.

PRACTICE 6

Complete each selection with an example word. Fill in each blank with a word or phrase from the "Words and Phrases That Introduce Examples" box. Use each choice only once.

1. Some popular video games send the message that killing is fun.

   _____, the ads for the video game *Carmageddon* state that playing the game is "as easy as killing babies with axes."

2. The Chrysler 300M is a sports luxury car that comes with extra options,

   _____ front seats that heat up and an Infinity sound system.

3. To compete in the sport of basketball, a player needs many skills,

   _____ quick thinking, running speed, jumping power, and sharp aim.

4. Kim is always willing to help others; _____ she cooked and delivered meals every night to a family for two weeks while the mother was in the hospital.

5. During deep breathing exercises, it is important to relax every part of the

   body; _____, loosening up a clenched jaw helps the whole body relax.

Textbook Skills: The Definition-and-Example Pattern

Textbooks are full of new words and special terms. Even if the word is common, it can take on a special meaning in a specific course. To help students understand their ideas, authors often include a definition of the new or special term. Then, to make sure the meaning of the word or concept is clear, the author may also give examples. Thus, at times an author gives just the definition, and other times a definition and example.

> **Self-disclosure** is a type of communication in which you reveal information about yourself. *For example,* slips of the tongue and gestures may send self-disclosing messages. Self-disclosure may also include your reactions to the feelings of others, *as* when you tell your friend you are sorry she was fired.
>
> —DeVito, *Messages: Building Interpersonal Communication Skills,* p. 45
> © 1999. Reproduced by permission of Pearson Education, Inc.

In this paragraph, the term *self-disclosure* is defined in the first sentence. Then the author gives two examples to make the term clear to the reader.

Definition Pattern
Term and definition Example Example

- The **definition** explains the meaning of new, difficult, or special terms. Definitions include words like *is* and *means:* "Self-disclosure *is* a type of communication in which you reveal information about yourself."

- The **examples** follow a definition to show how the word is used or applied in the content course. Examples are signaled by words like *for example* and *such as:* "For example, slips of the tongue and gestures may send self-disclosing messages."

EXAMPLE Annotate the paragraph. Circle the term being defined. Also circle key words in the definition of the term. Underline the examples. Then, answer the questions that follow.

¹Flashbulb memories arise when people go through emotionally charged events. ²These memories are vivid and rich in detail. ³In fact, they seem to be photographs of the original event. ⁴Flashbulb memories apply

to both private and public events. [5]For example, people might have vivid memories of a car accident they have had. [6]The instance of the September 11 attacks also caused flashbulb memories for many.

—Adapted from Gerrig/Zimbardo, *Psychology and Life*, p. 221 © 2010 Pearson Education, Inc. Reproduced by permission of Pearson Education, Inc.

1. What two examples illustrate the term being defined? _____

_____

2. What are the words that signal the examples? _____

_____

EXPLANATION When you annotate your text, you highlight the most important information for easy review. To make the most of your annotations, only underline key words and examples. Compare your annotations to the following:

[1]Flashbulb memories arise when people go through emotionally charged events. [2]These memories are vivid and rich in detail. [3]In fact, they seem to be photographs of the original event. [4]Flashbulb memories apply to both private and public events. [5]For example, people might have vivid memories of a car accident they have had. [6]The instance of the September 11 attacks also caused flashbulb memories for many.

Circling and underlining key ideas creates an opportunity for a quick review of the material. The answers to the questions are as follows:

1. The examples are *a car accident* and *the September 11 attacks*.

2. The signal words for the examples are *For example*, *instance*, and *also*.

PRACTICE 7

Textbook Skills

This paragraph from a college science textbook uses the definition thought pattern. Annotate the paragraph: circle the terms being defined and their definitions. Underline the signal words for the examples as well as the examples. Then complete the concept map that follows by filling in the missing details in the proper order.

Dripstone Features in Caverns

[1]Of the various dripstone features found in caverns, perhaps the most familiar are **stalactites**. [2]These icicle-like pendants hang from the ceiling of the cavern. [3]They form where water seeps through cracks above. [4]When water reaches air from in the cave, some of the dissolved carbon dioxide escapes from the drop and calcite begins to precipitate. [5]A deposit of the mineral forms a ring around the edge of the water drop. [6]As drop after drop follows, each leaves an infinitesimal

trace of calcite behind. [7]And a hollow limestone tube is created. [8]One example of a stalactite is the soda straw formation. [9]Formations that develop on the floor of a cavern and reach upward toward the ceiling are called **stalagmites**. [10]The water supplying the calcite for stalagmite growth falls from the ceiling and splatters over the surface. [11]As a result, stalagmites do not have a central tube. [12]And they are usually more massive in appearance and rounded on their upper ends. [13]For example, pile-of-plates stalagmites look like piled-up plates with broken edges. [14]Other examples can look like candle-sticks or lily pads.

—Adapted from Lutgens & Tarbuck, *Foundations of Earth Science*, 5th ed., pp. 94–96.

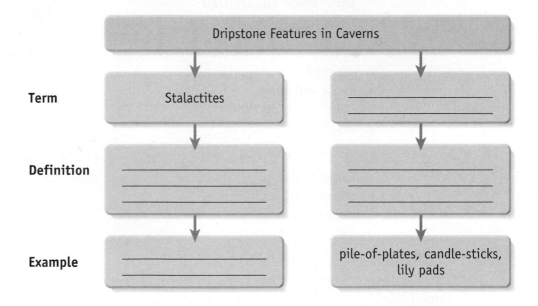

VISUAL VOCABULARY

_____ stand in the Coral Pool in the Mountain View Caverns, Ozark National Forest, Arkansas.

  a. Stalactites
  b. Stalagmites

A Final Note: Thought Patterns and Textbooks

Textbook
Skills

Textbook authors rely heavily on the use of transitions and thought patterns to make information clear and easy to understand.

EXAMPLES   The following topic sentences have been taken from college textbooks. Identify the thought pattern that each topic sentence suggests.

_____ **1.** People often develop poor listening skills for several reasons.
   a. cause and effect
   b. comparison and contrast
   c. definition

_____ **2.** Symmetry is the balanced arrangement of body parts around a center point.
   a. cause and effect
   b. comparison and contrast
   c. definition

_____ **3.** Unlike the South, the North's economy thrived during the Civil War.
   a. cause and effect
   b. comparison and contrast
   c. definition

EXPLANATIONS   Topic sentence 1, from a psychology textbook, suggests (a) cause and effect. Topic sentence 2, from a biology textbook, suggests (c) definition. Topic sentence 3, from a history textbook, suggests (b) comparison and contrast.

PRACTICE 8

Textbook
Skills

The following topic sentences have been taken from college textbooks. Identify the thought pattern that each topic sentence suggests. (The type of textbook is identified after each topic sentence.)

_____ **1.** Sandy and muddy shores appear empty of life at low tide, in contrast to the abundant life found on rocky shores. (_ecology_)
   a. cause and effect
   b. comparison and contrast
   c. generalization and example

_____ **2.** Unlike European railroads, the American railway system grew without government regulation or planning. (*history*)
   a. cause and effect
   b. comparison and contrast
   c. generalization and example

_____ **3.** Sickle cell disease is a blood disease. (*health*)
   a. cause and effect
   b. comparison and contrast
   c. definition

_____ **4.** Beethoven created program music, which is music that tells a story or describes a setting. (*humanities*)
   a. cause and effect
   b. comparison and contrast
   c. definition

_____ **5.** A family's image of itself affects the way it works. (*social science*)
   a. cause and effect
   b. comparison and contrast
   c. definition

APPLICATIONS

Application 1: Using Example and Definition Patterns

A. The following paragraph uses the generalization-and-example thought pattern. In the spaces provided, write the main idea and its example.

Shoppers' Choice

Most shoppers in America have an unbelievable number of choices. Just study the toothpaste aisle in a grocery store or drugstore as an example. First of all, there must be at least a dozen name brands of toothpaste. The best known include *Arm and Hammer*, *Crest*, *Colgate*, and *Aim*. Second, each of these brands offers another dozen choices, for each major brand offers a toothpaste to attack every imaginable problem. Labels shout that the toothpaste contains baking soda, mouthwash, cavity fighters, fluoride, and many other ingredients, singly or in combination. Choices fill several shelves, and this is just the toothpaste aisle!

1. Main idea: _____

_____

2. Example: _____

B. The following paragraph contains a definition and one example. In the spaces provided, write the term, its definition, and the example.

Survivor's Guilt

A person who survives a life-threatening event may experience survivor's guilt, the feeling that it is wrong to have survived. *Survivor's guilt* is made up of many feelings, including shame, confusion, and depression. For example, many of those who lived through the concentration camps of the Holocaust reported struggling with survivor's guilt. They could not come to grips with the fact that they had survived when so many of their family and friends were horribly killed.

3. Term: _____

4. Definition: _____

5. Example: _____

Application 2: Using the Contrast Pattern

The following paragraph uses the contrast thought pattern. Complete the idea map that follows the paragraph.

Native American Culture

Native American culture differs from the values and behaviors of mainstream American culture. The Native American way of life values the group more than the individual. However, the mainstream way of life values the individual more than the group. This contrast in values is seen in the role of the family. The extended family is the center of Native American life. (An extended family is made up of grandparents, aunts, uncles, cousins, nieces, and nephews.) In contrast, the nuclear family is the center of mainstream culture. (A nuclear family is made up of the mother, father, and children.) Native Americans behave differently than mainstream Americans. For example, Native Americans rely on and help others. In contrast, mainstream Americans rely on and look out for themselves. Native Americans respect humility. So they do not make direct eye contact. Mainstream Americans respect self-confidence. So they expect direct eye contact. In general, Native Americans cooperate with others to achieve a goal. Mainstream Americans compete with others to achieve a goal.

1. _____

Native American culture → Mainstream American culture

values **2.** _____ → **3.** _____

extended family → nuclear family

humility → self-confidence

behaviors **4.** _____ → **5.** _____

Cooperation → Competition

Application 3

Textbook
Skills

The following sentences come from college textbooks. Each sentence uses the cause-and-effect thought pattern. Identify the cause and effect in each item.

1. Sports teach not only physical skills but also values.

— Henslin, *Sociology: A Down to Earth Approach,* p. 87 © James M. Henslin.
Reproduced by permission of Pearson Education, Inc.

Cause: _____

Effect: _____

2. Religion may well have been the inspiration for farming.

— Fernandez-Armesto, *The World: A History,* 2nd ed., p. 52.

Cause: _____

Effect: _____

3. People can control pain through hypnosis.

—Gerrig/Zimbardo, *Psychology and Life*, p. 150 © 2010 Pearson Education,
Inc. Reproduced by permission of Pearson Education, Inc.

Cause: _____

Effect: _____

4. Arteries are narrowed by fatty deposits in their walls.

—Marieb, *Essentials of Human Anatomy & Physiology*, 9th ed., p. 392.

Cause: _____

Effect: _____

VISUAL VOCABULARY

A heart attack is the likely _____
of arteries narrowed by fatty deposits
in their walls.

  a. cause
  b. effect

REVIEW TEST 1

Score (number correct) _____ × 10 = _____%

Transitions and Thought Patterns

A. Read the following paragraph, and answer the questions that follow it.

Training for Success

¹On the first day of classes at American Motors Institute, the teacher began with a warning. ²"If you aren't serious about learning the trade, don't show up here tomorrow." ³He then went over the entire six-month course of study, and he didn't make it sound easy. ⁴He told the students that they would be expected to work on machines eight hours a day to

learn the trade. [5]They would also have to read and study written materials every night. [6]_____, he did encourage them with the news that the program is known for high job placement with good salaries.

    1. Fill in the blank in sentence 6 with a transition word or phrase that makes sense. _____

_____ **2.** The relationship between sentence 5 and sentence 6 is one of
    a. generalization and example.   c. cause and effect.
    b. comparison and contrast.

B. Read each paragraph, and answer the questions that follow it.

Latino Music

Music sensations like Selena, Jennifer Lopez, and Ricky Martin have brought the diversity of Latino music into the mainstream. Latino music has several different sounds. Contrasting the musical influences on salsa and Tejano music is interesting. Salsa first began in New York City in the 1970s. It blends Afro-Cuban and Puerto Rican music with rock and jazz. Salsa grew out of several types of dance rhythms such as the rhumba and the cha-cha. The use of claves, congos, horns, and guitars give salsa its dance rhythms. In contrast is the Latino sound of Tejano, which is Texan with Mexican roots. This music first came about in the early 1900s from the rhythms of the waltz and the polka. The use of the accordion, drums, the bajo sexto (a 12-stringed Spanish guitar), and the keyboard give Tejano its Tex-Mex sound.

_____ **3.** The thought pattern for this paragraph is
    a. generalization and example.   c. cause and effect.
    b. comparison and contrast.

Give two transition words or phrases from the paragraph:

4. _____

Yin and Yang

The Chinese use the terms *yin* and *yang* to define the balance in life. Yin is the feminine and passive side of nature. For example, the cold of winter, the darkness of night, the wetness of water, the moon, and death belong to yin. Yang is the masculine and active side of nature. For example, the heat of summer, the light of day, the energy of fire, the sun, and life belong to yang. For balance to occur, yin and yang come together and complete each other. One cannot exist without the other.

_____ **5.** The thought pattern for this paragraph is
a. process.   c. cause and effect.
b. definition.

6. Give one transition word or phrase from the paragraph:

_____

Philosophy

Philosophy is the study of thought or a search for meaning. For example, the mind-body philosophy came about mainly through the work of a man named René Descartes. Descartes was born in France in 1596. During his lifetime, many people were challenging widely accepted ideas. In response, Descartes created a method of logical thought for reaching the truth. He began with the idea "I think; therefore, I am." Then he divided a human into two parts: mind and body. The mind is the thinking being, and the body is only an extension of the mind. Next, he reasoned that the thinking part, the "I" of "I am," could outlive the body.

_____ **7.** The thought pattern for this paragraph is
a. definition.   c. cause and effect.
b. comparison and contrast.

8. Give one transition word or phrase from the paragraph:

_____

The Driverless Car of the Future

Cars of the future will be much different from cars of today. One difference is that in-car navigation systems, in only a few cars today, will be commonplace in the future. All cars will have a computer in the dashboard that stores maps, gets information from satellites in space, gives directions, and sends signals to rescuers if the driver is lost or hurt. Another difference will be the role of the driver; an automated highway may take the tasks of steering, speeding up, slowing down, and braking away from the driver. The cars that use these highways will have computers that pick up signals from magnets built into the road.

_____ **9.** The thought pattern for this paragraph is
a. generalization and example.   c. comparison and contrast.
b. cause and effect.

10. Give one transition word or phrase from the paragraph:

_____

REVIEW TEST 2

Topic Sentences and Thought Patterns

Read each of the following topic sentences. Then write the letter of the thought pattern that each topic sentence suggests.

_____ 1. Like African Americans, most Mexican Americans benefited from the New Deal.
   a. generalization and example   c. cause and effect
   b. comparison

_____ 2. Addiction to prescribed drugs is very similar to addiction to illegal drugs.
   a. cause and effect   c. generalization and example
   b. comparison

_____ 3. Energy can only be described by the effect it has on matter.
   a. generalization and example   c. cause and effect
   b. contrast

_____ 4. Today, political videos aim to produce very specific reactions in voters.
   a. generalization and example   c. comparison
   b. cause and effect

_____ 5. Self-affirming statements include phrases such as "I can do it" and "I can and I will succeed."
   a. generalization and example   c. cause and effect
   b. contrast

_____ 6. Toddlers and teenagers may face some of the same stresses as they try to separate from their parents.
   a. comparison   c. classification
   b. generalization and example

_____ 7. The way that people thought about and treated children in the 19th century stands in sharp contrast to their current treatment.
   a. cause and effect   c. contrast
   b. definition

_____ 8. Psychology is the science of mental processes and behavior; let's look at the key words in this definition.
   a. comparison   c. definition
   b. cause and effect

_____ **9.** Ambulances rushing to the rescue can lead to deadly results.
   a. cause and effect
   c. definition
   b. contrast

_____ **10.** The human body responds to stressful events by making extra energy available; for example, ordinary people have lifted cars off bodies trapped under them.
   a. comparison
   c. generalization and example
   b. cause and effect

REVIEW TEST 3

Score (number correct) _____ × 10 = _____%

Thought Patterns and Concept Maps

Read the following passage from a college biology textbook. Answer the questions and complete the concept map that follows.

Textbook
Skills

Dying to Be Thin

[1]In the most extreme cases, eating disorders can cause death from starvation. [2]However, long before they literally starve to death, people with eating disorders seriously damage their bodies. [3]And they often die of other causes. [4]According to Carre Otis, "It was common for the young girls I worked with to have a heart attack." [5]Most likely, their heart attacks were brought about by massive imbalances in the levels of sodium and potassium in the blood. [6]These problems were caused by malnutrition. [7]At age 30, Otis herself required surgery to repair her damaged heart.

[8]How do people develop eating disorders? [9]Anorexia and bulimia usually arise from a faulty self-image. [10]Or they come from anxiety due to the demands of family, friends, or career. [11]At her first foreign modeling assignment in 2004, Ana Reston was told that she was fat. [12]At the time, she weighed only about 110 pounds. [13]Friends and associates trace her descent to multiple organ failure from that time.

[14]Genes apparently play a role, too. [15]Women whose mother or sister suffers from anorexia are 12 times more likely to develop anorexia

than women without such a family history. [16]And they are 4 times more likely to develop bulimia. [17]If one member of a pair of identical twins develops an eating disorder, the other is highly likely to as well. [18]However, no one has yet found the link between any specific genes and eating disorders.

[19]Eating disorders are difficult to treat. [20]Victims usually get nutritional therapy to help them recover from malnutrition.

[21]Psychotherapy is often necessary. [22]And antidepressant drugs are helpful in some cases. [23]The majority of sufferers do not receive adequate treatment. [24]One reason is because many victims hide or deny their problem. [25]Another reason is because treatment is expensive. [26]Successes do occur, however. [27]The TV show *American Idol* may have saved the life of one of its stars, Katharine McPhee. [28]She also suffered from bulimia. [29]She worried that repeated vomiting might eat away at her vocal cords and hurt her chances to win the *Idol* singing competition. [30]Thus, McPhee spent 3 months, 6 days a week, at an eating disorder clinic. [31]It worked. [32]She is no longer bulimic. [33]She became the *Idol* runner-up. [34]And she released her first CD in January 2007.

—Adapted from Audesirk, Audesirk, & Byers, *Life on Earth,* 5th ed., p. 413.

_____ **1.** The relationship of ideas within sentence 9 is
    a. comparison.   c. cause and effect.
    b. generalization and example.

_____ **2.** The relationship between sentence 10 and sentence 11 is
    a. cause and effect.   c. generalization and example.
    b. contrast.

_____ **3.** The relationship of ideas within sentence 17 is
    a. comparison.   c. cause and effect.
    b. definition and example.

_____ **4.** The relationship between 17 and sentence 8 is
    a. contrast.   c. generalization and example.
    b. cause and effect.

_____ **5.** The overall thought pattern of the paragraph is
    a. comparison.   c. generalization and example.
    b. cause and effect.

Complete the following concept map with ideas from the paragraph.

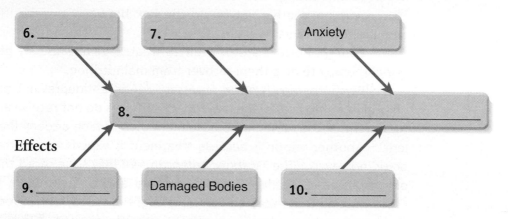

Causes

6. _____   7. _____   Anxiety

8. _____

Effects

9. _____   Damaged Bodies   10. _____

WHAT DO YOU THINK?

What do you think about the link between self-esteem and body image? Many think that the media fosters a faulty self-image. Do you agree with this opinion? Why or why not? Assume you are participating in a service project by volunteering as a mentor at a local girls club. The club is hosting a workshop about self-esteem. One session is about the link between a faulty self-image and eating disorders. You have been asked to open the workshop with a few remarks about this topic. Write a draft of your remarks. Discuss the causes of faulty self-esteem. Also warn your audience about the effects of eating disorders.

REVIEW TEST 4   Score (number correct) _____ × 5 = _____%

Transition Words and Phrases and Thought Patterns

Before you read, skim the passage and answer the Before Reading questions. Read the essay. Then answer the After Reading questions.

¹Some experts believe that birth order—the family position into which we are born—leads to many of our other traits. ²Whether we are the oldest, the youngest, or the middle child, the order in which we are

born can influence both the kinds of goals we set and the ways in which we relate to other people. [3]Understanding the effect of birth order may help us better understand others and ourselves.

[4]Being born first often results in leadership skills. [5]Only children are also included in this group. [6]Firstborns are often competitive, hardworking, and high-achieving. [7]Consequently, high numbers of firstborns earn degrees in higher education and become leaders in large corporations. [8]People in this group often **strive** for perfection. [9]They tend to be responsible, organized, and strong-minded.

[10]Middle children, by contrast, are often known as peacemakers. [11]They can see both sides of an issue and find the places where people can agree. [12]Middle children are good managers and leaders. [13]People in this group are often flexible, sociable, and generous. [14]They are often **tactful** even though they can be competitive. [15]Being the middle child results in a person who is balanced and skilled at getting along with others.

[16]Because of their position in the family, youngest children often love to be around people. [17]The baby of the family is likely to be outgoing and fun-loving. [18]Youngest children are direct and honest. [19]Many youngest children become highly successful salespeople as a result of their ability to motivate others. [20]In summary, birth order seems to have a strong effect on a person's nature.

Before Reading

Vocabulary in Context

_____ **1.** The word **strive** in sentence 8 means
   a. fight back.
   b. look around.
   c. work to achieve.
   d. go on.

_____ **2.** The best synonym for the word **tactful** in sentence 14 is
   a. rude.
   b. considerate.
   c. true.
   d. forceful.

After Reading

Concept Maps

Complete the concept map by filling in information from the essay.

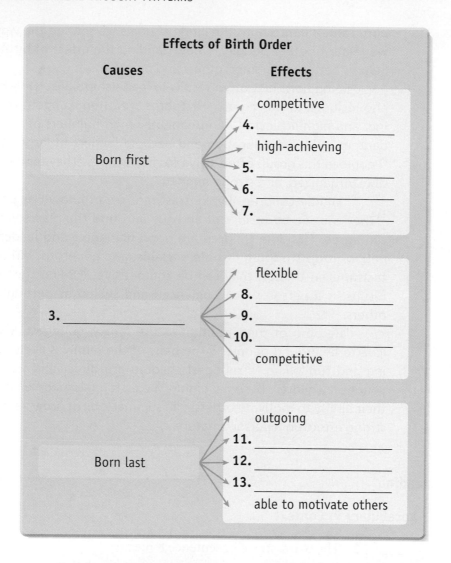

Effects of Birth Order

Causes — Effects

Born first

- competitive
- 4. _____
- high-achieving
- 5. _____
- 6. _____
- 7. _____

3. _____

- flexible
- 8. _____
- 9. _____
- 10. _____
- competitive

Born last

- outgoing
- 11. _____
- 12. _____
- 13. _____
- able to motivate others

Central Idea and Main Idea

_____ **14.** What is the central idea or thesis statement of the essay?
  a. Birth order is the single most important influence on our lives.
  b. Birth order determines our success or failure.
  c. Each birth order has its own problems.
  d. Understanding the effect of birth order will help us understand ourselves.

_____ **15.** What is the best statement of the main idea for the third paragraph (sentences 10–15)?
  a. The second group is the middle child.
  b. Middle children are peacemakers.
  c. Being a middle child leads to being pulled in different directions.
  d. Being a middle child results in a person who is balanced and skilled at getting along with others.

Supporting Details

_____ **16.** Sentence 5 is a
  a. major supporting detail.   b. minor supporting detail.

Transitions

_____ **17.** The phrase **leads to** in sentence 1 is a signal that shows
  a. definition.   c. comparison and contrast.
  b. cause and effect.

_____ **18.** The phrase **because of** in sentence 16 shows
  a. cause and effect.   c. definition.
  b. comparison and contrast.

Thought Patterns

_____ **19.** Identify the thought pattern that sentence 3 suggests.
  a. cause and effect   c. comparison and contrast
  b. generalization and example

_____ **20.** The main thought pattern used throughout the essay is
  a. cause and effect.   c. time order.
  b. definition.

WHAT DO YOU THINK?

Do you think that your birth order has influenced you? In what ways? Why do you think birth order might cause specific traits in people? What are some of the drawbacks of being a first born, middle, youngest, or only child? Assume your psychology teacher has assigned an oral and a written report on a topic of your choice. You have decided to speak about the effects of birth order. In your report, identify and discuss the traits and effects of each position of birth order. You may choose to use examples from your own life or observations of others. You may even want to analyze the personality of a famous person based on that person's birth order.

After Reading About More Thought Patterns

Before you move on to the Mastery Tests on more thought patterns, take time to reflect on your learning and performance by answering the following questions. Write your answers in your notebook.

- How has my knowledge base or prior knowledge about thought patterns changed?

- Based on my studies, how do I think I will perform on the Mastery Test(s)? Why do I think my scores will be above average, average, or below average?

- Would I recommend this chapter to other students who want to learn more about thought patterns? Why or why not?

Test your understanding of what you have learned about thought patterns by completing the Chapter 10 Review Card near the end of the textbook.

CONNECT TO **myreadinglab**

To check your progress in meeting Chapter 10's learning outcomes, log in to **www.myreadinglab.com**, and try the following activities:

- The "Patterns of Organization" section of MyReadingLab gives additional information about transitions and patterns of organization. The section provides a model, practices, activities, and tests. To access this resource, click on the "Study Plan" tab. Then click on "Patterns of Organization." Then click on the following links as needed: "Overview," "Model," "Signal Words (Flash Animation)," "Other Patterns of Organization (Flash Animation)," "Practice," and "Tests."

- To measure your mastery of the content of this chapter, complete the tests in the "Patterns of Organization" section and click on Gradebook to find your results.

Name _____ Section _____

Date _____ Score (number correct) _____ × 10 = _____%

A. Read each paragraph, and answer the questions that follow it.

The Hmong

The Hmong are a group of people originally from China. Their struggle to keep their culture and freedom has affected them deeply. In the early 1900s, many Hmong fled China because the government wanted to do away with Hmong traditions. When they fled China, many settled in the highland areas of Laos and Vietnam. During the Vietnam War in the 1960s and 1970s, thousands of Hmong died because they sided with the United States. After the war, the Hmong fled once more, this time to Thailand. There they waited in refugee camps until they could come to America.

_____ **1.** The main thought pattern is
   a. cause and effect.
   b. comparison and contrast.
   c. generalization and example.

2. What is one transition word that signals the main thought pattern?

_____

What's the Difference: Immigrant, Refugee, Illegal Alien?

To properly understand complex issue of immigration, we must know the differences between an immigrant, a refugee, and an illegal alien. Immigrants are persons who choose to leave their country of origin for any number of reasons. Often, immigrants are looking for better jobs. And they may live where they please as long as they abide by the laws of the land. By contrast, refugees are persons who fled their country of origin due to fear of persecution. Usually, refugees must leave behind their personal goods and fortunes. And many are forced to live in refugee camps for years. An illegal alien is an individual who enters a country without proper records or permission. Usually, illegal aliens are desperate to reunite with family or to escape war or poverty. And some are forced to become illegal aliens due to slavery and prostitution.

_____ **3.** The thought pattern is

a. comparison and contrast.

b. summary.

c. cause and effect.

What two words or phrases signal the thought pattern?

4. _____

5. _____

B. Read the paragraph. Then complete the chart that follows it.

Listening Skills

The difference between good and poor listening skills may mean the difference between success and failure. Poor listeners often do not hear what is being said. They are sidetracked by other tasks such as watching TV or daydreaming, and they miss needed information. Often they misunderstand what they do hear. Missing information leads to mistakes, problems, and failure. In contrast, good listeners hear what is being said, and they understand what they hear. They focus on ideas and ask questions when needed. They gather information. Listening helps a person avoid mistakes, solve problems, and achieve success.

Topic: The *difference* between poor and good listening skills

	Poor Listeners		Good Listeners
Listening:	**7.** _____	*differs from*	focused
Contrasts:	misunderstanding	*differs from*	**9.** _____
	8. _____	*differs from*	gathers information
	makes mistakes	*differs from*	solves problems
	failure	*differs from*	**10.** _____

Read the paragraph. Then answer the questions and complete the concept map that follows it.

Types of Abuse

Textbook
Skills

There are a number of differences between physical and sexual abuse. Typically, sexual abuse is mostly mentally harmful, while physical abuse is physically harmful. Society takes a strong stand against sexual abuse, yet violence is much more accepted. Health care workers tend to react differently to sexual and physical abuse as well. Sexual abuse does not get the same attention that physical abuse gets from doctors. Doctors are trained to deal with physical problems, but sexual abuse may not have any physical signs.

—Adapted from Mignon, Larson, & Holmes, *Family Abuse: Consequences, Theories, and Responses*, pp. 78–79.

_____ **1.** The thought pattern is
  a. cause and effect.
  b. generalization and example.
  c. comparison and contrast.

Complete the following chart with ideas from the passage:

Main idea: 2. _____

_____

	Sexual Abuse	Physical Abuse
Harm	3. _____	physical
Society's outlook	strongly against	violence more accepted
Health care workers' reaction	4. _____	5. _____

Health Care in North America

Although similar in many ways, the United States and Canada differ significantly in their health care systems. These two countries are very similar in their standard of living. Both have thriving economies. Both have their share of people who range from poor to wealthy. Major store and food chains have outlets in both places. Stores such as Sears and Wal-Mart and fast-food chains like Arby's and McDonald's are found in both countries. However, Canada and the United States differ in the way they deliver health care. In Canada, health care is supported by taxes, and nobody has to pay directly for services. Medicare, not the patient, pays all doctor visits, treatments, and surgeries. Even the poor have access to good health care. In contrast, in the United States, the patient pays for health care. Of course, health insurance helps, but the patient must pay for the insurance. Those who cannot pay are often left untreated.

_____ **6.** The thought pattern is
    a. generalization and example.
    b. cause and effect.
    c. comparison and contrast.

What four words or phrases signal the paragraph's thought pattern?

7. _____

8. _____

9. _____

10. _____

A. Read the following passage from a psychology textbook. Answer the questions, and finish the concept map that follows them.

Definition and Causes of Stress

Textbook
Skills

¹**Stress** is the general term describing the psychological and bodily response to an event. ²A **stressor** is a stimulus that throws the body out of balance. ³Stressors can be acute or chronic.

⁴The **stress response** causes physical changes in the nervous systems that get the body ready for physical effort and repair of injury. ⁵These effects include changes in the heart and breathing rates and the release of natural chemicals throughout the body. ⁶These changes occur during the **alarm stage** of the event. ⁷If the stressor continues, the body tries to adapt or resist. ⁸During the **exhaustion phase**, the stress response can cause damage and lead to stress-related diseases.

⁹Certain factors are likely to lead to a stress response. ¹⁰First, a sense of lack of control causes stress. ¹¹For example, jobs that do not allow a worker to have control over how the work is done and work that is too challenging or not challenging all cause stress. ¹²Another cause of stress is environmental factors such as noise and crowding. ¹³Finally, daily hassles and conflict result in stress.

—Adapted from Kosslyn/Rosenberg, *Psychology: The Brain, the Person, the World*, p. 432 © 2001 Allyn and Bacon. Reproduced by permission of Pearson Education, Inc.

_____ **1.** The thought pattern of the first paragraph (sentences 1–3) is
a. cause and effect.
b. comparison and contrast.
c. definition.

_____ **2.** The thought pattern of the second paragraph (sentences 4–8) is
a. cause and effect.
b. comparison and contrast.
c. definition.

_____ **3.** The main thought pattern of the third paragraph (sentences 9–13) is
a. cause and effect.
b. comparison and contrast.
c. definition.

B. What are three words that suggest the thought pattern used in the second paragraph (sentences 4–8)?

4. _____

5. _____

6. _____

C. Fill in the concept map using information from the passage.

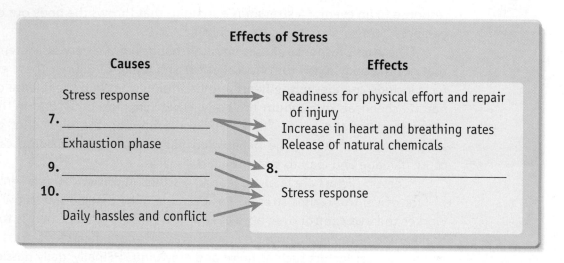

Effects of Stress

Causes

Stress response

7. _____

Exhaustion phase

9. _____

10. _____

Daily hassles and conflict

Effects

Readiness for physical effort and repair of injury

Increase in heart and breathing rates

Release of natural chemicals

8. _____

Stress response

Name _____ Section _____

Date _____ **Score** (number correct) _____ × 20 = _____%

Textbook
Skills

Read the following paragraph from a college science textbook. Then answer the questions that follow.

Natural Resources Are Vital to Our Survival

[1]An island by definition is finite and bounded. [2]And its residents must cope with limitations in the materials they need. [3]On our island, Earth, human beings, like all living things, ultimately face the limits of the natural world. [4]For example, there are limits to many of our natural resources, the various substances and energy sources we need to survive. [5]Natural resources that are replenished over short periods are known as **renewable natural resources**. [6]Some renewable resources, such as sunlight, wind, and wave energy, are always available. [7]Others, such as timber, water, and soil, renew themselves over months, years, or decades. [8]In contrast, resources such as mineral ores and crude oil are in finite supply. [9]And they are formed much more slowly than we use them. [10]These are known as **nonrenewable natural resources**. [11]Once we deplete them, they are no longer available.

—Adapted from Withgott & Brennan, *Essential Environment*, 3rd ed., p. 3.

_____ **1.** The relationship between sentence 3 and sentence 4 is
   a. comparison.   c. cause and effect.
   b. generalization and example.

_____ **2.** The relationship within sentence 5 is
   a. cause and effect.   c. definition and example.
   b. contrast.

_____ **3.** The relationship between sentence 5 and sentence 6 is
   a. comparison.   c. cause and effect.
   b. definition and example.

_____ **4.** The relationship between sentence 7 and sentence 8 is
   a. contrast.   c. generalization and example.
   b. cause and effect.

_____ **5.** The relationship of ideas within sentence 11 is

a. comparison.
c. generalization and example.
b. cause and effect.

VISUAL VOCABULARY

Coal is a _____ natural resource.

a. renewable
b. nonrenewable

Inferences

After studying this chapter you should be able to do the following:

1. Define the term *inference*.
2. Understand the role of fact and opinion in making an inference.
3. Distinguish between a valid and an invalid inference.
4. Apply the five steps for making a VALID inference.
5. Form valid inferences.
6. Evaluate the importance of inferences.

Before Reading About Inferences

Study the learning outcomes and underline words that relate to ideas you have already studied or know about. Did you underline the following terms: *facts, prior knowledge,* and *bias?* What you already know about these topics will help you learn about inferences. Use the blanks that follow to write a one- or two-sentence summary that explains each topic:

Facts: _____

_____

Prior knowledge: _____

_____

_____

Bias: _____

_____

Now, skim the chapter to find three additional topics that you have already studied.

List those topics: _____

_____

Copy the following study outline in your notebook. Leave ample blank space between each topic. Use your own words to fill in the outline with information about each topic as you study about inferences.

Reading Skills Needed to Make VALID Inferences:

I. Verify Facts

II. Assess Prior Knowledge

III. Learn from the Text

    a. Context Clues

    b. Thought Patterns

    c. Implied Main Ideas

IV. Investigate for Bias

V. Detect Contradictions

 # Inferences: Educated Guesses

Read the following short paragraph.

> Katherine Collier was running late for class again. She knew all the good parking spaces in the student lots would be taken, so she turned in to the faculty parking lot that was always half empty. She located a parking space directly in front of the math building where her first-period class was on the ground floor. Since she had a very brief walk to class, she took the time to back into the parking space so that campus security could not easily see the parking sticker that indicated she was in the wrong lot. When she came back to her car after class, she was not surprised to see the yellow ticket under her windshield wipers. She was not even surprised that the ticket stated she was being charged $50 for this third violation.

Which of the following statements might be true based on the ideas in the passage?

_____ Katherine Collier is a teacher.

_____ Katherine Collier is a student.

_____ Katherine Collier expected to get a ticket.

Congratulations! You have just made a set of educated guesses or **inferences** about the paragraph. An author suggests or **implies** an idea, and the reader uses the facts and background knowledge to come to a conclusion and make an **inference** about what the author means.

> An **inference** is an unstated idea that is suggested by the facts or details in a passage.

In the paragraph about Katherine Collier, the second and third statements are based on the information in the passage. However, the first statement is not backed by the supporting details. The facts that she receives a ticket for parking in the faculty parking lot and that her car has a sticker indicating she is in the wrong lot suggest that she is a student, not a teacher. The facts that she was not surprised and had received two previous tickets suggest that she expected to get this ticket, too.

 ## Inferences: The Role of Fact and Opinion

Facts play an important role in making inferences. Skilled readers must be able to sort fact from opinion to infer an author's meaning. Consider the following definitions of fact and opinion.

> A **fact** is a specific detail that is proven true based on evidence.
>
> An **opinion** is belief that cannot be proved or disproved.

Opinion is often stated as fact. Thus, sorting fact from opinion requires you to think critically. The following clues will help you sort out facts from opinions.

Fact	Opinion
Is discovered	Is created
Is objective	Is personal
States reality	Interprets reality
Can be verified	Cannot be verified
Is presented with unbiased words	Is presented with biased words
Example of a fact:	*Example of an opinion:*
A horse needs daily care.	Horseback riding is fun.

To test whether a detail states a fact or an opinion, ask these three questions:

- Can the detail be proved or demonstrated to be true?
- Can the detail be observed in practice or in operation?
- Can the detail be verified by witnesses or records?

stress. However, the author qualifies yoga as the *best* way to reduce stress. Sentence 4 also mixes fact with opinion by including the biased word *great*.

PRACTICE 2

Read the following paragraph from a college textbook. Underline the words that state a bias or qualify an idea. Then, mark each sentence as **F** if it states a fact, **O** if it expresses an opinion, or **F/O** if it includes both fact and opinion.

Textbook
Skills

¹When you hear the word *status,* you are likely to think of prestige. ²These two words are always joined together in people's minds. ³However, sociologists use status in a different way. ⁴In the study of sociology, *status* refers to the position someone occupies. ⁵That position may carry a great deal of prestige, as in a judge or an astronaut. ⁶The status may be looked down on, as in ex-convict or a thief. ⁷We can occupy several positions at the same time. ⁸For example, you may be a son or daughter, a worker, or a student at the same time. ⁹Sociologists use the term *status set* to refer to all the positions you occupy. ¹⁰Obviously, your status set changes as your particular statuses change.

—Adapted from Henslin, *Sociology: A Down to Earth Approach,* p. 101 ©
James M. Henslin. Reproduced by permission of Pearson Education, Inc.

1. _____   6. _____

2. _____   7. _____

3. _____   8. _____

4. _____   9. _____

5. _____   10. _____

The rest of this chapter guides you through a step-by-step process for making valid inferences. As you will see, several of these steps build on what you now know about facts and opinions.

 ## What Is a Valid Inference?

We use the skill of making inferences countless times every day. For example, when we see gray clouds, we infer rain is coming, and a slammed door may imply anger.

Study the photo, and answer the question accompanying it.

VISUAL VOCABULARY

What do these images tell us about the people who painted them?

_____

▶ Cave paintings from 4000 B.C.–2000 B.C. in the Sahara Desert.

If you wrote "people raised livestock," you made a valid inference based on the clues given in the the details of the situation. A **valid inference** is a thoughtful judgment based on details and evidence. For example, if you are bitten by an insect such as a spider or tick, you must pay careful attention to the effects of the bite. Some bites lead to serious, long-term diseases. Lyme disease is one example of the harmful effects of a tick bite. Lyme disease requires immediate medical attention. Many other bites can easily be treated at home. The decision to go to a doctor (or not) is based on making valid inferences. If you or someone you know has been bitten, you must make a set of wise decisions based on the evidence. The most effective inferences are based on a careful study the details provided.

> A **valid inference** is a logical conclusion based on evidence.

The ability to make a valid inference is a vital life skill. Making valid inferences aids us in our efforts to care for our families, succeed in our jobs, and even guard our health.

EXAMPLE Read the following paragraph. Write the letter **V** beside the *two* valid inferences. Remember that valid inferences are firmly supported by the details in the passage.

Only in the fifth grade, Roxanne already stood a full head and shoulders above most of her peers, including the boys. Constant exposure to the chlorine in the family swimming pool had given her hair a distinct greenish tint. In addition, she had to wear both orthodontic braces and thick eyeglasses. When Josh saw her on the first day of school, he immediately began harassing her. His favorite taunt to her was the nickname "The

Step 1: Verify and Value the Facts

Develop a devotion to finding and examining the facts. Valid inferences are firmly based on the facts. However, authors often mix fact with opinion. Facts are details that can be verified. Opinions are stated with biased words. A skilled reader first separates facts from opinion. Then, a skilled reader takes a close look at the facts. Once you verify the facts, you can decide if you agree or disagree with an opinion.

Read the following sentence. Answer the questions that follow it.

> Katherine Collier *should* break her *disrespectful* habit of being late to all her classes.

What are the facts in this sentence that can be verified? _____

_____

_____

What are the biased words that reveal an opinion? _____

This sentence blends fact and opinion. We can check with the registrar or the class rolls to verify that Collier is a student. We can also contact each of her teachers and verify the number of times she has been late to all of her classes. The biased words of opinion are *should* and *disrespectful.* Once we verify the facts, we can then decide whether we agree with the opinion. Often the opinion is an interpretation of the facts. Some readers come to an invalid conclusion or opinion from a misunderstanding of the facts.

At times, authors use false information for their own purposes. Just as authors may make this kind of mistake, readers may, too. Readers may draw false inferences by mixing the author's fact with their own opinions, or by misreading the facts. It is very important to find, verify, and stick to factual details.

Textbook
Skills

EXAMPLE Read the following paragraph. Write **V** next to the *two* inferences supported by the facts in the paragraph.

> The state and federal governments set the ages at which you could get your driver's license, drink alcohol, and vote. Before you could get a job, the federal government had to give you a Social Security number. And you have been paying Social Security taxes every month in which you have been employed. If you worked a low-paying job, your starting wages were set by state and federal minimum-wage laws.

—Adapted from Edwards, Wattenberg, & Lineberry, *Government in America:
People, Politics, and Policy,* 5th ed., Brief Version, p. 1.

_____ **1.** The state and federal governments are unfair.

_____ **2.** The state and federal governments affect daily life.

_____ **3.** Governments have influence over people.

EXPLANATION The last two statements are valid inferences based on the facts. However, there is no hint or clue that the state or federal governments are unfair. Skilled readers draw conclusions that are supported by the facts. Notice that sentence 1 offers an opinion not based on the details in the paragraph.

Step 2: Assess Prior Knowledge

Once you are sure of the facts, the next step is to draw on your prior knowledge and use your sense of logic. What you have already learned and experienced can help you make valid inferences.

EXAMPLE Study the photo and its caption. Write **V** beside the *two* inferences supported by prior knowledge activated by the picture and information in the caption.

VISUAL VOCABULARY

_____ 1. De facto means "in fact or reality."

_____ 2. De facto means "by law."

_____ 3. Freedom of speech is a de facto right in the U.S.

_____ 4. English is the de facto language of the U.S.

▲ Some driving customs are guided by **de facto standards**. In the U.S., people drive on the right side of the road. In other countries, like Samoa, people drive on the left side of the road. Also, in many places, driving slightly above the legal speed limit is a de facto standard.

EXPLANATION Our everyday driving experiences give us prior knowledge that helps us define and apply the term *de facto*. Few of us think about why we drive on the right side of the road—it's an age-old custom that can vary from country to country. It's an accepted practice, not a formal law. Likewise, we all have seen or have taken part in the common practice of going slightly higher than the legal speed limit. So based on our prior knowledge, we can infer that de facto means "in fact or reality." Likewise we can infer that de facto does not mean "by law." We also know that freedom of speech is a legal right based on the Constitution. So freedom of speech is not a de facto right, but a right "by law." Finally, the United States does not have an official national language. But English is "in fact or reality" the language used by most. Thus, sentences 1 and 4 state valid inferences.

Step 3: Learn from the Text

When you verify and value facts, you are learning from the text. A valid inference is always based on what is stated or implied by the details in the text; in contrast, an invalid inference goes beyond the evidence. Thus, to make a valid inference, you must learn to rely on the information in the text. Many of the skills you have studied from previous chapters work together to enable you to learn from the text. For example, context clues unlock the meaning of an author's use of vocabulary. Becoming aware of thought patterns teaches you to look for the logical relationship between ideas. Learning about stated and implied main ideas teaches you to study supporting details. (In fact, you use inference skills to find the implied main idea.) In addition, you often use inference skills to grasp the author's opinion. As you apply these skills to your reading process, you are carefully listening to what the author has to say. You are learning from the text. Once you learn from the text, only then can you make a valid inference. The following example shows you how you learn from the text.

EXAMPLE Read the following paragraph from a college nursing textbook. Answer the questions.

Concept of Holism

Textbook
Skills

¹Nurses care for the individual as a whole, complete person. ²Nurses do not see a person just as an assembly of parts and processes. ³When applied in nursing, the concept of **holism** points out that nurses must keep the whole person in mind. ⁴The nurse strives to understand how one area of concern relates to the whole person. ⁵The nurse must also consider the relationship of the individual to the environment and to others. ⁶For example, in helping a man who is grieving over the death of his spouse, the nurse explores the impact of the loss on the whole person. ⁷Nursing

interventions are directed toward restoring overall harmony. [8]So the interventions depend on the man's sense of purpose and meaning of his life.

—Adapted from Kozier & Erb, *Fundamentals of Nursing: Concepts, Process, and Practice*, 8th ed., p. 271.

_____ **1.** Based on the general context, the best meaning of holism (when applied to nursing) is
   a. a focus mainly on symptoms.
   b. an approach that considers physical and emotional states as playing equal roles in a person's state of health.
   c. a belief that gives purpose and meaning to life.

_____ **2.** The overall thought pattern of the paragraph is
   a. spatial order.
   b. cause and effect.
   c. definition and example.

_____ **3.** The details of the paragraph are
   a. facts.   c. facts and opinions.
   b. opinions.

_____ **4.** The best statement of the implied main idea is
   a. When applied to nursing, holism is a concern for the whole, complete person.
   b. A person's environment plays a key role in his or her state of health.
   c. Nurses must practice holism.

_____ **5.** Which of the following sentences states a valid inference based on the details in the paragraph?
   a. Holism is not a common practice in nursing.
   b. Based on holism, a nurse thinks about a person's eating and sleeping habits, moods, and relationships.
   c. Holism is not concerned with specific symptoms of an illness.

Step 4: Investigate for Bias

One of the most important steps in making a valid inference is confronting your biases. Each of us possesses strong opinions that influence the way we process information. Often our personal views are based on prior experiences. For example, if we have had a negative prior experience with a used car salesperson, we may become suspicious and stereotype all used car salespeople as dishonest. Sometimes, our biases are based on the way in which we were raised. Some people register as Democrats or Republicans and vote for only Democratic or Republican candidates. They do so simply because their parents were members of either the Democratic or Republican party.

To make a valid inference, we must look for bias in our response to information. Our bias can shape our reading of the author's meaning. Test your inferences for bias. Note biased words and replace them with factual details as you form your conclusions.

EXAMPLE Read the following paragraph. Investigate the list of inferences that follow for bias. Underline the biased words. Write **V** in the blank if the inference is valid or **I** if the inference is invalid due to bias.

The Power of Self-Talk

Textbook Skills

[1]Disparaging statements such as "I'm a failure" or "I'm foolish" or "I'm stupid" are destructive. [2]These statements imply that failure, foolishness, and stupidity are in you and will always be in you. [3]Instead, use statements that refer to the here and now. [4]In addition, describe actions and reasons for your feelings. [5]Such statements might look like this:

[6]"I feel like a failure right now; I've erased this computer file three times today."

[7]"I felt foolish when I couldn't think of that formula."

[8]"I feel stupid when you point out my grammatical errors."

—Adapted from DeVito, *Messages: Building Interpersonal Communication Skills*, p. 187 © 1999. Reproduced by permission of Pearson Education, Inc.

_____ **1.** The word *disparaging* means "degrading" or "devaluing."

_____ **2.** Once we fail, we are most likely always going to fail.

_____ **3.** We often believe the statements we make about ourselves.

_____ **4.** You should keep criticisms about yourself general.

EXPLANATION Items 1 and 3 are (**V**) valid inferences based on the details in the paragraph. Item 1 states the correct meaning of the word *disparaging* based on the general context of the passage. Item 3 states the implied main idea of the passage. Items 2 and 4 are (**I**) invalid inferences. In sentence 2, the biased words *most likely always* and *fail* are not supported by the details in the passage. Sentence 4 is an opinion that contradicts the details stated in sentences 5–7.

Step 5: Detect Contradictions

Have you ever misjudged a situation or formed a wrong first impression? For example, have you ever assumed a person was conceited or rude only to find out later that he or she was acutely shy? You may find a better explanation for a set of facts than the first one that comes to mind. The skilled reader hunts for the most reasonable explanation. The best way to do this is to consider other explanations that could logically contradict your first impression.

EXAMPLE   Read the following list, which describes the behaviors of a young person. Then, in the blank, write as many explanations for the behaviors as you can think of.

> Making careless errors
>
> Not sitting still
>
> Talking excessively
>
> Always interrupting
>
> Being forgetful

_____

_____

_____

_____

_____

EXPLANATION   Some readers may think this list describes a rebellious or disrespectful child. It is actually a list of symptoms for attention deficit hyperactivity disorder (ADHD). This disorder affects almost 5 percent of all children. Often those who have ADHD face difficulties in their school and social lives. Without thinking about other possible views, anyone can easily jump to a wrong conclusion. Skilled readers consider all the facts and all the possible explanations for those facts. Skilled readers look for contradictions.

Use these five steps to think your way through to VALID conclusions based on sound inferences: (1) verify and value the facts, (2) assess prior knowledge, (3) learn from the text, (4) investigate for bias, and (5) detect contradictions.

PRACTICE 4

A. Read the following paragraph. Identify the facts. Check those facts against your own experience and understanding. Write **V** for valid beside *two* inferences supported by the facts in the paragraph.

Textbook
Skills

¹Sandra Rosado had known poverty most of her young life, but she was determined to go to college. ²She saved every dollar she could from her part-time job after school. ³Sandra seemed well on her way to providing for herself rather than ending up on welfare like her mother. ⁴When welfare officials found out about Sandra's $4,900 bank account, they told her mother that the family was no longer eligible for aid. ⁵Without means to support her eight children, Mrs. Rosado asked whether there wasn't some way to get around the problem. ⁶The easiest way, she was told, was simply for Sandra to spend the money quickly. ⁷Thus, rather than spending her money on a college education, Sandra ended up buying clothes, jewelry, shoes, and perfume.

—Adapted from Edwards, Wattenberg, & Lineberry, *Government in America:*
People, Politics, and Policy, 5th ed., p. 33.

_____ Sandra made unwise decisions.

_____ It is difficult to break the cycle of poverty.

_____ The government encourages the poor to spend their money to support themselves instead of saving their money.

_____ Poor people choose to be poor.

B. Write **V** next to a valid inference you can make about this "Peanuts" cartoon featuring Charlie Brown and Linus.

VISUAL VOCABULARY

_____ It's important to hold opinions.

_____ Opinions should be based on facts.

_____ Never changing an opinion once you have it makes you strong.

AND THAT'S THE WAY I SEE IT! ABSOLUTELY, FOR SURE!

ACTUALLY, YOU HAVE YOUR FACTS MIXED UP, CHARLIE BROWN...

I DO? I GUESS MAYBE YOU'RE RIGHT

I HAVE VERY STRONG OPINIONS, BUT THEY DON'T LAST LONG!

▲ Peanuts reprinted by permission of United Features Syndicate, Inc.

Inferences and Visual Aids

Textbook Skills

Textbook authors often include visual aids such as photographs, graphs, or charts. These visual aids can help you understand the main point of a passage or section in the text. A skilled reader will study these pictures and visual aids to make inferences about the author's main idea. Read the following paragraph, taken from a college communications textbook. Study the picture, and then answer the questions.

Harnessing Kinetic Energy

[1]A wind turbine changes the wind's energy of motion into electrical energy. [2]Wind causes the blades of a wind turbine to spin. [3]The spinning blades turn a shaft that goes into the nacelle. [4]The nacelle sits atop the tower. [5]The rotational speed of the blades can be up to 20 revolutions per minute (rpm). [6]Inside the nacelle, a gearbox converts the speed of the blades into much higher speeds (over 1,500 rpm). [7]These high speeds provide enough motion for a generator inside the nacelle to produce electricity.

—Adapted from Withgott & Brennan,
Essential Environment, 3rd ed., p. 367.

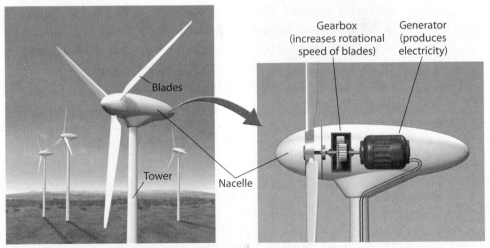

Source: Withgott, Jay H., Brennan, Scott R., *Essential Environment: The Science Behind the Stories*, 3rd, © 2009. Printed and Electronically reproduced by permission of Pearson Education, Inc., Upper Saddle River, New Jersey.

_____ **1.** Based on the general context of the passage, the term **kinetic** means
   a. electrical energy.
   b. man-made energy
   c. the energy of motion.

_____ **2.** Based on details in the paragraph and the visual aid, the **nacelle** is the
    a. mechanical device also known as a turbine.
    b. compartment in the turbine that holds a gearbox and a generator.
    c. shaft turned by the spinning blades.

_____ **3.** The best statement of the implied main idea is
    a. The three parts of a wind turbine are the tower, the blades, and the nacelle.
    b. We can harness power from the wind by using mechanical devices called wind turbines.
    c. A wind turbine creates clean, cheap energy.

APPLICATIONS

Application 1: Making Inferences

Read the paragraph; then answer the questions that follow it.

Manners in America

¹Several years ago, *A Status Report on Rudeness in America* revealed some interesting details about American manners. ²Nearly 8 out of 10 surveyed worried about the increasing lack of respect and courtesy in America. ³Most people agreed that they have to deal with people daily who treat them with **contempt**. ⁴Almost half of all shoppers said they have walked out of stores because of poor service. ⁵Over half of all drivers complained about hostile and reckless drivers. ⁶Many people complained about the public use of swear words. ⁷Still others resent those who hold loud cell phone conversations in public places. ⁸Finally, most admitted that they too have been rude. ⁹Everyone agreed that people used to be nicer to one another.

_____ **1.** Based on context clues, we can infer that the word **contempt** in sentence 3 means
    a. love.   c. boredom.
    b. disrespect.

_____ **2.** Based on the details of the paragraph, we can conclude that its implied main idea is
    a. Americans have become more rude.
    b. Americans are under too much stress.
    c. Americans have worse manners than people from other countries.
    d. Americans' rudeness is going to lead to violence.

Application 2: Making Inferences

Read the following list of facts, and write **V** beside *two* inferences based on the details in the list.

- Joan of Arc was only 17 years old when she led the French army to victory over the English.
- Marie Curie was an important scientist who won the Nobel Prize in chemistry and in physics.
- Margaret Thatcher became prime minister of Britain.
- Sally Ride traveled into space on the space shuttle.
- Two women writers, Pearl Buck and Toni Morrison, have won the Nobel Prize for literature.

_____ **1.** Women have made important contributions to history, science, politics, and literature.

_____ **2.** These women chose careers over family life.

_____ **3.** The Nobel Prize is given in several different fields.

_____ **4.** These women succeeded because of the fight for women's rights.

Application 3: Making Inferences

Read the following passage from a college anatomy textbook. Answer the questions that follow. Then, complete the visual vocabulary activity.

Textbook
Skills

Classification of Bones

[1]Bones come in many sizes and shapes. [2]For example, the tiny *pisiform* bone of the wrist is the size and shape of a pea, whereas the femur, or thigh bone, is nearly 2 feet long and has a large, ball-shaped head. [3]The unique shape of each bone fulfills a particular need.

[4]As their name suggests, **long bones** are typically longer than they are wide. [5]As a rule they have a shaft with heads at both ends. [6]Long bones are mostly compact bone. [7]All the bones of the limbs, except the patella (kneecap) and the wrist and ankle bones, are long bones.

[8]**Short bones** are generally cube-shaped and contain mostly spongy bone. [9]The bones of the wrist and ankle are short bones. [10]Sesamoid (ses'ahmoyd) bones, which form within tendons, are a special type of short bone. [11]The best-known example is the patella.

[12]**Flat bones** are thin, flattened, and usually curved. [13]They have two thin layers of compact bone sandwiching a layer of spongy bone between

female friends, men tend to confide more about their weaknesses. [6]However, they do include and enhance their strengths. [7]Men who are used to challenging each other believe that they do not have to compete with female friends. [8]Men rate their friendships with women as more enjoyable and higher in overall quality than their male friendships.

—Adapted from Gamble, Kwal, & Gamble, *The Gender Communication Connection*, pp. 156–156.

_____ Men are better friends than women.

_____ Men do not often talk with other men about their feelings or emotions.

_____ Men do not grow emotionally unless they have a female friend.

_____ Which of the following statements is the best implied main idea of the paragraph?
  a. Forming friendships with females offers men several benefits.
  b. Women are more supportive than men.
  c. Men trust women.

REVIEW TEST 2

Score (number correct) _____ × 25 = _____ %

Making Inferences

A. Read the paragraph. Write **V** beside *two* inferences that are based on the information in it.

Cable TV Companies in the City

[1]Every three years, the city council looks at the local cable TV companies and grants them the right to do business within the city limits. [2]During this review, new cable TV companies are allowed to bid for access. [3]The council also looks at the current company's rates and services. [4]The idea is to be sure that fair prices are charged for good service. [5]No new cable TV companies have been approved in many years. [6]The current cable TV company, which is the only company allowed access, pays a hefty fee to the city every year.

_____ The city council can help ensure fair prices for access to cable.

_____ The review process is fair and open.

_____ The cable company and the city council have made a deal with each other.

_____ The current cable company charges fair rates.

B. Read the paragraph. Write **V** beside *one* inference that is based on the information in the paragraph. Then answer the question.

Textbook Skills

> [1]Karen Quinlan was an active twenty-one-year-old when disaster struck. [2]She lapsed into a coma in the early morning hours of April 15, 1975, after drinking a few gin-and-tonics and possibly taking some drugs as well. [3]On the night before, Karen went with several friends to a roadside tavern. [4]They were to celebrate a friend's birthday. [5]She was seen "popping some pills," reportedly Quaaludes, earlier in the day. [6]And that evening, she had several drinks before even reaching the bar. [7]Karen "started to nod out" after only one drink at the tavern. [8]So she was driven home. [9]By the time they arrived, Karen had passed out entirely. [10]A few minutes later, the driver realized that she had stopped breathing. [11]He began to give her resuscitation. [12]An ambulance was called and Karen was carried off unconscious to the hospital, never to wake again. [13]Karen spent several years in a coma. [14]Meanwhile, her parents fought to discontinue the life support system that forced air into her lungs through an incision in her throat. [15]Karen remained in a "persistent vegetative state" until her death.

—Adapted from Fishbein/Pease, *The Dynamics of Drug Abuse*, p. 239 © 1996 Allyn and Bacon. Reproduced by permission of Pearson Education, Inc.

_____ Karen Quinlan was an alcoholic.

_____ Karen Quinlan's friends were partly responsible for her tragedy.

_____ Karen Quinlan's tragedy was avoidable.

_____ Which of the following statements is the best implied main idea of the paragraph?
  a. The Karen Quinlan case shows the harmful effects of taking a mixture of Quaaludes and alcohol.
  b. Karen Quinlan had the right to die.
  c. People shouldn't let others drive while under the influence of alcohol or drugs.

VISUAL VOCABULARY

Godzilla represents the damage caused by the _____ of the atomic bomb.

a. radiation
b. havoc
c. invasion

WHAT DO YOU THINK?

Do you think there is ever justification for using an atomic bomb or other nuclear weapons? Why or why not? Currently, many think that Iran is trying to develop nuclear weapons. Do you think they should? Why or why not? Does a country—any country—have the right to develop nuclear weapons? Should all countries, even the United States, get rid of nuclear weapons? Why or why not? Assume you have a strong opinion on one side of this debate. Write a letter to the editor of your local newspaper defending your side of the argument.

REVIEW TEST 4   Score (number correct) _____ × 10 = _____ %

Making Inferences

Textbook Skills

Before you read, skim the passage from a college textbook. Next answer the Before Reading questions. Read the passage. Then answer the After Reading questions that follow it.

Vocabulary Preview

notable (2)
outstanding, famous, important

Two Famous Black Journalists

[1]Two men figure strongly in the growth of the black press during the nineteenth and early twentieth centuries: Frederick Douglass and W. E. B. Du Bois.

rallied (4) brought together, united

protest (11) challenge, object to, disagree with

inferior (12) less than

[2]Frederick Douglass was the **notable** ex-slave who founded *The North Star* in 1847. [3]He became an **icon** of hope for blacks in his day. [4]He **rallied** the public against slavery. [5]His essays and speeches helped white men and women see the hardship of slavery through black eyes. [6]Around 3,000 people in the United States and Europe read *The North Star*. [7]Many readers were influential people. [8]After the Civil War, Douglass edited magazines for 15 years. [9]He also wrote three **autobiographies** retelling the events of his amazing life and career.

[10]In 1910, W. E. B. Du Bois founded *The Crisis*. [11]This new paper was the **protest** voice of the National Association for the Advancement of Colored People (NAACP). [12]"Mentally the Negro is **inferior** to the white," said the 1911 *Encyclopaedia Britannica*. [13]First, Du Bois knew, beliefs like this had to be changed. [14]Then the **bias** against blacks in education, housing, and social status could be defeated. [15]Under his leadership, *The Crisis* grew to have more than 100,000 readers. [16]He retired as editor in 1934.

—Agee, Ault, & Emery, *Introduction to Mass Communications*, 12th ed., p. 126.

Before Reading

Vocabulary in Context

_____ **1.** The word **icon** in sentence 3 means
  a. symbol.
  b. threat.
  c. topic.

_____ **2.** The word **autobiographies** in sentence 9 means that Douglass wrote
  a. books about the Civil War.
  b. books about himself.
  c. articles for newspapers.

After Reading

Concept Maps

Finish the concept map with information from the passage.

Read the following passage. Write **V** beside *ten* inferences that are based on the information in it.

[1]The local cable television company ran a **promotion** to sign up more homes to high-tech television. [2]The high-tech offer included the following: a smart box for digital TV access to hundreds of channels, a modem, and Road Runner high-speed cable connection to the Internet. [3]The offer also promised free hookup and free service for one month. [4]Shantel tried both the TV and Internet service for a few weeks. [5]Before the end of the one-month trial period, she returned the smart box and canceled Road Runner. [6]Her bill for that month showed that she was charged for a month. [7]She called the cable company and had the following discussion:

[8]"Thank you for choosing Acme Cable. [9]My name is Dorothy. [10]How may I help you?" the customer service woman said in a cool, polite voice.

[11]"My name is Shantel Adams, and I have a question about my bill," Shantel began in a cheerful voice.

[12]"Yes, ma'am," Dorothy cut her off. [13]"Could you please give me your phone number and the last three numbers of your Social Security number."

[14]Shantel, surprised at being cut off, gave the information and listened to the clicking sounds of typing at the other end of the line.

[15]"Yes, Ms. Adams, how may I help you?" Dorothy asked with a stifled yawn.

[16]"Well," Shantel explained, "I heard your ad on the TV about a one-month free trial offer for smart box digital TV and Road Runner . . ."

[17]"Yes, that is our upgrade package," Dorothy interrupted.

[18]"Well," Shantel continued, "I tried both of them for a couple of weeks. [19]But I don't want the services, so I took the **equipment** back to your office before the month was up."

[20]"So you returned the digital smart box and the modem?" Dorothy interrupted again.

[21]"Yes, ma'am," Shantel said, frustrated. [22]Then she snapped, "But my bill shows I owe a month's fee for the smart box and Road Runner."

[23]"We charge a month in advance," Dorothy explained.

[24]"What does that mean?" Shantel asked, surprised.

²⁵"We charge a month in advance," Dorothy repeated, saying each word very slowly as if talking to a child.

²⁶"So I was billed for next month? ²⁷I didn't know you charge a month in advance. ²⁸How could you possibly know if I would keep the stuff after the free trial was up?" Shantel asked in a puzzled voice. ²⁹Then she added in a sharp tone, "When I returned it, you should have taken it off my bill."

³⁰"Ms. Adams, most people keep the service," Dorothy said.

³¹Shantel cut Dorothy off and said sharply, "It's not really a free month, is it, if you are billing a month in advance."

³²"Ms. Adams, we will correct your bill," Dorothy replied.

³³"Good thing I called," Shantel said tersely, "or I would be paying for something I don't owe!"

³⁴"Please accept our apologies . . .," Dorothy began.

³⁵Shantel hung up abruptly.

_____ The word **promotion** in sentence 1 means "a raise in rank or status on a job."

_____ Shantel's attitude changed as she talked with Dorothy. (implied in sentences 11 and 22)

_____ Shantel was rude to Dorothy. (sentences 31 and 35)

_____ Dorothy was rude to Shantel.

_____ Shantel doesn't like to be interrupted.

_____ Dorothy became angry during the conversation.

_____ The word **equipment** in sentence 19 refers to a smart box and a modem.

_____ Shantel placed an order to upgrade her service from the cable company. (sentences 3–5)

_____ Shantel received a free month's trial of upgraded service.

_____ According to the cable company, few people cancel the upgrade when the free trial month is up.

_____ The cable company charges for services not yet used.

_____ The cable company acted illegally.

_____ The cable company charged Shantel without her approval.

A. Read the following paragraph from a college psychology textbook. Write **V** beside *five* inferences that are supported by the details in the paragraph.

Stress: A Response

Textbook Skills

[1]Physical stressors, such as a piece of glass stuck in your bare foot, are generally easy to identify. [2]But the definition of a psychological or social stressor is more subjective. [3]Maya is not bothered about the recent firings in her company. [4]She wants to spend more time with her children. [5]Part of her wouldn't mind being out of work and collecting unemployment. [6]Then, she could stay home for a while. [7]Between savings and her husband's paycheck, the family could get by for a few months. [8]So for Maya, the threat of being fired is not a psychological stressor. [9]It is the **perception** of whether or not a stimulus is a stressor that is crucial for determining whether the stress response will occur.

—Kosslyn/Rosenberg, *Psychology: The Brain, the Person, the World*, p. 434 © 2001 Allyn and Bacon. Reproduced by permission of Pearson Education, Inc.

_____ An injury or wound is an example of a physical stressor.

_____ A stressor can be physical or psychological.

_____ Maya is in no danger of being laid off from her job.

_____ Maya is afraid of losing her job.

_____ Unemployment benefits will give Maya time to be with her children.

_____ Maya is lazy.

_____ The word **perception** in sentence 9 means "thought, idea, view."

_____ Thoughts, ideas, and views about a situation can cause stress.

B. Read the following passage from the college textbook *Listening*. Write **V** beside *five* inferences that are supported by the details in the passage.

Two Views

Textbook Skills

[1]Linda Chou is a new receptionist at a busy downtown office. [2]She started work only two weeks ago after a week of orientation. [3]Lily Thomson is the office manager [4]She supervised Linda's orientation and

training. [5]She was satisfied with Linda's performance during training. [6]But she has kept an eye on Linda, particularly during peak hours. [7]For the past week, Lily has noticed that Linda sometimes hesitates to greet customers with a warm smile, as she was asked to do. [8]In fact, many times Linda doesn't even look at the male customers who come up to her desk. [9]In addition, she often speaks too softly and avoids dealing with the problems and questions that arise.

Manager's Viewpoint: [10]It has always been a policy for the receptionist to greet customers with a warm smile and friendly hello. [11]Linda acts almost uncaring when customers enter. [12]Therefore, Lily feels the need to coach Linda on this point. [13]She believes that Linda's behavior is likely the result of getting used to the workplace.

Employee Viewpoint: [14]Linda was brought up in a traditional Asian family. [15]She has always been taught that it is wrong for a woman to smile or look directly at a man. [16]Speaking too loudly is thought to be rude. [17]Therefore, Linda feels uneasy greeting customers the way Lily suggested, particularly since she did not have to do so when she worked in a similar position in Hong Kong.

—Adapted from Brownell, *Listening: Attitudes, Principles, and Skills*, p. 349 © 2002 by Pearson Education, Inc. Reproduced by permission of Pearson Education, Inc.

_____ Lily does not like Linda.

_____ Lily believes Linda is deliberately rude.

_____ A warm smile and a friendly hello are required behaviors for a receptionist in this office.

_____ Polite receptionist behavior is defined differently in Asia than it is in America.

_____ Linda was born and raised in America.

_____ Customers in Hong Kong do not expect a smile and a greeting.

_____ Linda has had experience working as a receptionist.

_____ It is helpful for managers to understand an employee's cultural background.

A. Read the following passage from the college textbook *Introduction to Mass Communications*. Answer the question in the photo caption, and then write **V** beside *five* inferences that are supported by the details in the passage.

Audiences Targeted on the Basis of Their Values and Lifestyles

[1]A research firm based in California created a system to study audiences based on their needs and desires. [2]This system is called the Values and Lifestyles Program (VALS 2). [3]The system divides people into two large groups. [4]The first large group is inner-directed; they take their cues from their own beliefs and values. [5]The second large group is outer-directed; they look to society to guide their choices.

[6]In addition, VALS 2 divides people into subgroups. [7]The research goal is to find out whether consumers in each of these subgroups can afford the things they need and want. [8]Advertisers use these categories as they design their advertising and marketing programs. [9]A few of the subgroups are described here:

[10]*Actualizers* are successful people with many resources; they are concerned with social issues and are open to change.

[11]*Experiencers* are young, enthusiastic, and impulsive; they savor the new, the offbeat, and the risky. [12]They are avid consumers.

[13]*Makers* are action-based and love to be self-supporting. [14]They are often found building their own houses, canning vegetables, or working on the car.

[15]*Strugglers* are almost fully concerned with meeting urgent needs of the moment.

—Agee, Ault, & Emery, *Introduction to Mass Communications*, 12th ed., p. 73.

VISUAL VOCABULARY

_____ Which audience group does the photo want to appeal to?

a. Actualizers
b. Experiencers
c. Makers

Textbook Skills

_____ Actualizers are better and stronger people than Strugglers.

_____ Actualizers probably earn high wages.

_____ Experiencers probably don't mind spending their money to have a good time.

_____ Makers work with their hands.

_____ Makers like to work more than Experiencers.

_____ Strugglers are driven by crisis.

_____ Advertisers rely on research to help them sell products.

B. Read the following passage from the college textbook *Listening*. Write **V** beside *five* inferences that are supported by the details in the passage.

Textbook
Skills

Listening to the Elderly

[1]Recognize that talking to an elderly person may take more time than talking to a young person. [2]If you need an answer in a hurry, try asking "closed" rather than "open" questions. [3]Or put your questions in an either-or format. [4]You cannot expect a quick answer to a question such as "What would you like to do tonight?" [5]Asking a more direct question such as "Would you like to take a ride after lunch?" or "Would you rather go look for that book you were talking about?" is less stressful and gives you more information.

[6]Let the older person know that she is important. [7]Rather than shouting a question from across the room, stand next to the person whenever you can. [8]People who have trouble hearing will appreciate the ability to see you as you speak with them.

[9]Ask questions. [10]Take the time to be interested in what an older person is doing and thinking. [11]Put yourself in the role of listener as much of the time as possible. [12]Share when it seems appropriate, but otherwise develop the attitude that you will gain more by listening than speaking.

—Adapted from Brownell, *Listening: Attitudes, Principles, and Skills*, p. 319 © 2002 by
Pearson Education, Inc. Reproduced by permission of Pearson Education, Inc.

_____ When talking with the elderly, a "closed" question is better than an "open" question.

_____ An example of a closed question is "Would you like to take a ride after lunch?"

_____ An example of an open question is "What would you like to do tonight?"

_____ Most older people are able to keep up with the activities of their families.

_____ Most older people ask a lot of questions.

_____ Older people often need extra time and attention.

_____ You can benefit from listening to older people.

A. Read the paragraph. Write **V** beside *three* inferences that are supported by the ideas in it.

The Importance of Clear Communication

¹David is a personal trainer, and Raul is a client of his. ²David gave Raul the following directions for a 4-mile run as the warm-up for Raul's daily workout. ³David told Raul to run all the way down the gravel path behind the gym until he saw a barn and a fence that followed a track for training horses. ⁴David said to turn right and follow the horse track until it looped around back to the gravel road and then run back to gym from there. ⁵Raul said he understood and began to run the course.

⁶During his run, Raul saw the barn but became confused about where to turn right. ⁷He saw two possible right turns—one before the barn and one after the barn at the end of the gravel path. ⁸The first right turn did look like a track for training horses. ⁹The second right turn was too far away to tell if it was a road or a training track. ¹⁰Both right turns followed fences. ¹¹Raul remembered David saying to "run all the way down the gravel path," so Raul passed by the first right turn and took the second right turn at the end of the gravel path. ¹²This gravel path did not look like a training track for horses, but it did bend as if it might loop around the barn, so Raul kept running instead of turning around.

¹³The path Raul chose was a long stretch that finally stopped in a dead-end. ¹⁴He turned around at the dead-end and ran back to the gym the way he had come. ¹⁵Raul ended up running 8 miles instead of 4 miles. ¹⁶After finishing his run, Raul was so tired and sore that he ended his workout session.

_____ Raul took the wrong turn.

_____ Raul did not listen carefully to David's directions.

_____ David's directions were incomplete.

_____ The longer run injured Raul.

_____ Raul's daily workout was supposed to include more than just the run.

_____ David is an ineffective trainer.

B. Read the following paragraph. Then write **V** beside *two* inferences that are supported by the ideas in it.

Changing Mores around Smoking

Textbook
Skills

[1]In the 1950s and 1960s, smoking was permitted virtually everywhere—in restaurants and bars, in airplanes, and offices. [2]Elevators had ashtrays because it was assumed people would smoke there. [3]If you held a dinner party in the 1950s, you would have been seen as an inconsiderate host if you failed to put out a box or holder containing cigarettes for your guests. [4]All the movie stars smoked. [5]It was cool. [6]Glamorous. [7]Sexy. [8]Since the 1980s, though, smoking has been increasingly **proscribed** for two reasons. [9]First, informal mores suggest that people who blow smoke in your direction are inconsiderate. [10]Second, formal laws now restrict where you can and cannot smoke. [11]Today, in your college or university, people are probably prohibited from smoking in their own offices. [12]Today, we might place health higher than pleasure on a hierarchy of values, and we believe that the rights of those who do not smoke are more significant than the rights of those who do.

—Adapted from Kimmel/Aronson, *Sociology Now*,
"Changing Mores around Smoking" p. 47, © 2009
Pearson/Allyn and Bacon. Reproduced by
permission of Pearson Education, Inc.

_____ Before the 1980s, smoking was a socially desirable activity.

_____ Smoking wasn't as dangerous in the 1950s and 1960s because tobacco products weren't as addictive then.

_____ The meaning of *proscribed* in sentence 8 is "allowed."

_____ The changes related to smoking have occurred because our understanding of the effects of smoking have changed and also because our values have changed.

1 Chapter Review

Summary of Key Concepts of A Reading System for Skilled Readers

LEARNING OUTCOME
1 4

Assess your comprehension of the key reading concepts described in the chapter.

- _____ is the understanding of information.

- _____ is the large body of information that is learned throughout a lifetime of experience. Use prior knowledge to increase comprehension:
  - Call up prior knowledge by asking _____
  - Check new information against prior knowledge by asking, _____ _____
  - Check for growth or change in your knowledge base by asking, _____ _____

- The reading process has three phases: _____ _____

- SQ3R, an acronym for a reading process, stands for Survey, Question, Read, Recite, and Review. SQ3R activates prior knowledge and offers strategies for each phase of the reading process:
  - Before Reading, _____: Skim titles, introductions, headings, bold and italic type, pictures, and graphs. Ask questions such as "What is my purpose for reading? What do I already know? What do I need to know?"
  - During Reading, _____: Annotate to understand. Repair confusion. Reread.
  - After Reading, Recite and Review: Recall key ideas and terms. Summarize. Answer questions: "What did I learn? What is the most important idea? How have my views changed?"

Test Your Comprehension of A Reading System for Skilled Readers

Respond to the following questions and prompts.

LEARNING
OUTCOME
1 **4**

In your own words, what is prior knowledge? _____

_____

LEARNING
OUTCOME
2 **3** **4**

Create a graph or draw a picture to illustrate SQ3R.

LEARNING
OUTCOME
3 **6**

Describe your reading process. How did you read before you studied this chapter? Will you change your reading process? If so, how? If not, why not? _____

_____

_____

_____

LEARNING
OUTCOME
4 **5** **6**

Identify the two most important ideas in this chapter that will help you improve your reading comprehension. _____

_____

_____

_____

_____

2 Chapter Review

Summary of Key Concepts of Vocabulary in Context

LEARNING OUTCOME ① ② ④ Assess your comprehension of context clues.

- _____ is all the words used or understood by a person.
- _____ is the information that surrounds a new word, used to understand its meaning.
- Skilled readers use _____ to learn new words.
- Four of the most common types of context clues and the traits of each context clue are as follows:
  - A(n) _____ is a word that has the same or nearly the same meaning as another word.
    - This context clue is often introduced by the signal words _____ and _____.
    - This clue may also be set off with a pair of _____, a pair of _____, or a pair of _____.
  - A(n) _____ is a word that has the opposite meaning of another word.
    - This context clue is often introduced by the signal words _____ _____ _____.
  - The _____ clue requires you to read the entire sentence, or to read ahead a few sentences, to determine the meaning of a new or unfamiliar word.
    - This context clue may offer information about a word in several ways such as by giving a _____, using vivid _____ or descriptions _____.

- _____ clues are often introduced with the signal words _____, *including*, _____, and _____.

- Many times, textbooks make information clearer by providing a visual image such as a _____.

Test Your Comprehension of Vocabulary in Context

Respond to the following questions and prompts.

LEARNING OUTCOME 1

In your own words, what is vocabulary? _____

_____

_____

LEARNING OUTCOME 2 6

Demonstrate your use of context clues. Use the headings below and create a chart based on the four types of context clues. Then, complete the chart with new words you have come across recently as you read for this class, another class, or any reading situation.

Type of Clue	New Word	Meaning of Word	Source Sentence of Word

LEARNING OUTCOME 3 5 6

Identify the two most important ideas in this chapter that will help you expand your vocabulary and improve your comprehension. Explain how these ideas have changed the way you learn new words.

_____

_____

_____

3 Chapter Review

Summary of Key Concepts of Vocabulary-Building Skills

LEARNING OUTCOME ❶ ❹ Assess your comprehension of vocabulary-building skills.

- _____ are the smaller parts of meaning in a word.
  - A _____ is the basic or main part of a word.
  - A _____ is a group of letters with a specific meaning added to the beginning of a word or root to make a new word.
  - A _____ is a group of letters with a specific meaning added to the end of a word or root to make a new word.
- _____ provide the following information about words:
  - _____ are a pair of words printed in bold at the top of every page of the dictionary.
  - A _____ is a unit of sound that includes a single vowel sound.
  - An _____ is a dark mark above a word that indicates which syllable gets the most emphasis when the word is spoken.
  - _____ indicate the sounds of consonants and vowels.
  - _____ is the study of a word's history.
- A textbook is written for a _____, such as math, history, or English.
  - _____ are words that take on new or different meanings in the context of the content or subject area.
  - A _____ is an alphabetical list of content words, their spellings, and their meanings.

Test Your Comprehension of Vocabulary-Building Skills

Respond to the following questions and prompts.

LEARNING
OUTCOME
1

In your own words, what are word parts? _____

_____

_____

LEARNING
OUTCOME
2 3 6

Create families of words using word parts. Choose a root word. Then create new words by adding prefixes and suffixes. Use your dictionary for the correct spelling of the new words you form. Complete the following vocabulary map as an example. Then use the roots, prefixes, and suffixes in Appendix C to create your own set of word families.

Vocabulary Word Map Based on Roots, Prefixes, and Suffixes

Prefix	**(Meaning)**	**Suffix**	**(Part of Speech) (Meaning)**
anti-	(against)	*-ic*	(adj.) (quality, trait)
auto-	(self)	*-ical*	(adj.) (of, like, relating to, being)
geo-	(earth, soil)	*-y*	(n.) (quality, trait)
tele-	(far, from a distance)		

Root   *bio* (life)   **Word family:** _____

_____

Root   *graph* (write)   **Word family:** _____

_____

LEARNING
OUTCOME
5 6

Identify the two most important ideas in this chapter that will help you improve your reading comprehension. _____

_____

_____

4 Chapter Review

Summary of Key Concepts of Topics and Main Ideas

LEARNING OUTCOME
1 **2** **5**

Assess your comprehension of topics and main ideas.

- A _____ is a broad subject that needs specific ideas to support or explain it.
- A _____ is a point used to support or explain a general idea.
- A _____ is the general subject matter of a reading passage.
- A _____ is the author's controlling point about the topic.
- A _____ is a single sentence in a paragraph that states the author's main idea.
- _____ are the specific ideas that develop, explain, support, or illustrate the main idea or controlling point.

Test Your Comprehension of Topics and Main Ideas

Respond to the following questions and prompts.

LEARNING OUTCOME
1

In your own words, what is the difference between a general and a specific idea? _____

_____

LEARNING OUTCOME
2

In your own words, what is the difference between a topic, main idea, and supporting details? _____

_____

_____

_____

_____

LEARNING
OUTCOME
① ② ③ ④   Create a picture that illustrates the flow of ideas among a topic, a main idea or topic sentence, and supporting details.

LEARNING
OUTCOME
⑥ ⑦   Describe how you will use topics and main ideas in your reading process to comprehend textbook material. For example, how could you use SQ3R to identify topics and main ideas? _____

_____

_____

_____

LEARNING
OUTCOME
③ ⑤ ⑥   Identify and discuss the two most important ideas in this chapter that will help you improve your reading comprehension. _____

_____

_____

_____

Summary of Key Concepts of Locating Stated Main Ideas

LEARNING OUTCOME 2 4 Assess your comprehension of locating stated main ideas.

- The _____ states the main idea of a paragraph.

- A _____ is the main idea of a passage made up of two or more paragraphs.

- The _____ is a sentence that states the central point of a longer passage.

- The stated main idea of a reading selection can be located _____ _____

- The flow of ideas from general to specific is known as _____ thinking.

- The flow of ideas from specific to general is known as _____ thinking.

Test Your Comprehension of Locating Stated Main Ideas

Respond to the following questions and prompts.

LEARNING OUTCOME 1 In your own words, what is the difference between deductive and inductive thinking? _____ _____ _____ _____

LEARNING
OUTCOME
2

In your own words, what is the difference between a topic sentence and a thesis statement? _____

_____

_____

_____

LEARNING
OUTCOME
1 3 6

Draw and label four graphs that show the possible locations of stated main ideas.

LEARNING
OUTCOME
5 6

Identify and discuss the two most important ideas in this chapter that will help you improve your reading comprehension. _____

_____

_____

_____

_____

_____

6 Chapter Review

LEARNING OUTCOME 1 Assess your comprehension of implied main ideas.

- A main idea that is not stated directly but is strongly suggested by the supporting details in a passage is a(n) _____.

- To determine an implied main idea, ask three questions:
  - What is the _____ of the passage?
  - What are the _____ in the passage?
  - What is the _____ of the passage?

- Implied main ideas must be neither too _____ nor too _____.

- To determine a main idea, _____ or mark the _____ and the words that reveal the author's _____ and thought patterns or types of _____ used in the passage.

Test Your Comprehension of Implied Main Ideas

Respond to the following questions and prompts.

LEARNING OUTCOME 1 In your own words, what is an implied main idea? _____
_____
_____

LEARNING OUTCOME 2 3 In your own words, how can the skills you use to identify the stated main idea help you determine the implied main idea? _____
_____
_____
_____

_____

_____

Study the following concept map. Then write the implied main idea suggested by the details in the map. Annotate the text in the map to show how you determined the implied main idea.

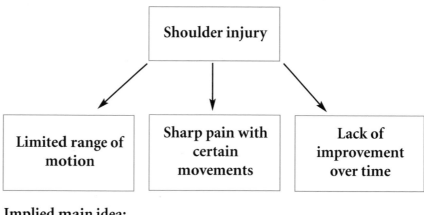

Shoulder injury

Limited range of motion

Sharp pain with certain movements

Lack of improvement over time

Implied main idea: _____

_____

Identify and discuss the two most important ideas in this chapter that will help you improve your reading comprehension. _____

_____

_____

_____

_____

7 Chapter Review

Summary of Key Concepts of Supporting Details

LEARNING OUTCOME ❶ Assess your comprehension of supporting details.

- To locate supporting details in a passage, a skilled reader turns the _____ _____ into a _____.

- A _____ directly explains, develops, or illustrates the _____ _____.

- A _____ explains, develops or illustrates a _____ _____.

- A summary is a brief, clear _____ of the _____ _____ of a paragraph or longer passage.

- Often you will want to _____ or restate the ideas in your own words.

- _____ or marking your text _____ reading will help you create a _____ after you read.

- To create a summary for a passage with a stated main idea, ask and answer questions based on the _____.

- To create a summary for a passage with an implied main idea, ask and answer questions based on the _____.

Test Your Comprehension of Supporting Details

Respond to the following questions and prompts.

LEARNING OUTCOME ❸ In your own words, how do major and minor supporting details differ? _____

_____

7-1

_____

_____

_____

**LEARNING
OUTCOME
3 4 7**

In the space below, outline the steps for creating a summary for stated and implied main ideas. See pages 246–249.

**LEARNING
OUTCOME
2 5 6**

Compose two questions and answers to summarize the two most important ideas in this chapter that will help you improve your reading comprehension.

Questions   Answers

_____   _____

_____   _____

8 Chapter Review

LEARNING OUTCOME ❶ Assess your comprehension of outlines and concept maps.

- An outline shows the relationships among the _____, _____, and _____.

- An author often uses _____ such as *a few causes*, *a number of reasons*, *several steps*, or *several kinds* of to introduce a _____.

- An author often uses signal words such as *first*, *second*, *furthermore*, *moreover*, *next*, or *finally* to introduce a _____.

- A formal outline uses _____ to indicate the _____, _____ to indicate the _____, and _____ to indicate the _____.

- A _____ is a diagram that shows the _____ of ideas from the main idea to the supporting details.

Test Your Comprehension of Outlines and Concept Maps

Respond to the following questions and prompts.

LEARNING OUTCOME ❶ In your own words, what is an outline? _____
_____
_____
_____
_____
_____

In your own words, what is a concept map? _____

_____

_____

_____

_____

In the space below, create an outline and a concept map for the following terms: Panic Attacks, Causes of Panic Attacks, Family History, Stress, Substance Abuse, Effects of Panic Attacks, Difficulty Breathing, Dizziness, Pounding Heart

Outline: Topic : Panic Attacks

I. _____

A. _____

B. _____

C. _____

II. _____

A. _____

B. _____

C. _____

Concept Map:

Panic Attacks

Causes of Panic Attacks

1. _____

2. _____

3. _____

Effects of Panic Attacks

1. _____

2. _____

3. _____

Summarize the two most important ideas in this chapter that will help you improve your reading comprehension. _____

_____

_____

9 Chapter Review

Summary of Key Concepts of Transitions and Thought Patterns

LEARNING OUTCOME
① ② ③ ④
⑥

Assess your comprehension of transitions and thought patterns.

- _____ are words and phrases that signal thought _____ by showing the _____ relationships within a sentence and between sentences.

- A thought pattern is established by using _____ to show the _____ relationship between ideas in a paragraph or passage.

- _____ and process are two uses of the _____ order thought pattern.

- In addition to showing a chain of events, the time order pattern is used to show _____, _____, or _____ that can be repeated at any time with similar results.

- The _____ order pattern allows authors to describe a person, place, or thing based on its location or the way it is arranged in space.

- Some of the words used to establish the space order pattern include adjacent, _____, and _____.

- Transitions of addition, such as _____, _____, and *furthermore*, are generally used to indicate a _____ pattern.

- Authors use the _____ pattern to sort ideas into smaller groups and describe the _____ of each group.

- Examples of classification signal words are _____, *second type*, or *another group*.

Test Your Comprehension of Transitions and Thought Patterns

Respond to the following questions and prompts.

LEARNING OUTCOME **1**

In your own words, what is a transition? _____

_____

_____

LEARNING OUTCOME **1**

In your own words, what is a thought pattern? _____

_____

_____

LEARNING OUTCOME **2 3 4 6**

In the space below, organize the following ideas from a college sociology textbook into a logical thought pattern. Create an outline or concept map.

Sigmund Freud's Three Levels of Personality. The **id** makes up the inborn basic drives. The **ego** balances the drive for basic needs and the demands of society. The **superego** is the conscience. The **id** demands immediate fulfillment of basic needs. Basic needs include food, safety, sleep, sex, and so on. The **ego** serves to balance the id and the superego. The conscience is the seat of morals and values. The **superego** causes feelings of shame or guilt when we break social rules.

—Adapted from Henslin, *Sociology: A Down-To-Earth Approach*, 9th ed., pp. 73–74.

Sigmund Freud's Three Levels of Personality

I. The basic level is the id.
    A. _____
    B. _____
II. Another level is the ego.
    A. _____
    B. _____
III. The third level is the superego.
    A. _____
    B. _____

LEARNING OUTCOME **5**

Summarize the two most important ideas in this chapter that will help you improve your reading comprehension. _____

_____

_____

10 Chapter Review

LEARNING OUTCOME
① ② ③ ④
⑥

Assess your comprehension of thought patterns.

- _____ points out the ways two or more ideas are alike.

- _____ points out the ways two or more ideas are different.

- The words *like, similarly*, and *likewise* signal the _____ pattern.

- A cause states _____.

- An effect states _____.

- An author will often begin with the _____ and then give the effects.

- The phrases *as a result, leads to*, and *therefore* signal the _____ pattern.

- _____ words signal that a writer is giving an instance of a general idea to clarify a point.

- _____ explains the meaning of new, difficult, or special terms.

- _____ often follow a definition to show how the word is used or applied.

Test Your Comprehension of More Thought Patterns

Respond to the following questions and prompts.

LEARNING OUTCOME
①

In your own words, what is the difference between comparison and contrast? _____

_____

_____

LEARNING
OUTCOME
❶

In your own words, what is the difference between a cause and an effect? _____

_____

LEARNING
OUTCOME
❷❸❹❻

In the space below, create a concept map based on the information in the paragraph.

Erosion moves soil from one place to another by the action of wind or water. Erosion becomes a problem because it often occurs more quickly than soil is formed. Grasslands, forests, and other plants protect soil from wind and water erosion. Vegetation breaks the wind and slows the water flow, and plant roots hold soil in place and take up water. Removing plant cover nearly always leads to erosion. Erosion removes topsoil, the most valuable soil layer for living things. People have caused erosion in several ways. One cause is the overfarming of fields through poor planning or too much tilling. Another cause is overgrazing rangelands with more livestock than the land can support. A third cause is clearing forest on steep slopes or with large clear-cuts.

—Adapted from Withgott & Brennan, *Essential Environment,* 3rd ed., p. 138.

LEARNING
OUTCOME
❺

Summarize the two most important ideas in this chapter that will help you improve your reading comprehension. _____

_____

_____

Summary of Key Concepts about Inferences

LEARNING OUTCOME
① ② ③ ④
⑤

Assess your comprehension of inferences.

- An inference is an _____ idea that is _____ by the facts or details in a passage.

- A skilled reader must sort _____ from _____ to infer the author's meaning.

- Biased words express opinions, _____, _____, or _____.

- A _____ signals an unchangeable idea, a command, the rightness of an action, or degrees of doubt.

- A(n) _____ inference is a logical conclusion based on evidence.

- A(n) _____ conclusion is a false inference that is not based on the details, facts, or reasonable thinking.

- The VALID approach consists of 5 thinking steps to take to make a valid inference.

  - Step 1: _____ and value the _____.

  - Step 2: _____ prior knowledge.

  - Step 3: Learn from the _____.

  - Step 4: Investigate for _____.

  - Step 5: _____.

 ## Test Your Comprehension of Inferences

Respond to the following questions and prompts.

LEARNING OUTCOME
① ③

In your own words, what is the difference between a valid and an invalid inference? _____

_____

_____

_____

Complete the following outline of the VALID approach.

I. _____

    A. Identify facts.

    B. Identify opinions.

       1. Identify opinions based on biased words.

       2. Identify opinions based on words that qualify ideas.

II. _____

III. _____

    A. Use context clues.

    B. Identify thought patterns.

    C. _____

IV. Investigate for bias.

    A. Note bias words in a reader's inference.

    B. Replace bias words in a reader's inference with factual details.

V. _____

Summarize the two most important ideas in this chapter that will help you improve your reading comprehension. _____

_____

_____

PART TWO

Additional Readings

The Connection Between Reading and Writing

The link between reading and writing is vital and natural. Written language allows an exchange of ideas between a writer and a reader. Thus, writing and reading are two equal parts of the communication process. In fact, reading is a form of listening or receiving information. And writing is like speaking—the sending of information. So a skilled reader makes every effort to understand and respond to the ideas of the writer. Likewise, a skilled writer makes every effort to make ideas clear so the reader can understand and respond to those ideas. Most writers find that reading improves their writing. Reading builds prior knowledge and fuels ideas for writing.

Because of this close relationship between reading and writing, both share similar thinking steps in their processes. In Chapter 1, you learned that the reading process has three phases: Before Reading, During Reading, and After Reading. The writing process also has three phases that occur before, during, and after writing: Prewriting, Drafting, and Proofing. By coordinating these two sets of process, you can improve both your reading and your writing. For example, the following statements sum up one way to connect reading and writing:

> Reading is a prewriting activity. Drafting is an after reading activity. Once you think of reading as a prewriting activity, you become a responsive or active reader during the reading process. In fact, you can begin using your writing skills as you read by annotating the text.

Annotating a Text

The word *annotate* suggests that you "take notes" in your book. Writing notes in the margin of a page as you read keeps you focused and improves your comprehension. You can quickly note questions where they occur, move on in your reading, and later return to clarify answers. In addition, after reading, your annotations help you review and respond to the material. The following suggestions offer one way to annotate a text:

How to Annotate a Text

- Circle important terms.
- Underline definitions and meanings.
- Note key ideas with a star or a check.
- Place question marks above words that are unknown or confusing.
- Number the steps in a process or items in a list.
- Write summaries at the end of long sections.
- Write recall questions in the margin near its answer.
- Write key words and meanings in margin.

EXAMPLE   The following passage from a college health textbook is marked up as an example of an annotated text. Read the passage. Study the annotations. Then work with a peer or in a small group and create a summary of the text based on the annotations.

HEALTH SKILLS

Avoiding Problem Drinking

Avoiding the problems associated with the consumption of alcohol is not complicated. It does, however, require basic knowledge of the effects of alcohol on the body, knowledge of how those effects can be minimized, and the skills needed to handle the social settings in which alcohol consumption takes place.

Practice Not Drinking

What is abstinence?

What are the two types of abstinence?

You have probably heard, and even made fun of, the saying "Just say no to drugs." Actually, this saying has its origin in reality. The most obvious and effective means of avoiding problem drinking is simply not to drink. Not drinking, often referred to as abstinence, is practiced by a large percentage of the population as a means of avoiding problem drinking. Two options are widely practiced: total abstinence to abstain from alcohol use at all times, and situational abstinence to abstain from alcohol use in situations in which use would present a risk.

People who totally abstain from alcohol use do so for a variety of reasons, including the following:

Why do people use total abstinence?

1. • Their religion forbids it.
2. • They have an allergic reaction to some of the components in alcohol products.   ?
3. • They have a genetic predisposition to problem drinking.
4. • They are aware of the health and social effects of drinking and do not want to have anything to do with it.
5. • They simply do not like the taste or smell of alcohol.

People use 2 types of abstinence to avoid drinking problems: Total abstinence means no drinking at any time. Situational abstinence avoids drinking at certain times such as when driving.

Situational abstinence is far more prevalent. ① One common situation in which it is not appropriate to drink alcohol is just before driving. The reasons for this are obvious: to avoid a potential automobile crash and to obey the law. Another ② situation in which abstinence is appropriate is when entering a risky social situation, such as a party where there is a lot of drinking. As you have read, alcohol is a contributing factor in unwanted sexual practices, including unprotected sex and date rape. Abstinence can help reduce the risks associated with such situations.

Pace Your Drinking

If you choose to drink, there are some practices that can help you drink wisely and reduce the risks of drinking. One important practice is to pace the amount of alcohol you consume. By doing so, you can avoid intoxication and the problems that result.

When alcohol is consumed at the pace of one drink per hour, the body is generally able to process the alcohol. One drink is measured as one and a half ounces of eighty-proof liquor, five ounces of 12 percent wine, or twelve ounces of five percent beer (this usually means one jigger of liquor, one glass of wine, or one bottle of beer). **Proof** refers to the percentage of pure alcohol in a beverage. The percentage of alcohol is half the proof: 40 percent alcohol is 80 proof.

total abstinence   The choice never to consume alcoholic beverages.

situational drinking   The choice not to consume alcoholic beverages in situations in which the consumption of alcohol would present a health risk.

proof   The percentage of pure alcohol in a beverage; the percentage of alcohol is half the proof.

—Pruitt & Stein, *HealthStyles: Decisions for Living Well*, 2nd ed., p. 224.

A Reading-Writing Plan of Action

Can you see how annotating a text lays the ground upon which you can build a written response? The steps you take during reading feeds into the process of writing a response after reading.

Remember, reading and writing is a conversation between the writer and the reader. One writes; the other reads. But the conversation often doesn't end there. A reader's response to a piece of writing keeps the dialogue going. When you write a summary, your response is to restate the author's ideas. It's like saying to the author, "If I understood you, you said . . ." When you offer your own views about the author's ideas, you are answering the author's implied question, "What do you think?" In your reading and writing classes, your teacher often steps into the conversation. He or she stands in for the author and becomes the reader of your written response. In this case, your teacher evaluates both your reading and writing abilities. Your teacher checks your response for accuracy in comprehension of the author's message and development of your ability to write. The following chart illustrates this exchange of ideas.

The Conversation among Writers and Readers

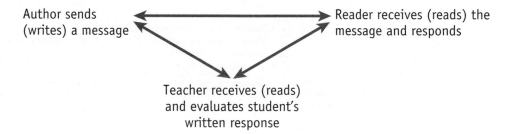

Author sends (writes) a message

Reader receives (reads) the message and responds

Teacher receives (reads) and evaluates student's written response

In each skill chapter of this textbook, the question "What Do You Think?" is posed after Review Tests 3 and 4. This question also appears after each reading selection in this section. The "What Do You Think?" writing assignments prompt you to respond to what you have read. This activity creates a writing situation and gives you a purpose for your written response. Just like a vocabulary word makes more sense in context than in a list, a writing assignment in context is more meaningful than an isolated topic or set of disconnected questions. The goal of "What Do You Think?" is to strengthen your connection between reading and writing. Because reading and writing are two distinct processes, it is helpful to have a guide that shows how to efficiently coordinate them. The following chart lays out a reading-writing plan of action. Note that the chart breaks the reading-writing process into a series of 6 steps. Keep in mind that any step can be repeated as needed. Also, you can move back and forth between steps as needed.

Study the 6-Step Reading-Writing Action Plan. Then work with a peer or small group of classmates and discuss the relationship between reading and writing, and how you will put this plan to use.

A 6-Step Reading-Writing Action Plan

Read		Write
1. Survey and Question	BEFORE	**4. Prewrite**

Read — BEFORE

1. Survey and Question

Call on Prior Knowledge
Identify Topic
Identify Key or New Words
Identify Patterns of Organization
Note Visual Aids
Skim Introductions and
    Conclusions

Write — BEFORE

4. Prewrite

Build Prior Knowledge*
Gather Information*
Read and Annotate*
Brainstorm Ideas
Choose Your Topic
Generate Your Details
Create a Concept Map
Outline Ideas

Read — DURING

2. Read

Monitor Comprehension
Fix Confusion
Annotate Text

Write — DURING

5. Draft

Write Introduction, Body,
    and Conclusion

Read — AFTER

3. Review and Recite

Recall Key Words and Ideas
Create Concept Maps
Create Outlines
Write a Summary
Write a Response

Write — AFTER

6. Revise and Proofread

Revise to Organize
Revise for Exact Wording
Correct Errors
    Fragments and Run-ons
    Spelling
    Punctuation

---

* Prewriting steps accomplished during reading

Shoulders

Nels Gould

Each of us has a deep need to be loved and to belong; we need the cycle of connection that comes from both receiving and giving respect and acceptance. And we spend much time and energy seeking to fill these needs. The following essay taken from a psychology textbook explores the significance of the human need for connectedness. The author Nels Gould, Indiana University-Purdue University at Indianapolis, offers his insights about our compelling need for each other.

Vocabulary Preview

modified (paragraph 2): adapted, changed
ungratified (paragraph 4): unmet
perseverance (paragraph 4): resolve, determination
obligatory (paragraph 4): required, mandatory
omnipotence (paragraph 5): all powerful
pseudosolution (paragraph 5): fake, or false, solution
alienation (paragraph 5): isolation
contemplations (paragraph 6): thoughts

1 I was about six years old when my parents took me to a parade. Standing there in a crowd of giants all I could see were knees and belt buckles. The bands, floats, and zany clowns passed by unseen. "I can't see! I want to see!" I yelled. Within a couple of seconds two strong arms lifted me up high above the crowd. I had the best seat in the house up there on my father's shoulders. He didn't seem to mind at all that he was half strangled each time I got excited.

2 Two weeks ago I took some college students through a **modified** Outward Bound initiatives course. One task was to figure out how to get over a sheer 13-foot wall using only their minds and bodies. Gradually they decided to place a couple of people at the base of the wall. Sandy was elected to climb up on their shoulders. Sandy stretched and still was six inches from reaching the upper ledge. The two classmates she was standing on then pushed her up until she caught hold of the ledge and scrambled over. The rest of the class cheered Sandy. No one gave a hand to the two below with dirty shirts and sore shoulders.

3   It took actual shoulders to see the parade and climb the wall. Shoulders come in many other forms—teachings, models and mentors, others' past efforts. Our most accomplished persons readily acknowledged shoulders. "Many times a day I realize how much my life is built upon the labors of my fellow men, both living and dead," said Einstein. Eddie Robinson, immediately before the game which made him college football's winningest coach, said to his players "It's a record made up of men like you for the last 40 years."

4   Why is it, then, that most of us, most of the time, forget that we stand on shoulders? It appears that once our foundations are established, they are dropped from waking consciousness. Our attention becomes fully focused on current struggles, unattained goals, and **ungratified** needs. Successes are seen as the result of personal resourcefulness, **perseverance,** and possibly a few breaks. Occasionally we might throw in a plaudit for those we stand on, but it generally rings of the **obligatory.** I was reminded of this when someone asked me how I achieved a certain style of trumpet playing. My response centered on individual effort and practice. Later reflection revealed gaping holes in this answer. I forgot my shoulders. Any current trumpeting skill would have to be traced to my mom's encouragement while hearing me butcher pieces like "The Carnival of Venice" in the back room; to Hendrik Buytendorp, the music teacher who made it clear that trumpet scales were just as important as little

league practice; and to Ferguson, Severinsen, Hirt, Mangione.* An honest and true answer would have to acknowledge all these influences. Try it yourself—just attempt to fully explain how you are able to do something well. The answer will unveil a vast network of shoulders.

5   Forgetting shoulders may be linked to distorted notions of self-sufficiency. We value and reward self-direction, individual initiative, and taking responsibility. A healthy person possesses these qualities. It is when these traits are exaggerated out of proportion that problems begin. Healthy autonomy turns into neurotic self-reliance. A person gradually begins to believe he/she can master life's challenges by relying solely on personal resources, and that to even acknowledge the help of others is a "weakness." It may even work for awhile. Then prices must be paid. Some develop illusions of **omnipotence** or step into the trap Karen Horney called the **pseudosolution** of mastery. This "I don't need anybody, never had, never will" orientation propels one to the outpost of **alienation.**

6   One does not lose uniqueness by tracing an accomplishment or ability to the influence of others. The actual idea and action is an individual one; it has your stamp. That is what shoulders are for; they permit a stretching of the limits of what has gone on before. By remembering shoulders while perched up there, you get the bonus of profound sense of belonging. One may even realize Thoreau's advice: "If I devote myself to pursuits and **contemplations,** I

*The last names of four accomplished trumpeters.

must first see, at least, that I do not pursue them sitting upon another man's shoulders. I must get off him first, that he may pursue his contemplations, too."

7   Sometimes I realize my part in this shoulders network in simple ways. I am watching the Indianapolis 500 parade with 250,000 other giants. The bands, floats, and clowns pass by and I hear my four year old son hollering, "I can't see! I want to see!" I hoist him up on my shoulders and he half strangles me.

—Gould/Arkoff, *Psychology and Personal Growth*, "Shoulders" pp. 197–198 © 2003 Pearson Education, Inc. Reproduced by permission of Pearson Education, Inc.

Fill in the blank in each sentence with a word from the "Vocabulary Preview."

Vocabulary Preview
1. Sticking to a physical fitness program requires _____ based on resolve.

Vocabulary Preview
2. Lanedra enjoys keeping a journal of her _____ or thoughts about current events and daily life.

Vocabulary Preview
3. Maria _____ her work schedule by switching to the late night shift so that she could spend time with her children before and after school.

Vocabulary Preview
4. Roderick overcame social _____ by taking responsibility for and changing the angry and rude behavior that isolated him from others.

Vocabulary Preview
5. Heather gladly wrote the _____ thank you notes to her family and friends who had showered her with wedding gifts.

Write the letter of the best meaning of each of the words in *italics*. Use context clues to make your choice.

Vocabulary in Context
_____ **6.** "The bands, floats, and *zany* clowns passed by unseen." (paragraph 1)
    a. stupid   c. funny
    b. embarrassing   d. tall

Vocabulary in Context
_____ **7.** "Our most *accomplished* persons readily acknowledged shoulders." (paragraph 3)
    a. fearful   c. hopeful
    b. successful   d. grateful

Vocabulary in Context
_____ **8.** "Occasionally we might throw in a *plaudit* for those we stand on, but it generally rings of the obligatory." (paragraph 4)
    a. criticism   c. compliment
    b. gift   d. glance

Vocabulary in Context _____ **9.** "Healthy *autonomy* turns into neurotic self-reliance." (paragraph 5)
   a. immune system
   b. dependence
   c. independence
   d. relationship

Vocabulary in Context _____ **10.** "One does not lose *uniqueness* by tracing an accomplishment or ability to the influence of others." (paragraph 6)
   a. individuality
   b. humility
   c. uniformity
   d. curiosity

Implied Central Idea _____ **11.** Which sentence is the best statement of the implied central idea of the passage?
   a. Successes are seen as the result of personal resourcefulness, perseverance, and possibly a few breaks.
   b. Forgetting shoulders may lead to distorted notions of self-sufficiency.
   c. Our successes come because we stand on the shoulders of others.
   d. One must have strong "shoulders" to survive in this world.

Implied Main Idea _____ **12.** Which sentence is the best statement of the implied main idea of paragraph 2?
   a. It takes everyone working together to succeed.
   b. Those who give a helping hand are often overlooked when success occurs.
   c. Outward Bound is an excellent initative course.
   d. Sandy is a young lady of determination.

Supporting Details _____ **13.** Speaking of his winning record, football coach Eddie Robinson said,
   a. "Many times a day I realize how much my life is built upon the labors of my fellow men."
   b. "I can't see! I want to see."
   c. "We stand on the shoulders of giants."
   d. "It's a record made up of men like you for the last 40 years."

Supporting Details _____ **14.** The author knows how to play
   a. football.
   b. the corporate game to get ahead.
   c. on the guilt of other people.
   d. trumpet.

Thought
Patterns _____ **15.** The main thought pattern for the overall passage is
- a. a list and explanation of examples of those who have made the author successful.
- b. an argument that gives supports for the point that each of us has relied on others to become the person we are today.
- c. a discussion of the causes of belonging.
- d. a comparison and contrast between self-reliance and dependence on others.

Thought
Patterns _____ **16.** The thought pattern for paragraph 2 is
- a. cause and effect.
- b. generalization and example.
- c. time order.

Transitions _____ **17.** "Our most accomplished persons readily acknowledged shoulders. 'Many times a day I realize how much my life is built upon the labors of my fellow men, both living and dead,' said Einstein." The relationship of ideas between these two sentences is
- a. time order.
- b. contrast.
- c. example.

Transitions _____ **18.** "It appears that once our foundations are established, they are dropped from waking consciousness." (paragraph 4) The relationship of ideas within this sentence is
- a. time order.
- b. example.
- c. cause and effect.

Inferences _____ **19.** Which of the following statements is a valid conclusion based on the ideas in paragraph 7?
- a. The author is annoyed at his son.
- b. The author is an avid Indianapolis 500 fan.
- c. The author is happily married.
- d. The author understands that his son's success in life will be in part because of his own successes.

Inferences _____ **20.** From the passage, we can conclude that
- a. we need each other in order to succeed.
- b. the author is a successful businessman.
- c. even some level of self-reliance is an impossible goal.
- d. we have the potential to do each other great harm.

Mapping

Complete the following concept map. Fill in the blanks with the central idea and the missing major supporting details from "Shoulders."

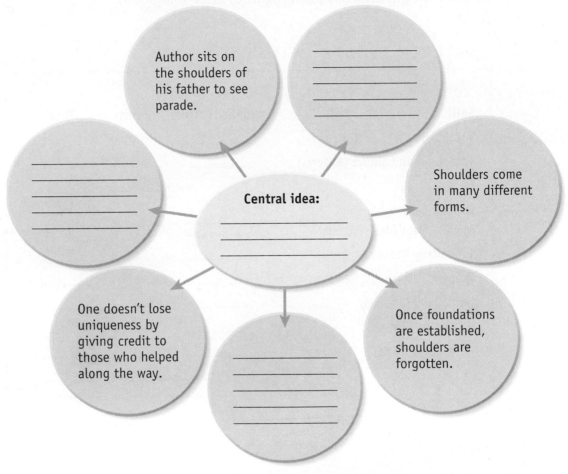

Author sits on the shoulders of his father to see parade.

_____
_____
_____
_____

Shoulders come in many different forms.

_____
_____
_____

Central idea:
_____
_____
_____

Once foundations are established, shoulders are forgotten.

One doesn't lose uniqueness by giving credit to those who helped along the way.

_____
_____
_____
_____

WHAT DO YOU THINK?

Do you agree with Gould's point about the origin of success? Why or why not? Why do some people think it is a sign of weakness to give credit to those who have helped them? Gould suggests that we trace the origin of a skill or accomplishment of a public figure. For example, upon whose shoulders does President Barack Obama stand? Or Secretary of State Hillary Clinton? Upon whose shoulders do certain current comedians or musicians stand? Assume you are involved in service learning and you earn academic credit for acting as a mentor at a local youth organization. As a mentor, you have been asked to speak to the youth. You have chosen the following topic for your speech. "Success: Standing on the Shoulders of Others." Use your own personal experience or the experience of a public figure to make your point.

SKILLED READER Scorecard

"Shoulders"

Skill	Number Correct	Points		Total
Vocabulary Preview (5 items)	_____	× 10	=	_____
Vocabulary in Context (5 items)	_____	× 10	=	_____
		Vocabulary Score		_____
Implied Central Idea and Implied Main Idea (2 items)	_____	× 8	=	_____
Supporting Details (2 items)	_____	× 8	=	_____
Thought Patterns (2 items)	_____	× 8	=	_____
Transitions (2 items)	_____	× 8	=	_____
Inferences (2 items)	_____	× 8	=	_____
Mapping (4 items)	_____	× 5	=	_____
		Comprehension Score		_____

Women of Courage
Remarks by the First Lady Michelle Obama At the State Department Women of Courage Awards

Imagine that you had been sold into slavery at the age of 12 for $500. Or suppose that as a 12-year-old you were forced to marry your 30-year-old cousin. Imagine you fought for your freedom and escaped. Would you run away or would you stand and fight for others like you who suffer the same fate? Every year, the Secretary of State gives an award to outstanding women leaders from around the world. The award is called the Secretary of State's Award for International Women of Courage. This award honors the struggle of women for social justice. It honors their fight for human rights. In 2009, women from Afghanistan, Guatemala, Iraq, Malaysia, Niger, Russia, Uzbekistan, and Yemen received this award. Read the tribute First Lady Michelle Obama gave to these women at the awards ceremony in the White House.

Vocabulary Preview

ambassador (paragraph 3): an appointed official of the highest rank who represents a country or organization to another country or to the world

phenomenal (paragraph 3): remarkable, out of the ordinary, rare, unique

psychological (paragraph 4): mental

motivates (paragraph 12): causes, inspires, encourages

generations (paragraph 14): groups of people, eras, time periods, stages in development

1   I am honored to be on this stage. So thank you for the invitation to participate in International Women's Day here at the State Department.

2   As Secretary Clinton mentioned earlier today at the White House, President Obama announced the **formation** of the White House Council on Women and Girls. Again, the goal of this Council is to **ensure** that young girls have no limits on their dreams and no obstacles to their achievements.

3   Secretary Clinton has also made this issue of particular importance right here at the State Department by creating a new position and nominating Melanne Verveer as **Ambassador**-at-large for global women's issues, and I again want to give her a round of applause. We are grateful for her participation. We thank her for her service in advance. She is going to do a **phenomenal** job.

4   The President and I share the belief that communities are only as strong as the health of their women. Every day, we see

what happens to families, communities and countries when women don't have access to health and medical care; when they don't have the resources to properly care for their children; when they are oppressed and struggling with emotional, physical, sexual and **psychological** abuse; when they have no access to education or fair treatment in the justice system.

5 The difference between a struggling family and a healthy one is often the presence of a strong woman or women at the center of that family.

6 The difference between a broken community and a thriving one is the presence of women who are valued; where relationships among women and between women and men are based on mutual respect.

7 The women we honor today teach us three very important lessons. One, that as women, we must stand up for ourselves. The second, as women, we must stand up for each other. And finally, as women, we must stand up for justice for all.

8 The women we honor here, standing on this stage today, risk their lives to fight for themselves and for their mothers, daughters, sisters, grandmothers, and friends. And in doing so, they create a better society not just for them, but for their fathers, sons, brothers, grandfathers, and husbands.

9 The women we honor today are not just changing their own **circumstances**; they're changing the world.

10 When 12-year-old girls fight for their freedom—and win—they change the future for millions of girls just like them.

11 When **advocates** are beaten and jailed and still raise their voice, they inspire and **nourish** hope.

12 When one woman with a phone in her apartment starts a movement that **motivates** thousands, her cause can no longer be ignored.

13 When brave women challenge thousands of years of tradition and history and become leaders in their religious communities, they change minds.

14 And, when women fight to be educated and then reach out to bring their sisters along, they change the future for **generations** to come.

15 This is how real change occurs—one determined woman at a time. And change is coming. Women have made great strides with regard to equality at all levels of society from families, communities to businesses and government. But the stories of the women we honor today remind us that we still have work to do.

16 And I am so very proud to be here today to celebrate these brave women who have fought for themselves and, in the process, made the way so much easier for other women and girls.

17 Again, I thank you for the honor to be here. I am so proud to be a woman today and every single day.

—Michelle Obama. "Remarks of the First Lady at the State Department Women of Courage Awards. U. S. State Department. Washington D.C. 11 March 2009. 4 Nov. 2009. http://www.whitehouse.gov/the_press_office/Remarks-by-the-First-Lady-at-the-State-Department-Women-of-Courage-Awards.

VISUAL VOCABULARY

This _____ two-year-old girl eats lunch in her hospital bed in Guatemala. Almost half of the children in Guatemala suffer starvation. Most mothers can't afford medical treatment for their children.

a. nourished
b. malnourished

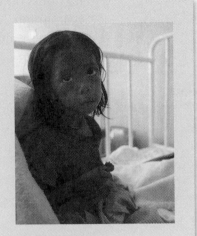

Fill in the blank in each sentence with a word from the "Vocabulary Preview."

Vocabulary Preview

1. Denying someone access to money or economic support is _____ abuse.

Vocabulary Preview

2. For _____, many women around the world have had to fight for fair treatment.

Vocabulary Preview

3. Taking a stand for justice may call for _____ courage and strength.

Vocabulary Preview

4. Nicole Kidman serves as a Goodwill _____ for the United Nations Development Fund for Women.

Vocabulary Preview

5. Violence against women likely affects as many as 6 out of 10 women. This fact _____ Kidman in her work with the United Nations.

For items 6 through 10, choose the best meaning of each word in italics. Use context clues to make your choice.

Vocabulary in Context

_____ **6.** "As Secretary Clinton mentioned earlier today at the White House, President Obama announced the *formation* of the White House Council on Women and Girls." (paragraph 2)
a. shape
b. design
c. creation
d. group

Vocabulary in Context _____ **7.** "Again, the goal of this Council is to *ensure* that young girls have no limits on their dreams and no obstacles to their achievements." (paragraph 2)

    a. understand   c. witness

    b. explain   d. make certain

Vocabulary in Context _____ **8.** "The women we honor today are not just changing their own *circumstances*; they're changing the world." (paragraph 9)

    a. situations   c. fates

    b. accidents   d. minds

Vocabulary in Context _____ **9.** "When *advocates* are beaten and jailed and still raise their voice, they inspire and nourish hope." (paragraph 11)

    a. enemies   c. supporters

    b. women   d. officials

Vocabulary in Context _____ **10.** "When advocates are beaten and jailed and still raise their voice, they inspire and *nourish* hope." (paragraph 11)

    a. feel   c. deprive

    b. feed   d. have

Central Idea _____ **11.** Which sentence best states the central idea of the passage?

    a. "I am honored to be on this stage." (paragraph 1)

    b. "The President and I share the belief that communities are only as strong as the health of their women." (paragraph 4)

    c. "The women we honor here today teach us three very important lessons." (paragraph 7)

    d. "And I am so very proud to be here today to celebrate these brave women who have fought for themselves and, in the process, made the way so much easier for other women and girls." (paragraph 16)

Supporting Detail _____ **12.** Earlier in the day, President Obama had announced

    a. the winners of the Women of Courage Awards.

    b. the three lessons taught by the women who won the awards.

    c. the formation of the White House Council on Women and Girls.

    d. the appointment of Melanne Verveer as Ambassador-at-large for global issues.

Transitions _____ **13.** "The difference between a struggling family and a healthy one is often the presence of a strong woman or women at the center of that family." (paragraph 5)

The relationship of ideas within this sentence is
a. cause and effect.
b. classification.
c. definition and example.
d. comparison and contrast.

Transitions _____ **14.** "One, that as women, we must stand up for ourselves. The second, as women, we must stand up for each other." (paragraph 7)

The relationship of ideas between these sentences is
a. cause and effect.
b. addition.
c. comparison and contrast.
d. time order.

Thought Patterns _____ **15.** The thought pattern for paragraphs 8 through 15 is
a. cause and effect.
b. listing.
c. comparison and contrast.
d. time order.

Fact and Opinion _____ **16.** "As Secretary Clinton mentioned earlier today at the White House, President Obama announced the formation of the White House Council on Women and Girls."

This sentence from paragraph 2 states
a. a fact.
b. an opinion.
c. fact and opinion.

Fact and Opinion _____ **17.** "The women we honor today teach us three very important lessons."

This sentence from paragraph 7 states
a. a fact.
b. an opinion.
c. fact and opinion.

Fact and Opinion _____ **18.** "This is how real change occurs—one determined woman at a time."

This sentence from paragraph 15 states
a. a fact.
b. an opinion.
c. fact and opinion.

Inference _____ **19.** From the details in the speech, we can conclude that
  a. women's issues are important to the Obama administration.
  b. American women do not suffer as much as do women in other countries.
  c. issues about women are more important than issues about men.
  d. the most important issue for women is education.

Inference _____ **20.** The details in paragraphs 7 through 15 imply that
  a. the efforts of women to improve society are often overlooked.
  b. the women being honored have achieved their goals.
  c. women cannot help themselves.
  d. one person can make a difference in the fight for a better society.

Outlining

Complete the following outline with information from Michelle Obama's speech "Remarks by the First Lady at the State Department Women of Courage Awards."

I. Issues of Importance to Women

   A. Access to health care

   B. _____

   C. _____

   D. Access to education

   E. _____

II. Lessons Taught by Women of Courage

   A. _____

   B. _____

   C. To stand up for justice for all

WHAT DO YOU THINK?

Why is "the presence of a strong woman or women" so important to a family? Why is the presence of a strong woman or women important to a community? Do you know a woman who has risen above circumstances to make the best of her life? Do you know a woman who works every day, often against great odds, to make life better for someone else? Do you know a woman who has stood up for justice for all? Assume a civic club such as The National Organization of Women or the Rotary Club is going to give a Woman of Courage award to a local woman. Write an essay nominating a woman worthy of recognition.

SKILLED READER Scorecard

"Women of Courage"

Skill	Number Correct	Points	Total
Vocabulary Preview (5 items)	_____	× 4 =	_____
Vocabulary in Context (5 items)	_____	× 4 =	_____
	Vocabulary Score		_____
Central Idea (1 item)	_____	× 4 =	_____
Supporting Detail (1 item)	_____	× 4 =	_____
Transitions (2 items)	_____	× 4 =	_____
Thought Patterns (1 item)	_____	× 4 =	_____
Fact and Opinion (3 items)	_____	× 4 =	_____
Inferences (2 items)	_____	× 4 =	_____
Outlining (5 items)	_____	× 4 =	_____
	Comprehension Score		_____

A Dad at the Final Frontier

Marc Parent

> Change has affected all aspects of our lives, from how we conduct our business to how we keep in touch with one another to how we cook our food. Families and the roles each member plays are also changing. The following essay appeared in the *New York Times*. In it, Marc Parent talks about society's reactions to his view of his role as a new kind of father.

Vocabulary Preview

accounting for (paragraph 1): explaining
nanny (paragraph 2): children's caregiver
provider (paragraph 2): supplier of income, goods, or services
putting in the hard time (paragraph 6): enduring a punishment
queasiness (paragraph 6): uneasiness
peppering (paragraph 10): showering, overwhelming

1   Things may be getting easier for me and my kind. In the last 10 years the number of fathers acting as primary custodians of children under 18 rose 62 percent—there are now 2.2 million of us, **accounting for** 2.1 percent of all American households. Of course, national statistics are one thing, and the midday grocery aisles are quite another.

2   If you want to assess America's adjustment to care-giving fathers, step into a city playground on a Wednesday afternoon and watch the reaction of the nearest **nanny**. As a stay-at-home father to sons 1 and 3 years old, I was often approached by well-meaning women who were certain I was between child-care **providers**, "Excuse me, do you need a nanny?"

3   "No thanks," I'd tell them. "I'm the father and the nanny."

4   And then I'd leave to go see the man at the deli, who asked every day, no matter what time, no matter how draped with children or how weighed down with stroller and diaper bag I was, "You on your lunch break?"

5   The curiosity is always the same: What business could a man in his mid-30's, midweek and midday, possibly have with his children?

6   Of course, some people see nothing at all remarkable about a man caring for his children, but most men **putting in the hard time** will tell you there are many who seem to harbor an unspoken **queasiness** about it.

7   My wife is a teacher with a paycheck like a small, steady train. I'm a writer who brings feast or famine. There are no hidden agendas surrounding our decision about who stays home—you keep the job with the better health plan.

8   Still there's a feeling that if a man dons a baby carrier, he does so at the cost of some measure of manhood. It's perhaps no coincidence that I became obsessed with hand-splitting wood around the same time I got really good with a Diaper Genie.

9   The problem is that unless men find their own way to care for their children, they are left to imitate their wives or their own mothers. There are still very few well-worn paths to full-time fatherhood. In our household, we've found that the parent who spends the time does it better. I'm better with the demands of parenting in winter, and my wife is better on summer break. But though I've found a way to make fatherhood relevant before the first game of catch, the rest of the world may not buy it yet.

10   I recently joined a conversation with a group of mothers as we waited to pick up our children from preschool. One of them was pregnant, and the women were **peppering** her with advice. I stayed quiet through the part about breast pads and swollen ankles but spoke up when they reached the topic of diaper rash.

11   "I don't suggest using powder for a rash," I said, hoisting my youngest to my hip. They smiled and nodded politely with eyes wide, as if I'd just told them I liked to rob banks. "And the cream is much better than the ointment," I continued as they looked from my son to my two-day beard. "I use it with every diaper."

—Parent, Marc, "A Dad at the Final Frontier"
from *The New York Times*, June 16,
2001, © 2001 The New York Times.
Reprinted with permission.

Fill in the blank in each sentence with a word from the "Vocabulary Preview."

Vocabulary Preview **1.** Jerome always felt a _____ in his stomach after he rode the roller coaster.

Vocabulary Preview **2.** It is very important to check the references of a _____ before you hire one.

Vocabulary Preview **3.** Dr. Nancy Bailey is an excellent _____ for her family.

Vocabulary Preview **4.** The boxer Muhammad Ali was known for _____ his opponents with quick, hard blows.

Vocabulary Preview **5.** The police had all the family members _____ their actions over the past few days.

Write the letter of the best meaning of the word in *italics*. Use context clues to make your choice.

_____ **6.** "Things may be getting easier for me and my kind. In the last 10 years the number of fathers acting as primary *custodians* of children under 18 rose 62 percent—there are now 2.2 million of us, accounting for 2.1 percent of all American households." (paragraph 1)

   a. janitors   c. families
   b. guardians   d. lawyers

_____ **7.** "And then I'd leave to go see the man at the deli, who asked every day, no matter what time, no matter how *draped* with children or how weighed down with stroller and diaper bag I was, 'You on your lunch break?'" (paragraph 4)

   a. covered   c. trapped
   b. stuck   d. good

_____ **8.** "The problem is that unless men find their own way to care for their children, they are left to *imitate* their wives or their own mothers." (paragraph 9)

   a. tease   c. copy
   b. frighten   d. see

_____ **9.** "But though I've found a way to make fatherhood *relevant* before the first game of catch, the rest of the world may not buy it yet." (paragraph 9)

   a. fun   c. useful
   b. relaxed   d. outdated

_____ **10.** "'I don't suggest using powder for a rash,' I said, *hoisting* my youngest to my hip." (paragraph 11)

   a. lifting   c. shouting
   b. shoving   d. dropping

_____ **11.** Which sentence is the best statement of the central idea of the passage?

   a. Fathers can be excellent caregivers.
   b. The rising number of men who choose to be full-time caregivers for their children face several challenges.
   c. Women in the workforce put stress on the family.
   d. There are very few role models for men who are the main caregivers for their children.

Implied
Main Idea   _____ **12.** What is the implied main idea of the final paragraph?

    a. The author gets along well with the other mothers.

    b. The author wants to go back to work outside the home.

    c. The author is an experienced caregiver for children.

    d. The author's children are often sick.

Supporting
Details   _____ **13.** The author stays home to care for his children because

    a. as a writer, he doesn't bring in a regular paycheck or have benefits.

    b. his wife insists on working outside the home.

    c. he is unemployed.

    d. he and his wife cannot afford child care.

Supporting
Details   _____ **14.** The author is a stay-at-home father to

    a. one son and one daughter.

    b. two daughters.

    c. two sons.

    d. two sons and one daughter.

Thought
Patterns   _____ **15.** The main thought pattern for paragraphs 2 through 5 is

    a. comparison.   c. cause and effect.

    b. time order.   d. listing.

Thought
Patterns   _____ **16.** The thought pattern for paragraphs 10 and 11 is

    a. comparison.   c. cause and effect.

    b. effect.   d. time order.

Transitions   _____ **17.** "Of course, some people see nothing at all remarkable about a man caring for his children, but most men putting in the hard time will tell you there are many who seem to harbor an unspoken queasiness about it." (paragraph 6)

The relationship of ideas in this sentence is one of

    a. time.   c. contrast.

    b. effect.   d. comparison.

Transitions   _____ **18.** "I recently joined a conversation with a group of mothers as we waited to pick up our children from preschool." (paragraph 10)

The relationship of ideas within this sentence is one of

    a. time order.   c. addition.

    b. effect.   d. comparison.

Inferences   Choose the two inferences that are most clearly based on information from the following passage.

> "Still there's a feeling that if a man dons a baby carrier, he does so at the cost of some measure of manhood. It's perhaps no coincidence that I became obsessed with hand-splitting wood around the same time I got really good with a Diaper Genie." (paragraph 8)

19. _____

20. _____

    a. The author felt that he had to prove he was manly.
    b. Others may think of a man as less than manly if he is the main caregiver for his children.
    c. The author is embarrassed to be the main caregiver for his children.
    d. The author refused to change diapers.

Outlining

Complete the following outline with ideas from the passage.

Central Idea: (**1**)_____

_____

I. More men than ever are the primary caregivers of their children.

    A. The number of fathers acting as primary caregivers rose (**2**)_____ in the last 10 years.

    B. 2.2 million men are primary caregivers of their children.

    C. 2.1 percent of all American households have fathers as the primary caregivers of the children.

II. Society does not expect men to be the primary caregivers of their children.

    A. In the park, (**3**)_____ often approach the author to offer their services.

    B. The man at the deli assumes the author with his children is on a lunch break.

    C. Some men harbor an unspoken queasiness about being a primary caregiver.

    D. Even when men find a way to make (**4**)_____ relevant before the first game of catch, the rest of the world may not understand.

WHAT DO YOU THINK?

Is Marc Parent an unusual father? Do you think that the traditional roles of men and women have changed? If so, in what ways are women taking on roles usually fulfilled by men? Do you think that men and women who choose to break away from traditional roles face prejudice and misunderstanding? Assume you are taking a sociology class. And each week you are required to write an essay about a current issue. Write an essay in which you take a stand for or against nontraditional roles for men and women. For example, defend a man's decision to be a stay-at-home parent while his spouse supports the family. Or explain why specific jobs or roles are better suited to men or women.

SKILLED READER Scorecard

"A Dad at the Final Frontier"

Skill	Number Correct	Points	Total
Vocabulary Preview (5 items)	_____	× 10 =	_____
Vocabulary in Context (5 items)	_____	× 10 =	_____
		Vocabulary Score	_____
Central Idea and Implied Main Idea (2 items)	_____	× 8 =	_____
Supporting Details (2 items)	_____	× 8 =	_____
Thought Patterns (2 items)	_____	× 8 =	_____
Transitions (2 items)	_____	× 8 =	_____
Inferences (2 items)	_____	× 8 =	_____
Outlining (4 items)	_____	× 5 =	_____
		Comprehension Score	_____

led a rich life, full of friends and interesting experiences, and she shared all of them with me. She devoted so much attention to me I never felt as if I were missing out because I didn't have both parents around. Why, then, couldn't I seem to give her what she needed now? I longed for her to have new stories, new friends, new experiences. She deserved to be living a rich life still, not spending her days closeted in her room.

16 "Hi, hon!" a voice rang out. It was Veronica, making her usual house call. She gave me a smile and headed to Mother's room. From down the hall I heard the two of them talking and laughing, old friends after nearly four years together. Mother should be enjoying herself like this all the time, I thought guiltily.

17 On her way out Veronica caught me **brooding.** "Marion, you might not want to hear this," she began, "but I have to say, it just doesn't feel right in this house anymore. Your mother needs to be in her own place. I told her so today."

18 It hurt to hear that, but at the same time I felt a **tremendous** sense of relief. Maybe now Mother and I could get the whole thing out in the open.

19 The next day, when I brought her breakfast, I asked as nonchalantly as I could, "What do you think of Veronica's suggestion?"

20 "What suggestion?" Mother said, snapping her napkin open on her lap.

21 Taking a deep breath, I replied, "About your moving into your own place . . . a home where you can mix with other folks."

22 "Forget it!" she declared, in a voice the whole neighborhood could probably hear. "I'm not moving."

23 "But, Mother, you might like . . ."

24 "Leave me alone."

25 "That's the problem," I said. "You're a people person. You're not made to spend all day alone. And I worry about what this is doing to us."

26 "You don't seem worried to me."

27 "Well, I am. We hardly talk, and we're getting short with each other."

28 "Then I'll go back to my house in Elberton," Mother said.

29 "You can't live on your own anymore," I reminded her. She glared at me. "Mother, please give this some thought," I said. "OK?"

30 Although she didn't answer, when I closed her door behind me, the tension between us didn't seem as impenetrable as before. We'd actually had our version of a fight, and it wasn't as bad as I had dreaded.

31 I made inquiries about Magnolia Estates, a new assisted-living home right down the road. They were having an open-house picnic the following Sunday. I showed Mother the handsomely printed invitation. She glanced at it, then flung it into her wastebasket. "I'm not about to go to some picnic for **pathetic** old ladies nobody wants."

32 "Gene and I want you to come with us," I said. I walked over to her closet. "What would you like to wear?"

33 "Oh, just shut up," she snapped.

34 She'd never said anything like that to me before, but this was the spunky mother I loved. "You know what?" I said, hiding a smile. "You're never going to turn into a pitiful old lady. That's just not you." I hung the outfit I'd given her the previous Mother's Day on the closet door, a silent ultimatum—we would attend that picnic.

35　　　Folding her arms, Mother regarded me coolly. "If you and Gene are set on going to that picnic," she allowed, "I guess I might go along."

36　　　When I went to her room Saturday morning, Mother was waiting, perfectly made-up, coiffed and dressed in the outfit I'd given her, looking like a *Modern Maturity* cover girl.

37　　　At the picnic we were greeted by the tangy aroma of barbecue and the tune of "Georgia on My Mind." I saw a smile cross Mother's lips. Then she started waving eagerly. Two ladies at a picnic table waved back. "Jewette Grogan," they called to her, "you'd better be coming to sit by us!" They were old friends of hers from Elberton. Gene and I went to get some food, and by the time we came back so many people were enjoying Mother's company I could hardly squeeze in at the table to hand her a plate.

38　　　Not long after that, Mother moved to Magnolia Estates, into a room that Gene and I decorated with some of her favorite things from her home in Elberton.

39　　　I visit her every day, and honestly, I think we spend more time together now than when she lived with me. I should have known our relationship was strong enough to survive even that test; after all, Mother had instilled in me the courage to do difficult things.

40　　　One afternoon recently, I was standing outside Mother's door, my hand lifted to knock, when an old, familiar feeling came over me. Looking at the "Bless This Home" lace banner she'd hung on the door, I realized what it was. That same delicious sense of love and anticipation I felt blessed by years ago, every time I'd stopped by the bank after school.

41　　　I knocked. "Come in," Mother called out.

42　　　When I walked into her room, her face lit up. "Mannie," she exclaimed, "I'm so glad to see you!"

43　　　I wasn't a bit surprised.

Fill in the blank in each sentence with a word from the "Vocabulary Preview."

Vocabulary Preview

1. The champion skater fell three times and stumbled twice; his performance was _____.

Vocabulary Preview

2. After years of taking medicine to prevent anxiety attacks, last week Jamie suffered a(n) _____.

Vocabulary Preview

3. _____ about a problem doesn't help find its solution.

Vocabulary
Preview
4. Jerome enjoyed the _____ with other students that he gained by working with the student government association.

Vocabulary
Preview
5. Development of the vaccine against smallpox was a _____ scientific achievement.

Write the letter of the best meaning of the word in *italics*. Use context clues to make your choice.

Vocabulary
in Context
_____   **6.** "From five different boxes of cereal lined up on my kitchen counter, I measured *precise* amounts into a bowl and added sliced bananas, sugar, and milk." (paragraph 1)

    a. small   c. large
    b. exact   d. daily

Vocabulary
in Context
_____   **7.** "I held the tray and *glared* at her bedroom door." (paragraph 6)

    a. looked lovingly   c. looked as though disappointed
    b. looked angrily   d. looked patiently

Vocabulary
in Context
_____   **8.** "I hung the outfit I'd given her the previous Mother's Day on the closet door, a silent *ultimatum*—we would attend that picnic." (paragraph 34)

    a. plea   c. demand
    b. question   d. thought

Vocabulary
in Context
_____   **9.** "At the picnic we were greeted by the tangy *aroma* of barbecue and the tune of 'Georgia on My Mind.'" (paragraph 37)

    a. sight   c. taste
    b. sound   d. smell

Vocabulary
in Context
_____   **10.** "That same delicious sense of love and *anticipation* I felt blessed by years ago, every time I'd stopped by the bank after school." (paragraph 40)

    a. eagerness   c. peace
    b. regret   d. anger

Central
Idea
_____   **11.** Which sentence is the best statement of the central idea of the passage?

    a. Close relationships are the result of love, patience, and communication.
    b. Mothers and daughters often disagree.
    c. Growing older is difficult for most people.
    d. Caregivers are often under a great deal of stress.

Main Idea _____ **12.** Which sentence is the best statement of the main idea of paragraph 15?
    a. I loved Mother to the point of fierceness for all she'd done for me.
    b. She made sure I wanted for nothing growing up.
    c. She led a rich life, full of friends and interesting experiences, and she shared all of them with me.
    d. I longed for her to have new stories, new friends, new experiences.

Supporting Details _____ **13.** When the author was a young girl, her mother
    a. worked late and neglected her.
    b. punished her often.
    c. fixed her breakfast and sat and talked with her as she ate.
    d. stayed home to raise her.

Supporting Details _____ **14.** When the author took her mother to visit the assisted-living home for the first time, her mother
    a. sat by herself and brooded.
    b. ignored her daughter.
    c. met old friends and enjoyed meeting new people.
    d. moved in and stayed.

Thought Patterns _____ **15.** The main thought pattern for paragraph 1 is
    a. comparison.   c. cause and effect.
    b. classification.   d. time order.

Thought Patterns _____ **16.** The overall thought pattern for the entire passage is
    a. comparison.   c. cause and effect.
    b. listing.   d. time order.

Transitions _____ **17.** "When I went to her room Saturday morning, Mother was waiting, perfectly made-up, coiffed and dressed in the outfit I'd given her, looking like a *Modern Maturity* cover girl." (paragraph 36)

The relationship of ideas in this sentence is one of
    a. time order.   c. contrast.
    b. effect.   d. classification.

Transitions _____ **18.** "Mother was as strong-willed and independent-minded as ever, but she could no longer live on her own." (paragraph 12)

The relationship of ideas in this sentence is one of
    a. time order.   c. contrast.
    b. cause and effect.   d. comparison.

Inferences   Choose the two inferences that are most clearly based on information from the passage.

19. _____

20. _____

a. The author felt guilty that her mother was being cut off from other people.
b. The author and her mother often fought.
c. The author's mother was a successful career woman.
d. The author disliked her mother.

Outlining

Complete the outline with details from the passage.

"Close Again"

I. Fixing __ _____ for mother (paragraphs 1–2)

II. Memories of closeness (paragraphs 3–4)

III. Tension in the house (paragraphs 5–7)

IV. Talking to _____ (paragraphs 8–10)

V. Brooding in the kitchen (paragraphs 11–18)

VI. Suggesting a visit to _____ (paragraphs 19–35)

VII. Visiting Magnolia Estates (paragraphs 36–38)

VIII. Close _____ (paragraphs 39–43)

WHAT DO YOU THINK?

Have you witnessed or experienced the demands of caring for an elderly person? In addition to the issues raised by Marion Bond West in "Close Again," what are some of the other challenges the elderly face as they grow older? What advice would you give the caregiver of an elderly person? How can we prepare ourselves as we face the aging process? Assume you are an advocate for the elderly. Write a letter to the editor of your local newspaper to draw attention to the challenges of the elderly and the role of caregivers in their lives. Consider discussing one or more of the following topics: challenges the elderly face; challenges caregivers for the elderly face; ways to make a positive difference in the life of an elder; ways to help relieve the stress of a caregiver.

SKILLED READER Scorecard

"Close Again"

Skill	Number Correct	Points		Total
Vocabulary Preview (5 items)	_____	$\times$ 10	=	_____
Vocabulary in Context (5 items)	_____	$\times$ 10	=	_____
		Vocabulary Score		_____
Central Idea and Main Idea (2 items)	_____	$\times$ 8	=	_____
Supporting Details (2 items)	_____	$\times$ 8	=	_____
Thought Patterns (2 items)	_____	$\times$ 8	=	_____
Transitions (2 items)	_____	$\times$ 8	=	_____
Inferences (2 items)	_____	$\times$ 8	=	_____
Outlining (4 items)	_____	$\times$ 5	=	_____
		Comprehension Score		_____

READING 5

I've Seen the Worst That War Can Do

Nikolay Palchikoff

The following essay appeared in *Newsweek* magazine toward the end of 2001. Each issue of *Newsweek* features an essay written by a reader of the magazine, in a regular column called "My Turn." In an introduction to this essay, the author summarizes his firsthand experience with the horrors of war by saying, "One month after the bomb dropped on Hiroshima, I stepped off the train and into a nuclear ground zero."

Vocabulary Preview

psychologically (paragraph 1): mentally
indescribable (paragraph 2): beyond words
begets (paragraph 3): causes, leads to
tsar (paragraph 4): emperor of Russia until 1917
imprisoned (paragraph 5): locked up, confined
preconditions (paragraph 7): requirements, terms to be met
negotiating (paragraph 9): bargaining, attempting to reach agreement

1   I remember getting off the train in Hiroshima in September 1945, one month after the city had been destroyed by the atom bomb. I was 21 years old. I stood there in my U.S. Army uniform, looking around at the world's first nuclear ground zero. The ground was covered with ashes that had once been my hometown. There were no search-and-rescue squads or policemen recovering bodies because there were none to recover. There were no memorial **shrines,** noisy tractors or visitors flocking to the site. Instead there were images of bodies burned like photographic negatives into the concrete and an utter silence so **psychologically traumatic** that it would be 40 years before I ever spoke about it.

2   When the train rolled away, I was overwhelmed by an **indescribable** emotion. Flashbacks of my childhood ran through my mind: drinking green tea and laughing with my mother; running through the local Sentai gardens; going to the annual cherry blossom festival each spring. As I looked at the wasteland where I once rode my bicycle, I wondered what had happened to the food **vendors** who brought tofu and fish to our house every week.

3   Watching the television coverage of the September 11 attacks brought back the

agony of that day. The scenes of devastation made me remember what it was like to be able to see clear across Hiroshima to the bay on the other side because there was nothing left standing in between. I can relate to the pain and confusion of the families who lost loved ones. My heart goes out to them. But 56 years after the tragedy of Hiroshima, I've come to the conclusion that violence only **begets** more violence, and war is not a solution to anything.

4   I didn't always think this way. For many years war was a part of my life. I was born in Hiroshima in 1924. My father was an officer in the **tsar's** White Army, a member of the Russian nobility who moved to Japan with my mother after the revolution in 1917. He would tell me bedtime stories about what it was like to fight in Siberia and encourage me to become an officer. My friends and I loved to imitate the Japanese soldiers marching off to the Manchurian War. We would run around the yard with sticks pretending to conquer our imaginary enemies.

5   When I was 16, a group of missionaries offered to take me to the United States so that I could continue my education. I arrived in San Francisco by ship. I wanted to become a doctor, so I went to high school during the day and worked as a janitor in a hospital each night. Within the year, two things happened that changed my plans: the Japanese bombed Pearl Harbor and **imprisoned** my father because I was living in America. My native country was now the enemy, and I was eager to join the war effort. Because of my ability to speak **fluent** Japanese, I became a member of U.S. Army intelligence.

I was translating Japanese radio in 6 the Philippines on August 6, 1945, when they announced that the entire city of Hiroshima had been destroyed by a single bomb. I was shocked. I never thought that war might mean death for innocent civilians like my family, and for other living creatures whose only crime was to be in the wrong place at the wrong time.

The Army sent me to Japan to make 7 sure its government was meeting the **preconditions** of the peace treaty. I took the opportunity to pay my last respects to my family. When I arrived in Hiroshima, I walked from the train station to the site where our home had stood. I recognized the fish-shaped pond that had been in the front yard and the twisted metal that was once my wrought-iron bed. Later that same day, I came across a family friend who had survived the attack by jumping into the river. He explained that my family had left the city just two days before the bomb was dropped. Miraculously, my parents and my brother and sister had survived and were living just a few miles away.

Despite the horror I had witnessed, I 8 returned to America believing that a strong military was needed to maintain world peace. But by the mid-'80s, my **perspective** began to change. The arms race was out of control, and I felt something had to be done. In 1986 I returned to Hiroshima with my wife as part of an antinuclear peace mission and to put to rest my emotions about that tragic event, something that has proved impossible.

Now, at 77, I continue to work for 9 peace. I believe that all countries, including the United States, must stop using the threat of war as a **negotiating** tool and find a way to solve global conflicts without killing more people. It is my hope that by speaking out about the horror of Hiroshima, I will help ensure that it is never repeated.

Fill in the blank in each sentence with a word from the "Vocabulary Preview."

Vocabulary Preview

1. Stress affects us both physically and _____.

Vocabulary Preview

2. _____ a deal with the car salesman saved Rob and Sue $2,000.

Vocabulary Preview

3. French silk pie is so delicious, it's _____.

Vocabulary Preview

4. Some very rich people set _____ before they marry to protect their wealth in case of a divorce.

Vocabulary Preview

5. Many convicted criminals are _____ for years while their cases are appealed.

Write the letter of the best meaning of the word in *italics*. Use context clues to make your choice.

Vocabulary in Context

_____ **6.** "There were no memorial *shrines*, noisy tractors or visitors flocking to the site." (paragraph 1)
a. churches
b. speeches
c. sacred places
d. crowds of mourners

Vocabulary in Context

_____ **7.** "Instead there were images of bodies burned like photographic negatives into the concrete and an utter silence so psychologically *traumatic* that it would be 40 years before I ever spoke about it." (paragraph 1)
a. hurtful
b. fatal
c. important
d. helpful

Vocabulary in Context _____ **8.** "As I looked at the wasteland where I once rode my bicycle, I wondered what had happened to the food *vendors* who brought tofu and fish to our house every week." (paragraph 2)

    a. cooks   c. buyers

    b. sellers   d. customers

Vocabulary in Context _____ **9.** "Because of my ability to speak *fluent* Japanese, I became a member of U.S. Army intelligence." (paragraph 5)

    a. a little   c. smooth and clear

    b. no   d. broken

Vocabulary in Context _____ **10.** "But by the mid-'80s, my *perspective* began to change." (paragraph 8)

    a. viewpoint   c. career

    b. love   d. fortune

Central Idea _____ **11.** Which sentence is the best statement of the central idea of the passage?

    a. Hiroshima in 1946 and New York on September 11, 2001, had many similarities.

    b. War is brutal.

    c. Speaking about horrors such as the bombing of Hiroshima may help prevent war in the future.

    d. War is not a solution to anything.

Implied Main Idea _____ **12.** Which sentence is the best statement of the implied main idea of paragraph 8?

    a. The author works for peace.

    b. The author is still upset about Hiroshima.

    c. The author is trying to deal with his pain by working for world peace.

    d. The author is opposed to the military.

Supporting Details _____ **13.** When the author saw the nuclear destruction at Hiroshima, his hometown, he was

    a. 77 years old.   c. 21 years old.

    b. 16 years old.   d. 56 years old.

Supporting Details _____ **14.** The author's father was imprisoned in Japan because

    a. his father was a war criminal.

    b. his father tried to escape Japan.

    c. the author was a war criminal.

    d. the author lived in America.

Thought
Patterns
_____ **15.** The main thought pattern of the passage is
   a. comparison.   c. contrast.
   b. time order.   d. listing.

Transitions _____ **16.** "There were no memorial shrines, noisy tractors or visitors flock-ing to the site. Instead there were images of bodies burned like photographic negatives into the concrete and an utter silence so psychologically traumatic that it would be 40 years before I ever spoke about it." (paragraph 1)

The relationship of ideas between these two sentences is one of
   a. contrast.   c. time order.
   b. cause and effect.   d. listing.

Transitions _____ **17.** "When I arrived in Hiroshima, I walked from the train station to the site where our home had stood." (paragraph 7)

The relationship of ideas in this sentence is one of
   a. time order.   c. addition.
   b. cause and effect.   d. comparison.

Transitions _____ **18.** "Despite the horror I had witnessed, I returned to America believ-ing that a strong military was needed to maintain world peace." (paragraph 8)

The relationship of ideas in this sentence is one of
   a. time order.   c. contrast.
   b. cause and effect.   d. comparison.

Inferences Choose the two inferences that are most clearly based on information from the following passage.

"Despite the horror I had witnessed, I returned to America believing that a strong military was needed to maintain world peace. But by the mid-'80s, my perspective began to change. The arms race was out of control, and I felt something had to be done. In 1986 I returned to Hiroshima with my wife as part of an anti-nuclear peace mission and to put to rest my emotions about that tragic event, something that has proved impossible." (paragraph 8)

19. _____

20. _____

   a. The author no longer believes military force ensures peace.
   b. The author believes that military force ensures peace.

    c. The author still struggles with the trauma of Hiroshima.

    d. The author refuses to return to his homeland.

Mapping

Complete the following timeline with details from the passage.

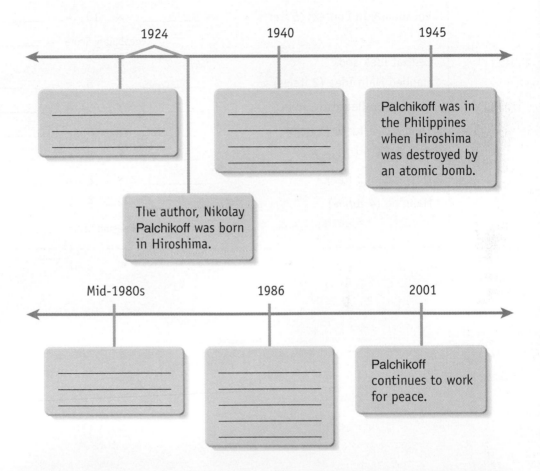

1924

1940

1945

Palchikoff was in the Philippines when Hiroshima was destroyed by an atomic bomb.

The author, Nikolay Palchikoff was born in Hiroshima.

Mid-1980s

1986

2001

Palchikoff continues to work for peace.

WHAT DO YOU THINK?

For many, recent history has been filled with disastrous events with profound effects, such as September 11, Hurricane Katrina, the Gulf oil spill, and the on-going war in the Middle East. Have you ever had an experience in life that changed the way you thought about or believed in something? What was your first belief? What happened to change your view? What is your current view about that idea? Assume you are an eyewitness to a life-changing event. Write a three-paragraph article for a newspaper that records your eyewitness account.

SKILLED READER Scorecard

"I've Seen the Worst That War Can Do"

Skill	Number Correct	Points		Total
Vocabulary Preview (5 items)	_____	× 10	=	_____
Vocabulary in Context (5 items)	_____	× 10	=	_____
		Vocabulary Score		_____
Central Idea and Implied Main Idea (2 items)	_____	× 8	=	_____
Supporting Details (2 items)	_____	× 8	=	_____
Thought Patterns (1 item)	_____	× 8	=	_____
Transitions (3 items)	_____	× 8	=	_____
Inferences (2 items)	_____	× 8	=	_____
Mapping (4 items)	_____	× 5	=	_____
		Comprehension Score		_____

To Tell the Truth

Maya Angelou

Maya Angelou is a well-known and highly praised poet, author, performer, teacher, director, and civil rights activist. In her book *Letter to My Daughter*, Angelou shares some of the important lessons she has learned from her life. In the following essay, she shares about the importance of telling the truth and the reasons we tell "little lies." Do you think we should always tell the truth? Is there a difference between a little lie and big lie? Are there times when it's okay to tell a little lie?

Vocabulary Preview

social (paragraph 2): relating to the way in which people in groups behave and interact: public, shared, common

frank (paragraph 3): truthful, honest, outspoken

unkempt (paragraph 4): messy, neglected, in need of combing or grooming

fashionistas (paragraph 4): followers of the fashion industry

discarded (paragraph 5): thrown away, useless

1   My mother, Vivian Baxter, warned me often not to believe that people really want the truth when they ask, "How are you?" She said that question was asked around the world in thousands of languages and most people knew that it is simply a conversation starter. No one really expects to be answered, or even wants to know "Well my knees feel like they are broken, and my back hurts so bad I could fall down and cry." A response like that would be a conversation stopper. It would end before it could begin. So, we all say; "Fine, thank you, and you?"

2   I believe in that way we learn to give and receive **social** lies.

3   We look at friends who have lost dangerous amounts of weight or who have added **ungainly** pounds and we say, "You're looking good." Everybody knows the statement is a **blatant** lie but we all swallow the untruth in part to keep the peace and in part because we do not wish to deal with the truth. I wish we could stop the little lies. I don't mean that one has to be brutally **frank**. I don't believe that we should be brutal about anything; however, it is wonderfully liberating to be honest. One does not have to tell all

Vocabulary
in Context _____ **10.** "But think of it this way; if people avoid you, you will have more
time to meditate and do fine research on a cure for whatever truly
afflicts you." (paragraph 6)

a. troubles   c. teaches
b. soothes   d. confuses

Central Idea _____ **11.** Which of the following sentences states the central idea of the
passage?

a. "My mother, Vivian Baxter, warned me often not to believe that
people really want the truth when they ask, 'How are you?'"
(paragraph 1)

b. "I believe in that way we learn to give and receive social lies."
(paragraph 2)

c. "One does not have to tell all that one knows, but we should be
careful what we do say is the truth." (paragraph 3)

d. "But think of it this way; if people avoid you, you will have
more time to meditate and do fine research on a cure for whatever truly afflicts you." (paragraph 6)

Supporting
Details _____ **12.** What style did the fashionistas label as sexy?

a. nose, nipple, and tongue rings
b. a raggedy but trendy hairstyle
c. a shirttail hanging out from under a jacket
d. wrinkled clothes and half-shaven faces

Supporting
Details _____ **13.** According to Angelou, which of the following is a conversation
starter?

a. "How are you?"   c. "You're looking good."
b. "Fine, thank you, and you?" d. the truth

Transitions _____ **14.** "I don't believe that we should be brutal about anything; however,
it is wonderfully liberating to be honest." (paragraph 3)

The relationship of ideas within this sentence is

a. cause and effect.   c. comparison and contrast.
b. time order.   d. generalization and example.

Transitions _____ **15.** "It would end before it could begin. So, we all say; 'Fine, thank you,
and you?'" (paragraph 1)

The relationship of ideas between these sentences is

a. cause and effect.   c. comparison and contrast.
b. time order.   d. generalization and example.

Thought Patterns

_____ **16.** The overall thought pattern for the passage is
  a. cause and effect.
  b. time order.
  c. comparison and contrast.
  d. generalization and example.

Fact and Opinion

_____ **17.** "I believe in that way we learn to give and receive social lies."

This sentence from paragraph 2 states
  a. a fact.
  b. an opinion.
  c. fact and opinion.

Fact and Opinion

_____ **18.** Overall, what does Maya Angelou mostly use to make her point?
  a. fact
  b. opinion
  c. fact and opinion

Inferences

_____ **19.** Based on the details in paragraph 5, we can infer that
  a. young people tell social lies.
  b. only defiant youth get body piercings.
  c. as they age, young people will regret getting body piercings.
  d. body piercings are a form of art.

Inferences

_____ **20.** Based on the details in paragraph 6, we can conclude that
  a. social lies are unavoidable.
  b. we should look for solutions instead of complaining.
  c. telling the truth will end friendships.
  d. we should become better listeners.

Mapping

Complete the following definition concept map with information from the passage "To Tell the Truth."

Term	Definition	Examples
_____	Questions people don't expect or want answers to	_____
_____	An untruth to told to keep peace and to avoid the truth	"Fine, thank you, and you?" _____

WHAT DO YOU THINK?

Has life taught you important lessons worth passing on to someone else? Think of one lesson you have learned. How did you learn this lesson and whom do you think would benefit most from what you have learned? Assume your local newspaper is sponsoring a writing contest for a $250 prize. The topic is "An Important Lesson Everyone Should Learn," and the length of the essay is limited to 500–600 words.

SKILLED READER Scorecard

"To Tell the Truth"

Skill	Number Correct	Points	Total
Vocabulary Preview (5 items)	_____	× 10 =	_____
Vocabulary in Context (5 items)	_____	× 10 =	_____
		Vocabulary Score	_____
Central Idea (1 item)	_____	× 8 =	_____
Supporting Details (2 items)	_____	× 8 =	_____
Transitions (2 items)	_____	× 8 =	_____
Thought Patterns (1 item)	_____	× 8 =	_____
Fact and Opinion (2 items)	_____	× 8 =	_____
Inferences (2 items)	_____	× 8 =	_____
Mapping (4 items)	_____	× 5 =	_____
		Comprehension Score	_____

READING 7

Want to Do Better on the Job? Listen Up!

Textbook Skills *Diane Cole*

> Have you ever found yourself wondering if the person you are talking to is really listening? Or have you found it difficult to concentrate when someone is talking to you? The following reading, reprinted in a college communication textbook, offers useful suggestions for listening more effectively in business situations. The suggestions, however, can easily be applied to the classroom or the home.

Vocabulary Preview

dividends (paragraph 6): benefits
perceptive (paragraph 7): aware
deliberate (paragraph 16): thoughtful
reluctant (paragraph 19): unwilling
studiously (paragraph 20): carefully

1   When Linda S., an Ohio banking executive, learned she would not be promoted, she asked her boss why. He had barely begun to speak when she blurted out, "I know whatever the reason, I can do better."

2   **Exasperated,** he replied, "You always interrupt before you even know what I'm going to say! How can you do better if you never listen?"

3   "Most people value speaking—which is seen as active—over listening, which is seen as **passive,**" explains Nancy Wyatt, professor of speech communication at Penn State University and coauthor with Carol Ashburn of *Successful Listening*.

4   And there are other reasons we might fail to tune in.

5   We may become so fixed on what *we* think that we tune out important information. Or we may react emotionally to a phrase or style the speaker uses and miss the main point. Or we're just too busy to pay attention to what is being said.

6   Sound familiar? If so, listen up, for changing your ways will pay big **dividends.**

7   You'll stop wasting time on misunderstood assignments at work. People will start to see you as a **perceptive,** smart, and sensitive person who understands their needs. And that will open new opportunities on the job, suggests Lyman K. Steil, Ph.D., president of Communication Development Inc., a consulting firm based in St. Paul, Minnesota.

8   You can also develop an ear for the crucial but unspoken words in conversation that signal problems in your business relationships. Here are some suggestions for learning to listen to what is said—and not said—more effectively.

9   • *Control distractions:* Give a speaker your full attention, or you're likely to miss the main point. Many interruptions can't be avoided, but you can limit their effect.

10   If you must take a call while a coworker is explaining something important, make a choice and devote yourself to one conversation at a time.

11   • *Identify the speaker's purpose:* Tune in to the speaker's agenda. Is he or she there to let off steam, solve a problem, share information, or just schmooze?

12   Once you know, you can respond in the way he or she wants and expects. Learning to listen may also keep you from inadvertently getting caught in the crossfire of office politics.

13   • *Don't finish other people's sentences:* Many people have this bad habit. Just observe yourself: Do you cut people off before they finish a thought? Are you so busy thinking about what you want to say that you can't resist breaking in?

14   "That often happens because the interrupter is bright, thinks she has grasped the point, and wants to show off how much she knows," says Dee Soder, Ph.D., president of Endymion, a New York City–based executive consulting firm. "What happens instead is that interrupters are perceived as being **arrogant** and interested only in themselves."

15   To break the habit of interrupting, bite your tongue and follow up with your comments only after the other person has had his or her say. Soder suggests you might even have to literally sit on your hands to keep your gestures from speaking for you. Finally, if you're not certain that the speaker has finished, ask!

16   • *Don't let the speaker's style turn you off:* It's easy to tune out when less-than-favorite speakers clear their throats. One high school teacher confesses that for a long time she found a colleague's slow, **deliberate** drawl so grating that she simply could not listen to him.

17   "It was only when I was forced to work with him and had to concentrate on what he was saying rather than how that I realized how smart and helpful he was, and now we're best friends at work."

18   • *Don't be distracted by buzzwords:* What springs to mind when you hear the label "feminist" or "right-to-life"? If you're like most people, emotions take over, and you stop paying careful attention to the point the speaker is trying to make.

19   • *Listen to what is not being said:* Sometimes it's important to hear between the lines. "Many people like to avoid conflict, and so the person speaking is very **reluctant** to say anything negative," says Soder.

20   When you suspect that a delicate or negative subject is being **studiously** avoided, you have to be prepared to delve deeper and ask the speaker, "Tell me more about that. Could you please explain?"

21 • *Show you are listening:* Think about what your body language is revealing. Are you making good eye contact and leaning slightly forward in a way that **indicates** "I'm open to what you're saying"? Or are you tapping your foot and looking out the window as if to say, "I have more important things to do than listen to you"?

22 • *Make a note of it:* Jotting down a word or two can remind you later of the main purpose behind the assignment your boss is giving you. A brief note can also help you remember the point you would like to raise after the speaker finishes.

• *Make sure you heard it right:* Many 23 misunderstandings could be **prevented** if we'd just make sure we heard what we thought we heard. So when in doubt, don't be afraid to ask, "Let me make sure I understand what you are saying." It's a hearing test well worth taking.

—Cole, Diane. "Want to Do Better on the Job? Listen Up!" First appeared in *Working Mother Magazine*, March 1991, © 1991 Diane Cole. Reprinted by permission of *Working Mother Magazine*.

Fill in the blank in each sentence with a word from the "Vocabulary Preview."

Vocabulary Preview **1.** Janine was _____ to drink the milk after it had been left on the counter all day.

Vocabulary Preview **2.** Many people invest in the stock market hoping for large _____.

Vocabulary Preview **3.** Maxine is _____ about her children's needs and strengths.

Vocabulary Preview **4.** Trey _____ recopies his class notes as a review of the day's lesson.

Vocabulary Preview **5.** Natalie Gulbis is _____ and accurate when she makes her putts.

Write the letter of the best meaning of the word in *italics*. Use context clues to make your choice.

Vocabulary in Context _____ **6.** "*Exasperated*, he replied, 'You always interrupt before you even know what I'm going to say! How can you do better if you never listen?'" (paragraph 2)
    a. annoyed   c. interested
    b. pleased   d. patiently

Vocabulary in Context _____ **7.** "Most people value speaking—which is seen as active—over listening, which is seen as *passive* . . ." (paragraph 3)
    a. bored   c. interested
    b. inactive   d. rude

Mapping

Complete the idea map with details from the passage.

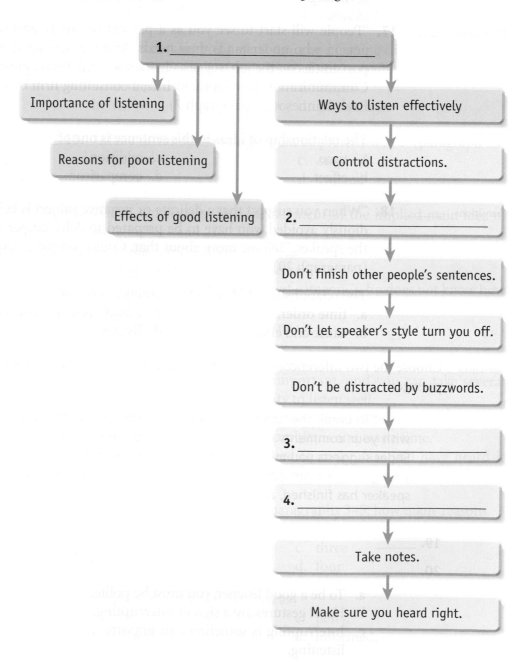

1. _____

Importance of listening

Reasons for poor listening

Effects of good listening

Ways to listen effectively

Control distractions.

2. _____

Don't finish other people's sentences.

Don't let speaker's style turn you off.

Don't be distracted by buzzwords.

3. _____

4. _____

Take notes.

Make sure you heard right.

WHAT DO YOU THINK?

Do you think you are a good listener? Are there certain situations in which you are a better listener than others? For example, are you a better listener with your friends than you are with your parents or professors? How many of the suggestions listed in paragraphs 9 through 23 do you already use as you listen to others? Assume you are taking a college course in communications. You have been assigned an independent project. You are to choose a topic, conduct some informal research, and share your findings in an oral presentation to the class. Your professor also wants a written draft in essay form of your remarks. You have decided to analyze your own listening abilities based on the nine suggestions listed by Diane Cole in her article. In your essay, rate yourself from 1 to 5 on your use of each of the nine suggestions. Give examples to support your rating. In addition, identify and explain any changes you plan to make to improve your listening skills.

SKILLED READER Scorecard

"Want to Do Better on the Job? Listen Up!"

Skill	Number Correct	Points	Total
Vocabulary Preview (5 items)	_____	× 10 =	_____
Vocabulary in Context (5 items)	_____	× 10 =	_____
		Vocabulary Score	_____
Implied Main Idea and Central Idea (2 items)	_____	× 8 =	_____
Supporting Details (2 items)	_____	× 8 =	_____
Thought Patterns (2 items)	_____	× 8 =	_____
Transitions (2 items)	_____	× 8 =	_____
Inferences (2 items)	_____	× 8 =	_____
Mapping (4 items)	_____	× 5 =	_____
		Comprehension Score	_____

Excerpt from *Essentials of Human Anatomy & Physiology,* 9th Edition

Textbook
Skills

Elaine N. Marieb

Have you thought about how complex the human body is? Did you know that the human body is made up of almost a dozen different systems? Did you also know that each system within the body is made up of precisely formed parts? And that each part carries out specific tasks for our well-being? In the preface to the book from which this passage is taken, Elaine N. Marieb says "human anatomy and physiology is more than just interesting—it is fascinating."

Vocabulary Preview

integumentary (paragraph 10): the external covering of the body, or the skin

endocrine (paragraph 14): the system of glands that produce hormones that regulate other body structures

cardiovascular (paragraph 16): the system of the heart and blood vessels

lymphatic (paragraph 17): the system that keeps blood moving throughout the body

respiratory (paragraph 18): the system that supplies the body with oxygen and removes carbon dioxide

An Overview of Anatomy and Physiology

1   Most of us are naturally curious about our bodies. We want to know what makes us tick. This curiosity is even seen in infants, who can keep themselves happy for a long time staring at their own hands or pulling their mother's nose. Older children wonder where food goes when they swallow it. And some believe that they will grow a watermelon in their belly if they swallow the seeds. They scream loudly when approached by medical personnel (fearing shots that sting). But they like to play doctor. Adults become upset when their hearts pound, when they have uncontrollable hot flashes, or when they cannot keep their weight down.

2   Anatomy and physiology, subdivisions of biology, explore many of these topics as they describe how our bodies are put together and how they work.

Anatomy

3   Anatomy (ah-nat' o-me) is the study of the structure and shape of the body and its parts and their relationships to one another. When we look at our own body or study large body structures such as the heart or bones, we are observing **gross**

anatomy. We are studying large, easily seen structures. Indeed, the term anatomy comes from the Greek words meaning to cut (*tomy*) apart (*ana*). In gross anatomical studies, preserved animals or their organs are dissected (*cut up*) to be examined. *Microscopic* anatomy, in contrast, is the study of body structures that are too small to be seen with the naked eye. The cells and tissues of the body can only be seen through a microscope.

Physiology

4   **Physiology** (fiz" e-ol' o-je) is the study of how the body and its parts work or function (*physio* = nature; *ology* = the study of). Like anatomy, physiology has many subtopics. For example, *neurophysiology* explains the workings of the nervous system. And *cardiac physiology* studies the function of the heart. The heart acts as a muscular pump to keep blood flowing throughout the body.

Relationship between Anatomy and Physiology

5   Anatomy and physiology are always related. The parts of your body form a well-organized unit. And each of those parts has a job to do to make the body operate as a whole. Structure determines what functions can take place. For example, the lungs are not muscular chambers like the heart and cannot pump blood through the body. But because the walls of their air sacs are very thin, they can exchange gases and provide oxygen to the body. The intimate relationship between anatomy and physiology is stressed throughout this book to make your learning meaningful.

Levels of Structural Organization

From Atoms to Organisms

The human body exhibits many levels 6 of structural complexity. The simplest level of the structural ladder is the chemical level. At this level, atoms are tiny building blocks of matter. They combine to form molecules such as water, sugar, and proteins. Molecules, in turn, connect in specific ways to form microscopic cells, the smallest units of all living things. This level is the *cellular level*. All cells have some common functions. But individual cells vary widely in size and shape. Their sizes and shapes reflect their particular functions in the body.

The simplest living creatures are com- 7 posed of single cells. But in complex organisms such as trees or human beings, the structural ladder continues on to the *tissue level*. Tissues consist of groups of similar cells that have a common function. The four basic tissue types are epithelial, connective, muscular, and neural. Each plays a definite but different role in the body.

An organ is a structure composed of 8 two or more tissue types that performs a specific function for the body. At the *organ level* of organization, extremely complex functions become possible. For example, the small intestine digests and absorbs food. And it is composed of all four tissue types. An organ system is a group of organs that work together to accomplish a common purpose. For example, the digestive system includes the esophagus, the stomach, and the small and large intestines (to name a few of its organs). Each organ has its own job. By working together, all of these organs keep food moving through the digestive system. Thus, food is properly broken down and absorbed into the blood and used as fuel for all the body's cells.

9   In all, 11 organ systems make up the living body, or the organism. This highest level of structural organization is called the **organismal** *level*.

Organ System Overview

Integumentary System

10   The **integumentary** (in-teg"u-men'-tar-e) system is the external covering of the body, or the skin. It waterproofs the body. It cushions and protects the deeper tissues from injury. It also excretes salts and urea in perspiration. And it helps control body temperature. Temperature, pressure, and pain receptors are located in the skin. They alert us to what is happening at the body surface.

Skeletal System

11   The skeletal system consists of bones, cartilages, ligaments, and joints. It supports the body. And it provides a framework that the skeletal muscles use to cause movement. It also has a protective function. For example, the skull encloses and protects the brain. *Hematopoiesis* (hem"ah-to-poi-e'sis) is the formation of blood cells. This process takes place within the cavities of the skeleton. The hard substance of bones acts as a storehouse for minerals.

Muscular System

12   The muscles of the body have only one function—to *contract*, or shorten. When this happens, movement occurs. Hence, muscles can be viewed as the "machines" of the body. The mobility of the body as a whole reflects the activity of *skeletal muscles*, the large, fleshy muscles attached to bones. When these contract, you are able to stand erect, walk, leap, grasp, throw a ball, or smile. The skeletal muscles form the muscular system. These muscles are distinct from the muscles of the heart and of other hollow organs, which move fluids (blood, urine) or other substances (such as food) along definite pathways within the body.

Nervous System

13   The nervous system is the body's fast-acting control system. It is made up of the brain, spinal cord, nerves, and sensory receptors. The body must be able to respond to irritants or stimuli coming from outside the body and inside the body. Examples of stimuli outside the body include light, sound, or changes in temperature. Examples of stimuli from inside the body include decreases in oxygen or stretching of tissue. The sensory **receptors** detect these changes. And they send messages to the central nervous system. The central nervous system is made up of the brain and spinal cord. And the messages are sent to it by electrical signals called *nerve impulses*. Thus, it is constantly informed about what is going on. The central nervous system then assesses this information. And it responds by activating the appropriate body effectors (muscles or glands).

Endocrine System

14   Like the nervous system, the **endocrine** (en'dokrin) system controls body activities. But it acts much more slowly. The endocrine glands produce chemical molecules called **hormones**. Hormones are released into the blood to travel to relatively distant target organs.

15   The endocrine glands include the pituitary, thyroid, parathyroids, adrenals, thymus, pancreas, pineal, ovaries (in the female), and testes (in the male). The endocrine glands are not connected anatomically in the same way that parts of the other organ systems are. What they have in common is that they all secrete hormones. And hormones regulate other structures. The body functions controlled by hormones are many and varied. They involve every cell in the body. Growth, reproduction, and food use by cells are all controlled (at least in part) by hormones.

Cardiovascular System

16   The primary organs of the **cardiovascular** system are the heart and blood vessels. The cardiovascular system uses blood as the transporting fluid. And it carries oxygen, nutrients, hormones, and other substances to and from the tissue cells. In tissue cells exchanges are made. White blood cells and chemicals in the blood help to protect the body from foreign invaders. Examples of foreign invaders are bacteria, toxins, and tumor cells. The heart acts as the blood pump. It propels blood out of its chambers into the blood vessels to be carried to all body tissues.

Lymphatic System

17   The role of the **lymphatic** system complements that of the cardiovascular system. Its organs include lymphatic vessels, lymph nodes, and other lymphoid organs such as the spleen and tonsils. The lymphatic vessels return fluid leaked from the blood back to the blood vessels. Thus, blood can be kept continuously circulating through the body. The lymph nodes and other lymphoid organs help to cleanse the blood. They also house cells involved in immunity.

Respiratory System

18   The job of the **respiratory** system is to keep the body constantly supplied with oxygen and to remove carbon dioxide. The respiratory system consists of the nasal passages, pharynx, larynx, trachea, bronchi, and lungs. Within the lungs are tiny air sacs. It is through the thin walls of these air sacs that gases are transported to and from the blood.

Digestive System

19   The **digestive** system is basically a tube running through the body from mouth to anus. The organs of the digestive system include the oral cavity (mouth), esophagus, stomach, small and large intestines, and rectum. Their role is to break down food and deliver the products to the blood for dispersal to the body cells. The undigested food that remains in the tract leaves the body through the anus as feces. The breakdown activities that begin in the mouth are completed in the small intestine. From that point on, the major function of the digestive system is to reclaim water. The liver is considered a digestive organ. The bile it produces helps to break down fats. The pancreas delivers digestive enzymes to the small intestine. It also acts as a digestive organ.

Urinary System

20   The body produces wastes as by-products of its normal functions. And

these wastes must be disposed of. One type of waste contains nitrogen. Examples are urea and uric acid. Nitrogen results when the body cells break down proteins and nucleic acids. The **urinary** system removes the nitrogen-containing wastes from the blood. And it flushes them from the body in urine. This system is often called the **excretory** system. It is composed of the kidneys, ureters, bladder, and urethra. Other important functions of this system include maintaining the body's water and salt (electrolyte) balance and regulating the acid-base balance of the blood.

Reproductive System

The **reproductive** system exists primarily to produce offspring. The testes of the male produce sperm. Other male reproductive system structures are the scrotum, penis, accessory glands, and the duct system. The duct system carries sperm to the outside of the body. The ovaries of the female produce eggs, or ova. The female duct system is made up of the uterine tubes, uterus, and vagina. The uterus provides the site for the development of the fetus (immature infant) once fertilization has occurred. 21

—Excerpt adapted from Marieb, Elaine N., *Essentials of Human Anatomy and Physiology*, pp. 2–7, Edition 9, © 2009. Reprinted by permission of Pearson Education, Inc.

VISUAL VOCABULARY

A doctor studying this X-ray of a narrowed artery on the surface of the heart is assessing the health of the patient's _____ system.

   a. nervous
   b. respiratory
   c. cardiovascular

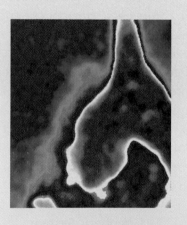

Fill in the blank in each sentence with a word from the Vocabulary Preview.

Vocabulary Preview

1. The _____ system cleanses the blood, helps keep blood moving throughout the body, and helps the body's ability to resist disease.

Vocabulary Preview

2. The _____ system carries oxygen, nutrients, and hormones to and from the tissue cells.

Vocabulary Preview

3. Along with supplying the body with oxygen, the _____ system also removes carbon dioxide from the body.

Vocabulary Preview

4. The _____ system is a protective covering that has temperature, pressure, and pain receptors.

Vocabulary Preview

5. Glands in the _____ system produce hormones that regulate other body structures.

For items 6 through 10, choose the best meaning of each word in italics. Use context clues to make your choice.

Vocabulary in Context

_____ **6.** "When we look at our own body or study large body structures such as the heart or bones, we are observing *gross* anatomy." (paragraph 3)
a. obvious   c. hidden
b. disgusting   d. extreme

Vocabulary in Context

_____ **7.** "This highest level of structural organization is called the *organismal* level." (paragraph 9)
a. bodily structure   c. bodily function
b. smallest unit of life   d. form of life

Vocabulary in Context

_____ **8.** "The sensory *receptors* detect these changes." (paragraph 13)
a. cells   c. irritations
b. electrical signals   d. sensitive nerve endings

Vocabulary in Context

_____ **9.** "The endocrine glands produce chemical molecules called *hormones*." (paragraph 14)
a. small cells   c. controlling substances
b. mass of cells   d. fluids

Vocabulary in Context

_____ **10.** "This system is often called the *excretory* system." (paragraph 20)
a. waste sifting   c. waste storage
b. sweat   d. urine

Central Idea

_____ **11.** Which of the following sentences states the central idea of the passage?
a. "Anatomy and physiology, subdivisions of biology, explore many of these topics as they describe how our bodies are put together and how they work." (paragraph 2)
b. "Anatomy and physiology are always related." (paragraph 5)
c. "Structure determines what functions can take place." (paragraph 5)
d. "The human body exhibits many levels of structural complexity." (paragraph 6)

Supporting
Details
_____ **12.** The smallest units of all living things are
    a. atoms.   c. tissues.
    b. cells.   d. organs.

Supporting
Details
_____ **13.** Extremely complex functions become possible at the
    a. chemical level.   c. tissue level.
    b. cellular level.   d. organ level.

Supporting
Details
_____ **14.** Hematopoiesis is
    a. the storehouse for minerals.
    b. the hard substance of bones.
    c. the formation of blood cells.
    d. the skeleton.

Supporting
Details
_____ **15.** The ability of the body to move is due to
    a. nerve impulses.   c. sensory receptors.
    b. skeletal muscles.   d. endocrine glands.

Transitions
_____ **16.** "The human body exhibits many levels of structural complexity."
(paragraph 6)

The relationship of ideas within this sentence is
    a. cause and effect.   c. comparison and contrast.
    b. classification.   d. generalization and example.

Transitions
_____ **17.** "The nervous system is the body's fast-acting control system. It is made
up of the brain, spinal cord, and sensory receptors." (paragraph 13)

The relationship of ideas between these sentences is
    a. cause and effect.   c. comparison and contrast.
    b. classification.   d. definition and example.

Thought
Patterns
_____ **18.** The main thought pattern for paragraphs 6 through 21 is
    a. cause and effect.
    b. classification.
    c. comparison and contrast.
    d. definition and example.

Inferences
_____ **19.** Based on the details in paragraph 10, we can infer that
    a. sweat glands are located in the skin.
    b. it is hard to injure the integumentary system.
    c. the integumentary system is the most important organ of the
body.
    d. the skin supports the body.

Inferences _____ **20.** Based on the details in the passage, we can conclude that

    a. some organ systems are more necessary than other organ systems.

    b. we can study the structure of the body without studying the function of its different parts.

    c. organ systems work independently of each other.

    d. organ systems work together for the well-being of the body.

Outlining

Complete the following outline with information from the passage "An Overview of Anatomy and Physiology."

I. Anatomy

II. Physiology

III. _____

IV. Levels of Organization

    A. From Atoms to Organisms

       1. Atoms—the _____

       2. Cells—the cellular level

       3. Tissues—the tissue level

       4. Organs—the organismal level

V. _____

    A. Integumentary System

    B. Skeletal System

    C. Muscular System

    D. Nervous System

    E. Endocrine System

    F. Cardiovascular System

    G. Lymphatic System

    H. Respiratory System

    I. Digestive System

    J. Urinary System

    K. _____

WHAT DO YOU THINK?

Why is the study of Anatomy and Physiology important? Who should know this information and why? Assume you are taking the college course Anatomy and Physiology. Part of your final grade depends on how well you do on a series of exams based on key chapters from your textbook. As you study the textbook for the chapter exam on "An Overview of Anatomy and Physiology," you notice the following question in the review material at the end of the chapter:

> "Why would you have a hard time learning and understanding physiology if you did not also understand anatomy?"

Write a short-answer essay in response to this question. In your essay, include details that achieve the following: Define anatomy and physiology. Identify the 11 organ systems of the body. Briefly describe the function of each. And then name two organs in each system.

SKILLED READER Scorecard

Excerpt from *Essentials of Human Anatomy & Physiology*

Skill	Number Correct	Points		Total
Vocabulary Preview (5 items)	_____	× 10	=	_____
Vocabulary in Context (5 items)	_____	× 10	=	_____
		Vocabulary Score		_____
Central Idea (1 item)	_____	× 8	=	_____
Supporting Details (4 items)	_____	× 8	=	_____
Transitions (2 items)	_____	× 8	=	_____
Thought Patterns (1 item)	_____	× 8	=	_____
Inferences (2 items)	_____	× 8	=	_____
Outlining (4 items)	_____	× 5	=	_____
		Comprehension Score		_____

The Secrets of the Bedroom

Malcolm Gladwell

Have you ever made a decision that you knew was the right choice? Have you ever made a decision that you regretted? Are you a good judge of character? Or have you ever misjudged someone else? Do you make decisions or form opinions quickly, or do you take time to gather information and think over your options and views? In his book *Blink*, best-selling author Malcolm Gladwell explores how we think without thinking, about choices and opinions that we seem to make in an instant—in the blink of an eye—but really aren't as simple as they seem. As you read the following passage from *Blink*, think about how you form opinions about others.

Vocabulary Preview

skeptical (paragraph 2): cynical, disbelieving, doubtful

inhabitant (paragraph 4): resident, occupant, a person or animal that lives in a particular place or area

animated (paragraph 5): something or someone that is active; something that is brought to life

incredible (paragraph 6): beyond belief, amazing, unexpected

magna cum laude (paragraph 6): with great distinction, the second-highest level of academic honors at graduation

---

1   Imagine that you are considering me for a job. You've seen my resume and think I have the necessary **credentials**. But you want to know whether I am the right fit for your organization. Am I a hard worker? Am I honest? Am I open to new ideas? In order to answer those questions about my personality, your boss gives you two options. The first is to meet with me twice a week for a year—to have lunch or dinner or go to a movie with me—to the point where you become one of my closest friends. (Your boss is quite demanding.) The second option is to drop by my house when I'm not there and spend half an hour or so looking around. Which would you choose?

2   The seemingly obvious answer is that you should take the first option: the thick slice. The more time you spend with me and the more information you gather, the better off you are. Right? I hope by now that you are at least a little bit **skeptical** of that approach. Sure enough, as the psychologist

Samuel Gosling has shown, judging people's personalities is a really good example of how surprisingly effective thin-slicing can be.

3   Gosling began his experiment by doing a personality workup on eighty college students. For this, he used what is called the Big Five Inventory, a highly respected, multi-item questionnaire that measures people across five dimensions:

1. **Extraversion**. Are you sociable or retiring? Fun-loving or reserved?
2. Agreeableness. Are you trusting or suspicious? Helpful or uncooperative?
3. **Conscientiousness**. Are you organized or disorganized? Self-disciplined or weak willed?
4. Emotional stability. Are you worried or calm? Insecure or secure?
5. Openness to new experiences. Are you imaginative or down-to-earth? Independent or conforming?

Then Gosling had close friends of those eighty students fill out the same questionnaire.

4   When our friends rank us on the Big Five, Gosling wanted to know, how closely do they come to the truth? The answer is, not surprisingly, that our friends can describe us fairly accurately. They have a thick slice of experience with us, and that translates to a real sense of who we are. Then Gosling repeated the process, but this time he didn't call on close friends. He used total strangers who had never even met the students they were judging. All they saw were their dorm rooms. He gave his raters clipboards and told them they had fifteen minutes to look around and answer a series of very basic questions about the occupant of the room: On a scale of 1 to 5, does the **inhabitant** of this room seem to be the kind of person who is talkative? Tends to find fault with others? Does a thorough job? Is original? Is reserved? Is helpful and unselfish with others? And so on. "I was trying to study everyday impressions," Gosling says. "So I was quite careful not to tell my subjects what to do. I just said, 'Here is your questionnaire. Go into the room and drink it in.' I was just trying to look at **intuitive** judgment processes."

5   How did they do? The dorm room observers weren't nearly as good as friends in measuring extraversion. If you want to know how **animated** and talkative and outgoing someone is, clearly, you have to meet him or her in person. The friends also did slightly better than the dorm room visitors at accurately estimating agreeableness—how helpful and trusting someone is. I think that also makes sense. But on the remaining three traits of the Big Five, the strangers with the clipboards came out on top. They were more accurate at measuring conscientiousness, and they were much more accurate at predicting both the students' emotional stability and their openness to new experiences. On balance, then, the strangers ended up doing a much better job. What this suggests is that it is quite possible for people who have never met us and who have spent only twenty minutes thinking about us to come to a better understanding of who we are than people who have known us for years. Forget the endless "getting to know" meetings and lunches, then. If you want to get a good idea of whether I'd make a good employee, drop by my house one day and take a look around.

6   If you are like most people, I imagine that you find Gosling's conclusions quite **incredible**. But the truth is that they shouldn't be, not after the lessons of John Gottman.* This is just another example of thin-slicing. The observers were looking at the students' most personal belongings, and our personal belongings contain a wealth of very telling information. Gosling says, for example, that a person's bedroom gives three kinds of clues to his or her personality. There are, first of all, identity claims, which are deliberate expressions about how we would like to be seen by the world: a framed copy of a **magna cum laude** degree from Harvard, for example. Then there is behavioral residue, which is defined as the **inadvertent** clues we leave behind: dirty laundry on the floor, for instance, or an alphabetized CD collection. Finally, there are thoughts and feelings regulators, which are changes we make to our most personal spaces to affect the way we feel when we inhabit them: a scented candle in the corner, for example, or a pile of artfully placed decorative pillows on the bed. If you see alphabetized CDs, a Harvard diploma on the wall, incense on a side table, and laundry neatly stacked in a hamper, you know certain aspects about that individual's personality instantly, in a way that you may not be able to grasp if all you ever do is spend time with him or her directly. Anyone who has ever scanned the bookshelves of a new girlfriend or boyfriend—or peeked inside his or her medicine cabinet—understands this implicitly: you can learn as much—or more—from one glance at a private space as you can from hours of exposure to a public face.

—From *Blink* by Malcolm Gladwell. Copyright © 2005 by Malcolm Gladwell. By permission of Little, Brown and Company. All rights reserved.

VISUAL VOCABULARY

Green living is _____ lifestyle.

a. an animated
b. an intuitive
c. a conscientious

---

*John Gottman has written widely on marriage and relationships including "Predicting Divorce Among Newlyweds from the First Three Minutes of Marital Conflict Discussions," *Family Process* 38, no. 3 (1999): 203–242.

Fill in the blank in each sentence with a word from the Vocabulary Preview.

Vocabulary
Preview
1. Jennifer Wang graduated _____ with a bachelor of fine arts.

Vocabulary
Preview
2. One of Ms. Wang's goals is to work as an artist to create _____ films similar to Disney's *The Lion King* and *The Princess and The Frog*.

Vocabulary
Preview
3. She also wants to make public service films; for example, she wants to make a film to overcome _____ views about the danger of residuals of pesticides in food.

Vocabulary
Preview
4. An _____ of a developed country in this age eats many foods that have been treated with pesticides.

Vocabulary
Preview
5. Ms. Wang believes her films will have an _____ impact on society through the lessons they teach.

For items 6 through 10, choose the best meaning of each word in italics. Use context clues to make your choice.

Vocabulary
in Context
_____ **6.** "You've seen my resume and think I have the necessary *credentials*." (paragraph 1)
   a. badges   c. qualifications
   b. identifications   d. traits

Vocabulary
in Context
_____ **7.** "*Extraversion*. Are you sociable or retiring? Fun-loving or reserved?" (paragraph 3)
   a. self-confidence   c. loveable
   b. friendliness   d. shyness

Vocabulary
in Context
_____ **8.** "*Conscientiousness*. Are you organized or disorganized? Self-disciplined or weak willed?" (paragraph 3)
   a. carefulness   c. fairness
   b. indifference   d. willfulness

Vocabulary
in Context
_____ **9.** "I was just trying to look at *intuitive* judgement processes." (paragraph 4)
   a. thoughtful   c. unthinking
   b. reasonable   d. foolish

Vocabulary
in Context
_____ **10.** Then there is behavioral residue, which is defined as the *inadvertent* clues we leave behind." (paragraph 6)
   a. deliberate   c. clear
   b. small   d. unplanned

Central Idea _____ **11.** Which of the following sentences states the central idea of the passage?
    a. "Sure enough, as the psychologist Samuel Gosling has shown, judging people's personalities is a really good example of how surprisingly effective thin-slicing can be." (paragraph 2)
    b. "If you want to know how **animated** and talkative and outgoing someone is, clearly, you have to meet him or her in person." (paragraph 5)
    c. "If you want to get a good idea of whether I'd make a good employee, drop by my house one day and take a look around." (paragraph 5)
    d. "Gosling says, for example, that a person's bedroom gives three kinds of clues to his or her personality." (paragraph 6)

Supporting Details _____ **12.** The "Big Five" is
    a. a questionnaire that measures people on several levels.
    b. the groups of students who participated in Samuel Gosling's research.
    c. the clues found in a bedroom about a person's personality.
    d. the number of respected experts who study how people form opinions.

Supporting Details _____ **13.** Whom did Gosling ask to rank the students in his study by answering a questionnaire after looking around their dorm rooms for 15 minutes?
    a. close friends of the students in the study
    b. experts in psychology who analyzed the students in the study
    c. people who did not know the students in the study
    d. possible future employers of the students in the study

Transitions _____ **14.** "The dorm room observers weren't nearly as good as friends in measuring extraversion." (paragraph 5)

The relationship of ideas within this sentence is
    a. cause and effect.
    b. classification.
    c. comparison and contrast.
    d. generalization and example.

Transitions _____ **15.** "In order to answer those questions about my personality, your boss gives you two options. The first is to meet with me twice a week for a year—to have lunch or dinner or go to a movie with me—to the point where you become one of my closest friends." (paragraph 1)

The relationship of ideas between these sentences is
a. listing.
b. cause and effect.
c. comparison and contrast.
d. time order.

Thought Patterns _____ **16.** The main thought pattern for paragraph 3 is
a. cause and effect.
b. classification.
c. comparison and contrast.
d. definition and example.

Fact and Opinion _____ **17.** "Gosling began his experiment by doing a personality workup on eighty college students." (paragraph 3)

This sentence is a statement of
a. fact.
b. opinion.
c. fact and opinion.

Fact and Opinion _____ **18.** "If you are like most people, I imagine that you find Gosling's conclusions quite incredible." (paragraph 6)

This sentence is a statement of
a. fact.
b. opinion.
c. fact and opinion.

Inferences _____ **19.** Based on the details in the passage, we can conclude that
a. first impressions are often accurate.
b. we should never trust our first impression of someone.
c. we cannot change someone's first impression of us.
d. we should never make a quick judgment or decision.

Inferences _____ **20.** Based on the details in the passage, we can infer the meaning of "thin slicing" to be
a. narrow mindedness.
b. deliberately thinking before making a decision or forming an opinion.

c. cutting people down to size or criticizing them based on their behaviors or the situation.

d. seeing patterns in situations and behaviors based on a narrow slice of experience.

Concept Map

Complete the following concept map with information from the passage "The Secrets of the Bedroom."

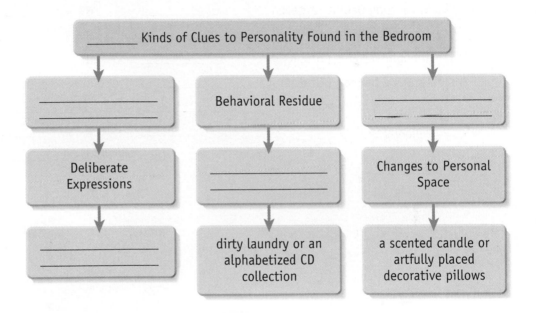

_____ Kinds of Clues to Personality Found in the Bedroom

Behavioral Residue

Deliberate Expressions

Changes to Personal Space

dirty laundry or an alphabetized CD collection

a scented candle or artfully placed decorative pillows

WHAT DO YOU THINK?

In the passage Malcolm Gladwell states, "You can learn as much—or more—from one glance at a private space as you can from hours of exposure to a public face." Do you agree with this statement? Why or why not? Assume you are taking a psychology course. Your professor has assigned this passage by Malcolm Gladwell for you to read. In addition, your professor has assigned a written response to the passage worth 10% of your final grade. Write an essay that describes you or someone you know based on the "Big Five Inventory" as listed in paragraph 3. Use details from your bedroom or the bedroom of the person you have chosen to describe in support of your opinions.

SKILLED READER Scorecard

"The Secrets of the Bedroom"

Skill	Number Correct	Points	Total
Vocabulary Preview (5 items)	_____	× 10 =	_____
Vocabulary in Context (5 items)	_____	× 10 =	_____
	Vocabulary Score		_____
Central Idea (1 item)	_____	× 8 =	_____
Supporting Details (2 items)	_____	× 8 =	_____
Transitions (2 items)	_____	× 8 =	_____
Thought Patterns (1 item)	_____	× 8 =	_____
Fact and Opinion (2 items)	_____	× 8 =	_____
Inferences (2 items)	_____	× 8 =	_____
Mapping (5 items)	_____	× 4 =	_____
	Comprehension Score		_____

READING 10

To Walk in Beauty

Bear Heart

According to his Web site, Marcellus Williams, 87, is a spiritual leader of the Muskogee Nation-Creek Tribe. One of the last traditionally trained medicine men, Bear Heart speaks thirteen native languages, is an American Baptist Minister, and holds an honorary Ph.D. in humanities. He served for seven years as a member of the advisory board for the Institute of Public Health-Native American and Alaskan Natives at Johns Hopkins School of Medicine. He is the author of *The Wind Is My Mother*, Random House, which is now published in fourteen languages. "To Walk in Beauty" is the opening passage of his inspirational book about his life and the wisdom of his people.

Vocabulary Preview

elements (paragraph 1): parts
environment (paragraph 8): climate, atmosphere, surroundings
ravines (paragraph 13): gullies, valleys
endurance (paragraph 13): staying power, stamina
dilapidated (paragraph 14): rundown, decaying
intentionally (paragraph 14): on purpose
gangrene (paragraph 16): death of soft tissue due to loss of blood supply

1   When I was three days old, my mother took me to a hilltop near our home and introduced me to the **elements**. First she introduced me to the Four Directions—East, South, West, and North. "I'm asking special blessings for this child. You surround our lives and keep us going. Please protect him and bring balance into his life."

2   Then, she touched my tiny feet to this Mother Earth. "Dear Mother and Grandmother Earth, one day this child will walk, play, and run on you. I will try to teach him to have respect for you as he grows up. Wherever he may go, please be there supporting and taking care of him."

3   I was introduced to the sun. "Grandfather Sun, shine upon this child as he grows. Let every portion of his body be normal and strong in every way, not only physically but mentally. Wherever he is, surround him with your warm, loving energy. We know that there will be cloudy days in his life, but you, are always constant

and, shining—please shine through to this child and keep him safe at all times."

4   She lifted me up to be embraced by the breeze as she spoke to the wind: "Please recognize this child. Sometimes you will blow strong. Sometimes you'll be very gentle, but let him grow up knowing the value of your presence at all times as he lives upon this planet."

5   Next I was introduced to the water. "Water, we do not live without you. Water is life. I ask that this child never know thirst."

6   She put some ashes on my forehead, saying, "Fire, burn away the obstacles of life for this child. Make the way clear so that he will not stumble in walking a path of learning to love and respect all of life."

7   And that night, I was introduced to the full moon and the stars. These elements were to watch over me as I grew up, running around on the carpet of grass that my Mother and Grandmother Earth provided, breathing in the air that sustains life and flows within my body, taking away all the toxins as I exhaled.

8   I had a sense of belonging as I grew up because of my people's relationship with these elements, and I imagine that's why most of our people related to the **environment** so easily. We recognized a long time ago that there was life all around us—in the water, in the ground, in the vegetation. Children were introduced to the elements so that as we grew up, we were not looking down upon nature or looking up to nature. We felt a part of nature, on the same level. We respected each blade of grass, one leaf on a tree among many other leaves, everything.

My name is *Nokus Feke Ematha* 9 *Tustanaki*—in your language it means "Bear Heart." I'm also known as Marcellus Williams and I was born in the state of Oklahoma in 1918.

My tribe is Muskogee, and we origi- 10 nally lived along the waterways of what is now Georgia and Alabama. The Europeans who eventually settled in that area didn't know of us as Muskogeans; they simply referred to us by our habitat, "the Indians who live by the creeks." The name prevailed, so we are commonly known as Creek Indians, but in fact we are the Muskogee Nation.

In 1832, President Andrew Jackson 11 signed an order to remove the native tribes from the southeastern United States, and it was then that the Muskogee were moved, along with the Chickasaws, Choctaws, and Cherokees. We walked all the way from our homes to "Indian Territory," which later became *Oklahoma*—that's a Choctaw word meaning "land of the red man." History has recorded that removal, but never once have the emotions been included in that record—what our people felt, what they had to leave behind, the hardships they had to **endure**.

The removal was forced; we were 12 given no choice about it. When our people refused to leave their homes, soldiers would **wrench** a little child from the arms of his mother and bash his head against a tree, saying, "Go or we'll do likewise to all the children here." It's said that some of the soldiers took their sabers and slashed pregnant women down the front, cut them open. That's how our people were forced from their homeland.

13   Our people walked the entire distance, from sunup to sundown, herded along by soldiers on horseback. When our old people died along the way, there was no time allowed to give them a decent burial. Many of our loved ones were left in **ravines,** their bodies covered with leaves and brush because our people were forced to go on. It was a long walk, people got very tired, and the young children could not keep *up* with the adults, so people would carry them, handing them back and forth. But they didn't have the **endurance** to carry them all the time, so some children and their mothers had to be left behind. Those are just some of the hardships our people endured on that walk, and out of those injustices came much **lamenting** and crying, so our people called it "The Trail of Tears."

14   I knew a man who went on that long walk as a child and he told me about it. At one point the people and the few horses they had were put on twelve **dilapidated** ferryboats to cross the Mississippi River. The ferry started sinking; so he grabbed his little sister, got on a horse, and headed for shore, all the while chased by soldiers who didn't want him riding. He was trying to hurry but the horse had to swim and was frightened from the **commotion,** so it was slow going. He had seen how brutal the soldiers could be and how the ferries were **intentionally** overloaded to make them sink, so he was making a break for his life. Someone came up behind him on another horse and grabbed his sister. "I was crying when I got to the shore," he said, "because I thought the soldiers took my sister, but I found out later one of my own people had helped me out."

15   Many of our people died crossing the Mississippi. When the survivors got across the river, many were soaked from swimming and it was freezing cold. One old woman, confused and exhausted from the **ordeal**, had no idea where she was—she thought she was back home and started giving instructions to the young ones. "Follow that trail and where it forks. There's some dry sticks on the ground. Gather them and build a fire to warm the people." She remembered where to find firewood at home and, in her own mind, she thought she was there. Surely she wished she was there.

16   My great-great-grandmother was on that forced march. No matter what kind of weather, they had to go on and, walking in the snow without any shoes, her feet froze. **Gangrene** set in and her feet literally dropped from her legs. She's buried at Fort Gibson, Oklahoma; but there's no name on those markers, just many, many crosses where our people died without recognition. I don't know where her grave is, but she's there among them.

17   Even after we were settled, that was not the end of our problems. Our children were taken from their parents and forced to go to boarding school, where they were not allowed to speak their native tongues— they had to speak English. The boarding school was a government school, so they had to march to and from class, make up their beds, do everything as if it were a military camp. This was forced upon our young children. Back then Native people took pride in their long hair, but the children had to have their hair cut short. Sometimes the administrators would just

put a bowl over a child's head and cut around it. Then they would laugh at the child.

19   Those are just some of the things that we endured. And yet today in our ceremonies, many of our people still pray for all mankind, whether they be black, yellow, red, or white. How is it possible, with a background like that among our people, to put out such love?

Fill in the blank in each sentence with a word from the "Vocabulary Preview."

Vocabulary Preview

1. Ari Swari bought a _____ house, fixed it up, and sold it for a profit.

Vocabulary Preview

2. Josiah trained to build his _____ in preparation to run a marathon.

Vocabulary Preview

3. To graduate in the spring, Justine _____ registered for six classes.

Vocabulary Preview

4. Many animals change colors to blend into their _____.

Vocabulary Preview

5. The _____ of water are hydrogen and oxygen.

Write the letter of the best meaning of the word in *italics*. Use context clues to make your choice.

Vocabulary in Context

_____ **6.** "History has recorded that removal, but never once have the emotions been included in that record—what our people felt, what they had to leave behind, the hardships they had to *endure*." (paragraph 11)
a. suffer
b. create
c. see
d. enjoy

Vocabulary in Context

_____ **7.** "When our people refused to leave their homes, soldiers would *wrench* a little child from the arms of his mother and bash his head against a tree, saying, 'Go or we'll do likewise to all the children here.'" (paragraph 12)
a. turn
b. give
c. yank
d. hold

Vocabulary in Context _____ **8.** "Those are just some of the hardships our people endured on that walk, and out of those injustices came much *lamenting* and crying, so our people called it 'The Trail of Tears.'" (paragraph 13)
a. talking
b. singing
c. remembering
d. mourning

Vocabulary in Context _____ **9.** "The ferry started sinking; so he grabbed his little sister, got on a horse, and headed for shore, all the while chased by soldiers who didn't want him riding. He was trying to hurry but the horse had to swim and was frightened from the *commotion*, so it was slow going." (paragraph 14)
a. current
b. disturbance
c. quarrel
d. soldiers

Vocabulary in Context _____ **10.** "One old woman, confused and exhausted from the *ordeal*, had no idea where she was—she thought she was back home and started giving instructions to the young ones." (paragraph 15)
a. hardship
b. memory
c. walk
d. society

Implied Main Idea _____ **11.** Which sentence is the best statement of the implied main idea of paragraph 18?
a. Native people have many reasons to be bitter.
b. Native people are able to love and pray for those who mistreated them.
c. Native people still celebrate their traditional ceremonies.
d. Native people pray for all mankind.

Implied Central Idea _____ **12.** What is the best statement of the implied central idea of the passage?
a. The Muskogee tribe are a spiritual people.
b. Bear Heart is a wise medicine man.
c. The Muskogee tribe are a spiritual people who have overcome brutal oppression and prejudice.
d. The Muskogee tribe were forced to walk the "Trail of Tears."

Supporting Details _____ **13.** The Muskogee tribe is also known as
a. Creek Indians.
b. Choctaws.
c. Cherokee.
d. Chickasaws.

Supporting Details _____ **14.** Who first called the Muskogee tribe "the Indians who live by the creeks"?
a. Andrew Jackson
b. the Americans
c. the Europeans
d. Marcellus Williams

Thought
Patterns

_____ **15.** The main thought pattern for paragraphs 1–8 is
a. comparison and contrast.   c. classification.
b. cause and effect.   d. time order.

Transitions _____ **16.** "But they didn't have the endurance to carry them all the time, so some children and their mothers had to be left behind." (paragraph 13)

The relationship of ideas between these sentences is one of
a. time order.   c. cause and effect.
b. contrast.   d. definition.

Transitions _____ **17.** "When I was three days old, my mother took me to a hilltop near our home and introduced me to the elements." (paragraph 1)

The relationship of ideas within this sentence is one of
a. time order.
b. cause and effect.
c. comparison and contrast.
d. listing.

Transitions _____ **18.** "Back then Native people took pride in their long hair, but the children had to have their hair cut short." (paragraph 17)

The relationship of ideas within this sentence is one of
a. time order.
b. cause and effect.
c. addition.
d. contrast.

Inferences Choose the two inferences that are most clearly based on the information in the following passage.

"The ferry started sinking; so he grabbed his little sister, got on a horse, and headed for shore, all the while chased by soldiers who didn't want him riding. He was trying to hurry but the horse had to swim and was frightened from the commotion, so it was slow going. He had seen how brutal the soldiers could be and how the ferries were intentionally overloaded to make them sink, so he was making a break for his life. Someone came up behind him on another horse and grabbed his sister. 'I was crying when I got to the shore,' he said, 'because I thought the soldiers took my sister, but I found out later one of my own people had helped me out.'" (paragraph 14)

19. _____

20. _____

    a. The speaker had difficulty controlling the horse as they crossed the river.

    b. The speaker was a coward.

    c. The soldiers wanted the ferry to sink.

    d. The speaker owned the horse he was riding.

Mapping

Complete the concept map using details from the narrative.

Timeline of Events in "To Walk in Beauty"

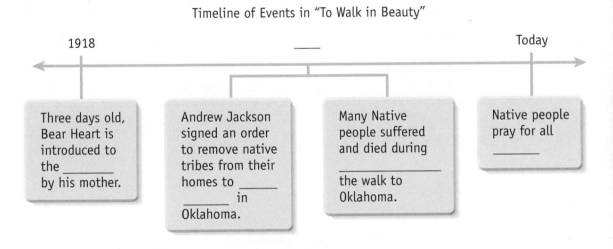

WHAT DO YOU THINK?

In the first seven paragraphs of the passage, Bear Heart shares a ritual of his people that reveals the values of his culture. What do we learn about his culture through this ritual? In what ways do you think the values taught in this ceremony helped his people endure their suffering? Does your family observe certain ceremonies based on your culture? What is a specific ceremony your family observes? What values does this ceremony reveal about your family or culture? Assume your college newspaper has called for articles to honor cultural diversity. Write an article about a specific ceremony that reveals the values of a culture or group of people.

SKILLED READER Scorecard

"To Walk in Beauty"

Skill	Number Correct	Points		Total
Vocabulary Preview (5 items)	_____	× 10	=	_____
Vocabulary in Context (5 items)	_____	× 10	=	_____
		Vocabulary Score		_____
Implied Main Idea and Central Idea (2 items)	_____	× 8	=	_____
Supporting Details (2 items)	_____	× 8	=	_____
Thought Patterns (1 item)	_____	× 8	=	_____
Transitions (3 items)	_____	× 8	=	_____
Inferences (2 items)	_____	× 8	=	_____
Mapping (5 items)	_____	× 4	=	_____
		Comprehension Score		_____

PART THREE

Combined-Skills Tests

Part Three contains 10 tests. The purpose of these tests is twofold: to track your growth as a reader and to prepare you for the formal tests you will face as you take college courses. Each test presents a reading passage and questions that cover some or all of the following skills: vocabulary in context, main ideas, supporting details, thought patterns, and inferences.

TEST 1

Read the paragraph, and answer the questions that follow it.

Triple E Communicators

Textbook Skills

[1]**Dynamic** professionals are usually smart readers. [2]They seek out new ideas. [3]No wonder others compete to include them on teams and join forces with them in business. [4]These lifelong learners have the same amount of time as everyone else does. [5]Their power lies in their ability to find excellent material. [6]Good research skills support ethical, effective and expressive communication. [7]These three traits help us to inform and persuade others. [8]"Triple E communicators" have all three traits. [9]First, **ethical** communicators care about the quality of information that they give to others. [10]And they respect the length of time a listener has to give to them. [11]Next, effective communicators think about the amount of information that is needed to make a point. [12]They know enough to back the claims they make. [13]And they know how the information fits together reasonably. [14]Finally, expressive communicators choose meaningful material for their listeners. [15]They use interesting information. [16]They also allow listeners to see the speaker's connection with the material.

—Adapted from Kelly, *Communication@work*. Allyn & Bacon, 2006, p. 139.

Vocabulary   _____   **1.** The best meaning of the word *dynamic* as used in sentence 1 is
   a. powerful.   c. explosive.
   b. controlling.   d. changing.

Vocabulary   _____   **2.** The best meaning of the word *ethical* as used in sentence 9 is
   a. informed.   c. unfair.
   b. expert.   d. moral.

Main Idea   _____   **3.** Choose the sentence that best states the main idea of the paragraph.
   a. Dynamic professionals are usually smart readers. (sentence 1)
   b. Good research skills support ethical, effective and expressive communication. (sentence 6)
   c. "Triple E communicators" have all three traits. (sentence 8)
   d. Finally, expressive communicators choose meaningful material for their listeners. (sentence 14)

Main Idea/   _____   **4.** Sentence 11, "Next, effective communicators think about the amount
Details   of information that is needed to make a point," is a
   a. main idea.   c. minor supporting detail.
   b. major supporting detail.

Thought _____ **5.** The thought pattern for this paragraph is
   a. cause and effect.   c. definition.
   b. classification.   d. comparison and contrast.

Inference _____ **6.** Choose the inference that is most clearly based on sentence 4,
Patterns   "These lifelong learners have the same amount of time as everyone
                 else does."
   a. Lifelong learners are busier than other people.
   b. Lifelong learners manage their time wisely.
   c. Lifelong learners make time for learning.
   d. Lifelong learners are smarter than other people.

Use ideas from the passage to complete the outline.

Triple E Communicators

7. I. _____

        A. care about quality of information they give to others.

        B. respect the length of time a listener has to give.

8. II. _____

        A. think about the quantity of information needed to make a point.

        B. know enough to back the claims they make.

9. III. _____

10.   A. _____

        B. use interesting information.

        C. allow listeners to see the speaker's connection with the material.

TEST 2

Read the paragraph, and answer the questions that follow it.

How Learners Learn

¹Too many people believe the ability to learn is a gift received at birth and measured by intelligence. ²Actually, learning is a process. ³This process consists of seven steps. ⁴First, learners set goals based on the need to know. ⁵The need to know goes beyond learning facts and looks at the

Vocabulary _____ **1.** The best meaning of the word *passive* as used in the title and sentence 1 is
a. weak.   c. nonviolent.
b. silent.   d. hateful.

Vocabulary _____ **2.** The best meaning of the word *protest* as used in sentence 3 is
a. strong disagreement.   c. embarrassment.
b. approval.   d. victory.

Vocabulary _____ **3.** The best meaning of the expression *submitted to* as used in sentence 14 is
a. created.   c. reacted against.
b. avoided.   d. endured.

Central Idea _____ **4.** What is the best statement of the central idea of this passage?
a. Thoreau, Gandhi, and King all used passive resistance.
b. Passive resistance is a powerful way to confront an unfair society.
c. African American students in the South used passive resistance.
d. Passive resistance does not often bring about the needed change.

Thought
Patterns _____ **5.** The thought pattern for this passage is
a. time order.   c. comparison and contrast.
b. definition.   d. cause and effect.

Inference _____ **6.** Choose the inference that is most clearly based on the information in the passage.
a. Passive resistance is nonviolent.
b. Passive resistance uses violence as its force.
c. Passive resistance is not effective.
d. Passive resistance was used by Thoreau, Gandhi, and King.

Complete the concept map, based on the information in the passage.

7. _____

Three leaders:
8. _____
9. _____
10. _____

Example:
African American
students in the South

TEST 4

Read the paragraph, and answer the questions that follow it.

Good and Poor Listeners

[1]Good listeners and poor listeners can be recognized by their behavior. [2]Good listeners look at the speaker, for they know that eye contact is a way to stay focused on what the speaker is saying. [3]In contrast, poor listeners allow their eyes to **wander** all over the place. [4]As their eyes wander, so do their minds. [5]Once their mind wanders, they miss important information. [6]Good listeners wait to hear the speaker's point, and they don't interrupt. [7]In contrast, poor listeners constantly interrupt with their own ideas, requests for information to be repeated, or premature questions that would be answered by listening. [8]Good listeners do ask questions at the appropriate time. [9]However, unlike poor listeners, good listeners ask questions that bring out more details or **clarify** confusing ideas. [10]Good listeners stay on the same subject as the speaker. [11]In contrast, poor listeners use the speaker's words as an opportunity to jump off into a topic of their own choice. [12]Good listeners keep their emotions under control so that they can understand the speaker's point of view. [13]In contrast, poor listeners become **agitated** or upset at ideas that are different from their own. [14]Finally, good listeners make the speaker feel valued; poor listeners show little respect for others or their ideas.

Vocabulary _____ **1.** The best meaning of the word *wander* as used in sentence 3 is
    a. focus.   c. move around.
    b. blink.   d. stare.

Vocabulary _____ **2.** The best meaning of the word *clarify* as used in sentence 9 is
    a. stir up.   c. question.
    b. clear up.   d. study.

Vocabulary _____ **3.** The best meaning of the word *agitated* as used in sentence 13 is
    a. calm.   c. disturbed.
    b. sad.   d. hurtful.

Inference _____ **4.** Sentence 9, "However, unlike poor listeners, good listeners ask questions that bring out more details or clarify confusing ideas," implies that
    a. good listeners ask questions that clarify.
    b. poor listeners don't usually ask good questions.
    c. poor listeners can ask good questions.
    d. good listeners can ask poor questions.

Implied
Central Idea
_____   **3.** What is the best statement of the implied central idea of this passage?

    a. Sibling status is the chief factor in a child's life.

    b. Older children are dethroned by a new sibling.

    c. The length of time between births affects the status of siblings.

    d. Parents care more about their firstborn child.

Main Idea/
Details
_____   **4.** "Infants cannot grasp the impact of a new sibling on their special position" (sentence 9) is a

    a. main idea.

    b. minor supporting detail.

    c. major supporting detail.

Thought
Patterns
_____   **5.** The overall thought pattern used in the passage is

    a. time order.   c. cause and effect.

    b. comparison.   d. contrast.

Inference
_____   **6.** The details in the second paragraph (sentences 6–12) imply that

    a. it is better to have children less than two years or more than five years apart.

    b. infants require a great deal of time and attention.

    c. five-year-olds are jealous of a new baby.

    d. it is harder to have children that are spaced two years apart.

Complete the following list, based on the information in the passage.

Positive Effects of Longer Spacing Intervals between Births

7. Five- and six-year-olds can better cope with _____

8. Parents will treat a newborn _____

9. Parents and children have more _____

10. Only one child at a time will be _____

TEST 6

Read the passage, and answer the questions that follow it.

The A-B-C's of Air Bag Safety

Air Bag Safety: Buckle Everyone! Children in Back!

[1]Air bags save lives. [2]They work best when everyone is buckled and children are properly restrained in the back seat. [3]Children riding in the

front seat can be seriously injured or killed when an air bag comes out in a crash. [4]An air bag is not a soft, billowy pillow. [5]To do its important job, an air bag comes out of the dashboard at up to 200 miles per hour—faster than the blink of an eye. [6]The force of an air bag can hurt those who are too close to it. [7]Drivers can prevent air bag-related injuries to adults and children by following the critical safety points.

Child Safety Points

- [8]Children 12 and under should ride buckled up in a rear seat.
- [9]Infants in rear facing child safety seats should NEVER ride in the front seat of a vehicle with a passenger side air bag.
- [10]Small children should ride in a rear seat in child safety seats approved for their age and size.
- [11]If a child over one year old must ride in the front seat with a passenger side air bag, put the child in a front facing child safety seat, a booster seat, or a correct fitting lap/shoulder belt—AND move the seat as far back as possible.

Adult Safety Points

- [12]Everyone should buckle up with both lap and shoulder belts on every trip. [13]Air bags are **supplemental** protection devices.
- [14]The lap belt should be worn under the abdomen and low across the hips. [15]The shoulder portion should come over the collar bone away from the neck and cross over the breast bone. [16]The shoulder belt in most new cars can be adjusted on the side pillar to improve fit.
- [17]Driver and front passenger seats should be moved as far back as practical, particularly for shorter **stature** people.

—"A-B-C's of Airbag Safety." National Highway Traffic Administration. United States Department of Transportation. Online. 4 Nov. 2009.

Vocabulary _____ **1.** The word *supplemental* as used in sentence 13 means
  a. necessary.   c. important.
  b. additional.   d. expensive.

Vocabulary _____ **2.** The word *stature* as used in sentence 17 means
  a. build.   c. looking.
  b. temper.   d. sighted.

Central Idea _____ **3.** The central idea of the passage is
  a. knowing how airbags work will ensure safety.
  b. airbags should be used in addition to seat belts.
  c. airbags can cause harm when they are deployed.
  d. drivers can take precautions to minimize the risks of airbags.

Details   _____   **4.** Sentence 4 is a
                        a. major supporting detail.
                        b. minor supporting detail.

Thought   _____   **5.** The thought pattern used in sentences 8–17 is
Patterns
                        a. time order.   c. listing.
                        b. comparison and contrast.   d. cause and effect.

TEST 7

Read the following passage, adapted from the college textbook *Access to Health*, and answer the questions that follow it.

Communicating as a Couple

Textbook
Skills

¹Lack of communication in intimate relationships is often a source of trouble. ²When two people cannot communicate, the couple's ability to solve problems is harmed. ³Two skills—leveling and editing—can help couples talk and listen to each other.

⁴**Leveling** refers to sending your partner a clear, simple, and honest message. ⁵Leveling serves several purposes. ⁶The overall purpose is to make communications clear. ⁷The next purpose is to make clear the expectations partners have of each other. ⁸Another purpose is to clear up unpleasant feelings and thoughts from past incidents. ⁹A similar purpose is to make clear what is relevant and what is irrelevant. ¹⁰And the final purpose is to become aware of the things that draw you together or push you apart. ¹¹Telling your partner that you expect a phone call if he or she is going to be late is an example of leveling.

¹²*Editing* or **censoring** remarks is another useful skill. ¹³Couples should hold back comments that are hurtful or irrelevant. ¹⁴Often when people are upset, they let everything fly. ¹⁵Bringing up old issues and incidents causes pain and puts the partner on the defensive. ¹⁶Editing means taking the time and making the effort not to say inflammatory things. ¹⁷Leveling and editing are ways for couples to be caring and sensitive as they communicate with each other.

—Adapted from Donatelle, *Access to Health*,
7th ed., pp. 136–137.

Vocabulary _____ **1.** The best meaning of the word *leveling* as used in sentence 4 is
    a. sending clear, simple, honest messages.
    b. demanding attention.
    c. facing disappointments.
    d. clearing up problems.

Vocabulary _____ **2.** The best meaning of the word *censoring* as used in sentence 12 is
    a. oppressing.   c. whispering.
    b. leaving parts out.   d. sharing.

Central
Idea _____ **3.** The central idea of the passage is found in
    a. sentence 1.   c. sentence 3.
    b. sentence 2.   d. sentence 4.

Thought
Patterns _____ **4.** The relationship between sentences 7 and 8 is
    a. cause.   c. addition.
    b. effect.   d. time order.

5. Complete the concept map with a detail from the passage.

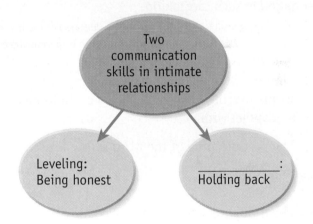

Two communication skills in intimate relationships

Leveling: Being honest

_____: Holding back

TEST 8

Textbook
Skills

Read the following passage, adapted from a college psychology textbook, and answer the questions that follow it.

Effects of Stress on the Immune System

¹Stress can affect the immune system, which functions to defend the body against infection. ²Two types of white blood cells are critical to the

immune system. ³The B cells mature in the bone marrow. ⁴And the T cells mature in the thymus, an organ located in the chest. ⁵Some of the T cells detect and destroy damaged or altered cells, such as precancerous cells, before they become tumors. ⁶Glucocorticoids, which are released when the stress response is triggered, can kill or stop the growth of new white blood cells.

⁷Even day-to-day events and stresses, such as taking exams, can affect the functioning of the immune system. ⁸A study looked at the relationship between stress and catching a cold. ⁹The study found that the more stress a participant reported before **exposure** to a cold virus, the more likely he or she was to catch a cold. ¹⁰The aspects of stress that best predicted whether participants would get a cold were how likely they were to experience negative feelings like guilt, anger, and being upset. ¹¹Another factor was how out of control and unpredictable they rated their lives.

¹²Stress can play a role in the length of time it takes a wound to heal. ¹³The wounds of women who experienced high levels of stress by caring for a relative with Alzheimer's disease took nine days longer to heal than those of women of similar age and economic **status** who were not engaged in such caretaking.

—Adapted from Kosslyn/Rosenberg, *Psychology: The Brain, the Person, the World*, p. 443
© 2001 Allyn and Bacon. Reproduced by permission of Pearson Education, Inc.

Vocabulary _____ **1.** The best meaning of the expression *exposure to* as used in sentence 9 is
    a. uncovering of.   c. holding of.
    b. contact with.   d. removal of.

Vocabulary _____ **2.** The best meaning of the word *status* as used in sentence 13 is
    a. style.   c. level.
    b. need.   d. goal.

Thought Patterns _____ **3.** The thought pattern for this passage is
    a. time order.   c. cause and effect.
    b. classification.   d. comparison and contrast.

Main Idea/ Details _____ **4.** Sentence 4 is a
    a. main idea.   c. minor supporting detail.
    b. major supporting detail.

Central Idea _____ **5.** What is the best statement of the central idea of this passage?
    a. White blood cells are crucial to the immune system.
    b. Stress affects the immune system.
    c. Stress lengthens the time it takes a wound to heal.
    d. Catching a cold is often stress-related.

TEST 9

Read the following passage written by Charles A. Eastman, also known by his Sioux name Ohiyesa, from his book *Indian Heroes and Great Chieftains*. Then, answer the questions that follow.

Crazy Horse

[1]Big-heartedness, generosity, courage, and self-denial are the qualifications of a public servant, and the average Indian was keen to follow this **ideal**. [2]As everyone knows, these characteristic traits become a weakness when he enters a life founded upon commerce and gain. [3]Under such conditions the life of Crazy Horse began. [4]His mother, like other mothers, tender and watchful of her boy, would never once place an obstacle in the way of his father's severe physical training. [5]They laid the spiritual and patriotic foundations of his education in such a way that he early became conscious of the demands of public service.

[6]He was perhaps four or five years old when the band was snowed in one severe winter. [7]They were very short of food, but his father was a tireless hunter. [8]The buffalo, their main dependence, were not to be found, but he was out in the storm and cold every day and finally brought in two antelopes. [9]The little boy got on his pet pony and rode through the camp, telling the old folks to come to his mother's teepee for meat. [10]It turned out that neither his father nor mother had authorized him to do this. [11]Before they knew it, old men and women were lined up before the teepee home, ready to receive the meat, in answer to his invitation. [12]As a result, the mother had to distribute nearly all of it, keeping only enough for two meals.

[13]On the following day the child asked for food. [14]His mother told him that the old folks had taken it all, and added: "Remember, my son, they went home singing praises in your name, not my name or your father's. [15]You must be brave. [16]You must live up to your reputation."

—Eastman, Charles A. "Crazy Horse." *Indian Heroes and Great Chieftains.* Little Brown and Co. 1918 pp. 33–34. *The Project Gutenberg EBook of Indian Heroes and Great Chieftains.* 4 Nov. 2009 http://www .gutenberg.org/files/336/336-h/336-h.htm#2H_4_0007.

Vocabulary _____ **1.** Based on the context of the passage, the best meaning of the word *ideal* (sentence 1) is

    a. perfection.   c. value.

    b. reality.   d. path.

Central
Idea

_____ **2.** Which sentence best states the central idea of the passage?

    a. sentence 1   c. sentence 5

    b. sentence 2   d. sentence 16

Transitions _____ **3.** The relationship of ideas between sentence 11 and sentence 12 is

    a. time order.   c. definition and example.

    b. classification.   d. cause and effect.

Fact and
Opinion

_____ **4.** Sentence 9 is a statement of

    a. fact.   c. fact and opinion.

    b. opinion.

Inference _____ **5.** Choose the inference most soundly based on the information in the passage.

    a. Crazy Horse's mother disagreed with his father about how to discipline Crazy Horse.

    b. As a child, Crazy Horse possessed the qualities of a public servant.

    c. Crazy Horse got his name because of his foolish acts.

    d. Crazy Horse caused his family to go hungry for the rest of the winter.

TEST 10

Textbook
Skills

Read the following passage from a college science textbook. Answer the questions that follow.

Early Greeks and Ancient Astronomy

[1]The "Golden Age" of early astronomy was centered in Greece from 600 B.C. through 150 A.D. [2]The early Greeks have been criticized, and rightly so, for using ideas, values, and beliefs to explain natural fact. [3]However, they did rely on recorded data as well. [4]They had developed the basics of geometry and trigonometry. [5]They used these to measure the sizes and distances of the largest-appearing bodies in the heavens—the Sun and the Moon.

[6]Many astronomical discoveries have been credited to the Greeks. [7]They held the **geocentric** view. [8]They believed that Earth was a sphere that stayed motionless at the center of the universe. [9]Orbiting Earth were the Moon, the Sun, and the known planets—Mercury, Venus, Mars, Jupiter, and Saturn. [10]Beyond the planets was a transparent and hollow

celestial sphere. [11]On this sphere, the stars traveled daily around Earth. [12](This is how it looks, but, of course, the effect is actually caused by Earth's rotation about its axis.) [13]Some early Greeks realized that the motion of the stars could be explained just as easily by a rotating Earth. [14]However, Earth exhibited no sense of motion. [15]And it seemed too large to be movable. [16]So they rejected that idea. [17]In fact, Earth's rotation was not proven until 1851.

[18]To the Greeks, most of the heavenly bodies appeared to remain in the same position in relation to one another. [19]Seven did not. These seven "wanderers" (*planetai* in Greek) included the Sun, the Moon, Mercury, Venus, Mars, Jupiter, and Saturn. [20]Each was thought to have a circular orbit around Earth. [21]This system was incorrect. [22]Yet the Greeks refined it to the point that it explained the movements of all celestial bodies.

[23]Many of the Greek discoveries were lost during the Middle Ages. [24]Yet the Earth-centered view of the Greeks became established in Europe. [25]Presented in its finest form by Claudius Ptolemy, this geocentric outlook became known as the *Ptolemaic* system.

—Adapted from Lutgens & Tarbuck, *Foundations of Earth Science*, 5th ed., Prentice Hall 2008 p. 396

Vocabulary _____ **1.** Based on the context of the passage the best meaning of the term *geocentric* (sentences 7 and 25) is
a. sun centered.   c. universe centered.
b. sphere centered.   d. earth centered.

Central Idea _____ **2.** The best statement of the central idea of the passage is
a. sentence 1.   c. sentence 8.
b. sentence 6.   d. sentence 25.

Supporting Details _____ **3.** In the second paragraph, sentence 10 is a
a. major detail.
b. minor detail.

Thought Patterns _____ **4.** The overall thought pattern of the passage is
a. definition and example.   c. classification.
b. cause and effect.   d. comparison and contrast.

Fact and Opinion _____ **5.** In the third paragraph, sentence 21 states
a. a fact.   c. fact and opinion.
b. an opinion.

PART FOUR

Reading Enrichment

ESL Reading Tips

Knowing more than one language is a tremendous advantage. A language is closely tied to the culture of its people. Thus, when you learn an additional language, you learn about the values and customs of a way of life different from your own. The differences among cultures can be seen in the differences among their languages. For example, three of the most frequently used words in the English language are the articles *the, an,* and *a.* Yet many other languages do not use articles at all. Some say that learning English as an additional language offers some specific challenges.

English as a Second Language (ESL) refers to teaching English to a person whose native or main language is not English. The following ESL reading tips are designed to aid you in your admirable quest to acquire English.

General Hints

Every chapter of *The Skilled Reader,* Third Edition, teaches specific skills and strategies that are helpful to students learning to read English. The following chart lists a few of the specific lessons that directly support ESL instruction. Use this chart to survey or review information that will help you learn to read English. Complete the chart by writing in the page numbers you will study.

> **Skills and Strategies in *The Skilled Reader* that support ESL**
> Use a reading plan like SQ3R. [Chapter 1] pages 4–17
> Skim or read rapidly for main ideas. [Chapter 4] pages 129–133
> Scan or read rapidly for specific details. [Chapter 7] pages 238–245
> Use the general sense of the passage to figure out the meaning of unfamiliar words and phrases. [Chapter 2] pages 42–51
> Annotate the passage. [Part II] pages 428–429
> Create graphic organizers based on thought patterns from information in the text. [Chapter 9] pages 312–324

In addition, form a study group that includes native speakers of English. The more you hear and speak the language, the more quickly you will learn it.

Figurative Language: Idioms, Similes, and Metaphors

Consider the following well-known phrases:

catch some Zs	sharp as a tack	eats like a bird
burn the midnight oil	an icy stare	raining cats and dogs

Each one of these sayings creates a vivid word picture that deepens the reader's understanding of the author's meaning. To understand how an author creates and uses vivid word pictures, you need to know about literal and figurative language.

> **Literal language**   uses the exact meaning of a word or phrase.
> **Figurative language**   uses a word or phrase to imply or mean something different from its literal definition; also known as "figures of speech."

Literal language expresses the exact meaning of a word or phrase. For example, if you were out hiking with a friend and told him to "go jump in a lake," he could take your words *literally* and immerse himself in a nearby body of water. However, if you were having an argument and said, "Go jump in a lake," your friend would understand that you were using **figurative language** and were saying something like "go away." Hundreds of figures of speech exist, but understanding three commonly used types will make you a more skilled reader. The three types are *idioms, similes,* and *metaphors.*

> **Idiom**—a phrase (a group of words) that cannot be understood based on the individual words in the phrase
> **Simile**—an indirect comparison between two ideas that uses *like, as, as if,* or *as though*
> **Metaphor**—a direct comparison between two ideas that does not use *like, as, as if,* or *as though*

Idiom

An **idiom** is a phrase (a group of words) that cannot be understood based on the individual words in the phrase.

EXAMPLE Read the following two sentences. Underline the idioms in each sentence. Use your own words to write the meaning of the idioms.

1. Last night, Enrico and Carlos burned the midnight oil studying for final exams. _____

2. Enrico was exhausted after the exam, so he went home to catch some Zs.

   _____

EXPLANATION The phrases *burned the midnight oil* and *to catch some Zs* are idioms. In sentence 1, the phrase *burned the midnight oil* implies that Enrico and Carlos stayed up late into the night studying. The expression refers to the time before electricity when oil lamps were used for light. In sentence 2, the phrase *to catch some Zs* implies sleep. This meaning is implied with the context clue "exhausted." The expression most likely came from the way cartoons depict the sound of someone snoring with a string of Zs coming from a character's mouth: Zzzzzzzz indicates snoring.

PRACTICE 1 **Idioms**

Use your own words to write the meaning of each idiom in bold print. Compare your answers with those of your classmates and discuss them.

1. Anna's **eyes were bigger than her stomach**.

   Anna _____

2. After winning the championship, the team **painted the town red**.

   The team _____

3. After giving instructions to the sales force, the manager said, **"Let's get the ball rolling."**

   The manager said, _____

4. Jonathan is so vain. He always **blows his own horn**.

   Jonathan always _____

5. I can never tell when Rodney is **pulling my leg** because he has **a poker face**.

   When Rodney is _____ he has _____

Simile

A **simile** is an indirect comparison between two ideas that uses *like, as, as if*, or *as though*.

EXAMPLE Read the following two sentences. Underline the similes in each sentence. Use your own words to write the meaning of the similes.

1. Jamie is sharp as a tack; she always knows the right thing to say.

   _____

2. Elaine, who is always worried about her weight, eats like a bird.

   _____

EXPLANATION The phrases *sharp as a tack* and *eats like a bird* are similes. They use the words *as* and *like,* which are words of indirect comparison. In sentence 1, the phrase *sharp as a tack* means that Jamie is smart or quick-minded. Jamie is not a tack. Perhaps Jamie is compared to a sharp tack because her ideas pierce through to the main point. In sentence 2, the phrase *eats like a bird* implies that Elaine eats small portions. Elaine is not a bird. Perhaps Elaine's eating style is compared to a bird's because she picks at her food and takes tiny bites of it. In both examples, Jamie and Elaine are described in *similes* as *similar* to these things.

Because a simile is a figure of speech that cannot be taken literally, the skilled reader must interpret the author's implied meaning.

PRACTICE 2 Similes

Write the meaning of each simile in bold print. Compare and discuss your answers with those of your classmates.

1. A gallbladder attack feels **like labor contractions during the last phase of childbirth**.

   A gallbladder attack is _____

2. Justine accepts new ideas **as well as a cat accepts a bath**.

   Justine accepts a new idea with _____

3. New love breaks into one's life **like a brilliant sunrise**.

   New love is _____

4. The tornado sounded **as though a freight train were coming straight at me**.

   The tornado had a _____ sound.

5. One stage of grief is **like the eye of a hurricane**.

   One stage of grief is _____

Metaphor

A **metaphor** is a direct comparison between two ideas that does *not* use *like*, *as*, *as if*, or *as though*. Often a metaphor is created by using the verb *is* to set up a direct comparison between ideas.

EXAMPLE Read the following three sentences. Underline the metaphors in each sentence. Use your own words to write the meaning of the metaphors.

1. Alita gave the naughty child an icy stare.

_____

2. It is raining cats and dogs.

_____

3. Faith is my anchor in life.

_____

EXPLANATION The three metaphors are an *icy stare*, *raining cats and dogs*, and *Faith is my anchor*. Note that none of these examples uses the word *like* or *as*. Instead, the first idea in each metaphor is directly compared to the second idea. In sentence 1, the word *icy* is used to directly describe Alita's stare, to paint a picture of a "cold look." In sentence 2, the phrase *raining cats and dogs* makes a comparison between cats and dogs and rain and wind. In some ancient myths, cats represented rain and dogs represented wind (for example, in Nordic mythology, both animals were associated with the storm god, Odin). The author's purpose is to suggest a storm.

Often a metaphor uses words such as *is*, *are*, or *were* to make the direct comparison between the two ideas. In sentence 3, *Faith is my anchor* sets up a direct link between faith and the traits of an anchor. Thus the metaphor paints a picture of faith as an ideal that lies beneath a person's everyday life, out of sight, yet holds that person's life steady so that it cannot drift.

Because a metaphor is a figure of speech that cannot be taken literally, the skilled reader must figure out the author's implied meaning.

PRACTICE 3   **Metaphors**

Write the meaning of each metaphor in bold print. Compare and discuss your answers with your classmates.

1. When April drives, she tailgates, darts in and out of traffic, and speeds through yellow lights.

She is **a road hog**.

_____

2. Daniel is a **couch potato**. He doesn't help around the house or go outside; instead, he watches television and refuses to exercise.

_____

3. Forgiveness is a **gift**, yet trust is a **reward**.

_____

_____

4. Love **quenches the fires** of greed.

_____

5. Fame is a **vapor that quickly vanishes**.

_____

Distinguishing Between Similes and Metaphors

Both similes and metaphors use comparisons between ideas to deepen meaning. Almost any expression that can be worded as a simile could also be worded as a metaphor. Remember the main difference between a simile and a metaphor is the use of the words *like*, *as*, *as if*, and *as though*. Similes use these words; metaphors do not. Authors must carefully choose whether the indirect comparison of a simile or the direct comparison of a metaphor is better suited for their purposes. Thus skilled readers pay close attention to the author's careful application of these two figures of speech.

EXAMPLE Read the following two sentences. Underline the figures of speech. Identify each one as a metaphor or a simile. Write **M** for metaphor and **S** for simile.

_____ 1. The stock market sank like a rock.

_____ 2. His mop of hair hung limp and stringy.

EXPLANATION In sentence 1, the phrase *sank like a rock* is a simile (**S**). The word *like* sets up an indirect comparison between the behavior of the stock market and a rock. In this case, both fall rapidly from high places. In sentence 2, the phrase *mop of hair* is a metaphor (**M**) that directly compares his hair to a limp and stringy mop.

PRACTICE 4

Each of the following sentences contains a figure of speech. Identify each figure of speech as a metaphor or a simile. Write **M** for metaphor and **S** for simile.

_____   **1.** Marie was as frightened as a deer caught in a car's headlights on a dark country road.

_____   **2.** Some military leaders are hawks; others are doves.

_____   **3.** Karl Marx said, "Religion is the opiate of the masses."

_____   **4.** Your words skim across my heart like small stones skipping across the smooth surface of water.

_____   **5.** I am as hungry as a horse.

VISUAL VOCABULARY

Investing in the stock market

is like _____.
Complete the caption.
This figure of speech is a

_____.

a. simile.
b. metaphor.

REVIEW TEST 1

Understanding Figures of Speech

A. Idioms   Use your own words to write the meaning of each idiom in bold print.

1. Samantha is **fed up with** Anita because Anita is always late.

Samantha is _____

2. Ricky almost missed the deadline to file his taxes, but he made it **by the skin of his teeth**.

   Ricky _____

B. Similes   For each simile choose a meaning from the box. Use each meaning once.

boastful	discipline	grow	valuable

3. Wisdom is as good as gold.

   Wisdom is _____

4. Talent is like a plant that needs to be fed, watered, and pruned.

   Talent can _____

5. William struts like a rooster.

   William is _____

6. Achieving success is like training for a marathon.

   Success requires _____

C. Metaphors   For each metaphor, choose a meaning from the box. Use each meaning once.

confusing	guardian	painful	short time

7. In George Orwell's novel *1984*, government becomes everybody's feared "Big Brother."

   Government becomes everyone's _____

8. The thorn of failure pricks self-confidence.

   Failure is _____

9. Grief is but a passing season.

   Grief lasts a _____

10. Surely life is a jewelry box; yet guilt, fear, love, and hope are tangled necklaces, hopelessly knotted together.

    Life is _____

REVIEW TEST 2

Understanding Figures of Speech

A. Idioms   Use your own words to write the meaning of each idiom in bold print.

1. She **bent over backwards** to please her boyfriend, but he never seemed satisfied.

   _____

2. If you let me **give you a hand**, we can finish the project by noon.

   _____

3. Joe sends text messages to his friends **twenty-four/seven**.

   _____

4. During the recession, our business was **in the black**. We even hired new employees.

   _____

5. When I become discouraged, I remember Grandmother's advice, "**Keep your chin up.**"

   _____

B. Similes and Metaphors   Identify each item as a simile or metaphor. Write S for simile or M for metaphor.

_____ 6. "What happens to a dream deferred? Does it dry up like a raisin in the sun?"—Langston Hughes

_____ 7. "All the world's a stage. And all the men and women merely players." —Shakespeare

_____ 8. "Medicine is my lawful wife and literature my mistress; when I tire of one, I spend the night with the other." —Anton Chekhov

_____ 9. "We are two eagles flying together, under the heavens, over the mountains, stretched on the wind.." —Sara Teasdale

_____ 10. "My love is like a red, red rose." —Robert Burns

Reading Graphics

Reading comprehension involves reading more than just words. Authors also use visual images such as photographs, cartoons, and graphics to relay ideas. Graphics are helpful for several reasons. First, graphics can simplify difficult ideas and make relationships easier to see. Second, graphics can sum up ideas so that they can be more quickly digested. Third, graphics can sway a reader by pointing out trends or gaps in information. A skilled reader should know how to read different types of graphics. This appendix will discuss three basic types: tables, graphs, and diagrams. Although a variety of graphics exist, a few basic guidelines can be applied as a reading process for any graphic.

Basic Guidelines for Reading Graphics

Graphics give a great deal of information in a smaller space than it would take to write the ideas in the form of words. The following suggestions will help you understand the general format of a graphic. Apply the SQ3R strategies discussed in Chapter 1. Remember to skim, question, read, recite, and review the information.

Read the Words Printed with the Graphic

Just as in a paragraph or passage, a graphic has a main idea and supporting details.

Read the title or caption. The title or caption is usually at the top of the graphic. The title or caption states the main idea of the graphic.

Ask: What is this graphic about? What is being described?

Note the source. The source is usually at the bottom of the graphic. The source is the author or publisher of the ideas in the graphic.

Ask: Who collected the information? Is the source a trusted authority? If the graphic reports the results of a survey, how many people took part? Who were they?

Read any footnotes. Footnotes are also found at the bottom of a graphic. Footnotes can include important supporting details.

Ask: Do the footnotes explain what any numbers or headings mean? How was the data collected?

Read the labels. Many graphics use columns and rows. Other graphics use horizontal or vertical axes. Columns, rows, and axes are labeled. These labels give important supporting details for the graphic's main idea. Look up any words you do not know in a dictionary.

Ask: Do the labels tell what the columns and rows represent? Are any symbols or abbreviations used? If so, what do they mean?

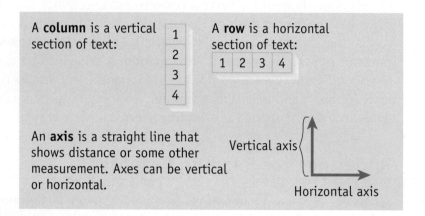

A **column** is a vertical section of text:

A **row** is a horizontal section of text:

An **axis** is a straight line that shows distance or some other measurement. Axes can be vertical or horizontal.

Vertical axis

Horizontal axis

Analyze the Graphic

Analyze the format. Each type of chart has its own organization. For example, a table uses columns and rows. A pie chart is a circle divided into parts.

Ask: How is the graphic organized? Why did the author use this type of graphic?

Analyze the unit of measurement. Study the legend. A legend will list and explain symbols used as labels. Study the labels of rows, columns, and axes.

Ask: Do the numbers represent hundreds? Thousands? Millions? Inches? Feet? Miles? Pounds? Ounces? Are metric units used?

Analyze trends and patterns. Trends and patterns suggest or imply important ideas that support the graphic's main idea.

Ask: What are the extremes? How do the extremes compare to the total? What are the averages? What and how much are the increases? What and how much are the decreases?

EXAMPLE   Study the graphic. Complete the statements that follow it with information from the graph.

Type of Home Internet Connection by Region, 2003

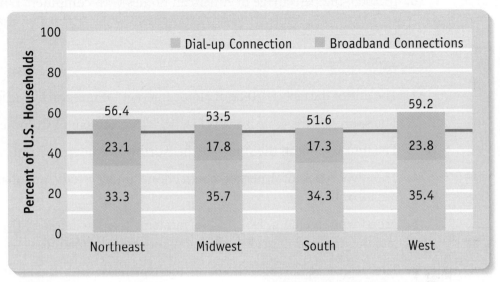

Note: Broadband includes DSL, cable modem, fixed wireless (MMDS), and satellite.

Source: National Telecommunications and Information Administration (NTIA), U.S. Department of Commerce, *A Nation Online: Entering the Broadband Age* (2004). 22 Nov. 2009. http://www.ntia.doc.gov/reports/anol/ NationOnlineBroadband04.htm.

1. The title of the table is _____.

2. The source of the table is _____.

3. The four regions in the study are the _____.

4. The two types of Internet connections under study are _____

_____.

5. Broadband includes _____.

6. The percentage of households in the Northeast with a dial-up Internet

connection is _____.

7. Overall, the rates of dial-up usage are roughly _____ across all regions.

8. Broadband rates are higher in the _____ and _____

than in the _____ and _____.

9. In 2003, in these regions, _____ usage was higher than

_____ usage.

10. In 2003, the percentage of American homes with computers ranged from

_____ to _____.

1. The title of the table is "Type of Home Internet Connection by Region, 2003."

2. The source of the table is the NTIA, U.S. Department of Commerce.

3. The four regions in the study are the Northeast, Midwest, South, and West.

4. The two types of Internet connections under study are dial-up and broadband.

5. Broadband includes DSL, cable modem, fixed wireless (MMDS), and satellite. You had to read the footnote for this information.

6. The percentage of households in the Northeast with a dial-up Internet connection is 33.3%.

7. Overall, the rates of dial-up usage are roughly the same across all regions.

8. Broadband rates are higher in the West and Northeast than in the South and Midwest.

9. In 2003, in these regions, dial-up usage was higher than broadband usage.

10. In 2003, the percentage of American homes with computers ranged from 51.6% to 59.2%. Although the information in the table focuses on the type of Internet connection, you may infer that the study had to identify how many people had computers in order to identify the type of Internet connection they used.

Three Basic Types of Graphics

Many magazines, newspapers, and textbooks use tables, graphs, and diagrams. These graphics call attention to key concepts. Thus a skilled reader takes time to study the ideas within them.

Tables

The graphic on U.S. households' usage of Internet connections is a table. Social science, health, and business textbooks often use tables. A **table** is a systematic ordering of facts in rows and columns for easy reference. The purpose of a table is to allow the reader to compare the given facts. Often the facts are given as numbers or statistics. The basic guidelines to reading graphics apply to reading a table. In addition, some tables require that you study the places where columns and rows intersect.

EXAMPLE Study the following table. Based on the data in the table, mark each numbered statement **T** if it is true, **F** if it is false, or **DK** if you don't know, based on the given data.

Approximate Energy Consumed by a 150-Pound Person Performing Different Activities

Activity	Calories/ Hour	Time to "Work Off"			
		500 Calories (Cheeseburger)	300 Calories (Ice Cream Cone)	70 Calories (Apple)	40 Calories (1 Cup Broccoli)
Running (6 mph)	700	43 min	26 min	6 min	3 min
Cross-country skiing (moderate)	560	54 min	32 min	7.5 min	4 min
Roller skating	490	1 hr 1 min	37 min	8.6 min	5 min
Bicycling (11 mph)	420	1 hr 11 min	43 min	10 min	6 min
Walking (3 mph)	250	2 hr	1 hr 12 min	17 min	10 min
Frisbee® playing	210	2 hr 23 min	1 hr 26 min	20 min	11 min
Studying	100	5 hr	3 hr	42 min	24 min

Source: Audesirk, Teresa, Audesirk, Gerald, & Byers, Bruce E., *Life on Earth*, 5th, © 2009. Electronically reproduced by permission of Pearson Education, Inc., Upper Saddle River, New Jersey.

_____ **1.** The body needs minerals such as iron, calcium, sodium, and potassium to proper perform activities.

_____ **2.** A 150-pound person would have to run for 43 minutes to burn off the calories consumed by eating a meal of a 500-calorie cheeseburger and a 300-calorie ice cream cone.

_____ **3.** A 150-pound person has to bicycle for over an hour to consume the 500 calories in a cheeseburger.

_____ **4.** Running causes weight loss.

_____ **5.** Studying is an activity that consumes calories.

EXPLANATION

1. DK: The chart does not address what the body needs to perform these activities.

2. F: A 150-pound person would have to run for 69 minutes (1 hr and 9 min) to burn off the calories consumed by eating both a 500-calorie cheeseburger and a 300-calorie ice cream cone.

3. T: The chart indicates that a 150-pound person would have to bike for 11 minutes more than one hour (1 hr 11 min).

4. DK: The chart does not address the effect the performance of any activity has on weight.

5. T: Based on the chart, studying consumes 100 calories an hour.

PRACTICE 1

Study the following table. Then mark each numbered statement **T** if it is true, **F** if it is false, or **DK** if you don't know, based on the given data.

Dietary Guidelines for Americans, 2000
Recommended Number of Servings

	1,600 Calories	2,200 Calories	2,800 Calories
Grains group	6	9	11
Vegetables group	3	4	5
Fruit group	2	3	4
Milk group	2 or 3	2 or 3	2 or 3
Meat and beans group	2 (5 oz. total)	2 (6 oz. total)	3 (7oz. total)

Source: USDA Center for Nutrition Policy and Promotion.

_____ 1. Eleven servings of grains is recommended for a diet of 1,600 calories.

_____ 2. Four servings of fruit is recommended for a diet of 2,800 calories.

_____ 3. Six ounces is recommended for one serving of meat for a diet of 2,200 calories.

_____ 4. A healthy diet should include two or three servings from the milk group.

_____ **5.** Individuals who need to lose weight should follow the recommendations for a 1,600-calorie diet.

Graphs

Graphs show the relationship between two or more sets of ideas. The most common types of graphs you will come across in your reading are line graphs, bar graphs, and pie charts.

Line Graphs A **line graph** plots two or more sets of facts on vertical and horizontal axes. The vertical axis sets out a scale to measure one set of data, and the horizontal axis offers another scale to measure the other set of data. These features make a line graph ideal to show the curve, shifts, or trends in data. As the information varies, the line changes to show dips and surges. If the information does not change, the line remains steady. Remember to use the guidelines for reading graphics from pages 535–536, and pay special attention to the labels on the vertical and horizontal axes.

EXAMPLE Study the following line graph. Based on the data in the graph, mark each numbered statement **T** if it is true, **F** if it is false, or **DK** if you don't know, based on the given data.

Prisoners on Death Row by Race, 1968-2007

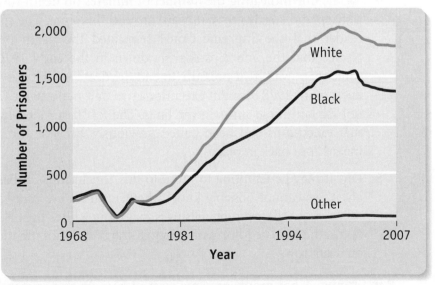

Source: _Capital Punishment, 2007-Statistical Tables._ U.S. Department of Justice, Bureau of Justice Statistics.

The death penalty was reinstated by the U.S. Supreme Court in 1976.

_____ **1.** Only two groups of people on death row are tracked on this line graph.

_____ **2.** The horizontal axis plots the timeline of death row in ten-year periods.

_____ **3.** The vertical axis plots the numbers of people on death row.

_____ **4.** The number of people on death row began to rise around 1976 when the U.S. Supreme Court reinstated the death penalty.

_____ **5.** Whites are more violent than all other races.

EXPLANATION   Compare your answers to the ones that follow.

1. F: Three groups of people by race are tracked on this graph. The third group is labeled "other."

2. F: The horizontal axis does plot the timeline of the death penalty, but it is plotted by five-year, not ten-year, periods. The time span is important because it gives the reader a sense of how many people face the death penalty during a given time.

3. T: The vertical axis does plot the number of people on death row. The numbers are marked off in groups of 500.

4. T: The line indicating the number of inmates on death row begins to take a sharp and steady curve upward around this time. The footnote tells the reader that the Supreme Court reinstated the death penalty in 1976. Notice that the line dips sharply down in the early 1970s. During this time, there was great pressure to end the death penalty. A Supreme Court decision in 1972 brought executions to a halt nationwide. The graph does not explain these shifts in the lines. The footnote does, however, suggest that executions had been halted previously, because the word *reinstated* means "put back in place."

5. DK: It may be tempting to jump to this conclusion. Yet based on the data given, we cannot possibly know whether whites are more violent than all other races. All the graph tells us is that more whites than all other races are on death row. The information in this graph does not mention why they are on death row.

Bar Graphs   A **bar graph** presents a set of bars. Each bar stands for a specific quantity, amount, or measurement of information. The bars allow you to compare the quantity of each item represented on the graph. The bars on bar graphs can be arranged horizontally or vertically. Remember to use the guidelines for reading graphics (pages 535–536) when you read bar graphs.

EXAMPLE Study the following bar graph. Based on the data in the graph, mark each numbered statement **T** if it is true, **F** if it is false, or **DK** if you don't know, based on the given data.

Percentage of Persons Under Age 65 Years Without Health Insurance Coverage at the Time of Interview, by Age Group and Sex: United States, 2008

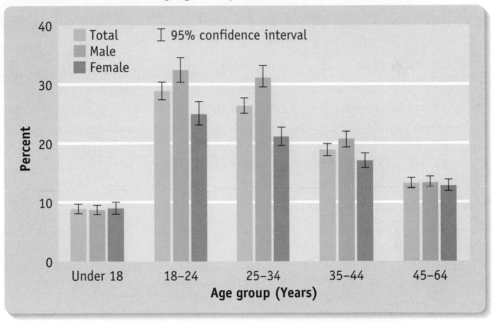

Source: *Early Release of Selected Estimates Based on Data from the 2008 National Health Interview Survey.* Center for Disease Control and Prevention.

_____ **1.** The blue bar tracks the percentage of males without health insurance coverage.

_____ **2.** The horizontal axis shows the percent of people without insurance as percentages.

_____ **3.** The horizontal axis shows people grouped by race.

_____ **4.** The highest percentage of people without health insurance in 2008 were under the age of 18.

_____ **5.** About 15 percent of the people aged 45 to 64 years were without health insurance in 2008.

EXPLANATION

1. T: The point of the graph is to track the percent of people without health-care, and the key to the graph indicates that males are represented by the blue bar.

2. F: The *vertical* axis shows the number of people as percentages.

3. F: The horizontal axis groups people by age, not race.

4. F: The group with the highest bar shows the largest group without health insurance, which is the 18- to 24-year-old group.

5. T: The 45- to 64-year-old group is represented by the green bar, which rests between 10 and 20 percent.

Pie Charts A **pie chart**, also known as a *circle graph,* shows a whole group as a circle and divides the circle into smaller units that look like slices of the pie. Each smaller slice is a part, percentage, or fraction of the whole. Pie graphs are used to show proportions and the importance of each smaller unit to the whole.

EXAMPLE Study the following pie chart. Based on the data shown, mark each numbered statement **T** if it is true, **F** if it is false, or **DK** if you don't know, based on the given data.

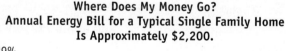

Where Does My Money Go?
Annual Energy Bill for a Typical Single Family Home
Is Approximately $2,200.

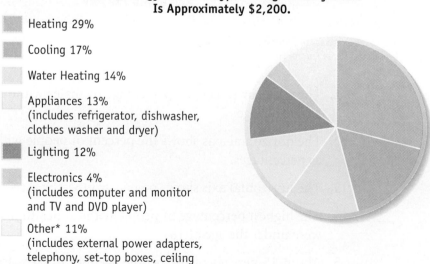

Heating 29%

Cooling 17%

Water Heating 14%

Appliances 13%
(includes refrigerator, dishwasher,
clothes washer and dryer)

Lighting 12%

Electronics 4%
(includes computer and monitor
and TV and DVD player)

Other* 11%
(includes external power adapters,
telephony, set-top boxes, ceiling
fans, vent fans and home audio)

Source: Typical House memo, Lawrence Berkeley National Laboratory, 2009 and Typical
house_2009_Reference.xls spreadsheet.

_____ **1.** The chart is divided into seven parts.

_____ **2.** More money is spent on running appliances than on heating water.

_____ **3.** The most money spent on energy goes to heating.

_____ **4.** The least percentage of money spent on energy goes to an assortment of other items such as power adapters and ceiling fans.

_____ **5.** The majority of single family homes spend at least $2000 a year on energy.

1. T: The pie chart is divided into seven groups based on the percentage of spending on energy in a typical home each year.

2. F: A larger percentage of money is spent on heating water than on running appliances. A typical single family home spends 14% on heating water in contrast to only 13% using appliances.

3. T: The greatest expense in energy for a typical single family home is heating at 29%.

4. F: The least percentage of money spent on energy goes to electronics, such as computers and televisions, at 4%.

5. T: The title of the chart indicates that the data represents a *typical* single family home. The word typical means average, common, or mainstream. So it is valid to infer that the majority of single family homes pay over $2000 each year in energy costs.

PRACTICE 2

Study the following graphic. Then mark each numbered statement **T** if it is true, **F** if it is false, or **DK** if you don't know, based on the given data.

_____ **1.** This graphic is a line graph.

_____ **2.** The vertical axis indicates places around the world.

_____ **3.** Africa is the continent with the highest percentage of AIDS cases.

_____ **4.** North America has more cases of AIDS than Central and South America.

_____ **5.** Millions of new cases of AIDS occur each year.

AIDS: A Global Glimpse

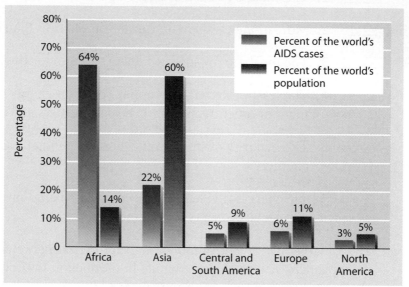

Source: Henslin, *Sociology: A Down to Earth Approach*, p. 557 © James M. Henslin. Reproduced by permission of Pearson Education, Inc.

Diagrams

A **diagram** is a graphic that explains in detail the relationships of the parts of an idea to the whole idea. Diagrams include flowcharts, pictograms, and drawings.

Flowcharts A **flowchart** is a diagram that shows a step-by-step process. Each step or phase of the process is typically shown in a box or circle, and the shapes are connected with lines and arrows to show the proper order or flow of the steps. Flowcharts are used in a number of subject areas, including social sciences, science, history, and English.

EXAMPLE Study the following flowchart. Based on the data in the diagram, mark each numbered statement **T** if it is true, **F** if it is false, or **DK** if you don't know, based on the given information.

_____ **1.** Either a federal or state court can apply for a case to be heard by the Supreme Court.

_____ **2.** Most of the cases the Supreme Court argues come from state courts.

_____ **3.** Clerks of the Supreme Court have an important role in deciding which cases are heard by the Supreme Court.

How a Case Goes to the Supreme Court

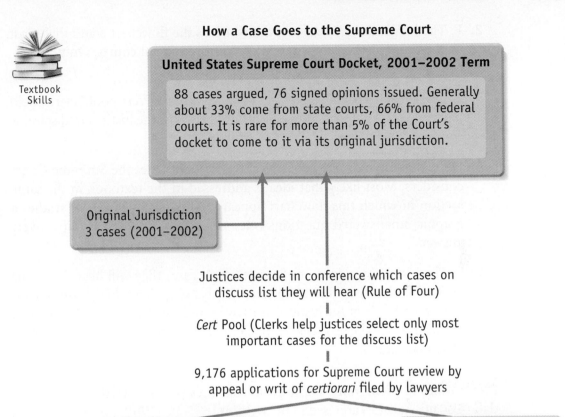

Textbook
Skills

United States Supreme Court Docket, 2001–2002 Term

88 cases argued, 76 signed opinions issued. Generally about 33% come from state courts, 66% from federal courts. It is rare for more than 5% of the Court's docket to come to it via its original jurisdiction.

Original Jurisdiction
3 cases (2001–2002)

Justices decide in conference which cases on discuss list they will hear (Rule of Four)

Cert Pool (Clerks help justices select only most important cases for the discuss list)

9,176 applications for Supreme Court review by appeal or writ of *certiorari* filed by lawyers

Federal Courts

Cases involving the interpretation of federal laws, treaties, or the U.S. Constitution

State Courts

Over 92 million cases initially filed in U.S. state and federal trial courts

Source: Karen O'Connor and Larry J. Sabato, *American Government: Continuity and Change* (New York: Longman, 2004), Fig. 10.6.

_____ **4.** Most of the Supreme Court cases deal with the Bill of Rights.

_____ **5.** A single Supreme Court justice can insist that the Supreme Court hear a case.

EXPLANATION

1. T: The lines that are drawn from the boxes that are labeled "Federal Courts" and "State Courts" show that both courts can send cases to be considered by the Supreme Court.

2. F: The information in the box at the top of the flowchart states that most of the cases (66 percent) argued come from federal courts. Only 33 percent come from state courts.

3. T: The flowchart states that when cases reach the "*cert* pool," clerks help justices select "only the most important cases" for the justices to discuss as a group.

4. DK: The flowchart does not reveal the types of cases the Supreme Court considers. Most likely that idea is addressed in the textbook in the same section in which this flowchart appears. When a skilled reader studies a graphic, unanswered questions often arise that the text can most likely answer.

5. F: The justices decide in conference which cases they will hear. The "rule of four" is also noted in the flowchart at this stage. The rule of four means that at least four of the justices must agree to hear the case, or the case will not be heard. (The text tells the reader that the Supreme Court is made up of nine justices.)

Pictograms　A **pictogram** is a diagram that uses pictorial forms to represent data. Usually statistics are used in pictograms.

EXAMPLE　Study the following pictogram. Based on the ideas in the diagram, mark each numbered statement **T** if it is true, **F** if it is false, or **DK** if you don't know, based on the given information.

_____　**1.** The Cascade Range is a mountain range that stretches 1,000 miles across three states and part of Canada.

_____　**2.** Mount St. Helens has had more eruptions over the past 4,000 years than the other volcanoes of the Cascades.

_____　**3.** Newberry Volcano has had the fewest eruptions over the past 4,000 years.

_____　**4.** The volcano Three Sisters is located in the state of Washington.

_____　**5.** In the last 200 years, Mount St. Helens has had the most violent and destructive eruptions of any of the volcanoes in the Cascade Range.

Cascades Eruptions During the Past 4,000 Years

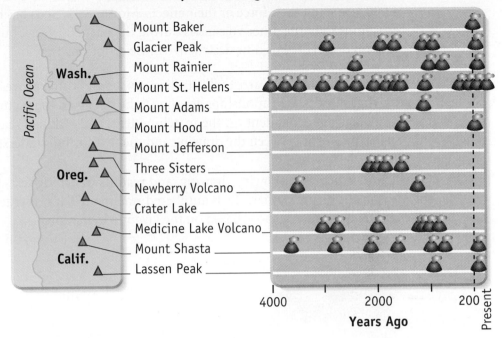

Source: Cascades Volcano Observatory, U.S. Geological Survey, Department of the Interior, 2000.

The Cascade Range includes numerous volcanoes and covers about 1,000 miles from Mount Garibaldi in British Columbia, Canada, to Lassen Peak in northern California.

EXPLANATION

1. T: This information is found in two places on the pictogram. The map shows that the range covers three states. The footnote tells you that the range is also in Canada and covers a distance of about 1,000 miles.

2. T: The pictogram shows a total of 15 eruptions for Mount St. Helens, more than any of the other volcanoes. Each volcano picture represents one eruption.

3. F: Newberry Volcano has two volcano icons. However, both Mount Baker and Mount Adams have only one each. So Mount Baker and Mount Adams have had the fewest number of eruptions.

4. F: The line from Three Sisters to the map points to a volcano in the middle of the state of Oregon.

5. DK: The pictogram depicts only the number of eruptions over the past 4,000 years, not their force or their effects. Mount St. Helens has had more eruptions than the other volcanoes during the past 200 years, but the pictogram doesn't tell us how destructive those eruptions were.

Drawings A **drawing** is an artist's illustration of a complicated process or idea. The drawing shows the relationships among all the details in the picture. Often these drawings are dependent on the matching text, and a skilled reader must move back and forth between the drawing and the text for full understanding.

EXAMPLE   Study the following drawing, and read its matching text. Based on the ideas in the diagram, mark each numbered statement **T** if it is true, **F** if it is false, or **DK** if you don't know, based on the given information.

Coral Reef Structure

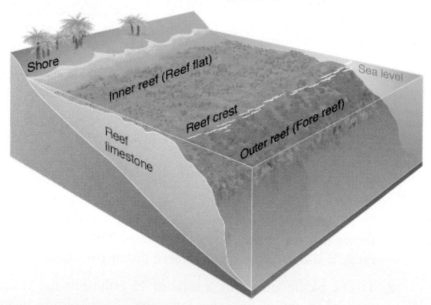

Source: U.S. Department of the Interior, *U.S. Coral Reefs—Imperiled National Treasures.* U.S. Geological Survey Fact Sheet no. 025-02, Oct. 30, 2008.

Coral Reefs Develop in Clear, Warm Seas

[1]Colonial "hard corals" can take on several different forms. [2]Hard corals become elaborate finger-shaped, branching, or mound-shaped structures. [3]These structures can create masses of limestone that stretch for tens or even hundreds of miles. [4]Many coral reefs fringing coasts

consist of near-shore inner reef flats. ⁵These inner reefs slope to deeper water fore reefs farther offshore. ⁶The reef crest lies in very shallow water between the inner reef flat and outer fore reef. ⁷The reef crest may be exposed during the lowest tides. ⁸Waves commonly crash against or break on the reef crest.

—Adapted from U.S. Department of the Interior, *U.S. Coral Reefs—Imperiled National Treasures*. U.S. Geological Survey Fact Sheet no. 025-02, Oct. 2, 2002.

_____ **1.** Coral reefs have a limestone base.

_____ **2.** The fore reef lies close to shore.

_____ **3.** The reef crest lies between the inner reef and the fore reef.

_____ **4.** Coral reefs are home to 25 percent of all marine species.

_____ **5.** All coral reefs develop into a mound shape.

EXPLANATION

1. T: This idea is verified in both the text and the drawing. Sentence 3 tells us that coral structures "create masses of limestone." In addition, the drawing clearly shows that the living coral is supported by "reef limestone."

2. F: The fore reef is another name for the "outer reef," which is farther out in deeper water. Sentence 5 states this idea, and the drawing clearly labels the fore reef as the outer reef in deeper water.

3. T: This fact is clearly stated in sentence 6 and depicted in the drawing.

4. DK: This may well be a fact; however, this idea is not mentioned in the text, and the drawing gives us no details for its support.

5. F: The drawing shows a mound-shaped coral reef. However, sentence 2 states that coral reefs can develop into three shapes: finger, branching, and mound. The drawing is just an example of one type.

PRACTICE 3

Study the following graphic. Then mark each numbered statement **T** if it is true, **F** if it is false, or **DK** if you don't know, based on the given information.

_____ **1.** This graphic is a pie chart, also known as a circle graph.

_____ **2.** Food waste makes up the majority of our trash.

Total MSW Generation (by Material), 2008
250 Million Tons (Before Recycling)

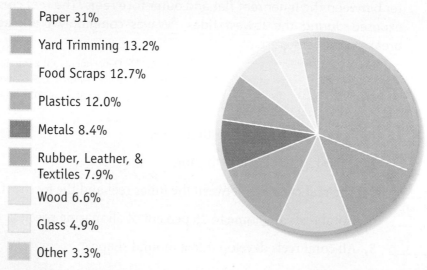

Paper 31%

Yard Trimming 13.2%

Food Scraps 12.7%

Plastics 12.0%

Metals 8.4%

Rubber, Leather, & Textiles 7.9%

Wood 6.6%

Glass 4.9%

Other 3.3%

Source: Environmental Protection Agency. "Basic Facts: Municipal Solid Waste (MSW)." 25 Nov. 2009. http://www.epa.gov/osw/basic-solid.htm.

_____ **3.** Paper makes up the highest percentage of daily trash.

_____ **4.** Plastic items make up the smallest percentage of daily trash.

_____ **5.** The United States is running out of landfills in which to dump trash.

REVIEW TEST 1

A. Based on the ideas in the following graphic, mark each numbered statement **T** if it is true, **F** if it is false, or **DK** if you don't know, based on the given information.

_____ **1.** This graphic is a pictogram.

_____ **2.** A healthy diet is mostly made up of meats and beans.

_____ **3.** A healthy diet contains a number of servings from each food group.

_____ **4.** Exercise is an important part of a healthy diet.

_____ **5.** A healthy diet avoids all fat.

Source: U.S. Department of Agriculture, Center for Policy and Promotion. Home and Garden Bulletin no. 267-1.

B. Based on the ideas in the graphic, mark each numbered statement **T** if it is true, **F** if it is false, or **DK** if you don't know, based on the given information.

_____ **6.** This graphic is a flowchart.

_____ **7.** The purpose of this graphic is to show how easy it is to eat more than the food pyramid recommends for a healthy diet.

_____ **8.** One 4½-inch-sized bagel is equivalent to four servings as defined by the food pyramid.

_____ **9.** The column labeled "Approximate Pyramid Servings in This Portion" refers to the column labeled "Sample Portion You Receive."

_____ **10.** People who eat the portions of food listed in the column "Sample Portion You Receive" are overweight.

Sample Food Portions Larger Than One Pyramid Serving

Food Grains Group	Sample Portion You Receive	Compare to Pyramid Serving Size	Approximate Pyramid Servings in This Portion
Bagel	1 bagel 4^1/$_2$" in diameter (4 ounces)	1/2 bagel 3" in diameter (1 ounce)	4
Muffin	1 muffin 3^1/$_2$" in diameter (4 ounces)	1 muffin 2^1/$_2$" in diameter (1^1/$_2$ ounces)	3
English muffin	1 whole muffin	1/2 muffin	2
Sweet roll or cinnamon bun	1 large from bakery (6 ounces)	1 small (1^1/$_2$ ounces)	4
Pancakes	4 pancakes 5" in diameter (10 ounces)	1 pancake 4" in diameter (1^1/$_2$ ounces)	6
Burrito-sized flour tortilla	1 tortilla 9" in diameter (2 ounces)	1 tortilla 7" in diameter (1 ounce)	2
Individual bag of tortilla chips	1^3/$_4$ ounces	12 tortilla chips (^{3}/$_4$ ounce)	2
Popcorn	16 cups (movie theater, medium)	2 cups	8
Hamburger bun	1 bun	1/2 bun	2
Spaghetti	2 cups (cooked)	1/2 cup (cooked)	4
Rice	1 cup (cooked)	1/2 cup (cooked)	2

Source: U.S. Department of Agriculture, Center for Policy and Promotion. Home and Garden Bulletin no. 267-1.

REVIEW TEST 2

A. Study the following graphic. Then mark each numbered statement **T** if it is true, **F** if it is false, or **DK** if you don't know, based on the given information.

_____ **1.** This graphic is a flowchart.

_____ **2.** Step 4 shows that a solution can be either accepted or rejected.

_____ **3.** If a solution is rejected, the process ends.

Stages of Conflict Resolution

Textbook
Skills

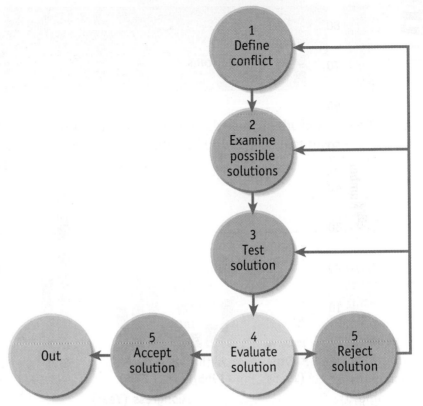

DeVito, *Messages: Building Interpersonal Communication Skills*, p. 300 © 1999. Reproduced by permission of Pearson Education, Inc.

_____ **4.** If a solution is rejected, a person can repeat any one or all of the first three steps.

_____ **5.** Most tested solutions are accepted.

B. Study the following graphic. Then mark each numbered statement **T** if it is true, **F** if it is false, or **DK** if you don't know, based on the given information.

_____ **6.** This graphic is a line graph.

_____ **7.** The 79th Congress had the fewest numbers of women and minorities of the Congresses shown.

_____ **8.** Between 1985 and 1993, the number of African Americans in Congress nearly doubled.

-lat-	carry	translate
-log-, -logue-	thought	logic
-luc-	light	lucid, translucent
-man-, -manu-	hand	manual
-mand-, -mend-	order	mandate
-mis-, -mit-	send, let go	transmit
-path-	feel	empathy
-phil-	love	philosophy
-phon-	sound	cellphone
-photo-	light	photograph
-plic-, -plicat-, -plicit-	fold	complicate
-pli-, -ply-, -plex-	fold	complex
-pon-, -pos-, -posit-	place, put	dispose, deposit
-port-	carry	import, portable
-quit-	quiet, resist	acquit, tranquil
-sanct-	holy	sanctuary
-scrib-, -script-	write	inscription, script
-sens-, -sent-	feel	sensitive, sensory
-spec-, -spic-	look	aspect, prospect
-stare, -sta-, -stat-, -sti-, - sist-	to take a stand, be firm	insist
-tain-, -tene-, -tin-	hold	contain
-tend-, -tent, -tens-	offer, direct, stretch	contend
-tele-	far off	telecast
-terr-	earth	territory
-tract-	drag, draw	extract
-vac-	empty	vacate
-vert-	turn	divert
-vid-, -vis-	see	video, visible

25 Prefixes

Prefix	Meaning	Example
ab-	from	abduct
ad-	to, toward	admit
be-	around, on, over, thoroughly	beside, belittle
col-, co-, com-, con-	together, with	collate, comply
de-	downward, reversal, undoing	detract, destruction
dis-, dif-	not, reversal	disquiet

e-, ex-	away, out of, former	extend
en-, em-	in, into, to cover or contain	empathy
epi-	after, besides, among, at, on, over	epilogue
in-, im-	into, not	import
inter-	among, between	interfere
non-	not	nonsense
mal-	bad, wrong	malpractice
mis-	wrong	mistake
mono-	one	monotone
multi-	many	multiply
omni-	all	omnipresent
over-	above, exceed, excessive	oversee
per-	through, thoroughly, throughout	peruse
pre-	before, in front of	precede
pro-	before, forward, in favor of	promote
re-	again, restore	retract
sub-	beneath, under	submit
trans-	across	transfer
un-	not, opposite of	unnecessary

37 Suffixes

Suffix	**Meaning**	**Example**
Noun suffixes		
-acy	state or quality	privacy
-ance, -ence, -ency	state or quality	residence, residency
-ant	person or thing acting as an agent	descendant
-ation	the act of, process	education
-dom	place or state of being	freedom, kingdom
-eer, -er, -es, -or	doer or person	contractor, princess
-en	made of	wooden
-es, -s	plural, more than one	books, boxes
-hood	condition, state of being	brotherhood
-ism	belief	capitalism
-ist	one who	materialist
-it, -ity	quality, condition, state of	sincerity

Photo Credits

Pp. vi, 6 (top): Al Tielemans/Sports Illustrated/Getty Images; p. 6 (bottom): Adam Pretty/Getty Images Sport; p. 9: Car Culture/Corbis; p. 23: Karen Kasmauski/Corbis; p. 25: Ann Johansson/Corbis; p. 27: Frans Lanting/Corbis; p. 40: ©Jonathan Ernst/Reuters/Corbis; p. 44: Mark Hamilton/Corbis; p. 45: Thom Lang/Corbis; p. 48: Bob Daemmrich/Corbis; p. 55: Jason Hosking/Corbis; p. 56: Skyscan/Corbis; pp. vii, 80: Enrique castro-Mendivil/ Reuters/Corbis; p. 82: Sara DeBoer/Retna/ Corbis; p. 84: Ann Boyajian/Illustration Works/Corbis; p. 86: Chris Giovanni/Corbis; p. 97: Peggy Heard/Frank Lane Agency/ Corbis; p. 123: Medical RF.com/Corbis; p. 126: Gary I. Rothstein/Retuers/Corbis; p. 132: Harish Tyagi/epa/Corbis; p. 160: Alberto Ruggieri/Corbis; p. 175: B. Anthony Stewart/National Georgraphic Society/Corbis; p. 177: Randy Faris/Corbis; p. vii, 182: Andy Aitchison/Corbis; p. 192: Image Source/Corbis; pp. vii, 203: Paul A. Souders/Corbis; p. 206: Tanya Constantine/ Corbis; p. 208: Jeff Foott/Science Faction/Corbis; p. 214 (both): Nick Clements/Getty Images; p. 220: Maher Attar/Sygma/ Corbis; p. 224: Robert Wallis/Corbis; pp. viii, 268: Car Culture/Corbis; p. 270: A2582Frank Leonhardt/ dpa/Corbis; p. 278: Visuals Unlimited/Corbis; p. 293: Araldo De Luca/Corbis; p. 299: Lawrence Migdale/Stock Boston; pp. ix,311: Paul A. Souders/Corbis; p. 318: Courtesy of Earth Sciences and Image Analysis Laboratory, NASA Johnson Space Center; p. 325: Envision/Corbis; p. 330: Wolfgang Kaehler/Corbis; p. 343: David Pollack/Corbis; p. 346: Visuals Unlimited/Corbis; p.357: Jonathan Blair/Corbis; pp. ix, 365: Jonathan Blair/Corbis; p. 370: Images.com/ Corbis RF; p. 388: Bill Ross/Corbis; pp. x, 395: Kazuyoshi Nomachi/Corbis; 399: Samoa Observer/epa/Corbis; p. 404: *Peanuts* reprinted by permission of United Features Syndicate, Inc.; p, 414: Stocktrek/Corbis; p. 423: Larry Dale Gordon; p. 441: Daniel Le Clair/Reuters/Corbis; p. 468: Flint/Corbis; p. 484: Gilles Rodevins/spl/ Corbis; p. 491: Ariel Skelley/Blend Images/Corbis; p. 531: Mark Weiss/Corbis.